G. M. B. Maughs

Souvenirs of Travel

G. M. B. Maughs

Souvenirs of Travel

ISBN/EAN: 9783337210250

Printed in Europe, USA, Canada, Australia, Japan

Cover: Foto ©Andreas Hilbeck / pixelio.de

More available books at **www.hansebooks.com**

SOUVENIRS OF TRAVEL

—BY—

G. M. B. MAUGHS, M. D.

ST. LOUIS:
FARRIS, SMITH & CO. PRINT.

Entered according to Act of Congress, in the year 1887, by
G. M. B. MAUGHS, M. D.,
In the office of the Librarian of Congress, at Washington, D. C.

TO MY WIFE

My Constant Companion in all these Wanderings

TO WHOSE BETTER TASTE IS DUE

Whatever of Merit there may be in reflections on Works of Art

AND

Whose Devotion and Tender Care

for more than Forty Years have known no cessation

MAKING

November pleasant as was May

THIS BOOK

IS AFFECTIONATELY DEDICATED BY

THE AUTHOR.

PREFACE.

Some apology may be thought due for throwing upon the world another Book of Travels: none, however, will be given. It consists of the random thoughts of a stray M. D., wandering over Europe, thinking about things he saw. And if there seem to be too much enthusiasm or gush, I may state that this was most natural for one transported from the backwoods of the Far West, where his youth had been spent in philosophizing upon the mysteries of the plow, to the transcendent glories of the Vatican Frescoes. And some may not like the style: let me assure such that this is a matter of taste, that the style is good and the matter as varied as excellent. Yet others may not like some of the remarks: let such rest assured that these are as honest as true, and were not written to please any one. There are some errors that might have been corrected had health permitted, and will be corrected in the 10th or 20th edition which the book will soon reach, as every person will read it. And should any one have the misfortune not to do so, he will die ignorant of many things he should have known.

LEAVING HOME.

July 1st, 1884.—After bidding adieu to kind friends, some of whom accompanied us to, and others met us at, the depot, we left St. Louis at 7 P. M., on the Vandalia Railway, for New York, on our way to Europe, a journey we had long intended making, but which had been deferred until passing years and declining health warned us against further delay.

We had a pleasant section on a Pullman Car with several friends and acquaintances on the same sleeper. During the night, we passed through Illinois and Western Indiana. The morning of July 2nd found us in the eastern portion of Indiana; took breakfast at Richmond, and during the day passed through the rich agricultural portion of Ohio, dining at Columbus. the State capital; through the less inviting western portion of Pennsylvania, arriving at the smoky, dingy, dirty manufacturing town of Pittsburgh at 8 P. M., at which time the sombre appearance of the smoky city was rendered more so by the gathering shades of evening; supped at Pittsburgh, and during the night passed through the western and middle portions of Pennsylvania, arriving at the city of brotherly love, Philadelphia, early in the morning of July 3rd, where we took breakfast, and continued our journey into and through the State of New Jersey, with its beautiful highly-cultivated fields, comfortable farm houses and pleasant villages, to New ork City, where we arrived at 11 A. M., and put up at the Grand Central Hotel, Thirty-first and Broadway, where we met our friends, Dr. and Mrs. E., who will accompany us to Europe.

NEW YORK.

New York City is one of the marvels of our new and rapidly developing country. Only 150 years ago it was an obscure Dutch village, and indeed only one hundred years ago it was but a small town, the centre of a fur trade, the treasures of which were gathered from the unknown rivers and unexplored wilderness of an unknown region extending to an unknown distance towards the setting sun, and perhaps to the North pole, certainly to arctic snows, and possibly to the tropics. Now it is the third city in Europe or America in population, wealth and commercial importance, with costly private palaces and public buildings, that vie in splendor with those of kings, while her warehouses are filled with the costly products of the civilized world, and her merchant princes extend their trade to the ends of the earth, and the world feels the throbbings of this money centre.

Fortunately, I was enabled to transact some banking business, after which, late in the evening, in company with Dr. and Mrs. E., we had a trip on the elevated railroad to Harlem and return. Next morning, July 4th, being a holiday and also rainy, we remained in the hotel; wife busy packing trunks and arranging for our long voyage. The next day, Saturday, July 5th, contrary to the custom in St. Louis, being also a holiday, we were unable to make some needful purchases, previous to embarking. Indeed, so entirely had we been engaged up to the moment of our leaving home that we had not even a map or guide book, as well as many little necessaries we had intended getting in New York, and none of which could we get, on account of this awkward intervention of the holidays.

ON THE SEA.

July 5th.—At 11 A. M. left our hotel and went on board the staunch steamer Rhyneland, to trust our lives for the next twelve days to the, to us, unknown dangers of the ocean. At 3 P. M. the ship weighed anchor and amidst the waving of hats and handkerchiefs, started on her long voyage, steaming down the Hudson and out through Long Island Sound, in company with five other ocean steamers, making a grand sight. These six ocean steamships, leaving port at the same time, each bound for widely different parts of the world, and each freighted with its living cargo, was beautiful, grand, impressive. What multitudinous hopes and fears were here! Alas! how many of the former like morning mists will vanish, and how many of the latter may find full fruition, can only be determined by the unknown future. Off Sandy Hook we parted with our pilot and entered the stormy waves of the seemingly shoreless Atlantic. The sea was so rough, the waves so chopped, and our vessel rocked so much, that scarcely were we fairly out on the sea when almost every lady and child on board was sea-sick, and vomiting as though seized with some sudden epidemic.

At 6 P. M. dinner was announced, when only a few ladies were enabled to get to the table and long before the meal was finished, every one of these, with the single exception of my wife, were compelled to leave the table and hasten on deck or were prostrated in their cabins. It was really pitiable to see these poor sufferers, many of whom were not able to come to their meals for many days. Up to this time neither of us has been in the least nauseated, and with appetites sharpened by the sea breeze we do such ample justice to the excellent cuisane of the Rhyneland that we fear the Captain almost wishes that we, too, had a brush of sea-sickness.

July 6th.—The night continued stormy, with the waves rolling mountain high, dashing against the sides of the ship and port hole window of our birth, as shown by the faint phosphorescent light these breaking, foaming waves produce. All night long the spray dashed over the deck, driving the passengers from the lee side of the ship or to their rooms. The noise of the waves and rolling of the ship so frightened wife that she had me get up to see if we were not sinking or had not struck a whale or iceberg, or grounded.

Sunday, July 6th.—We are fairly out of sight of land. Ocean! illimitable ocean! everywhere, bounded only by the horizon. How fearfully moan the waves as they roll in upon our vessel from the eternity of waters that lie beyond—nothing but darkness, mists and storms, the fitting emblem and home of terrors. But our good ship, a floating palace, is of iron with ribs of steel, and though the work of puny man, seems at home amidst this waste of waters, laughing at winds and riding down storm and waves. Our course is slightly south of east, running down to north latitude 40, bearing directly for the Gulf Stream. This direction is taken in part to avoid icebergs, the terror of the North Atlantic at this season of the year. These floating mountains of ice, broken off from arctic glaciers. float down south as far as the Gulf Stream, where they are rapidly melted away by this mighty river of warm salt water, heated up in the sea of Sargossa and intertropical portions of the South Atlantic to a temperature of 90, and heaped up by its expansion, flowing as a mighty river, more than equal to all the fresh water rivers of the world. with a velocity of from four to six miles an hour off the Keys of Florida, being deflected further from our coast until off the banks of Newfoundland it is divided, a portion running as an undercurrent up through Behring Straits to the Polar Sea, where it comes to the surface, giving, most probably, an open sea immediately around the North Pole, while the greater portion runs across to northern Europe, warming up and rendering habitable England, Scotland and other parts of northern Europe, producing the beautiful green of the Emerald Isle. All of these, though in high northern latitudes, to which belong the inhospitable climate of

Labrador, are so warmed by this ocean furnace, whose heat is bottled up in intertropical seas, as to spread their fields with laughing plenty. How wonderful and beneficent is this aqueous furnace is seen in the fact that from opposite causes we have even in lower latitudes the inhospitable wastes of Labrador. Our rapid approach to this warm river is shown in the rise of the temperature of the sea, which has risen from 69 to 77.

Monday, July 7th.—Weather continues stormy, waves breaking over the deck, and as our room is to the windward we are compelled to keep the windows closed, thus cutting off all currents of air, which, with the vessel running through hot water, renders the nights uncomfortably warm. In the day, however, when not confined to our room, the fresh, balmy sea air almost compensates for the disagreeable nights. Towards evening of this day the sea became more calm and we all remained on deck until near midnight. The younger passengers entertaining us with songs and with music on the piano in the saloon, making us feel much at home. Really this life on the ocean wave with smooth seas and no storm is rather pleasant, so much so that, forgetting stormy weather, we feel that we would soon become fond of life upon the sea.

Tuesday, 8th.—The subsidence of the rough weather has produced a happy change in our ship's crew, nearly all of whom now get to the table, and with appetites so much sharpened by previous privation as to threaten an exhaustion of provisions, if from any cause our journey should be prolonged a few days. Met to-day two steamers and one sail-vessel on this great highway of nations which. without trees or mile-posts, is blocked out by the mariner's compass with unerring certitude. A few stormy petrels and sea gulls still follow our steamer. One whale was seen, and shoals or flocks of flying-fish start up in front of the ship's bow and, after flying a few hundred feet or as many yards, drop down again into the water. To see these tiny creatures while playing the bird is both interesting and instructive, as they evidently represent in some manner, in the world's history, the primogenitors of birds, or of flying, half-sea, half-land serpents, the immediate primogenitors of birds. Only a little development would fit them for extensive flights in the air, while a metamorphosis not greater than that which forms the air-breathing frog from the gilled, water-breathing tadpole would qualify them for a change of life from water to dry-land animals. A few porpoises were also seen, but this was all of life anywhere visible outside the ship. Evidently we are in a desert waste as void of life as the alkaline plains of Colorado or the sandy wastes of the Sahara. How or why is this? Cannot fish live in the deep sea? Or is the temperature of the Gulf stream, now as high as $89°$, unfavorable to animal life? Whatever be the cause certain it is, that there is an absence of animal life in this mid-ocean highway that is painfully tangible. On mentioning this fact to some of the passengers they thought I must be mistaken, but on appealing to the Captain, he confirmed our observations, which with us, however, were not original, only confirmatory, having seen the fact stated by, perhaps, Lieutenant Mauray, in his "Physical Geography of the Sea," a work that does us great national credit.

Wednesday, July 9th.—Storms and waves have disappeared. The sea is smooth as glass and last night when the full-orbed moon lighted up this silver sheen, it shone as a vast mirror of molten silver, dispelling all fears of danger, so quiet, so smooth, calm, serene that it hardly presented the reflected image of past or gathering dangers. It is, however, becoming foggy, and gathering mists seem to float like ghastly shadows towards our vessel. Ominous tangible forms, as the shrouded spirits of night, are coming nearer, ever nearer, thicker, thicker. Hark!

what frightful sound is this! What does it mean? It is the coarse warning voice of the fog-horn. Again and again its wild screams, so big with warning dangers, startle the ship's crew, while great clouds of fog, the very embodiment of the spirit of night, roll in mountain masses in upon the ship, enveloping all in darkness so thick and tangible that the ship ploughs its way through this body of darkness, which stands over and around us, while every few seconds the fog-whistle, as if fearful that we might forget the danger, announces it with startling clearness; while the rapid fall of the thermometer indicates the immediate presence of an iceberg. The possibility of running into an iceberg or being run into by some lost ship presents itself to the most stolid of the ship's crew. All hands are on the lookout, the steamer's engines are slackened, the ship slowered; ship's crew and passengers alike feeling that they are in the immediate presence of a shrouded danger, born only of the briny deep. A feeling of general alarm or terror has taken the place of the fancied security of only a few moments ago. Wife, who is much afraid of water even without storms and darkness, now cried how much she wished she were at home. Had she thought of this she was sure she never would have tempted Providence by coming here. How dreadful to be thus lost at sea, and devoured by hungry sharks! Well, the iceberg is passed, the danger over, and the vessel is afloat with a brisk breeze and clear skies, which stand in beautiful contrast to these spectres of fog mists. The frightful fog-horn is no longer heard.

Thursday, July 10th.—After having run southeast to latitude 40°, longitude 40°, our course was changed to northeast, when we soon ran out of the Gulf Stream with a temperature of 81°, into the cold waters of the North Atlantic, where in latitude 43°, longitude 42°, the water temperature had fallen to

68. The wind has changed to northeast with freshening breeze, threatening a blow. Two sails were sighted to-day— really these passing sails, out here in this watery waste, give us the pleasant feelings of company; we feel that they are old acquaintances and are by their presence assured that we are not alone on this wild waste of waters. The moon is in its wane and does not now rise until 10 P. M. This leaves the beautifully phosphorescent wake of the vessel a most striking phenomenon. This wake or track behind the vessel appears as a great illuminated highway, flashing in phorescent light, caused by the millions of animalcules in the water—the disturbance of which, or change in their electric states, caused by the passage of the vessel, produces a light sufficient to read by—near the stern of the ship and fading in a long line of milky way—in the distant track of the ship. Truly, ocean as well as land hath its wonders, and among them this is not the least.

Friday, July 11th.—All day stormy, with waves running high; vessel rocked so much that the lady passengers were confined to their rooms, and most of them again sick, causing many vacant places at table; towards night the wind had increased to great violence, sea fearfully rough, causing the vessel to plunge so much as to really alarm many; the night continued stormy.

Saturday, July 12th.—We have been out from New York one week, and still in mid-ocean with a stormy deep stretching out as a shoreless eternity. Our course continues northeast, we are now in north latitude 46°, longitude 31°. The night continued stormy, sea very rough.

Sunday, July 13th.—This is our second Sunday at sea. With a subsidence of the storm the water is becoming smoother. We are now in north latitude 47°. Had a clever sermon from a Methodist minister—Professor in the Wesleyan University.

The subject of the discourse, of course, was the voyage and shipwreck of St. Paul, which in the midst of this wild waste of waters possessed an interest not felt at home—indeed any shipwreck would have interested here—where we were quite ready to believe in our own, as well as all others.

Monday, July 14th.—No ships seen to-day, to all appearances ours is the only one afloat; and really this long voyage is becoming monotonous. A few porpoises are playing around our ship. They look and act much as a drove of wild hogs, wonder if they are not the descendants of those that—when the evil spirits entered them—plunged down a steep precipice into the sea, or it may be that they are the primogenitors—prehistoric of course—of our present Berkshire. We are to-day in north latitude 48 , longitude 18°, and 2,626 miles from New York and 427 from Lizards Point, the nearest land at which we touch.

Tuesday, July 15th.—At noon to-day in latitude 48 50", longitude 11 , and 250 miles from Lizards Point. On nearing the British Channel there is a great increase of sails; some eight or ten were in sight at one time to-day. A feeling of discontent in being so long on the voyage is becoming general. and this feeling is aggravated by the fact that many articles of food are exhausted, the fare becoming bad, food stale, and then with many there is a want of appetite to give it relish. Conversation less animated, reading and writing tiresome.

Wednesday, July 16th.—Have been out from St. Louis sixteen days, on the sea eleven days. The morning dawned beautiful, clear and balmy. We were up and on the deck at daylight to catch a view of the long-wished-for land. At 5 A. M. the Scilla Islands were sighted, when the boatswain's shrill cry of " land ahoy " brought all the passengers on deck. The look of weariness rapidly gave place to bright faces and the conversation became more animated as each passenger saw, or

fancied he saw, some new feature in the small islands. At
9 A. M. we were off Lizards Point. We were now fairly in the
British Channel, with the beautiful undulating shores of Old
England in full view. The low coast has gradually risen into
a high ridge, the foot of which is lined with serpentine rock,
which gives it a sombre appearance. Above the lower rocky
border the sloping ridges are in a high state of cultivation,
with green fields and pastures to their summits, while neat
farm houses, or clusters of houses, checker them. Doubtless
this entire region was originally a heath, as no trees are seen
except along the borders of the stream or in cave-like depressions between the hills, and even these have the appearance of
having been planted. An old Gothic church with a square
tower—said to be the most southerly church in England—is
seen from the deck of the steamer. All the passengers are
now upon the deck and in high spirits, each anxious to discover something new, and as we run along, at no great distance
from the land, the entire coast-line with all its beauties real
or immaginary are beautifully given. At 11 P. M. the historic
Isle of Wight is passed with its outline coast distinctly indicated by long rows of gas lamps.

Thursday, July 17th.—Arose early to get a glimpse of the
wondrous historic white chalk cliffs of Dover, which rise in
perpendicular walls several hundred feet above the sea. Above
the town is the splendid castle of Dover, built in the middle
ages. To the west, and crowning the heights, are strong fortifications frowning destruction upon England's foes. Several
revenue cutters are lying off the town. These with the fleet
of fishing smacks and passing steamers give the Channel here
quite an animated appearance. At this point it has been proposed to construct a tunnel to connect England with La Belle
France. Thus far the project has not been favorably entertained by the English, who prefer their insular position with

the Channel between them and their hereditary foes, and fear, perhaps, that with too close a connection between them and their mercurial neighbors they might wake up some fine morning to find a French army on their side of the Channel. The Channel here is only twenty-five miles wide, and both coasts, England and France, are distinctly seen from the steamer. Passed the popular Belgian Spa Ostend, and took on a pilot at the old Dutch town of Flushings, a beautiful place with the old walls of fortification on the sea side still standing, though battled by the storms of more than a thousand years, and for several hundred years, since the introduction of gunpowder, utterly useless as a means of protection. The town with its wind-mills and red-tiled steep roofs presents a quaint and Dutch-like appearance.

BELGIUM.

This entire section of Belgium, like Holland, is below the level of the sea, intersected by canals, and drained by lifting the water into these by means of windmills. It is protected against inundations from the sea by high embankments along the entire coast and the banks of the river Schelde. This levee is lined the entire distance by tiles laid down as neatly and as continuously as the roof of a house. What an immense cost of time and labor this has necessitated!

The entire country, as far as can be seen from the steamer's deck—over a level district with its planted, cultivated trees, its neat garden-like farms, its wind-mills, villages, with the steep roofs covered by red tiles, is beautifully picturesque and quite unlike anything seen in America. We are now steaming up the river Schelde with Holland on one side and Belgium on the other, and both flat, level surfaces below the sea level and drained by numerous canals. Art has so triumphed over nature here, recovering from the ocean the land, building a wall against the waves, lifting into artificial canals by means of wind-mills, and carrying off by these canals the entire surplus waterfall, planting forests, making and cultivating rich fields, building farm houses and cities, where formerly was ocean, as to produce a beautiful country; for here, country, as well as its products, is artificial. The industry and skill that has created all this, excite our wonder and admiration for the people who have thus maintained the struggle for existence under circumstances so unfavorable.

The banks of the Schelde are lined with numerous fortifications, worthless and mostly in ruins now, but eloquent witnesses of the vigilance and fearful struggle by which these people have had to maintain their existence against human, as well as Neptunian foes. Indeed Belgium is a very gem that has excited the cupidity of surrounding nations, who have with overwhelming forces ravaged the land, sacking and burning its cities and fattening the ground with the blood of its brave defenders, whose bravery against fearful odds, often served no other purpose than securing their own destruction. Their struggles for liberty against formidable invasions have been almost constant for the last 1800 years. First the Romans under Cæsar, B. C. 50, in a pitched battle overcame the Servi, who yielded only after the destruction of their army by the conquerors of the world. Afterwards the country was invaded by the Danes, Normans, and other pirates; then by the Spaniards, who under the cruel, blood-thirsty and bigoted duke of Alva, overran and destroyed by fire and sword alike, cities and country, slaughtering without mercy men, women and children. Later the country was conquered and possessed by the French under Napoleon I.

But ever restless under all these oppressors, and with an inextinguishable love of freedom, these brave people stood ever ready to strike for liberty, and with lands devastated, cities burned, they continued the struggle until in 1830 their autonomy and independence were fully established.

Notwithstanding their many disasters, such was the native vigor, intellectual as well as physical, that from the 12th to the 18th century, Belgium was the most intellectual nation in Europe, producing even amidst the chaos and ruin that covered them, many of the most distinguished literary and scientific men of those times.

At 7 P. M. the old and now highly prosperous city of Antwerp was seen. Shortly after we ran alongside its spacious wharves, and landed amidst a very babel of people. We, with many of the ship's passengers, went to the Hotel St. Antoine, which is to Antwerp what the Southern Hotel is to St. Louis, and beautifully situated at the *Place Verte.*

ANTWERP.

July, 18th–21st.—Antwerp, the chief commercial city of Belgium, with a population of 175,000, is situated on the Schelde, sixty miles from its mouth. The river here is 700 yards wide and thirty or forty feet deep, allowing the largest-sized ocean steamers to come up alongside of its spacious wharves. It is a strongly-fortified town, and its walls have not been for ornament, nor of sufficient strength to secure it against conquest, as it has witnessed more scenes of blood than almost any other city in Europe. Near our hotel the bloody duke of Alva murdered 8,000 citizens, when the remainder fled the city to escape a like fate.

It is the third city in Europe in commercial importance, and has long been renowned for its art treasures, possessing to the tourist great interest. First among these is its old and fine Cathedral, first built in 800, again in 1124, it presents many peculiar traits of mediæval architecture.

This cathedral is 384 feet long and 214 feet wide and 90 feet high. The nave is 178 feet wide, with three aisles on either side, divided by lofty columns. The tapering, lace-like spire rises 407 feet above the ground and is ascended by 516 steps. It has forty-two bells, the largest weighing 1,600 pounds. Within the church are many carvings, statues and paintings. Three of the paintings are masterpieces by Rubens. One, the Ascension of Mary, is over the high altar; another the *Descent from the Cross*, is in the south transept, and the third, the Hoisting of the Cross, is in the north transept. The masterpiece of Rubens, and one of the great paintings of the world, is the *Descent from the Cross*. It is in three pieces and called a Triptych—in the center, taking of Jesus down from the cross. On the left the Child Jesus in the arms of Simeon; on the right the meeting of Mary and Elizabeth. Mary, a beautiful woman, dressed in blue, is Rubens' first wife. A beautiful flower-girl in the painting is his daughter. A St. Francis by Murillo, and the Marriage at Cana, by M de Vas, are masterpieces. There are also many other paintings and statuary of great merit, constituting this Cathedral an art or picture gallery of the first order, and quite worth a visit to Antwerp to see and study, and they would, were they sold at public auction, bring money enough to build this fine Cathedral. But in fact, no amount of money could purchase them, as these people are very proud of Rubens, who was, or is considered, their greatest native artist. Many tombs and monuments are in and around the Cathedral, which is also ornamented with frescoes, *bas* and *alto* reliefs and beautiful stained windows of the 15th century.

    The Museé or Picture Gallery contains many fine paintings by the old Flemish and Dutch masters. Among them the Crucifixion, and the Adoration of the Magi, by Rubens; Christ on the Cross, by VanDyck; Fisher Boy, by Hals; A Landscape, by Ruysdale; The Crucifixion, by VanWeiden; The Virgin Mary, by VanEyck; Portrait of his First Wife, by VanDyck; the chair and other souvenirs of Rubens, also a fine white marble bust of Rubens; hundreds of paintings and works of art constitute this gallery one of very great interest.

The Rubens chapel, also the Mary chapel contains many fine paintings, with the tombs of Rubens and others. We visited the house of Rubens held in great veneration. One of the places of most interest is the Museum Planter Moretus. This is the old house of the great Antwerp printers, Planter and his son-in-law Moretus, who carried on this great printing house, they and their descendants, from 1550 to 1804. It contains in its printing presses, fonts, etc., preserved here a complete history of the rise and development of printing nowhere else found, with many old manuscripts and copies of all the early books, with their beautiful and often quaint illuminations, published by the house of Planter & Moretus. Among these we noticed Vesalius' Anatomy, 1568.

HOLLAND.

July 21st.—Left Antwerp for the Hague, capital of Holland. The railroad runs through a level country intersected by numerous canals. We passed through Rotterdam, the streets of which are canals, deep enough to admit large steamers and sail vessels, which pass through all parts of the city, loading and unloading their wares on the side-walks or streets, as do wagons in other cities. It is a city of the first commercial importance, exporting to, and importing from, all parts of the world. This substitution of canals for streets gives the city a strange appearance, quite unlike anything we had seen, while the numerous wind-mills seen throughout the city increase the quaint picturesque oddity of this old Dutch town.

These great wind-mills, seen not only here, but dotting over the country in every direction, with their great moving wings, look like monstrous fabled birds of ill omen, or ghostly spectres of night. Nor do I wonder that Don Quixote put spurs to his spirited war horse Rozinante, and charged them with poised lance—that is, if he was not afraid to do so, and however much we may admire his courage, we must place a low estimate on the discretion of mortal man, though aided by as fierce a war horse as Rozinante, who would attempt thus to overthrow these winged monsters.

This entire country is not more strange than beautiful. These frugal industrious Dutch have made this the most artificial, highly cultivated and beautiful country in the world. All of Holland is a highly cultivated garden, with its fields scarcely larger than garden squares, not a square rood of ground is let go to waste, even to the very water's edge of the canals and ditches, and to the borders of the gravelled roads and walks, the earth is tilled, or long lines of trimmed trees fill in the space, and then they are as clean, as industrious. Here in the Hague—for we are now in the Hague—the streets are paved with the prettiest little bricks in the world, and kept washed and scoured until they are as clean as a house floor. And then the neat and tidy women, even of the poorer classes, as in their wooden shoes, they wash and scour the pavements, have their skirts and stockings so clean and neat, that we might suppose they had put them on that morning to attend church or a fair. Few, very few, rags are seen, and those seen are rendered almost pretty from their cleanness. Surely if cleanliness is next to godliness, these people are nearer the latter than any other nation under heaven.

Here in the Hague a heavy wagon is almost, or never, seen on the streets. Nearly all the carriages are light one-horse or dog carts, and most of the traffic is done in hand-carts, drawn by a dog, or if too heavy, by a dog and man, or more frequently a woman. These latter animals assist the dog by pushing the cart, but not unfrequently a dog and woman are harnessed side by side. The marketing from gardens near the city is brought in by dogs and women pulling the cart. That from a distance is brought not in wagons, as with us, but in boats, and placed in stores throughout the city whence it is distributed in hand-carts drawn by dogs. In the country I saw a two-dog team returning home after the contents of the cart had been distributed, with the dogs harnessed as horses in a full run, with a man and woman sitting in the wagon or cart. Wife remarked that this was the only country she had seen where dogs were useful, but really I felt indignant that so noble an animal should be treated thus.

But the picture changes—women are seen with heavy baskets on their heads or with a yoke across their shoulders, to each end of which is attached a great basket filled with vegetables, which in some instances has been brought for miles in this manner, and yet the poor creatures, tired as they must be, look cheerful, happy. How can they be? How patient and uncomplaining is helpless woman! And then the struggle for existence here enforces a toil unknown to us, and absolutely requires that every one be in some manner self-sustaining. But here more outrageous still—a poor woman of perhaps twenty-five years of age, neat and tidy, as all these women are, and of rather comely appearance, is actually pulling along a cart loaded with vegetables for the market, and not even aided by the dog. And here again, a poor woman and a dog hitched to a wagon and pulling it along the streets on perfect equality, the dog evidently feeling that he is the more important animal of the two. Well it may truly be said that in this country "woman is a help-mate," supporting not only herself, but often the worthless husband. At these sights an enthusiastic lady suffragist exclaimed, "Just wait until we suffragists get control of this country—control, as we should, the ballot box—and we will have the men and dogs haul us about in these carts we now pull, until the men, at least, will learn it were not well to treat us so!"

On our arrival here I called on our minister, Mr. Hayden, to whom I had a letter of introduction. I found him a polite and accomplished gentleman, who not only discharges well his duty as minister, but by his courteous manner and high accomplishments reflects honor on his country.

The *Museum Royal* is one of the finest picture galleries in Europe. It was first established by the House of Orange, in 1647. Of the 300 principal paintings here, 200 are by the old Dutch masters, 40 by French, 20 by German, and 40 by Italian masters. Among these are works by Rembrandt, Rubens, Potter, VanDyck, Terbury, Tenniers, Hans Holbien. One of the greatest of these paintings is the Young Bull, by Paul Potter. This is a rural scene, and represents a bull standing, with several sheep and cows lying down in a pasture, while a peasant is leaning against a tree admiring the beautiful stock. I am told its estimated value is 2,000,000 of guilders— but really no money would buy it—so nearly do these Hollanders associate it with their national glory. Napoleon in one of his Vandal raids having seized this picture and sent it to Paris as one of the treasures of the Louvre, as much impoverished as this people then were, they offered Napoleon $50,000 for the picture, which the glory-loving Emperor, as much as he needed money, refused to accept. After the downfall of Napoleon, this painting, with many other works of art, was restored. Some of these paintings are 350 years old—many of them 200 and 300 years old—and yet the colors are in many instances as bright and fresh as if painted last year. Indeed, so bright and fresh are some of the fruits and flowers painted by these old Dutch and French masters 300 years ago, that it is difficult to believe they have not been painted recently. How magical the touch of these old masters to thus smile through centuries, impressed as it were, with an immortality that bids defiance to the corroding tooth of time, outlasting the marble tombs that commemorate their dust. It was here and by these painters that oil was first used in mixing the colors, a discovery obtained by the great Italian painters from here. Previous to this, all colors, both on canvas and fresco painting had been mixed in water. Raphael's first paintings were thus prepared. Afterwards he painted in oil. By this discovery a smoother and finer finish was given the paintings, and then, perhaps, they were made more durable. And yet while this would appear reasonable, I am not at all certain of it, as I have seen frescoes where size or some glutinous substance—no oil—was used in Pompeii 1,900 or 2,000 years old, and also frescoes and papyrus scrolls from the ruins of Karnak in Egypt three or four thousand years old, with the colors quite fresh.

Thursday, July 23rd.—Visited to-day the Zoological and Botanical Gardens. The collection of animals is not so large or fine as we expected. There is, however, a beautiful collection of birds, some of them quite strange to us, and the flowers constitute a very paradise.

Friday, July 24th.—Left the Hague for Hamburg, Germany, at 7 A. M., passed through Holland, much of it like the portion near the sea, a low, flat country, intersected by canals and ditches, with wind-mills ever in sight. At one point I counted forty-nine of these in sight at the same time. The people are in the midst of harvest, which is evidently good—rye, oats, and some wheat, with large quantities of Irish potatoes, the latter evidently an important crop here as well as in Ireland. Large flocks of sheep and herds of cattle give their pastures a rich yield. Most of the cattle are spotted black and white, evidently some special and favorite breed. The entire country is under cultivation, not an acre is lying waste.

One thing that attracts the attention of an American, is the entire absence of fences. Sheep and cattle are seen grazing within a few feet of growing crops of grain, and as they are not attended or haltered, we wonder why they do not injure the grain, but upon closer attention we discover the cause in a narrow ditch, filled—as are all ditches here—with water, and these narrow ditches not only divide fields and pastures, but separate farms or estates, as do fences with us. The entire country is seen to be below the sea-level, as the water in the canals, which is pumped there for drainage, is seen to be above that in the field ditches. To lift this water from the field ditches into the higher canals, is the work of the innumerable wind mills. So much is the whole country below the water in the canals, that it would be quite easy to inundate all the country by breaking the canals—and indeed this has been done with large sections as a means of defense against the invasions of a powerful enemy. The entire country looks like a beautiful landscape garden. There is no dust, and the neatly trimmed trees, farm-houses and barns are as neat and tidy as the inhabitants. In the western portion of the State, next to Germany, the country becomes utterly sterile—unreclaimed, because unreclaimable—an extended sandy plain with low sand dunes. Here and there amidst the universal sterility a few stunted pines struggle for existence. But unforbiding as is this Sahara-like district, the exigencies of man have forced to the utmost the struggle against it until every little spot of even a few acres, not covered with sand, is the home of some toiling peasant family, who manage to wring from reluctant nature a scanty subsistence. But even here amidst the sand dunes, this home-loving people have surrounded themselves with vines and flowers, which give to their neat little homes an unsuspected appearance of comfort.

HAMBURG.

On crossing the border and fairly in Germany the country becomes more fertile and populous, with numerous villages or large towns. Passed the Custom House officers, polite and accommodating, giving us no trouble, not even opening our trunks; passed several large towns, one or two of these strongly fortified. We are traveling in a first-class car, which is quite as fine as, and for day traveling more comfortable than, a Pullman Car; traveled all day, and at 8 P. M., quite tired with a thirteen hours' journey, we arrived at Hamburg, the most important commercial city in Germany, put up at Hotel de l'Europe.

July 26th.—Hamburg has about 300,000 inhabitants, the largest of the Hanseatic or Free cities of the German Empire, and the fourth in commercial importance in Europe. Its extensive railroad system connects it with all parts of the continent, while its steamers and merchant vessels bring it in relation with all parts of the world. It is situated on the left bank of the Elbe, sixty miles from the mouth, on tide-water. Besides the Elbe, there are two small rivers passing through this city; one of these forms an extensive and picturesque lake, or square of clear, fresh water in the midst of the city. Charlemagne built a castle here in 811, at which time there was most probably a considerable city at this place, as its situation on this great river, and its proximity to the sea, with its safe and commodious harbor, presented inducements or advantages not likely to be overlooked by even a half-civilized, but sea-faring people such as these. Owing to its strong fortifications it fortunately escaped the ravages of the thirty years' war which devastated so many other cities of this part of Europe. It fell, however, with other cities of Germany, into the hands of Bonaparte, and when the citizens attempted to throw off the French yoke he wreaked a terrible vengeance, destroying much of the city, and plundering or killing the citizens. It possesses but little importance in the art world, its citizens being engaged in money-making, in which they have certainly succeeded.

The harbor presents a most busy and animated appearance; great forests of masts, with merchant vessels and ocean steamers receiving and discharging their valuable cargoes, for, and from, all parts of the world, give a ready explanation of its great prosperity and rapidly increasing wealth. It has a line of steamers direct with America, and its commerce with the United States is much the most important of any city in Germany. The English language is spoken in all the hotels and shops to such an extent that one unacquainted with German scarcely feels at a loss; even many of the cab drivers understand English. The living at our hotel—as indeed at all the first-class hotels we have thus far met with in Europe—is good. The rooms large, comfortable, well-furnished; but there is one convenience in all hotels in the United States—parlors—not found in this country. No large room is set apart for the especial purpose of parlors, where all the guests may meet. This is a serious objection, as it confines guests to their rooms without the means of becoming acquainted—especially the ladies, who never meet except at Table d'Hote, which is a rather formal, tedious and unsocial affair. Our hotel is situated in the most delightful part of Hamburg, immediately in front of the *Alster Basin*, a beautiful sheet of water, walled in, and surrounded with trees. Numerous small boats carry passengers across it in every direction, either for business or pleasure. It is in the midst of the city and surrounded by fine houses; numerous white swans upon its surface increase its interest. These swans are the gift of an old lady who on dying, a number of years since, left in her will these swans, with a considerable sum of money, to the city for their maintenance. How beautiful the thought; many strangers have with the natives blessed her for the gift.

We remained for some time at this hotel, until meeting our friend, Dr. B., of St. Louis, a Hamburger by birth, with relations living here, who kindly procured us boarding in an Anglo-German family, a Mrs. Simpson, No. 47 Besenbinderhof Strasse, where we met an English captain and his wife, who, as well as the landlady and her daughter, are most estimable people. With all these kind English-speaking people we felt quite at home.

August 3rd.—Took carriage, and with our English friends, made a protracted drive through the city and suburbs. It was Sunday, a beautiful day, and all the citizens out of doors. The gardens and parks were filled with happy men, women and children. We noticed one custom not common at home; at almost every house not opening on the street they had a few trees or pagoda, under which was a table with the entire family sitting around it. The men with a bottle of wine or beer, smoking and sipping their wine with their family; often some member of the family was reading aloud, and the women, cheerful, happy, were knitting or embroidering; and while this looked a little strange as it was Sunday, I am not sure but that it looked pretty. All this with the reading and conversation must make the day both pleasant and profitable; and while from education and the force of habit I could but feel that it was almost a desecration of the Sabbath, yet it was most likely but a much more rational and fitting observance of the day than to spend the day in enforced idleness.

These Germans are much more accustomed to living out of doors than are the Americans. With us domestic life is around the hearthstone; with them out of doors, in the manner observed, or at cafés or beer-gardens, where the men, at least, and often their families, spend almost every pleasant Sunday evening. But then these German cafés and beer-gardens are much more quiet, orderly, and respectable than with us.

August 5th.—Took carriage, and together with several members of our house, drove up the Elbe some six or eight miles, to Blankenese. The drive was along shaded avenues, and by the wondrously beautiful gardens of Hamburg merchant princes, who are the aristocracy here—this being a free city has no titled nobility; indeed all such have a distaste for the atmosphere of Hamburg—and surely there could be no more lovely drive. The lawns, palaces and flower-gardens of these wealthy citizens far surpass anything we had ever seen, or that can be seen at home. They are all open to the public, even more so than Shaw's Garden in St. Louis, the gates not being closed; the wealthy proprietors evidently taking pleasure in the enjoyment they afford the public, in all this rivalling our noble-minded, public-spirited citizen, Mr. Shaw, while these gardens are much larger, more variegated and beautiful than our wonderfully beautiful Shaw's Garden. We walked through one of the largest and most beautiful of these, belonging to a Mr. Bower. It is of great size, and truly a fairyland. In it landscape gardening is carried to the greatest perfection. Carpet squares, almost equaling in beauty of design and execution the most beautiful Aixminster carpets; while its palms, roses, flower borders and graveled walks, rendered it a very Eden, from which man would feel acutely the pang of expulsion, even though on his way to paradise. These gardens border, while the palace residences overlook, the majestic, beautiful Elbe, whose broad silver surface, covered with white sails, gives additional enchantment to the charming scene.

At Blankenese we ascended, by an elaborately ornamental and artificially as well as artistically constructed pathway, a lofty eminence, from the top of which we had an enchanting view of the winding river and adjacent country, dotted over with small towns, villas and neat, garden-like farms and comfortable farm houses. On our return we stopped at a neat, picturesque café on the banks of, and overlooking the Elbe, where we had most excellent coffee and bread; driving back home through the principal parts of the city, around the Alster Basin and by its palatial surroundings, reaching home at 8 P. M., after a drive of five hours, quite fatigued, after a most delightful drive.

August 6th.—Left Hamburg on the 7 A. M. train for Copenhagen by way of Kiel. The country over which we passed is populous, and, although the land is poor, through careful cultivation, yields good crops. Rye is the principal cereal of this high northern latitude, though small fields of oats and wheat are not uncommon, with an occasional field of buckwheat, while large sections here and there are utterly sterile wastes of peat bogs. But even these morasses, in this country where the struggle for existence permits no waste, are turned to good account, as the peat turf is cut out in bricks, dried in the sun, and burned as fuel.

KIEL.

The town of Kiel is the Baltic headquarters of the German Navy, and possesses considerable commercial importance; has some 90,000 inhabitants. It is picturesquely situated on the Kieler Föhrde near the Baltic, and gives evidence of great prosperity. Its University, founded in 1665, is at present in a most prosperous condition. We put up at the neat little hotel Stadt Hamburg. After dinner took carriage and with our friend, Dr. B., drove around the suburbs along the *Düsternbroohen Weg*, through a beautiful beech wood to an elevated position where we had a beautiful view of the Föhrde, around by the observatory, and back to the city by the University. Nothing can excel the picturesque beauty presented by this forest drive, with the enchanting views of sea and land given from its loftier heights. The evening was one of the loveliest of the year. The sun set in a cloudless sky, casting a golden sheen over the distant hill tops and forest heights, while the beautiful harbor, whitened by numerous sails, stretched out in transparent beauty as far as vision extended. At midnight we took steamer for Copenhagen, via Korsar. The Baltic, here called Oest Sea, not unfrequently stormy, was during our crossing, remarkably smooth. The moon was in its full, the sky cloudless, and not a breath of air disturbed the sleeping billows. We had a pleasant run to Korsar, in Den-, mark, where we arrived at 7 A. M., and took cars for Copenhagen, where we arrived at 11 A. M. and put up at Hotel Kongen af Denmark. We had fortunately engaged rooms by letter, as we found the hotels all full with delegates to the Eighth International Medical Congress to which I am an accredited member, and which meets next week.

COPENHAGEN.

August 8th, 1884.—Copenhagen, capital of Denmark, situated in North latitude 53 40', and immediately on the sound, has a population of 300,000. It had from times unknown been occupied by fishermen's huts, when in the twelfth century the city was founded by Axel. Its commercial importance caused the rapid growth of the city, which, in the fourteenth century, became the residence of the Danish kings. The greatest or most esteemed of them, Christian II., greatly added to the beauty of the city by the erection of palaces and public buildings, a citadel and naval establishments. Many of the nobility reside here; their palatial residences together with the palace of the king of Denmark, who also resides here, assist greatly in making this the most beautiful city in Northern Europe, indeed, the Paris of this Hyperborean region.

August 9th.—Visited the Thorwaldsen Museum, which

contains many works by the great Danish sculptor, Thorwaldsen who, after many years absence in Italy, studying and copying the works of great masters found there, and after having acquired a world-wide reputation, that shed glory alike on his native country and his art, returned home to give his mature labors in decorating his native city. He was received with royal honors, a triumphal procession met and conducted him to and through the city, amidst flowers, music, triumphal arches and the waving of banners with the shouts of the multitudes rising ever above the roar of artillery. This reception is immortalized by bas reliefs on the sides of the building, which is a large structure of the Renaissance style. On the front is a victory on a quadriga by Bessen. The building contains an almost countless number of statues and pieces of sculpture, many of these by Thorwaldsen, but mostly the works of Greek, Roman and native artists other than Thorwaldsen, consisting of Ganymedes, Cupids, The Seasons, Psyches, Day and Night, Jason, The Eagle of Jupiter, Shepherd Boy, Triumph of Alexander, Bachus and Hebe, etc.

The Ethnological Museum contains a large and valuable collection, illustrating the civilization or want of it, of different countries, Europe, Asia, Africa, North and South America and Oceanica. The cabinet of medals contains 30,000 pieces.

The Royal Library contains 550,000 volumes and 200,000 manuscripts. The Royal Picture Gallery contains 750 paintings, many of them by Dutch and Flemish artists, Rubens, Rembrandt and Ruysdale being represented.

Sunday, August 10th.—The grand opening of the Medical Congress took place to-day, under the patronage of his Royal Highness, the King of Denmark. It was a grand occasion. The King and Queen of Denmark, the King and Queen of Greece, and many royal persons present. The King of Denmark, who was ex-officio President of the Convention, was without any of the insignia of royalty, except a heavy gold chain and star, while the Queen and her daughters, though richly, were plainly dressed, and so entirely without ornaments or royal insignia, that one ignorant of their presence would not have recognized them as members of the royal family. The King was introduced to many members of the Convention, shaking hands and conversing familiarly, much as our President would do on a like occasion. I believe, however, the hand-shaking was confined to the American delegates, who unawed by the sanctity of royalty, *met him on terms of equality*, scarcely doubting that a king might be as good as an American citizen. Doubtless his majesty appreciated this acknowledgment, while the nobility with their gay decorations of stars and badges of honor, of knights and noblemen, members of the Congress, with their genuflexions indicated the, to them, awful, presence of royalty. With the exception of this flutter among the stars and garters, the royal family passed through the crowd and out of the room much as distinguished guests in America might have done. Now it struck me that nothing could be more appropriate than this dignified courteous action on the part of the American delegates, or the humble bowing and scraping of the nobility, who as physicians were delegates. The former owed nothing to kings or queens, while the latter were their creations. Any king or queen may make a thousand knights, but all the kings and queens in Europe could not make an American citizen, without themselves becoming such. The occasion was a very enjoyable one, and the courtesy and quiet, good breeding shown by the king and royal family impressed every one favorably. And were kings always as unpretentious and harmless, they would not be bad things to have in any country.

August 12th.—A grand excursion was given the delegates and their families to the old castle palace at Elsinore. The day was delightful and the excursion by water. A number of steamers were gaily decorated with flags of the different nations represented in the Congress, and as this included all the civilized nations of the earth, the world was represented in these flags, while gay streamers fluttered from every mast and sail and rope. Thousands of citizens arrayed in their gayest costumes lined the wharf both here and on our arrival at Elsinore, while a laughing, happy throng filled the six great steamers that left the wharf at Copenhagen amidst the waving of hats and handkerchiefs, the booming of artillery, shouts of the multitude and strains of martial music. At Elsinore we were received in like manner. The water was smooth as an interior lake. All the steamers and sail vessels we met, as well as those in the ports, were gaily decorated with flags and streamers. At Elsinore, where a royal banquet awaited us in the old palace, hundreds of banners were waving, small flags waved from every house-top and window, while gaily-prepared triumphal arches spanned the streets. It was indeed a lovely sight, such as we might expect at the reception of a Roman conqueror on his return with the spoils of a nation, these noble Danes kindly making this occasion a national fete.

The town of Elsinore, thirty-seven miles from Copenhagen, is an old Scandinavian town of some 10,000 inhabitants, situated upon the narrowest part of the sound, where strong battlements commanded the payment of sound dues from all passing vessels. The old castle in which we were entertained, Kronberg, a former residence of the Danish Kings, is in perfect preservation and royally furnished for the king and family when visiting it. It is fortified—or of itself is a fortress —with a deep moat running around it; was built by King Frederick XI. in 1570. The flag battery before the castle is where Shakespeare makes the ghost appear to the guards. No place is a more fitting home for ghosts than this old castle, whose walls have witnessed many a frightfully tragic scene, while its dark recesses are said even yet to hold the ghost or spirit of the guardian of Denmark, Holgen Danske, who, according to reliable legends, now only makes his appearance to warn his country of pressing danger. Of course he did not appear on this occasion, as ours was a mission of life, not of death. But while we did not make the acquaintance of Holgen Danske, we did enjoy the right royal hospitality and love of good cheer he bequeathed to his posterity in a royal feast, at which, though four or five thousands guests were entertained, there was no apparent dimunition of the supply, while the great number and size of the rooms permitted no crowding. The walls are hung with many fine paintings, portraits of kings and historical personages, with battle scenes, naval and land battles. After a most enjoyable day, we returned at 5 P. M., by rail, to Copenhagen.

August 14th.—Wonderfully grand and royal as were the excursion to, and feast at Elsinore, all were greatly surpassed by those of last evening. The business of the Medical Congress, which consisted mostly in eating and drinking, having been much of it disposed of in a satisfactory manner, the delegates were entertained with a grand banquet, music, songs, etc., given by the citizens. The grand pavilion with seats for 2,500 guests was gaily decorated for the occasion. Tens of thousands of citizens lined the roadway and entrance to the grand banqueting hall, or pavilion, which was situated immediately on the bank of the sound, the quay, scores of steamers, ships and barges, gaily decorated with flags and streamers and crowded with the elite of Denmark, flitted to and fro in front of the pavilion. Many of these had on board bands which discoursed sweet music during the feasting, while the members of the different musical societies sang songs prepared by Danish poets for the occasion, making this truly a feast of soul as well as body. The banquet was interspersed with toasts and speeches. Most of these were in foreign languages which we did not well understand, and of course less interesting than they would otherwise have been. The music, however, needed no interpretation, as its language is universal, speaking to the heart, which interprets it to the brain.

After the banquet, the entire assembly, consisting of many thousands, went on board the steamers, and amidst the waving of handkerchiefs and flags and shouts of the multitude, and with bands playing patriotic airs, we steamed along the quay to the *Tivoli*, the largest and finest gardens of the kind in the world. Thousands of lamps with innumerable colored gas jets lighted up the entire grounds as light as day. This open air resort or ornamental garden, with numerous halls and booths, was on our arrival already fairly filled with ladies and gentlemen, who had gathered here to do honor to the occasion; it really looked as though all Denmark was here. The ladies were in most handsome attire which well set off their beautiful forms and faces, and tens of thousands of men, civil and military, the many officers of the army and navy in their gayest uniforms, all of which was rendered the more wierd and beautiful by the thousands of bright lights that shone with variegated colors upon the vast assembly. The entire scene was that of an enchanted garden; Aladin's lamp never threw its magic rays upon such a marvelously enchanting, bewitching scene.

These hospitable, polite and handsome Scandinavians have quite won our affections, and we feel quite ready to pledge all America for their assistance in any and all future difficulties with, and against, any and all the powers of earth.

August 15th.—The closing of the labors of the Congress took place this evening at a royal banquet at the king's palace, which was of course a grand affair, truly becoming royalty.

The king and queen of Denmark, the king and queen of Greece and many members of the royal family were present. The king was dressed plainly and was only distinguished by the star on his breast. The ladies of the royal family, consisting of two queens and some three or four princesses, wore white satin with long trains. The dresses were decolette, with short sleeves. They had on a profusion of diamonds, pearls and precious stones, all of which were well set off by their beautiful forms and lovely complexions. The king was very polite and gracious, shaking hands and talking with the members as at the opening of the Congress. The palace is, of course, gorgeously furnished as it is the residence of the king and family. Many costly pictures hung upon the walls, mostly portraits of royal or distinguished Danes. The palace is not lighted with gas, but entirely with wax candles, ten thousand of which were burning in the great banqueting hall. All present were in full court dress, and the titled members of the Congress were gaily decorated with their stars and garters, among these the one who outshone all the rest, was a swarthy Arab from Egypt, who, if we may believe his badges, had done the Sultan, perhaps also the King of Dahomey, some distinguished service, but science, I believe, had never heard of these or of him.

THE MUSEUM OF NORTHERN ANTIQUITIES.

Visited this collection, the finest of the kind in the world. It consists largely of prehistoric collections from the kitchen middens, or rubbish heaps, constituting mounds along or near the sea shore. These long-neglected mounds have been found, what no one suspected, nor until lately could have properly interpreted, vast collections or deposits, dust heaps, made by towns, settlements or encampments of prehistoric man. Of course, they belong to the Stone Age, and contain quantities of flint and bone instruments, tools and domestic implements and utensils, together with the bones of animals and fish upon which they fed, with other vestiges of primitive man. These are classified and arranged as belonging to remote times, utterly unknown in its beginning, perhaps reaching back for tens of thousands of years before our era, down to B. C. 1,500 years. Then others from B. C. 1,500 to 500 B. C. when the Age of Stone is being replaced by that of Bronze. The exact time of the introduction of bronze among these Northern nations is not, nor can it be, shown in the kitchen middens, as these all belong to the Stone Age. The Ages of Bronze and Iron are, however, beautifully given in this ethnological collection and are so arranged as to show, as far as possible, their introduction and advance among these peoples. Of course, both bronze and iron were introduced by the Romans, so that here or elsewhere we are not able to trace the archaic period of these ages as we can do, for instance, the improvement in Etruscan and Grecian faces. Here again, in the garbage piles, or kitchen refuse, as in the caves of England and France, we meet with the bones of animals long since extinct in this part of Europe and indeed in all Europe. These remains of prehistoric man carry us back to the times of cave-dwellers and the cave-bear. One curious fact taught here is that these kitchen middens were commenced long anterior to the time when man had domesticated the dog. During the earlier periods of these people, as shown here, the dog had not yet become the companion of man.

ROSENBURG PALACE.

Aug. 16th.—Visited the old palace of Rosenburg, founded in 1604 by Christian IV. It is a fine, large, Renaissance structure with gables and towers 300 feet high. It was, and is, used as the Autumn and Summer residence of Danish kings, each of whom have furnished it, in part, according to their times, also keeping here their crowns, jewels etc. Of late the historical value of this collection has been greatly increased by removing here, from other palaces and places, precious things, heirlooms, bric-a-bracs, by which this old palace has become a most valuable, interesting and instructive historical museum, informing us, without the aid of books, as to the habits and customs of these people in bygone ages, extending in some instances beyond the times of Christian IV., half a thousand years even into the dim misty legendary, if not mythological times.

During the reign of Christian IV. the revival of learning, the Renaissance, reached this far-off land, and is beautifully seen in the improvements shown here. This new style was called by the older Danes the style of Christian IV., just as in France, from the same causes, the Renaissance was called the style of Francis I. The audience-room and bed chamber of Christian IV. are now much as he left them. In other rooms are shown the crown jewels, with diamonds and diamond setting of sword handles, all of great worth and beauty, porcelain, glass, state and coronation robes, uniforms, wedding-dresses of kings and queens, gold and silver ware, watches and clocks of the time of Christian IV., portraits of a long line of kings and queens extending through a period of 400 years. The palace walls in some of the rooms are lined with tapestries, representing seiges and battles, by sea and land, with numerous historical legendary and mythological scenes. Some of these are 300 years old, with their scenes representing the time when these powerful, fearless Northmen carried a *broom* at their masthead, as indicating that their navy *swept* the seas. Other of these old tapestries were the works of queens and princesses and show in their devices of *hearts* and *love knots*, that they were the works of love, as presents to husbands, lovers or children, and in many instances with their colors quite well preserved and with an elegance in design and finish rivalling oil paintings. The vast palace is filled with these emblems of the royal splendor of bygone ages, and yet the past appears to live in these things that bring us into the immediate presence of a long line of monarchs, queens, princesses and court beauties, while the loving hearts and cunning fingers that wrought these things have long since mouldered to common dust. How impressively these costly baubles of semi-barbaric splendor found in this collection speak the vanity of rulers. The carved silver drinking-cup, the jeweled sword, the diamond trappings are here, but those who owned them, where are they? Their very mausoleums fallen to dust, and in many instances even their names forgotten; surely

> Time deals alike with royal dust
>   As with more common clay.
> The small, the great, the vile, the just,
>   Are pageants of a day.
>
> Kings and vassals together fall,
>   The mighty pass away,
> And castles, towers, turrets, all
>   Are hastening to decay.
>
> All living men must yield to dust,
>   The vase that was given,
> To hold a far more precious trust,
>   Not for earth, but heaven.
>
> 'Tis only *deeds* that will outlive
>   The tinsel robes we wear,
> 'Tis only *actions* that can give
>   Us lasting presence here.

The labors of the Congress closed with the feast at the royal palace, and the delegates, those who are able to do so, are leaving for their homes, leaving Copenhagen's banquet-halls deserted. Indeed the labors of this Congress have been rendered quite onerous by these sharp-sighted Scandinavians, who, taking in the situation at first glance, have so plied us with feasts, that many of the delegates who came here thin as weasels, are returning home puffed up like bladders—so much so that their wives will not know them, and many must die of dropsies produced by the excessive labors of this Congress. While all leave with regret this fair city, whose splendid palaces and flower gardens were surpassed in beauty and loveliness by its surpassingly beautiful women, while the feats in arms of their ancestors were eclipsed by the arts of peace and triumph of hospitality of its present inhabitants. We leave with many wishes for the long life, prosperity and happiness of the king of Denmark and all the royal family, as well as the good people of Denmark. If the world must have kings, it would do well to get them here, while all will join me in the belief that here is the place all should get their queens.

STETTIN.

Aug. 18th.—Took steamer at 2 P. M. for Stettin. The Baltic, or Oest Sea, was again smooth, placid, beautiful, the steamer running as smoothly as if on a river. At sunrise next morning we were steaming up the beautiful Oder, with a fine view of the country, which much resembles the upper Mississippi, with, however, the difference, that here every foot of available land is under the highest cultivation. Arrived at Stettin at 8 A. M.

The town has 100,000 inhabitants, with some manufacturing and commercial importance. Its greatest activity was evidently in the Naval Department, and the building of torpedo boats the most active part of this. Without stopping in the city, we took cars for Berlin, stopping at the Grand Central Hotel, which is among the finest hotels in Europe. Being quite sick and tired, we did not go out. Left at 9 P. M. for Carlsbad, where we arrived next day at 11 A. M.

CARLSBAD.

August 20th, 1884.— These are the most important mineral springs in the world, and are visited by some 30,000 persons annually. They are said to have been discovered by the Emperor Charles XIV., whose statue is here near the rathhaus. But this is legendary; they have doubtless been known from time immemorial. There are some fifteen of these springs, all more or less hot; the hottest being the Sprudel, 167° Fahrenheit. The chemical composition of all the springs is much the same; Glauber's salts, common salt, potash, carbonate of lime, magnesia and an impure salt mixed with earthy matter derived from the desintegration of the rotten stone called sprudel. This name is a generic one from Sprudel, the great central spring, or the rotten composite stone which underlies the entire surface as a crust, and when pierced by boring, or otherwise, at any point in this immediate valley, gives origin to a sprudel spring. The stone, sprudelstein, deposited from these waters, is hard, many-colored, admits a high polish, and is manufactured into various ornaments. These several springs are recommended by the local doctors here according to the disease or strength of the patient; different springs we are assured having different properties; but in fact the springs are of one and the same water; and I found these physicians in almost every case found that spring near where the patient happened to be boarding best adapted to the complaint. Of course it would not do to send patients out of the way to another spring, as they would be tabooed by the numerous boarding-houses, who would send their inmates to another doctor.

These waters differ from all other mineral springs, and, possessing very decided therapeutical properties, should never be used by the uninitiated without consulting a local physician. This necessity exists however, only as to how and when you should use the water, and how much you should drink, and in regard to your habits, diet, etc. Having learned this, you have no further use for the doctor, as far as the use of the water is concerned, and the frequent calls of the physician to see how the waters are affecting you should be discouraged. And while the waters have positive therapeutical virtues, the value of which in many liver complaints it would be difficult to overestimate, they have by no means such peculiar or subtle or nicely-adjusted or dangerous properties as is often taught and believed here. The waters being all one and the same, differing only as they differ in temperature, the hotter the water the stronger it is; that is, the more salts it holds in solution. But this is of but little practical importance, and this difference would make but little or no difference upon the patient or his disease. It makes, therefore, little or no difference which spring we use, nor need we confine ourselves to the use of one spring, but had just as well drink out of half a dozen, or indeed all, of them in turn. And yet this is a point much insisted upon; of course it is, and by magnifying the properties of these waters, the local physicians may really honestly serve the best interest of his patients, who are thereby the better induced to observe strict rules of diet, etc. Nor is the amount of water drank of any great consequence, so long as it is not too active as a cathartic, and with most persons it does not act as a cathartic at all, being drank hot, the contained salts are absorbed. It is not, however, to be inferred from this that these waters are inert and to be drank in enormous quantities. Of course no one but a fool would do this were they only hot, or indeed cold waters. I have drank a tumbler full of water from each of half a dozen of these springs the same day, without any appreciable results only such as would have resulted from the same quantity of water drank from the same spring.

These physicians formerly practiced on the old system of making no specified charge, leaving it to the patient to pay what he thought proper, but it was very naturally discovered that many of these thought proper to pay nothing, while the others did not think proper to pay enough. This system, however well adapted to ante-railroad times, was found not in accordance with this more accurate age, and very properly they now here, as elsewhere, make out regular charges, according to services rendered. As I was not a water-cure physician and unwilling to suppose that I knew as much as those who had made these waters a special study, I consulted Dr. Segar, an eminent physician and professor from Vienna, who visits these springs and practices here during the season, who recommended my wife to use the Schlossbrunnen, which is one of the most popular, as it is one of the largest and hottest, of these springs, and as this spring had the additional advantage of being higher up the hill, some 2,000 feet above the valley and near our pension, we were well pleased with the selection. We boarded at the Englisher Hof, with front and back room, large, good, light and well-furnished ; one of the thousand logis or boarding houses here ; indeed the town of Carlsbad is made up of logis and hotels. The boarding-houses are built expressly for this purpose and with especial regard to sanitary conditions, which, being entirely under public inspection, are almost always good. These logis are fitted up with furnished rooms, where you can obtain rooms and breakfast, consisting of two boiled eggs, coffee, cold light-bread and butter. The coffee and bread, the latter under public inspection, are the best in the world ; the eggs always fresh, the butter fresh and good ; so much so is this the case that we soon become entirely satisfied with the fare, not wishing anything else. The charges for two furnished rooms, lights and breakfast, are quite reasonable. We pay for our two large, well-furnished rooms, fifteen guilders per week ; breakfast consisting of tea or coffee, bread and eggs, eighty kreutzers, and the same for supper, if obtained in the house. Dinner, and most generally supper, is obtained out of the house at reasonable rates. One can live well here with large, comfortable, well-furnished rooms, for $2.50 or $3 per day—indeed for less.

The cure and diet rules prescribed by physicians are, a glass of water, about six ounces, at 6 A. M., when, after walking about for half an hour, another glass is drank, and another at 9, after which we breakfast, drink another glass at 11 A. M., take dinner at 1:30 P. M., after which most persons, ourselves among them, devote the afternoon to light walks, visiting some one of the numerous cafés, where we listen to music, or take excursions to greater distances, to some one of the many resorts, walks or drives, in which Carlsbad surpasses all other places. The most popular of these resorts is the Alte Wiese, and a most delightful place—promenade—it is. Situated between the hill and the little mountain stream, the Tepel, and is lined on either side by bright stores and shops, presenting a fine assortment of fine or taking goods, sprudelstein wares, etc.

This delightful walk, some mile or more within the town, with numerous hotels and restaurants, continues as a beautiful shaded, graveled walk or drive severals miles up the valley of the Tepel to Pirkenhammer, with several beer gardens and cafés along the route. Indeed, in almost every direction we may walk there are beautifully prepared paths, with neat cafés cosily placed in pleasant groves with music.

Friday, Aug. 22nd.—Together with some St. Louis friends, Mr. and Mr. P., we made an excursion to one of the highest points around Carlsbad, and on which has been erected a tower, sixty feet high. From here we have an extensive view of the beautiful surrounding country with the valley of the Eger with its numerous neat little farms, picturesque bordering hill-sides, groves of trees and clusters of houses surrounding the numerous manufactories of porcelain or Bohemian glass, great quantities of which are made here and shipped to all parts of the world. But to my wife and Mrs. P. perhaps, the most interesting feature of this trip was the manner of making it. The hills, or mountains, surrounding Carlsbad are too steep for carriage roads. To meet this difficulty the city has a great number of esel (donkeys) not much larger than a Newfoundland dog, with small, low, two-wheeled carriages, much like large baby-carriages at home, but much stronger. Wife and Mrs. P. took each one of these esel outfits, with a boy walking by the head of the donkey as guide and driver, or rather leader. Mr. P. and I walked. To ladies unable to walk so far this makes a most enjoyable mode of travel. Wife became so fond of these donkey drives that she was never so well pleased as when in one of these carriages. These strong, patient, sure-footed animals pull the little carriages with one person along the narrow roads that wind around the hills covered with dense forests, tacking first one way then another, much as a ship at sea, sailing against the wind, each tack or turn carrying us a little higher up the steep hill-side until the summit is reached. The distance was two miles and we were one and a half hours in making it. After taking a cup of excellent coffee at the café on the summit and resting an hour or more enjoying the picturesque landscape, we returned to the town, having been out four or five hours.

Aug. 24th.—Took carriage and with some friends drove out to Gieshübel, some seven or eight miles. This is a very remarkable mineral water, pleasant-tasted, a natural soda-water which, with the addition of a little syrup, makes an effervescing soda-water, and when drank here at the spring, as pleasant a drink as that obtained at a soda fountain at home. Vast quantities of this mineral water are bottled and sent throughout Europe. I was told that last year the enormous quantity of five million bottles were put up here. The site of the springs, high up on a hill-side, with the extended view of the surrounding country, its beautiful dark forests, picturesque hill and dale, held us here for hours. The entire drive which was along the narrow, rock-walled valley, or over the high points of the projecting hills that wall in the Eger, was most delightful, enchanting—nothing in nature can be more picturesque, more beautiful. The whole afternoon was taken up with this pleasant excursion.

When well enough, we employ a part of almost every afternoon in walking down to, and along up, the Alte Wiese, taking supper at some one of the numerous cafés. A favorite one is Pupp's, situated at the upper end of the Alte Wiese.

Aug. 25th.—Wife not so well for some days past, not able to get to the spring for the water, which I bring to her; also have her meals sent from a neighboring restaurant, as she is confined to her room. Mr. and Mrs. P. left to-day for Munich on their way home. We shall miss them greatly, as they are most agreeable people, and then they formed a connecting-link with home, as we felt with them here that we were not so entirely alone in the world as we shall now be. How long and dreary the time must appear when sick in this far-off land and alone, and how gladly will we turn our faces homeward when our wanderings are over.

Aug. 29th.—Wife being somewhat better, I took an esel and carriage for her and went to the top of a lofty mountain hill overlooking the town. The road was very steep, winding around the hill through a thick forest wood, tacking back and forwards until the top was reached. The zigzag path more than doubles the distance. The view from the summit is somewhat obstructed, but at different points of the road, we had through openings in the forest, most enchanting panoramic views of the distant hills and valleys, with their beautiful little farms, as so many gardens. A café on the summit afforded us a pleasant rest and good cup of coffee. Several hours of the afternoon were spent in this excursion. We were entirely alone, not knowing a person we saw during the trip, and yet we hardly felt this, so lovely are these communings with nature, picturesque and lovely as it is here. There was a voice in the silent wood, in the whisperings of the breeze as it toyed with the lofty forest trees above us, that spoke in a familiar tone, and as it was the voice of nature speaking to the heart needed no interpretation.

Sept. 11th.—For some ten days past wife not so well, confined to her room. We had, however, been so fortunate as to make the acquaintance of several Americans, among them Mr. B., and his son, from Minneapolis, Minnesota, also Mr. R., of Philadelphia. To-day in company with these we visited Pirkenhammer to see the porcelain factory, also the Atelier of Gunther, a cunning worker in palm wood, and said to be the only person in possession of the art of giving to this wood its beautiful polish and fine finish, an art that has been kept as a secret in the family, and handed down from father to son for several generations. We purchased a glove-box of this beautiful wood, giving twenty guilders for it.

Sept. 13th.—In company with Mr. R., drove out some eight miles to the beautiful village of Dallwitz, where are three celebrated oaks. The largest of these is dedicated to the Bohemian poet and patriot Körner, whose patriotic poems did much in arousing his countrymen to resist the French, and who lost his life in defense of his country against Napoleon. He also wrote a beautiful poem on these oaks, which has hallowed them to the present day with all true Bohemians, inspiring by their majestic beauty and patriotic associations additional love for fatherland. The entire drive along the valley of the Eger is enchantingly beautiful. Perhaps but few places in the world present more lovely landscape, hill and dale, neat, small farms embossed by the dark pine forests. The winding Eger with its narrow, fertile valley, with bordering mountains, whose dark pine forests are broken only by an occasional small peasant farm, the houses of which, while rude, serve to diversify the scenery, while the clusters of birch with their lighter green give additional variety and beauty to the landscape, to all of which the changed autumn leaves of maples and ash, with which the forests are intermixed, presents us with a picture as much more beautiful than any oil landscape painting as it is larger. But here in this country it is only nature in its picturesque loveliness that is lovely; man with few exceptions lives in stolid ignorance unmoved by the stirring events of the nineteenth century. We took coffee in the open air at the *Zu den drei Eichen*, and drove home late in the afternoon, when hill and dale, forest and field, sparkled in their autumnal robes, mellowed by the rays of a setting sun.

Sept. 16th.—In company with Mr. R. and Prof. ——, an Anglo-Bohemian, we drove to Elbogen, eight or ten miles from Carlsbad. The road for the most part runs up the narrow picturesque valley of the Eger, which with the adjacent heights present a most lovely and variegated landscape, where every admissible acre of land is cultivated, small farms with many little villages diversify and beautify the lovely view. Elbogen is one of the oldest castle towns in Bohemia and one of the most picturesque. The Eger makes here a sharp elbow bend almost surrounding the high projecting rock upon which the castle and town stand. In most places this rock presents perpendicular walls from fifty to one hundred feet in height, and when the rock wall is deficient, a heavy stone wall has been built to the same height, making a most formidable stronghold, which before the invention of artillery must have been impregnable, and when defended by even a few brave men, capable of standing against the assaults of an army. Perched upon this lofty rock eminence, 250 feet above the river, this old castle, now used for a prison and poor-house, though neglected, stands, and will yet stand, for ages, while its walls must last forever, a very spectre standing out from the night of ages. When or by whom this old castle was built is utterly unknown, as it reaches far beyond the civilization of this part of the world—is prehistoric. It is known, however, to be over a thousand years old, and is first mentioned by the chroniclers of the eighth century, at which time it was old and its builders unknown.

Doubtless away back in the early settlement of the country this old castle was the stronghold of some rude robber chieftain, who was at the same time the protector and oppressor of his tribe, and in its old halls we may well imagine was enacted many a bloody tragedy, while its deep, gloomy, prison walls have heard the last sad moans of many a helpless captive. Doubtless, too, these old halls have been thronged with the elite of the forest land, where brave men and woman, gaily decorated in barbaric splendor, danced to the sound of untaught music. But as no chronicler was here to leave to posterity the manner of these revels, or the songs of these forest minstrels, nor the dresses worn by court beauties that assembled here, we are left to conjecture, and that, too, without the imagination being aided by even the most imperfect knowledge of the manners or customs of these people.

After getting an excellent dinner at the old, time-battered hotel, Zum Weisen, we returned home down the wild, narrow and weird gorge of the Eger, by Heiling Fels, where the river, forcing its way through a rocky defile, has left standing a number of rock columns, which, standing at the foot of a pine covered mountain, on the banks of the river, present a strange, weird appearance, spectre-like ghosts of other conditions. Tradition, here more fortunate than with the old castle, gives us the origin of these stone pillars. "Once upon a time a shepherd, while attending his flocks upon the banks of the

Eger, met with the genius of the river, a beautiful fairy, with whom he fell violently in love. His flocks were deserted for the society of the beautiful princess. The fairy agreed to marry him on the condition that he would forget all others and remain ever with her. To this he readily assented, as he had no pleasure of life except in her company, readily swearing to forget all others and remain always with her. For some time he lived contentedly and happy with his beautiful fairy bride, forgetting home and the companions of his youth. But after a time he began to tire of his seclusion where his only companion was his fairy bride. Thoughts of home and the long-absent but familiar faces of his former associates obtruded more and more upon his mind; he became restless, silent, gloomy. This condition his fair young bride endeavored to dissipate by songs and enchantments, but finally the desire to visit again the haunts of men became so urgent that he obtained permission from the fairy to do so if he would remain true in his love to his queen and return again within a given time. This he promised and swore to do, intending, no doubt, at the time, to keep his oath. But, unfortunately, at home he met with an old sweetheart, the beautiful companion of his youth and object of his first love, whose charms appeared to be only increased by long absence. Overcome by the return of his love for the beautiful companion of his youth he resolved to marry her and forget his fairy queen, not suspecting that as an invisible Fairy she was near by and fully aware of his perfidy, and, more fortunate than many a neglected bride, had the power to punish.

The day was appointed, the feast prepared, and with merry hearts the intended bride and bridegroom, with a gay company of wedding guests repaired to the church, where mitered priest stood ready at the altar to perform the ceremony. But like many other human hopes and expectations these were doomed to meet a sad, a terrible disappointment. The fairy, enraged at the loss of her lover, invoked the aid of her wild and ever-obedient river. Thick mists began to darken the air, the mountains trembled, and from the earth startling moanings were heard, while high up the valley the turbulent river rose in an angry flood. A watery wall higher than the hills rolled down towards the town and church, where, paralyzed with fear, all stood unable to move ; nearer and nearer came the angry flood, which—the Eger now the embodiment of destruction—rolled down and over the church and multitudes of people, all of whom, with the town and church, were destroyed. But in order that the perfidy of her shepherd-lover might stand in everlasting remembrance and warning to faithless lovers, instead of bearing all away in the flood they were turned into these stone pillars, where they stand as mute witnesses of all this to the present day." Now if anyone doubts the truth of this legend, let him visit this weird spot where he may see them all, just as the river left them on that fatal day. We returned home late in the evening by way of Aichs quite fatigued by our long but romantic drive.

Sept. 18th.—Early in the morning, wife in an esel-carriage, in company with Mr. R., we went up to the top of the Hirschensprung, a lofty eminence almost overhanging our boarding house, but two miles to the summit by the winding road, where we took breakfast at a neat little café almost hid away among woodbines and wild flowers. The view in the clear atmosphere of the early morning, from this height which overhangs the town is most beautiful. On the topmost point is a cross ; near by, a statue of Peter the Great, of Russia, a good work, by Geidon ; near this is a small pyramid erected to the memory of Theressa, of Austria, a little beyond this is a neatly executed bronze deer, commemorative of the occurrence which gives name to this mountain peak. It is related and held as an article of faith by all true Carlsbaders, that Charles

V., some hundreds of years ago, drove with his dogs to this point a mighty stag, where a perpendicular rock of hundreds of feet prevented a further flight, while all retreat was rendered impossible by the approach of the king and his retinue; hard-pressed by the blood-thirsty hounds, the monstrous stag leaped from this projecting rock into the valley, some half mile or more, and a thousand feet below. Alighting, it broke through the earth's crust at the point where the Sprudel now is. These healing waters springing up where the stag had disappeared, in the sprudelkessel deep below. Why not?

For some time the weather has been delightful. Every day we have walked or driven to some one of the many pleasant resorts around Carlsbad, sometimes taking breakfast at the Yager and dinner or supper at Kaiser Park or Pupps, the beautiful groves and picturesque hill-tops and variegated parks now rendered greatly more beautiful by autumn-colored leaves, and yet Carlsbad is not a place where one would wish to remain long. Its far-off and isolated situation shuts out the great world, and without the society of friends the communing with nature grows monotonous. We have been here now six weeks.

Sept. 30th.—Passed the morning pleasantly with some friends, Mr. and Mrs. T., formerly of St. Louis, now of London, both highly-cultivated and pleasant people. In the afternoon, wife in the esel carriage, we went up to the highest mountain-top surrounding Carlsbad, some two miles off, and called Francis Joseph Heights. The ascent is made by a narrow, winding path cut in the side of the mountain, along which the esel drew the little carriage with seeming ease, complaining not; indeed the patient. good-natured animal really seems to enjoy it, but not, I am sure, as much as wife does. The summit is crowned with a high tower, from the top of which Carlsbad and a long range of the Tepel valley and distant hills are seen, as on a map, at our feet. It would be difficult to imagine the beauty and loveliness of this view. The forests with their dark pines, light-green birches, bright, golden maples, crimson-colored ash and sumach leaves, while the little garden farms creeping up, or dotting the hill sides, break, with their manifest evidence of human life, the hushed beauty of nature. The evening was one of the loveliest of these northern autumn days, the sky cloudless, scarcely a breath of air disturbed the sleeping sere and yellow leaves, while the universal stillness was broken only by the song of birds, as they, gathered in the overhanging trees, were in softest musical notes of instructive tenderness discussing with their assembled friends and newly-fledged families the preparations for their long annual migration to the distant sunny South. A restaurant is here during the season, but this had closed with the waning year, and its inmates, like the wandering Arab, had silently folded their tents and fled. The winged spirits of other days now hang as shadows of the past over and around us, whispering to the lonely lingerer here, Ichabod. We returned home down the winding, but now almost deserted, valley of the babbling Tepel, whose crystal waters seemed to flash less brightly as it meandered through the meadows now that the flowers had faded at the touch of the waning year, and the festive halls, with garlands dead, were no longer pressed by strangers' feet. We took coffee at the restaurant Kaiser Hof. Here, 6,000 miles from home and kindred and friends, save only those of the passing hour, and yet in our companionship with nature almost forgetting that we were alone. Having spent the afternoon of the last day of our sojourn at Carlsbad in the most pleasant excursion of our lives, we returned home at 5 P. M., at which time the sun was hiding behind the Eger hills, and the evening shadows, like winged ghosts, were creeping athwart the dusky vale, and silently climbing the western slope of the hills to their fitting home in the dark pine forests.

PRAGUE.

Oct. 1st.—Left Carlsbad for Prague at 6 A. M. Morning cold, rainy. The hour of leaving was too early to get our breakfast before starting, an inconvenience felt the more acutely as we both were quite unwell, and this, added to the cold wet day, with the cars rather crowded by rough Bohemian boors, who would keep the windows up, gave us a most uncomfortable travel of five hours to Prague, where we arrived about eleven, cold, wet, sick and tired. Went to the hotel Englisher Hof, which we found to be both uncomfortable and unaccommodating; So much so, that we would not even stay to dinner, but sick and tired as we were, went to the Blauer Stern (Blue Star), a most excellent hotel, where we were made quite comfortable.

Prague is a rather handsome city, but not near so much so as we had been led to expect. It has some 200,000 inhabitants, is the ancient capital of Bohemia, and is rather quaint or picturesque than beautiful. It was founded in the midst of the dark ages, built in the middle, and imperfectly decorated in the Renaissance, and presents many of the characteristics of all of these, and generally, we thought, the worst features of them.

Took carriage and drove over the city. Visited the old Gothic Tower, built in 1470. Watched the complicated movements, while striking, of its old astronomical clock, made by Hanusch in 1790. The clock shows the globe-zodiac with the sun and month indices, shows the phases of the moon, the entrance of twilight, night and day. When it strikes small windows open of themselves and the twelve apostles appear at the windows. Death rings the bell and beckons to a man who, not wishing his acquaintance, turns his head. It is curious and interesting, without possessing an amount of usefulness to repay for so much mechanical ingenuity in constructing it, and yet as we watched its curiously complicated automatic movements, while striking, we could but feel glad that it had been constructed.

Few places have been more noted for religious factions than Prague. During the fifteenth and sixteenth century it was the stronghold of Protestants, who, known as Hussites, were, in their zeal, often guilty of great excesses. The burning at the stake of their great leaders, Huss and Jerome, failed, as is often the case, to suppress the reform movement, and with better-defined views as enunciated by Luther and Calvin, Prague, and indeed Bohemia, had become Protestant. But after the disastrous battle of White Hill, in which the Protestant army was destroyed, and its leaders afterwards beheaded by command of the bloody and bigoted Wallenstein, freedom of thought has been crushed out in this land.

Visited the Jesuit College, Clementinum, also the University, the oldest university in Austria, and at one time the most important, but through some intolerance a schism was produced when many students left Prague and founded the University of Leipsic, in 1409, since which time this University has been cursed with non-progressive ideas, and has gradually but constantly, declined until it is now of but little importance, while its rival at Leipsic, imbued with the spirit of progress and freedom of thought, has become one of the most important seats of learning in Europe.

The Carlsbrucke, over the Moldau, is a splendid old structure, but disfigured by a multitude of hideous statues of saints, which are scarcely less repulsive in their archaic execution than the heads of the decapitated Bohemian nobles and generals which they replaced.

The cathedral begun in 1395 is yet unfinished. It contains some good statues and paintings, with reliefs of saints, etc. By ascending the highest point in the town, the Abbey of Strakow, a really fine structure, containing some good statues and tombs with a good painting of the Virgin and Child by Dürer, we obtain a splendid view of the city, with its quaint structures dotting the valley and hill-sides of the Moldau, together with an extended view of the populous and fertile valley of the Moldau, a tributary of the Elbe. Visited the Jewish quarters and the old Synagogue, said to be the oldest Jewish temple in Europe, founded in the first century of our era, the lower part very old and built in the Byzantine style, the upper part, of the twelfth century, built in the Gothic style. To the Jew it is hallowed in its memories, to the tourist scarcely less so, as a connecting link between the present and the remote past, to the philanthropist even more so as a witness of their wrongs, and to the philosopher, most of all, as evidence of the persistence of a faith which no cruelty has been able to stamp out. In its old cemetery, for the last hundred years closed to further interments, are many time-worn, moss-covered tombs and gravestones with strange Hebrew inscriptions and devices more than a thousand years old. Indeed, some of them may have been placed over the contemporaries of Josephus. This crowded, dingy, antique Jewish quarter speaks in its appearance of the manners and customs of the land and race of Rachel. Not more of Rachel at the well than of Rachel weeping over the woes of her children, who for nearly 2,000 years have toiled and suffered here. These quaint old storm-battered houses that cluster around this old Synagogue have witnessed the storming, sacking and burning of the city through all the dark and middle ages, bidding defiance to the corroding tooth of time, while the religion, manners and customs they reflect in their oriental shadows maintain an adamantine firmness that has so blunted the tooth of time that in despair it would seem no longer to trouble them. Will not these that have outlived all the manners and customs of the world outlast time itself? The devout Jew believes so.

Oct. 3rd.—Weather being cold, wet, disagreeable, and not being well, and there being nothing particularly worth seeing in Prague, we left the city for Dresden. But not being willing to be again annoyed, we took a first-class car to ourselves, by which we secured great comfort in our six hours' travel to Dresden, when we stopped at the Hotel Belvue, a most excellent hotel situated near the Opera House.

DRESDEN.

Dresden, to the tourist the most important city in Germany, is situated on either side of the beautiful Elbe, which is here spanned by several fine bridges, the most important of which is the Augustenbrucke, first built in the thirteenth century. It is the capital of Saxony, whose king resides here; has a population of 250,000 inhabitants, with so large a number of Americans residing here, that they have what is known as the American Quarter. And for the purpose for which most of them live here, educating their children, there is perhaps no place more desirable. Aside from its beautiful public buildings, parks, gardens, drives, etc., its picture galleries and museums, constituting it the art city of Germany, attract here all lovers of art visiting Germany.

With commendable pride the city has erected a noble structure suitable for the preservation and exhibition of one of the finest collections of paintings, by the old masters, in the world. These grandest creations of art, annually attract great multitudes to Dresden. The crowning glory of this collection, and indeed would be of any like collection in the world, is the great work of the world's greatest painter Raphael's Cistine

Madonna. This, like most of the works of this great artist, is an altar piece, and was painted for the Black Friars at Piacenza. It is eight feet long and six feet wide, and is of such transcendent worth, of such marvelous splendor, that like the noonday sun, while illuminating all other objects, remains itself the brightest of all. The transcendent glory of this picture breaks upon us as we enter the gallery with the greater effect from the fact that here, for the first time, it may be, we are brought in contact with the divine as shown in the human. In all other paintings of men or women, no matter how beautiful or marvelous may be the form or finish of the work, the picture is only human, but here we have an addition of what we have perhaps not even conceived the possibility, the divine given not less clearly than the human. I know of but one other work of human hands where this blending of the divine and human is given, the Venus of Milo in the Louvre at Paris, and this not so clearly or perfectly or distinctly done as in this wondrous painting. Now how is this? and why do we recognize this introduction of the divine element when it is quite certain that we know, and can know, nothing of how divinity would look were we to see it? In the case of this divine Madonna the painter has produced a part of this effect by the position and surroundings, and completed it by enlarging the space between the eyes. The Virgin is seen standing on *nothing* but space, with the curtains that hide the infinite from mortal vision, drawn back and the Madonna with the Child in her arms appears as though just stepped to the front from infinite space, with her large eyes looking out, not upon the earth, but the universe, which spreads out in infinite space before her, and evidently included within the range of vision.

It is certain that if she were standing on something, even a cloud, and looking at something, even the world, this illusion would not exist. And as much as we may admire the lofty grandeur of the Child, yet we see that it is a child and not a God we are looking at, it is in the *Virgin*, not the Child, the divinity is manifested. Now the strange part of this is, that, while we do not know the divine, we here recognize it. I suppose this grows out of our anthropomorphic ideas. The sublimest form with which we are acquainted is the human, and as man is to us the noblest of all existing beings, we naturally suppose that if he could be exalted greatly above what he now is he would be a god. All the efforts of the ancient sculptors were upon this idea, as in the Jupiter of the Greeks, and as shown in the Venus of Milo. Here in this Madonna the something added is not simply more humanity, for this is given to the highest ideal conception in the beautiful woman, beyond which we can have no conception of humanity being more exalted, more perfect. The added something here is something more exalted, more perfect, more sublime than merely the human. The artist here without enlarging the figure has infinitely enlarged the capabilities, the possibilities, the attributes—has removed the figure from place into infinite space, while the drawn curtains are manifestly those that hide the habitation of the eternal. I have, as stated, never met with this marvelous effect in the same degree, in any other work—no, not even in Raphael's other Madonnas, which, though wondrously beautiful, are still women, with all the perfection, loveliness and beauty of surpassingly beautiful women, yet only women, while here is a goddess as well as woman. And the angels that hold back the curtains are manifestly not more a part of heaven or the unseen world than the figure that stands between the curtains with the Child in her arms and looks out upon immeasurable space, which we are here made to feel her vision embraces.

St. Sixtus is a grand figure intended to represent not a

saint alone, but Christianity; and as he stands meekly, reverently on her right hand, the spirit of Christianity is represented, while St. Barbara, a most beautiful and lovely young woman, though reverently kneeling on the left of the Virgin, and most manifestly quite devout and reverent, has a coquettish air that unconsciously betrays the fact that she knows she is very pretty, and herself worthy of much adoration. Now this thought so beautifully expressed in the coquettish appearance of this beautiful saint enhances the interest, as it increases the meaning of the painting. St. Barbara is religion, not entirely as it came from heaven, but as it is after being assimilated with humanity, still pure and good and true and holy, but all these as manifested by humanity. The two lovely cherubs at the lower part of the picture, with the brightest, prettiest faces ever known to earth or heaven, although also looking out over infinite space, fail to embrace it, as do the Madonna and Child, yet beautifully connect the eternal and the finite.

The more we study this picture, the more lovely, grand, majestic, glorious it becomes; and had Raphael never painted anything else, this alone would have given him a bright immortality. These opinions of mine I am quite sure are honest, and the result of impressions I have received in seeing and studying this painting; nor have they grown out of any love I had for Madonna pictures—in fact I had seen so many of these as mere daubs and the objects of superstitious regard that I had conceived a contempt, almost a horror, for these pictures, but this has so won upon heart and brain that I am quite ready to forgive anyone who may make it an object of adoration.

Here also is a celebrated Madonna and Child by the great German artist, Hans Holbien, which while it doubtless possesses much excellence, does not impress me favorably. The Madonna is certainly beautiful, but the Child has a rather peevish, sickly appearance, looking as though it might have *Cholera Infantum*, which certainly mars the effect of this much praised work of this truly great master. The picture is known as the Meyer Madonna, from the fact that it was painted for, and included the portraits of the Burgomaster, Meyer and his family. Since this criticism on this picture was made, it has been pronounced by competent authorities an early copy by some Dutch master, an opinion in which I heartily concur, as this might account for the imperfections pointed out in the Child; imperfections which we are glad to find Holbein is not accountable for. Here too, is Battoni's Penitent Magdalene, also a Magdalene reading by Correggio; two paintings of rival excellence, each beautiful to perfection, lovely beyond comparison, as each represents a different type of female beauty, and each too perfectly beautiful to be compared to anything but itself. Titian's Head of Christ, which has served as a model for all subsequent painters and sculptors, is one of the gems of this gallery. A Madonna by Murillo, one of his greatest pictures, and only second to the best of Raphael's Madonnas. Indeed, this Madonna by Murillo, is of the very highest perfection. The style is entirely different from that of Raphael, so much so that it would be difficult, and perhaps hardly fair, to compare this Madonna by Murillo to one by Raphael; both may be pronounced perfect in their style, permitting no alteration without injury, and forbidding any attempt at improvement.

We attended the Opera, which is one of the finest opera buildings in Europe. The Queen of Sheba was being performed, and had a successful run of several weeks. The music was very fine, the scenery truly gorgeous, and the dresses regal. I was astonished that such dresses and scenery, and so much musical talent of the highest order could be produced at the price of admission, and during a run of only four weeks, even in this city of so much culture, but was informed that the Kaiser gives this Opera House 200,000 marks ($50,000) annually, which of course renders such expense and such excellence possible.

Oct. 13th.—Visited the Moreau Monument, erected upon the spot where this commander fell mortally wounded. It is on an elevated ridge overlooking the entire city, and a long range of the Elbe, here quite a river, giving a beautiful panoramic view of the city and adjacent country. Returned by way of the palace, where we visited the Green Vault, which contains an immense collection of great value and beauty, consisting of the jewels and furniture of kings and queens of Saxony, among them the crown jewels, great diamonds and precious stones in incredible quantities, costly royal baubles sufficient to found a city, or indeed to support one, or feed the hungry and clothe the naked of a province. Visited also the Japanese collection, a rare and beautiful collection of Chinese, Japan, French, and Dresden porcelain, glass, etc., many of these of great size and fabulous price, the gift of kings and emperors, or royal purchases. Visited also the Archaelogical, Mineralogical, Geological and Ethnological Museum, a most valuable, interesting and instructive collection which the visitor to Dresden will not fail to see or appreciate.

BERLIN.

Berlin, the most important city within the German Empire, with a population of 1,200,000, dates back, as do nearly all of these German towns, not further than the ninth or tenth century, previous to which Germany only had existence as a vast forest, swarming with wild, semi-barbaric men, mostly known as Scandinavians, whose habitations stretched back into the unknown regions of the North, whose unknown forests seemed to swarm with men as multitudinous as its leaves.

True, we read of Goths, Ostrogoths, Huns, Alemani, but by the Romans these interminable swarms of warlike barbarians were classed as Scandinavians, belonging to the forests and not to cities. It is situated in the flat, sandy and unromantic plain of the Spree. The location is such as to prevent the city presenting so good an appearance as it would were it more favorably situated, while the entire absence of the mediæval appearance seen in some other of the German cities, gives it a less interesting appearance than it might otherwise possess, producing, in despite its many objects of interest, to one visiting it for the first time, a feeling of disappointment. It was until lately the capital of one of the German States only, and while this, Prussia, was the most important of these States, it was of small size. Yet such was the worth of this people that both their State and capital assumed great importance in Europe, waging war or defending themselves against the most powerful empires. But now that Berlin is not only the capital of Prussia, but practically that of the great German Empire, the vast resources of which centre here, it is rapidly becoming the most important city in Europe. And if, when the capital of the small kingdom of Prussia, it was able to maintain the successful rivalry with Vienna, the capital of the former mighty empire of Austria, may we not well expect that all rivalry will soon cease in the overwhelming importance of this, the capital of the great military empire of Europe.

The first place to which the comer to Berlin naturally resorts is the *Unter den Linden*, and this, while comparatively handsome from its great width (200 feet) and long lines of old linden and chestnut trees, with the emperor's and crown princes' palaces, Opera House, and other palatial buildings, statues and monuments, like the city in general, produces a feeling of disappointment. The street is really not improved by all these as much as we would suppose it must necessarily be. The lindens are uneven in size and height, are often unthrifty in appearance, and not unfrequently missing, while this defect is not supplied by the chestnut trees which often present the untidy appearance of the lindens; and then, perhaps, from the unfavorable topography of the city, the palaces and palatial buildings do not appear to the best advantage—fail to impress us as we would expect. And, then, while there are many things to be seen of great interest, with the exception of the Zoological Gardens and the Egyptian Museum, both of the highest merit, there is produced a painful feeling of disappointment, and this is further increased on visiting the picture galleries, where we find a great collection of paintings of much merit, but few or none of the first-class, and when even by the great masters, they are never their best works. Added to all these unfavorable facts, things really beautiful, as palaces, churches, etc., have no historical importance, are not hallowed by associations. We must leave the immediate city to become really interested.

POTSDAM.

Oct. 29th.—Visited Potsdam by way of the sylvan castle of Babelsberg, an old castle still occupied by the Emperor during a part of the summer, and containing many paintings, principally portraits of royal personages—a multitudinous host here in Germany. The palace is a beautiful Renaissance structure, picturesquely situated in a forest wilderness, the unbroken wildness of which gives no indications of the palace near by until, turning a sharp bend in the road, the old palace is immediately before us nestled away amidst grand old forest trees, which, with the tiny lake in front, give an air of quiet repose that must be most grateful to the aged emperor during his retreat here from the din and care of busy Berlin.

From here we drove on to Sanssouci, the former palace residence of Frederick the Great. It is a beautifully situated long range of one story buildings yet, notwithstanding the cheerful surroundings, rather gloomy-looking. This palace possesses great interest to all true Prussians from its intimate association with the Great Monarch, and is visited with much the same awe and reverence with which a crusader may be supposed to have approached the holy sepulcher at Jerusalem. We were politely shown through the palace by an intelligent attaché who pointed out and explained many things that might have escaped observation, and many more that would not have been so well understood.

In the death-bed chamber of Frederick the Great, stands a clock, with the hands pointing to twenty minutes past two o'clock, the moment of the great king's death. The clock stopped, we are told, at this moment and has stood, and still stands, as a mute but instructive guardian spirit of this chamber, pointing, and has for 100 years pointed all comers to the moment and the hour when in 1786 the spirit of this truly great king passed from the scenes of his earthly glory. It has been intimated by the unsympathetic sceptic, that this faithful sentinel was stopped, but I am quite ready to believe all that is here related of the illustrious monarch, and really felt a tender regard for this old clock that refused to move when he who had so long attended and loved it, was forever still, which I am sure the less credulous can not feel. Frederick William IV. also died here. Many of the paintings and much of the furniture of Frederick the Great are still here, and much as he left them 100 years ago. The room he fitted up for his mercurial friend, Voltaire, is much as when Voltaire last saw it, and in a rage left Sanssouci never to return. Frederick had a real attachment and love for this great Frenchman, however little he may have liked the French in general. There was much in common between these two great men, both monarchs in their line, Voltaire with his inexhaustible fund of humor and wit, a great writer and poet, was to the great warrior a most congenial companion, and then, perhaps, the great Frenchman's want of faith in the Christian religion, and hatred of priests, most of all made him a welcome guest at Sanssouci, as in this Frederick found sentiments in harmony with his own. During Voltaire's temporary absence, Frederick had this room in his palace fitted up with special reference to Voltaire's characteristics—numerous monkeys with distorted bodies and ludicrous grimaces, and parrots with open mouths and wriggling bodies, were worked into the walls as bas or alto reliefs. The room was fantastically furnished and ludicrously frescoed. This so disgusted and enraged Voltaire that he engaged in a violent quarrel with Frederick—and these two had had many quarrels—and left for France where he was when his friend Frederick the Great died. It were a pity that these two congenial spirits should have been thus separated, as it is highly probable that they had for each other more true affection than for anyone else. Both were truly great—Voltaire as mighty with the pen as was Frederick, the greatest warrior of his times, with the sword. Well there is a melancholy pleasure in thinking that these congenial spirits have long since joined company, where no monkey or parrot images will again separate them. Voltaire's picture, an excellent work of art, as well as most striking likeness, painted by the king himself, still hangs in this room, and is one of the palace's greatest ornaments, as it brings us by its presence in direct communion with the great king, and scarcely less great wit and poet. Indeed to me this picture possessed far greater interest than those of royal personages by great artists, that hung upon the palace walls.

The spirit of the great monarch so pervades these halls, chambers, the entire palace and grounds, that we are insensibly, as if by an unseen force, awed into a reverence for the place. Immediately in front of, and near to, the palace door are buried his faithful hounds and war-horse, and here too, the great king wished to be buried, that these faithful companions might keep him company, if not in the spirit world, surely in dust. And if these have spirits that also are immortal—and who can say they have not—surely the faithful attendance and devotion they gave in life are guarantees of watchful care in the spirit land that but few human friends could give. I could but look upon this striking instance of man's attachment to, and kind regard for, animals whose devotion to duty, watchful care, and desire to serve or please never tired, as one of the better traits of our nature, and more exalted the great monarch in my esteem than his exploits upon the battle-field. How unkind and how unwise in man to wish or willingly believe in a final separation at death from these, the most faithful and true, and often the only devoted and utterly unselfish friends, he had in life. What human spirit friends would more certainly scent from afar, and drive off the spirit terrors of an unseen world, then the spirits of these faithful dogs who through life had loved to battle with storm and darkness through the silent watches of the night in guarding their much loved master; and as they preceded the great king how gladly would their watchful spirits leap to meet him at his coming? I must confess that I viewed this burial place of his faithful war-horse and hounds with feelings scarce less reverent than those felt in his death-bed chamber, with its dumb sentinel clock that refused to measure time, when he, for whom it was so long accustomed to measure it, was no longer of time—had passed its bourne for a shoreless eternity, and I painfully regretted to know that Frederick's last wishes were not complied with—that he was not buried here.

From Sanssouci we drove to the new palace, built, it is said, by Frederick the Great to convince the world that he, nor his much-loved and loving Prussia, was not impoverished by the long wars that he had waged for the maintainance of the autonomy of Prussia. These long wars had been successfully maintained against the united and overwhelming armies of the two most powerful nations of Europe, France and Austria, whose irresistible forces overran and laid waste with fire and sword, his small kingdom of Prussia. But again and again when they thought they had certainly crushed the spirit and exhausted the resources of this war-like people, were they undeceived by Frederick and his small band of Spartan heroes, every man of whom fought

> "As though 'twere he,
> On whose sole arm hung victory."

Suddenly, and at an unexpected moment, like an eagle from his eyre, or a wounded lion from his lair he fell or sprung upon the spoiler, striking with the force of the fierce thunderbolt, at which whole armies went down before this unconquerable band of heroes, who fought for God and their native land, with a strength that 'twere suicide to meet.

Well, if this were indeed his object in building this palace, the proof was certainly convincing, as it manifestly cost a vast sum to erect this building and adorn its 200 rooms, many of them decorated in the most beautiful or gorgeous manner, and furnished with the most costly garniture of the times. Inlaid tables, fine vases, mirrors, clocks, paintings, frescoes, and many other articles of truly royal splendor, still remain in the rooms, some of which are occupied as a summer residence by the Crown Prince of Prussia. One room of great size has its entire walls finished with shells, minerals and precious stones, which of themselves cost large sums of money.

Just beyond the Bradenburg Gate, a structure of much interest standing at the terminus of the *Unter den Linden*, is the monument of Victory, erected to commemorate the destruction of the French Empire, and glorious triumph of the

German army, in the Franco-German war. It is a beautiful structure, 200 feet high, built of granite and ornamented with French cannon, on the sides are frescoes and bas reliefs of Sedan and other battles. From its lofty summit we have a fine view of Berlin, its palaces, churches and public buildings, the broad *Unter den Linden*, and adjoining country with the forest of the Tiergarten, which latter as seen from here presents the appearance of a primeval wilderness, the fitting habitation of wild beasts and savage men, but in fact is a beautiful cultivated forest park with its flower beds, trimmed trees and graveled roads and winding artistic paths, constituting it one of the most beautiful forest parks in the world, where, invited by the loveliness and quietude of its sylvan retreats, we fall into revery, when the imagination peoples its grottoes with fairies, and its streams and miniature lakes with nymphs who gambol to the dulcet notes of birds, quite unconscious of the immediate presence of the great city with its din and stir of human life.

CHARLOTTENBURG.

Nov. 8th.—Visited to-day the old suburban town of Charlottenburg, with its old palace, erected in 1699, long the residence of Sophia Charlotte, wife of Frederick the Great, and where are buried Queen Louise and her husband, William III., whose mausoleum we visited first before entering the palace. The mausoleum is approached through a long avenue lined on either side by rows of beautiful trees, covered all the way to their tops with ivy, which gives them a melancholy beauty, a quiet, sombre appearance, well becoming the surrounding of the dead. Indeed I never saw a spot that seemed more pervaded with that spirit of stillness so naturally associated with death. The very leaves were hushed to silence, lest by their rustling they might disturb the slumbering dust that reposes here.

The statues of the royal pair, in white Carrara marble, lie side byside, as though sleeping. They must have been quite handsome in life; the lovely queen images in this beautiful statue a sleeping angel. If their sleep is as quiet and peaceful as this lovely place, it were a pity to awaken them. A beautiful candelabra with three Fates is by Rausch, another, the three Horæ, by Tick. Returning to the palace, we passed through the beautiful small palace garden, laid out by the world-renowned landscape-gardener, De Nötre, landscape-gardener to Louis XIV., who planned the enchanting gardens at Marseilles.

   We were politely shown through the palace by an intelligent young woman, who, strange to say, refused any compensation for her trouble and really valuable services. This old palace is occupied at present by the crown Prince of Meiningen, who, though a Prince, can occupy but a small part of this immense structure, which is really large enough for several full-grown kings. Like all the palaces we have visited, whether inhabited or not, it contains many costly royal baubles, tapestries, inlaid tables, rare and beautiful ancient vases, clocks, and cabinets of rare and excellent workmanship, numerous old oil paintings, portraits of kings and queens, courtiers and court beauties. Many of these old paintings astonish us by the freshness of the colors.

   Our visit through these old halls was made the more pleasant and instructive, not alone by the intelligent guide, who pointed out and named the different portraits and objects of interest, but also by an old Anglo-German lady who had accepted our invitation to accompany us, and who seemed to have by heart the history, private and public, of the entire royal families of Germany, with their deeds, hopes and fears, virtues and vices, all of which was given with such clearness and minuteness of detail that at the time I felt quite competent to write a history of the court of Berlin. These royal portraits and royal baubles extend back to times antedating Frederick the Great, silent but impressive witnesses of other days. But all this royal splendor, inviting perpetual residence here, did not enable them to evade the great reaper Death, who seems to have revelled here as if in high carnival, loving, as it would appear, a royal mark, making these royal halls like those of a wayside inn, the transient abode of passing guests, where royal personages met and jostled each other on their great highway to the tomb, passed on, making room for others, who for more than 200 years have followed each other in mournful procession, the order of which these portraits give us.

Yet, in despite of all this. I am satisfied it is quite worth while being a king, for while these may not baffle death they certainly profit by baffling others, as of all this splendor none of it is the creation of their hands, but was wrung from the toiling masses. How different the fortunes of men! How many sow, in this land, who also reap, but the product of their honest harvest toil is not for them, but for the privileged classes.

Visited the Aquarium, a place of much interest, as we meet here with marine and fresh water animals gathered from every clime, with tanks so arranged, by an intelligent study of their habits and habitats, that they meet here all the requirements of their respective natures, and flourish as if at home, whether from arctic or tropical seas or rivers.

What strange inhabitants water, as well as the land, hath! For what possible purpose were some of these strange, imperfect and uncouth things created, or how developed? Doubtless they have their use in the great plan of the universe and also their allotment of happiness; but it is difficult, yea, often quite impossible, to see the one or the other. Indeed, the word *happiness* which I have here used, is entirely misapplied, is a misnomer, as it is impossible to suppose a stone or flower *happy,* and yet not more so than to suppose this of some of these things that are scarcely lifted out of the inorganic world, while others so closely form the connecting link between plants and animals that naturalists are divided as to which kingdom they belong. Who can say that a polyp or sponge is happy? These things exist, and in them we see life as 'tis in ocean, but how crude the forms, how strange the motions! and yet, "all are but parts of one stupendous whole." And perhaps there may be some satisfaction in knowing that if they exist without enjoyment, without happiness, they are without the want of it.

VIENNA.

On approaching Vienna next morning, we found the ground covered with snow, and it was still snowing. This was the first snow we had seen this season, and with the strange aspect of the country, the extended level plain dotted over with small farms and peasants' cottages, was really pretty. Arrived in Vienna at 8 A. M.

Vienna, the capital of Austria, is situated in the broad valley of the Danube, here a large river, contains 1,200,000 inhabitants, and next to Paris, is the most beautiful city in Europe. It has many broad and well-paved streets with its principal one, the Ring-strasse, of an average width of 160 feet. This beautiful street is much more handsome than the celebrated *Unter den Linden* of Berlin, and longer than the Champs Elysees of Paris, while the palatial houses that line it on either side, are more uniformly beautiful than those of either of these streets. This and the Graben-strasse are the principal shopping streets, and, with their bright shops filled with elegant and costly wares, with sidewalks and stores crowded with fashionably and costly-dressed ladies, quite rival the more fashionable boulevards of Paris. Indeed as a centre of taste and fashion. Vienna is only second to Paris, of which it constantly reminds us. It is celebrated for its handsome women.

Many of the public buildings are grand, beautiful, palatial. It can hardly be that the government could have built them, for this is bankrupt, with its currency at 20 per cent. discount. Many of these fine structures must have been built by public-spirited, wealthy individuals, or the money raised by some direct taxation on the industry of the city of Vienna, which is prosperous. Evidence of this local prosperity is seen in the splendid private villas, and long rows of palatial business houses, stores and shops, filled with bright wares, indicative of industry and thrift. A native vigor and industry inherent in this people have made them rich and prosperous in despite the shameful misrule of the land for centuries, and in despite the degrading and destructive subordination, practically at least, of the temporal to the spiritual powers. Kings and rulers have often been but puppets in the hands of their ecclesiastical advisers.

Great prosperity of the merchants, artizans and mechanics, has brought its attendent blessings of more commodious houses, and an art culture, as seen in the improved style of architecture and establishment of art galleries, museums, opera houses, etc. The Imperial Opera House, a beautiful Renaissance structure, and among the finest buildings of the kind in Europe, seats 3,000 spectators. The New Exchange, also a Renaissance structure, cost 8,000,000 florins.

So important have become the art treasures collected here, that they make this a most desirable point to the tourist, while their scientific attainments have made the Vienna medical schools and hospitals the most important of the age, the medical *Mecca*, to which flock medical students from all parts of the world.

Nov. 17th.—Visited the treasury, which contains the royal collections for 600 or 800 years, consisting of helmets, swords, pistols, goblets and drinking-horns, richly set with pearls and diamonds. These swords and pistols of kings were very properly ornamented with jewels, as they were only for show. Very few kings venture their precious lives by using them in defense of the country; those of heroes thus ornamented, detract from the merit of their owners. Strange and costly watches and clocks, among them the first clock made, in which the pendulum was used to measure time, the Austrian regalia crowns and crown jewels. The collection of diamonds, jewels and precious stones alone would buy a city. The crown of the empress is brilliantly ornamented with diamonds, one of these weighs 133 carats, and is valued at $300,000, numerous stars and garters covered with diamonds and precious stones. One order, that of the Golden Fleece, contains 150 brilliants, with one, the central piece, as large as an English walnut. A scarf of the Grand Order of Maria Theresa, contains 548 brilliants, many of these of great size and beauty. The coronation robe of Napoleon, the silver cradle of his son, the king of Rome, weighing 500 lbs. Indeed, after seeing this vast collection of royal baubles, one scarcely wonders that the government is bankrupt; whole generations have been plundered to administer to the vanity of Emperors.

Another room here is of great interest, containing many rare and valuable relics of unquestionable genuineness, being endorsed, proved by that most reliable of human testimony, legends, as given in dreams, visions, miracles, etc., and these endorsed by the guide who shows them. These objects are themselves often of great interest, and then the pleasure we feel in viewing them is greatly enhanced by the positive assurance we feel that, here at least, there is no mistake, and consequently no room for the doubt we feel in seeing and hearing some other things. All doubts which might lessen the pleasure the tourist would otherwise feel, being dismissed, we proceed to notice a few of these inestimable relics. In one case, we saw carefully preserved, as indeed it should be, a large piece of the true cross, the veritable cross on which Christ was crucified; no mistake here. The cross was carefully buried by the disciples, and a thousand years afterwards its place of secretion was revealed, in a dream, to an empress saint, and it was dug up by some pious monks; and then it is pleasant to feel that our faith in this piece being of the true cross, as thus revealed, is not affected by our knowledge that enough pieces of this true cross have been disposed of to build a man-of-war. Why not? Who would doubt that, like Prometheus' liver, it grows as fast as consumed? Also we were shown a piece of the apron Christ wore, as well as a piece of the cloth that covered the table at the Last Supper, and what is of perhaps even more interest, the spear-head that pierced the Savior's side, the very spear, proofs positive. Well it is a formidable instrument, that leaves no wonder that it killed.

Nov. 20th.—Visited the Belvidere Picture Gallery, which contains a large collection of the old masters, Perugino, Correggio, Titian, Raphael, Murillo, Rubens, Van Eyck, Van Dyck, Durer, Holbein and others. But while this gallery contains many works of much interest, yet very few great or firstclass works are found here; none of these are the best works of these artists. And yet this and other picture galleries of Vienna possess no secondary importance to lovers or students of art, as the great number of pieces from the different schools furnish a most excellent study of the different schools. There are a number of other collections of paintings here, but the want of a suitable place for collecting together and properly exhibiting these and other works of art now scattered through the city in numerous collections, private and public, has heretofore prevented Vienna taking her proper place in the art world. This want is being now met by the erection of two large and splendid buildings, separated by an open court. The one for paintings, the other as a museum. When these are completed and the works of art collected and properly arranged, Vienna will become to the art-loving tourist one of the most important places in Europe, outside of Italy.

Nov. 22nd.—Visited the collection of coins and antiquities. This is a large and valuable collection of curiosities, consisting of ancient bronzes, cut stones, Greek and Etruscan vases of great beauty, often of great value, many of them presents to the emperors of Austria, by potentates, as bridal or coronation gifts, others purchased or obtained by conquests. The collection of coins contain 40,000 pieces, gold, silver, copper, bronze, etc. The collection of Chinese and Japanese vases fills a large hall; many of these are of great size and beauty; many of these too, are bridal or coronation presents.

Nov. 26th.—Visited the votive church, a beautiful Renaissance structure, built as a votive offering for the escape of the Emperor Joseph, in 1883, who was fired at by a blundering Bohemian who, of course, missed his mark. Had it been an American backwoodsman this church would not have been built. Of course, it was well enough that the assasin failed, as assasination is perhaps never justifiable, but had he succeeded in his intent, the world would have lost nothing, nor would Austria, most probably, have gained anything, as these royal families swarm in multitudinous troops, are as prolific as rabbits, and as numerous, and have ever ready a more hungry aspirant who is willing to take the chances of being shot for the fatness connected with the royal robe. The church with its beautiful proportions, stained memorial windows and lofty, lace-like spires, is an ornament to the city. But we must believe that courtiers and priests had much more interest in its erection than heaven or the masses of the Austrian people had, as it is difficult to believe the Author of the universe takes any especial delight or interest in the well-being of the Austrian royal family, or that the people are tenderly attached to a line of rulers that have reduced the nation from one of the first powers of Europe to one of almost no importance.

Nov. 27th.—Visited Count Czernen's palace and picture gallery containing a large number of paintings by the old masters, mostly of small size, but many of them art gems, more beautiful than almost anything in the great Belvidere or Academy of Art picture galleries. Among the most beautiful we may mention, Christ on the Cross, by Murillo; Storm at Sea, by Ruysdale; Portraits, by Van Dyck; Bagpipe, by Tenniers; Players, by Doce; Portraits, by Helst; Landscape, by Claude Lorraine; Cattle, by Potter; Doge of Venice, by Titian; Return from the Chase, by Wouverman; Portrait of Philip of Spain, by Valesquez. How bright and new many of these old paintings appear, many of them are on wood, some on zinc, others on canvass, many of them three and four hundred years old, with their colors as fresh as though painted but last year. How strange this is! Are these beautiful productions immortal? If not, when will they fade?

Nov. 30th.—Visited the Augustine Kirche, an imposing Gothic structure, commenced in 1330, consequently between five and six hundred years old. How many human hopes and fears has it witnessed! How many rulers have come and gone, and what changes in the manners, customs and conditions of mankind have taken place since first its foundations were laid. But with all its memories, that which gave it especial interest to us, and in the presence of which we almost forgot to notice its lofty dome supported by double rows of immense marble columns, eighty feet in height, or its splendid altars, was the monumental tomb of the Archduchess Maria Christina, the lovely daughter of the mighty Maria Theresa, Empress of Austria, by Canova. This lovely daughter of the most mighty empress in Europe honored her high-born position, her sex and human nature in not forgetting that she had a common humanity with the humble poor, and of her abundance gave liberally to sweet charity, clothing the naked, feeding the hungry, and administering to the lowly, sick and helpless, so much so that her death was a personal and present loss to the poor and needy. This the sculptor has beautifully immortalized in this work. The monument of white Carrara marble is in front of an opening in the church wall, most likely the entrance into a small side chapel, representing a vault. This is reached by six or eight marble steps, some twenty feet in length. At one side of the vault lies a great marble lion slumberingly guarding, with half-closed eyes, the holy place from vulgar tread. Leaning, half sleeping, on the lion as if to guard the place against even the approach or gaze of spirits that prowl in darkness, is a most lovely angel wrapped in devotional sorrow. On the opposite side is a gronp of six or eight pilgrims of the poor, approaching with the little all they had to offer, garlands of sweet-scented flowers as immortelles to her memory. I could but believe these simple but appropriate offerings of the humble poor, whose misfortunes she had labored to alleviate, were more grateful to her sweet spirit than crowns of gold. Above the tomb is an angel flying to heaven with her imaged soul. The entire production is beautifully significant, impressive beyond description. I could have shed a tear to her sweet memory. Were all high-born men and women so thoughtful of those less fortunate, the world, methinks, would be a very Eden, where human sighs and tears would ne'er be shed as witnesses of man's inhumanity to his fellow-man. I breathed a prayer with full faith that her gentle spirit may rest as serenely beautiful as the sweet-imaged angel that guards her tomb. Our deeds live after us, and deeds of love and charity will outlive monuments of marble and of brass, are indeed like a river flowing on, ever widening, deepening, on and on forever. The choir sang, and the deep-toned organ, played by master hands, filled the vast church with sweetest melody, echoing back from aisle and nave and lofty, vaulted roof the music of the spheres. I thought that it was mellowed with a chant from the spirit of this sepulchre, which, perhaps, for the moment basking upon the borders of Paradise, had, with a bevy of angels, lingered there to join in the sweet requiem.

The everlasting hills with earth and the heavens may pass away, but love and charity, upon which is builded the eternal throne of God, shall last on and on, growing brighter and brighter, to and throughout the eternal day.

In another part of the church is a vault or room, a side-chapel with a tomb and altar. Upon the altar burned a wax-candle. It is closed by a lattice gate through which is seen the costly marble monument of Leopold II., who died in 1792. His statue in white marble, full-size and clothed in mailed armor, reposes on the tomb. Several other royal and distinguished persons are buried here, among them Dr. Von Gunter, physician to Maria Theresa. In the Loretto Chapel are the hearts of the imperial family in urns. This I like not. Had their bodies been burned and their ashes preserved in these urns, it would have been in better taste. Who cares for their worthless hearts, most of which never felt a noble or generous emotion during all their beating, and now when dried or fallen to dust are of no more importance than a hand or foot? And then I could but think it were a pity to separate these pride-inflated hearts of kings from their worthless bodies, which even the royal purple and diadem had failed to make better or less corruptible than those they despised.

"Thy scales, mortality, are just,
To all who pass away;
Weighed in thy ballance royal dust
Is vile as common clay."

The beautiful stained windows of this church are several hundred years old, the chair stalls of oak, richly carved, are of the fifteenth century. Beneath the church are catacombs containing the bones, skulls and dust of priests, monks and other holy men, but

>Time has dealt with these holy men,
>   As with less pious clay;
>They lived and ate and drank, and then
>   Like sinners passed away.

But the time approaches when we must bid adieu to beautiful Vienna with its miles of palatial marble rows of houses. No, they are not of marble, not even of stone, but solid brick structures, covered with plaster, but so beautifully and uniformly done, that the cheat is only detected by its very perfection. As art is more perfect than nature, often, here, as in a painted beauty, exciting suspicion by the absence of defects, which nature in the very wantonness of her resources despises to conceal, and if nature is creative, art is ever more so, as here, as in many other instances, unsightly crude matter is by the plastic touch of art transformed into images of beauty. With a passing sigh of regret that our stay in this beautiful city is not longer, we leave for the romantic, historic city of the Doges, where we may hope, at least, to have better weather. It is cold here, the ground hard frozen, and the public squares and fields covered with snow, which is kept swept up and hauled away from the streets.

THE SEMMERING PASS.

Dec. 1st.—Left Vienna at 6 A. M. for Venice. On leaving Vienna the morning was clear, bright and cold, with a slight snow covering the ground. Our route was over a wild mountainous country, the Semmering Pass. The ever deepening snow gave the pass a wilder and more weird appearance. I think I never saw a more beautiful day. Snow, deep snow, covered the vales and hill sides, while the neighboring mountains, rising 5,000 and 6,000 feet above the sea, wild and rugged, stood in white mantles on either side in truly Alpine grandeur. The road was built at great expense, and is a grand triumph of engineering skill over the seeming impossiblities which nature had here, as if in very wantonness, interposed. Winding now around some projecting mountain point, now plunging through the very heart of another that stood in stubborn grandeur refusing to be otherwise overcome, now spanning with a structure so frail as to yawn destruction some frightful chasm, whose dismal depths the fitful wintry sun reached not. Now as if tired of pursuing one course it would turn back, when creeping along under the overhanging heights of the opposite side of the ravine as if hunting a point of escape, then running back nearly parallel to the point just passed over, all the time, however, climbing higher and higher until the summit is reached, where, passing over the watershed we find ourselves descending the slopes of the Adriatic. The gathering shades of night hide from view the distant landscape, and give increased force to the cold which had been tempered by the rays of a cloudless sun. The road is long and tiresome, the tedious journey scarcely relieved by the beauties of the dimly-lighted hills and valleys as seen by the shadowy light of the full-orbed moon, aided by the clear, blue, serene Italian sky, in which every twinkling star glitters as the diamond settings of the Order of the Golden Fleece. On our line of travel, over these mountains, numerous ruined castles, the strongholds of robber-knights of the middle ages, hung like so many eagle nests on the brow of inaccessible mountain heights. These once strongholds of mailed knights, having outlived the age and customs that originated them, have like many other things one meets with in this country, fallen into decay, while chieftain and cohorts have alike been forgotten in the onward march of ages. The narrow valleys in the mountain, even where almost closed in by precipitous hills, are thickly inhabited, and the hill sides, when not too precipitous, are cultivated even to their rocky summits.

How hardly must toiling man wring from reluctant nature a scanty subsistence. Descending into the plain as we near the city, the road, by a long line of trestle-work and bridges, passes over the salt lagoons outlying the city, and runs, apparently, far out into the sea. Indeed, by the uncertain light of the moon, a watery waste stretches around us as though we were in the middle of the Adriatic. We arrived finally at the depot.

VENICE.

The City of Gondolas, Queen of the Adriatic, and formerly the home of the Doges, wonderful city, whose history is transcendently glorious or dark, gloomy or perfidious. The once proud mistress of the sea, in whose ample lap was poured the riches of sacked cities and plundered provinces, and whose coffers were filled to repletion with tribute money paid by a hundred cities for protection by, or mercy from, her formidable fleets that, issuing from her ports, swept the Mediterranean coast with fire and sword. Her great artery is the Grand Canal which passes like a river or arm of the sea quite through the midst of the city. On arriving at the depot we found gondolas awaiting the train, just as carriages do at other cities. Taking one of them as our carriage, we were conducted through the entire length of the Grand Canal to the Hotel Luna, situated at its mouth, ever and anon on our passage the gondola would make a cut off through some by canal just as would a carriage across a vacant square in a city. We flew along this highway undisturbed by the rolling of wheels, with the moon at its full, lighting up the often dark, half-decayed palaces that, rising from the water's edge, line the banks of this canal on either side. These marble palaces, shrouded in departed glory, stand as the ghosts of other days, mute but impressive witnesses, testifying, by their presence and condition alike to what Venice has been and now is. The night winds in their passage through these silent halls gave forth a requiem wail, eloquent in its funeral dirge over fallen greatness.

The salt lagoons upon the mud islands of which Venice is built, are protected on the land side, by an extensive system of piling, from mixture with the fresh water of the river, which also serve to prevent the mud, brought down by the river, gradually filling up this part of the canal, as it would otherwise do. By this extensive system of piling and embankments, the city is protected from the dangerous proximity of paludal swamps, and the filling up of the canals, which here are the streets. On the seaside the city had to be protected by an immense stone wall built out into the sea. The former, or land side, required 400 years to build, and cost 2,000,000 francs. And when it is stated that this was but a small part of the expense required to render these mud islands sufficiently stable to support the immense structures placed upon them, some idea may be obtained of the enormous amount of time and money expended in building this city. Indeed to get a stable place upon which to build cost more than the building of a city in other places.

The city thus protected is rendered quite healthy by the tide which rises and falls two feet every twelve hours, this, in running in and out, forms as many rivers as there are canals, carrying out the foul and replacing it with fresh sea water every twelve hour.

These mud islands, 114 in number, lie in the shallow Adriatic, some three miles from the mainland, so that it is literally a city rising out of the sea, with 150 canals crossed by numerous bridges. These canals constitute the streets and connect every part of the city. Most of the houses, like those on the Grand Canal, rise directly from the water, with their doors or piazzas opening out upon the canal, which often affords the inhabitants their only communication with other parts of the city, their gondolas waiting for them at the door as would a carriage in other cities. There are no horses or mules in Venice, consequently no wagons or carriages. The only horses in the city are the four bronze ones on St. Mark's.

The population of the city, which in the days of its glory was 250,000, is now mot more than half this number, and most of these are paupers.

But with all this decay in population and wealth, through decline of trade and commercial importance, with silent workshops and the ghosts of other days standing in vacant palaces, decaying houses, deserted wharves, like shrouded skeletons over and around her, like some mighty oak that has witnessed not only the decay of the forest, but its own, Venice stands proudly, majestically great, even in her ruins. Navies may go down at sea, ships rot at the wharves, and her marble palaces crumble to dust, but the glory of her works and deeds can never fade, while the impress given by her art-loving citizens to the Renaissance of art will live forever.

The former aristocratic quarters of the city were along the Grand Canal, both sides of which are lined by marble palaces. These were the residences of Doges, merchant princes, wealthy senators and State officials, and even now, with their beautiful columns, piazzas, carvings, statuary and frescoes, present a fairy appearance and evidence of taste and oppulence only to be met with in Venice.

To one acquainted with her history (and who is not?) it is not unexpected to find in the earlier forms of her sculpture and architecture a large mixture of the Orient, nor is he unprepared to find in her art forms, a lingering Byzantine influence, long after it had been replaced by the classical in other parts of

Italy, as Byzantium was itself a part of Venice, Constantinople having been conquered by the Venetians in 1204 under the Doge, Henrico Dondola. Therefore in cultivating and fostering Byzantine art, they felt that they were but cultivating their own. To all this was added the spoils of a hundred sacked eastern cities, while her commerce constantly added to her overfilled stores, and her navy that rode triumphant on the Mediterranean, while especially directed against the Moslem power, was ever ready to despoil a Christian church.

A knowledge of this history prepares us to account for the unusual amount of exotic works found here, and for the oriental cast of these. From their aggressive and irresistible expeditions, her fleets returned loaded with the spoils of Constantinople, including the doors and other costly spoils of the Christian church of St. Sophia. During these wars or plundering expeditions—for these Venetians were often but little better than freebooters—extending over centuries, they took and sacked most of the important Greek cities and added to their stores their invaluable works of art, until the city was filled with imported Ionic, Doric and Corinthian columns, marble and bronze statuary, freizes and stuccoes from the Greek and Saracene churches, temples and mosques, until we find here in her palaces, churches, museums, many of the most beautiful productions of the eastern cities, with a constant recurrence, in her native productions, mosaics and paintings, to the Greek or Byzantine style. Indeed most of their earlier works called native, as the Mosaics of St. Mark's, are native only in that they were done in Venice by Greek artists living here or imported for this purpose, conditions readily produced by the stimulus of high wages for works of art, which the great wealth brought by her conquests and commerce enabled Venice and Venetians to pay for such works.

Here on the Grand Canal is the palace in which Byron lived

while in Venice, and where he wrote his beautiful and immortal poem, Childe Harold—many passages of which are the finest in the English or any other language—and will be read when the marble palace in which they were written shall have crumbled to dust. Here, also, plunged in the excesses of Venetian society, he unfortunately wrote another work which no beauty of thought or expression can redeem, his Don Juan. The palace is a beautiful, fairy-like structure which, with its associations, doubtless gave inspiration to the poet's muse. Here also stands the palace of Desdemona, and close by that of Shylock, associated with the genius of the Bord of Avon. One can see and feel in passing here, the truthfulness of Shakespear's Merchant of Venice. The realities of this wonderful production meet us at every winding of the canal—stand out as ghostly images of the past from tesselated palaces—and yet, Shakespear was never here, which fact of itself increases our wonder and admiration for the godlike genius of the poet, who lived in all places, for all times. Other men, though great, belong to a place and an age, but he is of the world, and all subsequent time is his.

There is a fault observable in the architecture of Venice, a mixture of styles, a profusion, on overloading, not the fault of her architects, but the result of the superabundance of materials at their disposal, and which they were required to use-work in. And as this material, the spoils of conquest or plunder, was taken from churches, temples and public buildings of different designs and orders, it was often incongruous, and sometimes oddly placed together. We shall see this notably the case in St. Mark's, in the construction of which they used material from Jerusalem, Greek temples and Christian churches, as the doors and other spoils from St. Sophia at Constantinople. All these came alike to these Christian freebooters. At most it was only robbing St. Peter and Pau and other saints and apostles, to pay or enrich St. Mark, who, as the patron saint of Venice, was in especial favor with these devout people, who supposed his influence over the affairs of this world to be sufficient to protect their city and give to their armies and navies power to continue the spoils, and so long as this was done, they cared but little about his influence elsewhere.

But with all her acquirements and attainments in architecture, sculpture, etc., and rich as Venice is in these, it is to her great painters that modern Venice points with most pride, and whose immortal works most interest the present age. These great painters, stimulated, created, not less by the spirit of the age, than by the art associations of the city, carved for Venice, a higher, brighter niche in the roll of fame, and one more enduring than even her naval victories. These beautiful productions of their pencils, found here in the greatest profusion in the churches, palaces and picture galleries, as well as in every picture gallery in Europe, will outlast the spoils of war or the Doges' palace—will indeed delight and instruct mankind when these shall have failed.

There are, in the history of man, intellectual waves, movements or cycles, not less surely felt and known, though in their laws eluding our most searching inquiry, than those of the physical world. These manifest themselves now in great, prolonged and widely-extended religious revivals or excitements, in which, for the time being, it would seem that whole communities or peoples, moved by some great moral impulse, perhaps the near approach of the millenium, had mounted a higher plain of religious thought and action. During this movement, great pulpit orators preach with incalculable force and effect, while those less gifted, preach with a power and influence beyond the most gifted in other times. Again this movement shows itself in a seemingly quite opposite direction, in which, without any accord, or indeed uninfluenced by each other, many nations are engaged in internicene or foreign wars, in which fire and the sword seem to be the sport of nations, in which, an Alexander, Cæsar, Cambyses, Ghenghis Khan or Napoleon threaten, the conquest of the world, planning and fighting great battles that are the wonder of all succeeding ages, while their lieutenants perform greater military exploits than could the greatest general in other times. Now this movement manifests itself in a searching inquiry into physical phenomena, resulting in the cotemporary discoveries or invention, perhaps in remote and disconnected countries, of great and lasting importance. The telescope is discovered; the laws of gravity governing the world announced; the thunderbolt is caught and examined; the slumbering Titan existing in steam is discovered, startled from his slumbers, and set to work, the printing press invented, a passing sunbeam halted and made to paint an image, photograph the passing shadow, and all this with such startling suddenness that we are often, at a loss to determine the real author. Indeed the discoverer or inventor is not the man, but the age. Now the movement finds expression in the production of great orators, poets, sculptors, painters and architects, not singly or confined to any one people, but often in great numbers and in many nations, producing styles and works of beauty, that impress all future generations. These facts, while patent to all men as results, in the causes producing or influencing them are known to none, are possibly supersensual and in the absence of known causes are termed, "the genius or spirit of the age," *zeitgheist*. This *zeitgheist* or *spirit of the age*, running in a particular direction, produces in remote communities results of the greatest importance and works of the highest excellence, this spirit impressing the age so forcibly, that even men of moderate ability, in some of their best moods, or when least themselves and most under the influence of this spirit of the age, have produced works of the highest excellence, works surpassing in motive or beauty of execution those of the greatest masters of another age.

This was never more strikingly or lastingly shown than in the fine-arts movement of the 15th, 16th and early part of the 17th centuries. And this too, in despite of the absence of all the conditions admitted to be most favorable to the production of great works of art, freedom of thought and action, and the protection by the state of life and property. Indeed not only in the absence of these conditions, but in the actual presence of their contraries, with soul and body enslaved, and life and property jeopardized daily.

This spirit of the age, the spirit of painting, extended at this time over most of Europe, producing in Spain, Velasquez and Murillo, in Germany, Durer and Holbein, in England, Hogarth and Reynolds, in Holland and Belgium, among others, Van Dyck, Van Eyck, Rembrandt and Rubens, and in Italy, beginning, or receiving its impulse, with Cimabue and Giotto, culminated in Michael Angelo, Leonardi de Vinci and Raphael. This tidal wave of art, or zeitgeist, having produced not one, but an army, of the greatest painters, and a multitude of the finest paintings the world ever has, or ever will, produce, culminated in the three last named, and having run its cycle, rapidly passed away, possibly never to return, leaving these immortal productions, the wonder and admiration of all future ages. As is well known, it was in Italy this zeitgeist embraced the widest area, manifested the greatest force, and attained its highest excellence. And it was precisely here where the conditions were least favorable. And least of all, present with two of these, Michael Angelo and Raphael, who attained the highest excellence, as these two were but little better than the slaves of the most despotic of powers, Leo X., working often by actual dictation, and at all times amidst and under conditions admitted to be the least favorable to artistic eminence. It will then be seen that it was the *age* that produced these great works.

In all this, Venice contributed a part worthy of her glory in arms. Of these great paintings, stamped with the genius of the age, her churches, halls and art galleries contain enough to enrich the picture galleries of many cities.

We will notice in particular only a few of these great masters belonging to Venice, and only mention some of their greatest works found here, as these last will constantly recur in other cities. Titian, 1477–1576, was the greatest of the Venetian school; excelling perhaps all others in the richness of his colors and life-likeness of his flesh tints, and the beauty of his portraits. Some of his numerous paintings are found in every picture gallery in Europe, and here in Venice are in every church, hall and gallery and museum. His master-production, "The Ascension," painted on wood. is truly a great work, and in some points places Titian the equal of Raphael. "The Entombment," his last picture, painted in the ninety-ninth year of his age, is also a great work. Both of these are in the Accademia delle Belle Arti. Tintoretto, one of Titians pupils, whose richness of invention and perfection in coloring places him in the first rank of Venetian, if not indeed of Italian, painters, has numerous paintings here. The Doges' Palace has its walls covered with his paintings and frescoes. His " Paradise " covers one end of the great hall, is the largest oil painting in the world, and while possessing much excellence, is more remarkable for its size and the great multitude of figures it contains, than for its excellence of execution, and yet many of the figures are very fine. His "Miracle of St. Mark Saving a Slave From the Hands of the Heathens," a great work, is in the Academy. Palma Vecchio is remarkable for his portraits of Venetian beauties. Paul Veronese painted here, where many of his best pieces are found in the Academy.

The place of most interest in Venice, and in some respects, one of the most remarkable in Europe, is *St. Mark's*, the piazza of which, with the church, affords a study not less instructive than interesting. The piazza is an oblong square, 540 feet long by 250 feet wide, and is paved with dark grey freestone and white Istria marble, and has on three sides marble colonnades which form an unbroken arcade of 128 arches. The other side is bounded by St. Mark's church. These structures represent half a thousand years of Venetian architecture, illustrating her life-history, St. Mark's church constituting the illuminated pages.

We cannot describe this church—(who could ?) and shall only attempt to give some of its distinctive peculiarities, whereby it may be seen that it is really indescribable, also a vague idea given of its general appearance and importance in the history of this city. This strange, unique structure, while of no particular style, blends within itself, with more or less harmonious beauty, the wondrous excellence of the old Greek, or classical, the new or Byzantine and Saracenic, Syriac and Hindo styles. Its history runs back into the night of the dark ages to a time when the affrighted inhabitants of the adjacent hills and plains had secured a sure footing upon these mud islands to which they had fled in very terror to escape the irresistible and merciless slaughtering horde of Goths and Vandals who pressed down in countless numbers from the forests of the unknown North to complete the destruction of the Roman Empire. In the darkness and terror of that long night, when the intellectual light of the world, Rome, had been extinguished by the barbarian hordes led by Atilla, the Hun, and Allaric, the Goth, these peoples of Northern Italy, unable to protect themselves, sought and obtained kindly protection from the sea, and here, in 550, erected a chapel on the site where St. Mark's now stands. In the beginning of the ninth century, when Venice had become a strong city, whose navies were strong enough to ravage the Mediterranean coast, one of those miracles occurred not uncommon in those times when monkish legends or dreams of saints were proofs as strong as holy writ—the finding of the body of Saint Mark, the Apostle—of course, miracuously preserved for 800 years, and miraculously discovered, and therefore miraculously here in Venice, where it was conveyed from Egypt and supplanted the tutelar saint Theodore. The body was brought with great pomp, no one doubting its genuineness, and received and deposited with much ecclesiastical ceremony on this spot. Then, as a suitable mousoleum for a corpse of so much dignity as that of an apostle, the pious cut-throat Doge began, and his pious successors completed in 977, St. Mark's church, which, however, in despite the Saint's guardian care, took fire and burned down soon after its completion. Not in the least discouraged by this neglect, indifference or want of power on the part of their patron saint, the saintly Doge Pietro commenced to rebuild it on a grander scale than before, thinking perhaps the apostle had let the other burn down because not suiting his æsthetic tastes. This task the very pious Dodge undertook out of his private fortune, a fortune acquired by the very laudable and Christian means of plundering Greek temples, Moslem mosques and Christian churches.

For the erection of St. Mark's, the most distinguished architects were summoned to Venice, and under their guidance the pious work continued with the spoils of sacked cities, until after the lapse of one hundred years in 1071 A. D. it was completed under the pious Doge Dominico, so that as it now stands it is upwards of 800 years old. The bones of the saint—perhaps in fact those of a thief or crocodile from the catacombs of

Egypt have thus had a long and royal rest. The great time in building the church, with the wealth of material at their disposal, brought from plundered oriental temple, churches and mosques, with their different styles of architecture, necessitated an admixture of different styles in the building. The ground plan is Byzantine Christian, being that of a Greek cross, in which the transept or cross-bar is in the middle of the shaft, giving four bars of nearly equal length. The top of the church is strikingly Saracenic, so much so, with its five Moslem domes, that we are convinced at first sight that it is a mosque. This with its ground-plan and roof constitutes a structure that might be called Byzantine and Arabic, or Turko-Christian. Some of the other parts are Gothic and Lombardine, all these being not the work of one or any particular plan or style, but an ingenious adaptation of the architect to work in the often-beautiful but discordant material stolen from the cities of Greece and Asia Minor, including some beautiful marble columns said to be from Solomon's Temple, together with some highly-ornamented columns from the ruined capital of the splendor-loving Queen of Sheba. Who doubts that these beautiful columns were miraculously preserved to ornament this Christian temple, that stands as a trumpet-tongued witness to tell of the stormy times when the taking of helpless cities, with the rape and murder of the inhabitants, was a sport in which good Christians had a right to engage. And then who had a better right to the fatness of the land than the patron saint of the city, the Apostle Mark? What if he had preached a gospel of virtue and mercy! times had changed, and with them also customs and morals.

But the work of these pious Doges stands here none the less picturesque, grand, beautiful, from the fact that it was only their leisure hours that were given to this pious task, their official hours having been devoted to the not-less-pleasing task of directing the application of thumb-screws, the wheel and the rack, and other like modes of torture, to wring from their hapless victims the confession of crimes of which they were often quite ignorant. But if the bones of these pious Doges, like those of other saints, repose in consecrated ground, those of their victims rest not less quietly amidst the mud and slime of dark lagoons or deep sea.

The exterior front of the church is ornamented with wondrously-executed portraits of apostles and saints in mosaics on a bright gold ground, with a representation in mosaic of the embarkment of the body of St. Mark, at Alexandria, Egypt, and the landing of the body at Venice. Over the principal entrance is the Judgment of Solomon. Surrounding the body of St. Mark are a number of Doges, patriarchs, city magnates and others, all in mosaics. Upon the gallery in front of the great central window are the four bronze horses which all true Venetians look upon with reverence and awe. They are said to have at one time adorned Nero's triumphal arch at Rome. Taken from there to Constantinople, when this city was taken and sacked by the crusaders they were brought to Venice. When Napoleon I. took Venice, he sent these horses to Paris. After his fall they were returned to Venice.

The upper arches are filled with mosaics, The Descent from the Cross, The Resurrection, The Ascension. All these figures are of life size and well executed in bright mosaics on a gold ground. These, like all the older mosaics in this church, some of which date back to the tenth century, are of Byzantine style, a stiff, conventional manner of the figures and dress. All the Christs, Madonnas and Apostles, and many of the Saints, have a golden halo surrounding the head. Hundreds of figures of life size appear on the vast arch of the roof covering every square foot of its area. These figures, in despite their stiff, motionless appearance, are really beautiful, while the colors of many of them, though nearly a thousand years old, are as bright and, as seen from the vast distance to the dome, as handsome as if done in oil. There are *40,000 square feet* of mosaics in this church. The wagon roof and great dome are covered with mosaics. The whole history of creation, Noah's flood, the known and many unknown incidents in the life of Christ and the Apostles are given in these mosaics, while the figures of more saints than were ever known to heaven crowd the roof and extend into the curious recesses and niches of the walls.

The different times of doing these mosaics can be easily read in their gradual change from the stiff, motionless Byzantine style into the more natural, active, life-like, easy style with the flowing dresses of the classical or Renaissance.

Three great metal doors open from the piazza into the church. One of these elaborately-wrought doors, with Greek inscriptions upon it, was plundered from the Christian church, St. Sophia, at Constantinople, and placed here by these Christian marauders as a suitable offering to the Apostle St. Mark and appropriate decoration for his mausoleum. There are at the entrance of the church eight marble columns of beautiful Greek workmanship, four on either side, brought also from Constantinople, and back of the high altar there are four spiral columns of translucent alabaster of great beauty and of Greek finish, said to be from Solomon's Temple at Jerusalem, but their Greek workmanship prove them of a later origin and from a different place. The Altar of the Madonna with a very fine Greek painting of the Virgin, was taken from a Christian church in Constantinople and brought here in 1204 A. D. This picture is held in very great esteem, as indeed it should be; St. Luke himself being the painter? Well who knows but that this apostle might have employed his leisure time in painting portraits. History is silent upon this subject, so much so that it cannot be disproved from history. In the Iridon Chapel lie the relics of Saint Iride, brought from Chios in A. D. 1124. The mosaics of this chapel celebrate her life and virtues. They are of the fourteenth century.

The vast amount of mosaics, marble statuary, beautiful Ionic, Doric and Corinthian columns in this church is truly amazing. Had it been intended, as perhaps it was, as a depository for all the art treasures plundered from Eastern cities, for hundreds of years, it could hardly have been richer; a very store-house of the spoils of war. All ages, all nations, visited by their conquering fleets, all religions and all styles are represented by their spoils in this church, thus constituting it a library in which is contained, more or less complete, the history of the irresistible prowess of Venice in the days of her glory. And while these spoils, in their source, and the uses to which they were placed, are not always such as we can justify, yet much must be assigned to the time; and these Venetians, in robbing other Christian churches to ornament that of their tutelary saint, only did as they would have been done by, under like circumstances. Would that Venice was alone in thus plundering her fellow Christians.

The Bell Tower, which, according to the custom of the age, was built apart from the church, is an immense square pyramid, 300 feet high. It was commenced in the tenth, and completed in the latter part of the twelfth century. In company with some St. Louis friends I ascended to its summit, from which we had a panoramic view of the entire city. The ascent is not by steps but by an inclined plane running around on the inside of the Tower, making, we thought, the ascent much easier than by steps. The Clock Tower, built in 1219, contains a clock of scarcely less mechanical interest than that of Strasburg. The dial plate, next the piazza, shows the signs of the zodiac, with the moon's phases. In the second story sits a Madonna between two gilded door, the doors opening every hour for the egress and ingress of three sacred kings, who are preceded by an angel. All the figures reverently greet the Virgin. On the top are two giant Moors in bronze, who strike the hours upon a great bell.

The Doge's Palace forms one side of St. Mark Piazza, which here runs down to the wharf. This Palace, history informs us, was first built in 820. Like St. Mark's church, it was destroyed by fire, and rebuilt in 1430. Its beautiful works of art suffered greatly by the vandalism of the French during their occupancy of Venice, but it is still rich in many of the finer paintings of the world. The painting and frescoes of Titian, Paul Veronese and Tintaretto, ornament its halls. A volume would be required to describe its architecture, statues, statuetts, frescoes and paintings. The grand hall of the four doors was the room in which foreign embassadors, ministers and envoys were received, and was gorgeously decorated with frescoes and paintings with a high throne for the ruling Doge. This throne on state occasions was covered with cloth of gold, and nothing was left undone that might assist to impress embassadors and others with the glory and majesty and might and dominion of Venice. From the room of the inquisitors, a secret power in masks, to whom mercy was unknown, a dark, narrow passage leads to the Bridge of Sighs. The opening to this stairway, entering the hall, was concealed in the wall, and when they closed behind the hapless victim hope was left behind. Through this passage and over this bridge, many an innocent victim of envy, malice or jealousy passed to the dark, dismal dungeon, deep below. We traversed this passage, and crossing the bridge, which, with a high arch, spans one of the numerous canals, reached on the opposite side of the canal the Doges' palace, the entrance to the dungeon, and, lighted by a torch in the hand of the guide, explored its dismal depths. Thanks to the times and circumstances, with different feelings from the many who had gone here at the mandate of the masked inquisitors, and yet not without a shudder as we groped our way along the dark, narrow, mouldy way, to chambers in which confinement was worse than death.

The very stones seemed to give out sighs and groans as we descended quite to the water's edge, or even below that in the adjacent canals, where dark, dismal, damp cells, without a ray of light, with a stone bed, had received their unfortunate victims. Horror of horrors. To be immured here, without a hope of ever again seeing those they loved, were a living death. Welcome the axe of the executioner that released the hopeless victim from the horror of living. And then here lay the axe and the block, with and upon which their necks were severed, while the stain of the stream of human blood was still, or seemed to be, upon the rock channel along which it had run to the canal. A boat awaited, at dead of night, to conduct the headless body, and severed head, to be dropped in the deep sea. When once seized and dragged from home, no mother, wife, sister, friend, ever again saw these State victims while living or when dead. Well, here all is silent now. Informers, inquisitors and their victims have passed away. And is this the end of man? Shall these groans and tears of the innocent bear no fruit? and these bloody crimes go unwhipped of vengeance? Well it may be so. I could but hope not. On the opposite side of the piazza is the king's palace, with a front much like that of the Doges' palace. A long row of marble columns support the façade. Above this a row of lighter Corinthian columns support the roof. The palace is still the summer residence of the king of Italy, when he visits Venice. It is much as king Humbert's father, Victor Emanuel left it when last here, with his bed-room and bed just as he left them.

The palace contains a great number of rooms, furnished in princely style, costly furniture, mirrors, inlaid tables with sofas and chairs. We were shown through the entire palace, which though not as fine as many we have seen, it being only an occasional residence of royalty, is certainly rather extravagantly furnished for the small amount of use it is to any one. But then like old Caspar's notions of the battle of Blenheim,

> Such things you know must be
> In every land of royalty.

But we must bid farewell to this once-beautiful and art-loving city of the lagoons, with her history the brighest and darkest of any of the cities of the middle ages.

Dec. 10th.—Left Venice at 1 P. M. and arrived at Florence at 8 P. M. and put up at the very comfortable Hotel Chapman, No. 24 Via Pandolfini, kept by an American lady.

FLORENCE.

This is the art city of the world, and though Venice is a great store-house of art, much of it is *exotic*, plundered from other cities, while here in Florence it is the work of her native artists. Here is the cradle and nursery of the Renaissance, the birthplace of the modern Italian language, literature and art. Here lived and labored those remarkable men who have instructed and delighted the world. Here was the home of Dante, whose Comedia Divina has been translated into all the languages of modern Europe, and so intimately blended with our religious thought and literature, that it would be difficult to separate it from them without a revolution in religious thought. Here was the home of Galileo, also of Michael Angelo, Leonardi and Raphael, all of whom studied and worked at the same time in Florence. The long line of the Medici, a semi-royal family, by the encouragement they gave to men of genius, and as patrons of letters, did much to constitute, and continue for ages, Florence the focus of intellectual activity. Indeed, so great has been her production of genius, that the whole city is moulded by, and on, their art creations. So much so is this the case, that not a street, not a public square, but is adorned with their works, while every church is an art gallery. These churches contain of themselves so many works of great merit as to make Florence one of the most important art cities of Europe, even were her great picture galleries, the Uffizi and the Pitti, with their priceless treasures, not here.

The city has a mediæval appearance, with her narrow, crooked streets, lined on either side by walls of houses indicating the necessity that existed in the times of its erection for crowding the population into as small a compass as possible, that they might be within the walls, which the turbulent, lawless times it has witnessed, when might made right and no law or obligation was binding, except that of force, made fortress walls a necessity to the existence of all these Italian cities. Many of these houses are the former residences of men of letters, and some of them date back to the 12th and 14th centuries, having braved the storms of half a thousand years, during which time Europe has passed from the darkness of the feudal age to the intellectual light of the 19th century, in the development of which the inhabitants of this city have contributed more than those of any other. Perhaps the most potent of the agents through which they effected this, was the Platonic Academy, whose members, by diligently hunting up and translating the lost knowledge of the ancients, through which means the *artless* forms of art then in existence were replaced by the classical, created a new era, known as the revival of learning, the Renaissance. In their efforts in this, the members of the Platonic Academy labored with all the zeal and self-devotion of religious enthusiasts, while the strong native intellect of this people was stimulated by the example and encouraged by the means placed at their disposal through the labors of this academy, and the munificence of the *Medici* soon constituted Florence the literary center of Italy. Their artistic taste was alike stimulated by the genius of Cimabue and Giotto, whose departure from the stiff conventionalism of the Byzantine style continued ever greater, until it culminated in the classic and the productions of the greatest of painters Leonardi, Michael Angelo and Raphael, whose immortal works are found in all the galleries of Europe, and as things of beauty will constitute the gems of these through coming ages.

The city lies on both sides the Arno, a small stream, except when swollen by rains or melted snows from the adjacent Appenines. To prevent disaster, formerly frequent, from these causes, the river is enclosed on both sides by strong stone walls, some twenty feet in height. It is crossed by five stone bridges, the oldest of which dates back to the 13th century. The high stone walls which protected the city during the dark and middle ages, were strengthened by gates, battlements and towers by Michael Angelo, who, as engineer, defended the city for eleven months against the overwhelming armies of Charles V., of Spain and Germany. Famine, however, accomplished what all the force of Spain and Germany could not, and the city was finally compelled to capitulate for want of food. The greater part of these walls has been removed. However the line on the west side and extending north and south from the Roman gate, still exists in a good state of preservation, giving the town from this side much the same appearance it had 400 years ago, that of a walled city. The Porta Romano, erected in 1320, still stands in a good state of preservation, and gives a good idea of the strength and durability of the gates of an ancient walled city, where the lives and property of the inhabitants depended upon the strength of the gates and walls enclosing the city, not less than the skill and valor of those defending them.

The point to which the stranger most naturally first directs his attention, is the Piazza della Signoria, with its adjoining Palazzo Vecchio and Loggia del Lonzi, not more an account of their appearance than their memories, as here was enacted much of the history of Florence, being to this city, what the Forum was to Rome for six hundred years, the assembly place of the people, where was determined the life and fortune of individuals, as well as the affairs of state. The Piazza is a small, open space, only containing a few acres, walled in by high houses, and in approaching it from any direction we emerge from narrow alleys, called here via or straddi (streets), which again are so entirely closed on either side by a continuous line of high walls, houses, as to render it impossible to see any other part of the city than the immediate part we are in, which fact of itself gives this bright, open Piazza additional charm. And this is greatly enhanced by the many works of art here met with. Some of these are silent witnesses of many a dark and bloody deed, whose spectres throw their shadows across the past history of this Piazza.

The Palazzo Vecchio, which bounds this square on one side, was the residence of the Signoria or ruling power of the city, the residence and battle tower of Cosimo I. and subsequent rulers of the great, wise and magnanimous, or dark, bloody, cruel, despotic Medici, who, like the Doges of Venice, are associated with perhaps most that is grand, great, glorious, and also with much that is to be deplored, in the history of Florence. This castle was built by Arnalfo del Cambio, in A. D. 1298. In front of the castle is the beautiful, large fountain, with Neptune and Tritons, or sea-horses, beautifully executed. It occupies the spot where stood the stake at which was burned Savonnarola and two Dominican monks in the 15th century.

Savonnarola, a Dominican priest, was one of those rarely-gifted religious enthusiasts whose governing convictions are often mistaken by others, and sometimes by themselves as inspirations from heaven, and who, dominated and acting by these, honestly believing they are acting under the immediate commands of a higher power, may do great good or harm. Sometimes when this conviction dominating the individual, favorably impresses their cotemporaries, he becomes the founder of a religion, as Buddha, Moses and Mahomet. In other instances, new interpretations are given to old religions, which continue with more or less influence during their cycle, instance Luther, Calvin, Wesley and others.

This great man, dominated by the belief in his direct communications with heaven, aided by an intellect that was almost superhuman and an eloquence convincingly overwhelming, was long the Umpire of Florence, influencing its counsels and dictating or giving its laws, and controlling public opinion by declaring in his sermons against the extravagance and wickedness of his age, making his pulpit the rostrum from which were denounced the sins, both actual and imaginary, of this city of Florence. And as this wickedness was supposed to be in some especial manner connected with the rulers and wealthy classes, he very naturally became the idol of the masses. Most fortunately his earnest fanaticism was mostly directed for good, nor was this at all unlikely in a city where there was so much to be improved. But his unfortunate diabolical taking-off doubtless only came in time to prevent his fanaticism taking practical movement in lines that would forever have destroyed his good name. For instance, his sermons had more than once darkly pointed towards the destruction of works of art as idols, and such was his influence at this time, that his instruction to the populace might have made a bonfire of all or many of those great paintings at Florence that now delight the world and make much of the glory of Florence. Indeed so near was he upon this, that it is believed that some of those paintings possessed by his more devout friends were actually destroyed, Savonnarola setting the example. This constituted one of the charges brought against him by his enemies. It stands, at first sight, in rebuttal to this accusation that his own monastery, San Marco, was the nursery of these fine arts, and his dearest brother monks among the most gifted painters of his time. But it is quite possible that to a mind constituted and dominated by religious convictions, this very circumstance might have determined him to destroy all such idols as called off the mind from monastic devotion. Or while he may have determined upon this, it may be that in very love for his truly much-loved and loving brothers he deferred the fatal decree. To one believing as I do, in the earnestness of his convictions that he was acting under the direct guidance of heaven nothing is more probable than that he may have had some of these works destroyed, or than that he may have seriously contemplated declaring an iconoclastic war against all these works of art, as idolatrous and therefore to be destroyed.

Had Savonnarola confined his diatribes to the rulers and wealthy citizens, all might have gone well with him, but unfortunately for his continued success and influence, his pure and fearless soul revolted against the vices of the cloister and clergy whose pollutions rose rank against heaven, and therefore these too fell under his terrible denunciations. At first, most naturally, these denunciations met with the warm support of the populace, to whom the sins of these orders were not more known than hated. But Savonnarola learned, when too late, what many others have learned before and since, that the multitude are fickle, often turning against their greatest benefactors, while the *orders* he attacked were organized bodies acting in concert for a common support. These, by intrigue with the masses, through the infinite and potent means they possessed, with the aid of the Pope who was most naturally with them in suppressing any popular feeling against the religious orders, were not slow to undermine and destroy this great enemy, And this the more easily as they had the rulers and wealthy classes with them, and then their success was the more certain, as in all intrigue and dissimulation they had the field to themselves, as the pure and lofty soul of the seer, guided, as he verily believed, by divine direction and protected by the God whom he worshipped, could no more have made use of these means than it could have soiled itself with the pollutions he denounced. Had he boldly attacked the sins he denounced, as sins of the Church, rather than sins of the orders, he might have succeeded in the great work left for the more sagacious, though not more earnest or fearless, German reformer, but failing in this he fell between the upper and the nether millstone. And he who, when the city of Florence was at the mercy of a conquering Gallic army, whose legions occupied the city, with every vestige of liberty and autonomy stamped out, and the city in immediate danger of universal rapine and pillage, stood in the presence of the Emperor Francis I. to plead for the city, and by eloquently imploring him to treat them with mercy and leave the city, accompanying his prayer with fearful threatenings of divine vengeance, which he really believed and convinced the Emperor were at his bidding, succeeded in so far frightening this despotic conqueror that he withdrew his armies and retired from Florence leaving the people in full possession of their liberty and fortunes, was now in the power of those to whom mercy was a stranger.

While legends and myths give accounts of miraculous interposition producing like effects—works of the Church or oracles—this, in fact, is the only instance in the world's history of such a work having been accomplished by the unaided efforts or spiritual influence of an obscure priest or seer.

And now that the conqueror was conquered, and had fled when no man was pursuing, the city was most naturally in a state of anarchy. Savonnarola, by the wisdom of his councils, again saved it and restored law and order. But his enemies slept not. Their existence, or what to them amounted to the same thing, the corrupt means of existence, depended upon the destruction of this fearless champion of reform, who, now that the city was again free, hurled his anathemas against the corruptions of the times. But his days were numbered.

> And he, the prophet-priest, who had dared to wake
> The slumbering venom of the cloister snake,

was seized at midnight and dragged from his cloister, St. Marco, and from the midst of his brothers, many of whom would gladly have died for him, and some of them with tears begged the authorities that they might in mercy have the privilege of suffering in his stead. But in vain. Savonnarola was thrown into prison, where, with two of his fellow-monks, he was subjected to the most frightful tortures, was stretched upon the rack, broken upon the wheel, and when almost dead, with his two companions was dragged from prison and burned at the stake in this open square. The gloomy walls that surround this square were lighted up by the pale and sickly glare of these faggot fires, behind whose ghastly wreaths of smoke we may well believe the angels hid their faces and wept, while the night was rendered more hideous by the shouts of the insane multitude, who rejoiced in a deed the very fiends might well abhor to claim as their own.

Thus ended Florence's great priest and seer. In all its human aspects how wonderfully his closing scene reminds us of that of his Divine Master. Exchange the stake for the cross, the Florentines for the Jews, and the Piazza for Calvary, and all of these are mere accidents, and the similitude is wonderful—both alike innocent of the crimes of which they were accused, both alike had committed the acts for which they actually suffered, attempting to reform the abuses of their age and exalt and reform man and the Church, by making them more pure, more spiritual.

THE PALAZZO PITTI.

This splendid, or rather massive, palace stands on an eminence on the left bank of the Arno which divides Florence, a city of 160,000 inhabitants, into two unequal parts. It is connected with the Uffiza on the opposite side of the Arno by a covered passway which spans the river and is five or six hundred yards in length, this being the distance between these two picture galleries. The palace was built in 1440 by Luca Pitti, a gentleman of great wealth and rival of the Medici. His intention was to build the most imposing structure ever erected by a private individual. In as far as size is concerned he scarcely failed, but otherwise it certainly is neither fine nor imposing. The eye is unrelieved by columns, porticoes or ornamentation, a vast pile of stone, undressed except at their joints, utterly void of architectural beauty. It was long the residence of the reigning governors, and even now is the residence of the king of Italy when in summer he visits Florence. The upper floors contain the world-renowned Pitti Picture Gallery, which was formerly the property of Cardinal Leopold and Carlo de Medici and the Grand Duke Ferdinand II. In the Pitti Gallery there are 500 paintings, many of them art gems and some of them the finest paintings in the world.

It is impossible to spend even an hour here without feeling an elevation of soul, as we are here brought in communion with the impressive gifts of genius, the cunning touch of whose pencils have brought us in direct relation with much that is divine in the human, the unseen, the ideal, that here is more real than things that are tangible.

The best works of the Florentine period are a Madonna by Fillippo Lippi, The Adoration of the Magi by Gherlandago, A Pieta by Perugino, The Resurrection, an Annunciation, St. Mark, and a Pieta by FraBartolommeo, The Disputa, a Holy Family, and a Madonna by Andrea del Sarto.

On entering the Saloon of the Iliad, so named, as are the other saloons, from the frescoes on the ceilings, to the right of the entrance is a most beautiful portrait of a lady, formerly attributed to Raphael, and which would do this, the greatest of painters, no discredit. An Assumption, a grand painting by A. del Sarto. Mary and John adoring the Child by Perugino. The Nuptials of St. Catherine, by the almost-divine FraBartolommeo. This is the greatest of this master's productions, and in many points equal to a Raphael. Cardinal Ippolito de Medici, the warrior-saint in Hungarian costume, painted in 1532 after his return from the campaign against the Turks, by Titian. The Concert, an almost unequaled painting in which a handsome young monk has struck a cord on a musical instrument, a piano, with another monk and a handsome young knight standing by listening. The painting is most expressive. Action and motion are visible as the musical note thrills the three. Nothing could be more perfect or expressive. A very gem, by Giorgione!

Saloon of Saturn—Cleopatra with the asp on her breast, by Guido Reni. Vision of Ezekiel with God, the Father, enthroned upon the beasts of the Apocalypse, by Raphael, much admired, but I do not like it. The idea attempted is unreal, unnatural, unbelievable, monstrous, even if Raphael did paint it. Leo X and the Cardinals de Medici and de Rassi, by Raphael. A Madonna, by Del Sarto. Angelo Doni, by Raphael. Rembrandt, a portrait by himself. Portrait of Madelino Strozze Duni, by Raphael. Descent from the Cross, by A. del Sarto. Holy Family, by Murillo. Had this, the greatest of Spanish painters, never produced anything better, he would scarcely have been remembered. The picture is certainly commonplace. Know no other reason for its preservation here than that it is a Murillo. Christ at Emmaus, by Palma Vecchio. Adam, by Dürer, the great German artist, said to be a good work. Don't like it. La Belle Tiziano, a beautiful woman, by Titian. This is a perfect picture of female beauty, natural, real, earnest, with only enough of the divine to give it enchantment, while the earthly, or real, clothes it with all the loveliness of a surpassingly beautiful woman.

Saloon of Jupiter—Ceiling frescoes by Catoni. Madonna del Grande Duca, by Raphael. This beautiful picture is so named because long owned by the Grand Duke of Tuscany, with whose family it was an object of worship, their prayers being addressed to it, and no wonder, as it represents at least the most easily worshipped object of earth, an ideally lovely woman, while the beautiful Child Jesus is full of action and life. Had Raphael never painted any other, this picture alone would have placed him as the greatest of artists. Philip of Spain, by the preceptor of Murillo, and next to his pupil, Spain's greatest painter, Velasquez.

Saloon of Ulysses—Madonna and Saints, by A. del Sarto. In one of the side rooms are many excellent paintings and other art productions, among them a statue of Napoleon I., by Canova, two tables of oriental alabaster, and another of malachite, costly drinking cups of mediæval time, a round table of modern mosaics valued at $150,000. Another valuable gem is a life-size statue of Venus, by Canova. If this is not one of the most perfect, life-like statues of Venus ever produced, I fail to see it. This exquisitely beautiful statue is further beautified by the modestly disposed drapery which hangs in natural folds half revealing the beautifully rounded contour of her limbs. Returning to the room of Saturn, there is an Entombment, by Perugino, a grand work. Pope Julius, by Raphael, a grand portrait in which the noble, austere, selt-reliant physiognomy of this great man and Pope inspires us with awe. From such a physiognomy everything may be hoped for or feared.

Saloon of Jupiter—Battle Scene, by Salvator Rosa, a grand painting. Annunciation, by Del Sarto.

Saloon of Mars—Ceiling by Pietro da Cartona. Holy Family, by Raphael. Portrait of the immortal anatomist, Andreas Vesalius, by Titian. Madonna della Sedia, by Raphael. Perhaps no work of art, not even excepting his Cistine Madonna at Dresden, is better known or more admired than this, grand, beautiful, lovely almost beyond conception. The Madonna is seated in an arm-chair with the child in her arms, and the child John standing by them. It is said that more than fifty engravers have engraved it, while copies and photographs innumerable have transmitted its reflex throughout the world. No money could purchase it, as no art could reproduce it.

ACADEMIA DE BELLE ART.

This valuable collection presents the finest historical collection for the student in Italy. The characteristic features of the Byzantine-Umbrian styles are beautifully shown here, beginning with Cimabue of the thirteenth century, and father of the Florentine School, which during his lifetime rose to the first school of Tuscany. This gifted artist seems to have been the first to depart from the Greco-Christian, known as the Byzantine, style. The departure from this stiff, conventional, unreal and lifeless style, however important, is not great. We have in all his paintings the same gold background, the same halo, or glory, the same coppery tints, with the elongated, nun-like faces and stiff, motionless, motiveless attitude, with the ever-recurring stiff folds of the drapery, in which there is ever the same straight plaits which characterizes the Byzantine-

Christian, or sacred, style, which, endorsed by the Church, became stereotyped as the model from which no painter, however gifted, dared depart. But all this, while present in the works of this great master, is ever less and less so, until from an evident impossibility of motion the figures become ever more intent to action, while with the more naturalness of the drapery, movement becomes so manifest that we are not surprised when in the further development of this departure the figures start into active motion, as they do in the school of Cimabue's great pupil Giotto. This departure, made by the master, continued in the school of Giotto until the Byzantine style was lost in the natural, the classic, bursting into the glorious triumphs of the Renaissance.

Giotto, like many of the great painters of this age, was also a great sculptor and architect. His skill in these is immortalized in the Campinile of the Cathedral. The numerous great halls of this building are filled with fine paintings of the old masters, principally pre-Renaissance, and which we have not time to even mention. On the ground floor is the wonderful master work in stone of Michael Angelo, his great colossal statue of David. No work ever brought more immediate reputation or glory to its author. No work ever better deserved to do so. It has been called a miracle work, and surely is as near so as any other work of modern chisel. Among marvelous creations it is only equaled by Raphael's Cistine Madonna at Dresden.

But while this great work of Raphael awes, entrances, thrills us, by its divinity, bringing us in to the presence of the half unveiled glories of heaven, Michael Angelo's David subdues, awes us by its almost miraculous humanity, or life-likeness. With all we had heard and read of this marvelous production of Michael Angelo, we felt in its presence as did the Queen of Sheba in the Court of Solomon, that "the half had never been told." The look and attitude of Judea's champion becomes the godlike youth; composed, quiet, firm and noble, he stands in the immediate presence of Goliah, as if carefully weighing the might of his giant opponent, with his sling thrown over his left shoulder, the end grasped firmly in his left hand, which is lifted near the shoulder, while his right hand hangs by his side, carefully concealing, but firmly grasping a stone, which is to be hurled at the next moment with deadly effect against the mighty champion of Israel's foes. And while this, only a stone image, is all we have here, as we gaze upon it, so life-like is it, so quick with motion, and so big with meaning, that we quite readily see the two embattled armies resting on either side of their champions, awaiting with breathless eagerness the combat, and with feelings of emotion we almost ask ourselves, "Why is not the death-bearing pebble thrown?" We close our eyes; it is thrown and the mighty giant lies, gasping in death before us. The earth trembles at his gaspings.

CHURCH OF THE ANNUNCIATION.

This now time-worn and faded church was built in 1239, by the order of the Servi, or servants of the Virgin. The Atrium faces the piazza and contains seven arches, resting on slender Corinthian columns. The central arch was decorated with a fresco by Antonio de San Gallo, in 1513, representing Faith, Hope and Charity. This fresco, which so greatly charmed Michael Angelo, although greatly injured by exposure in an open façade for near 400 years, is still quite distinctly seen, revealing through the mist of ages, the genius of the youthful painter. The decorations within the Church are by the master artist Andrea Del Sarto and his pupils. The frescoes representing the life and miracles of San Phillippi Benezzi are now preserved under glass. This saint was a Florentine physician who left the cure of the body for the cure of souls, joined the order of the Servi and was beatified by Pope Leo X.

There are many other beautiful frescoes and paintings in this old church, which is indeed a very picture gallery. A Last Supper, by Del Sarto, and the Madonna Del Sacco, have been much admired. In the Madonna Del Sacco, the Holy Family are on their way to Egypt, and during the flight have stopped to rest. Mary, with the Infant in her arms, is seated. while Joseph has laid down the sack containing their wardrobe and is seated upon it. All this is pleasingly and beautifully rendered, and we find ourselves returning to this fresco to study it deeper. A pleasing anecdote is related of this fresco, which contains many female portraits of rare beauty. Many long years after the death of Del Sarto, and when it was supposed all who knew him and his were dead, it was being copied by a painter, when a decrepit old woman whom almost no one knew, passed by him on her way to mass, stopped, looked at the fresco, at the copy, then told the artist that a given beautiful young female figure was a portrait, was her portrait, that she was the widow, the once beautiful young wife of A. Del Sarto, the immortal artist, whose beautiful productions in this church and also in the picture gallery of Italy constitute some of the finest gems of art. His beautiful Madonna the Del Sacco was pronounced unequaled in grace and color.

CONVENT OF SAN MARCO.

This venerable structure was first built and occupied by monks, called Silvestrini, in 1299. In 1400, when the city was stricken by the plague, these monks, by the relaxation of their dicipline, fell into disfavor, and the monastery was given to the Dominicans. This order and their monastery are immortalized here, 1st. By the wonderfully-gifted, earnest, eloquent, fervent, pious, enthusiastic, inspired, fanatical Dominican friar, priest and martyr, Savonnarola, who entered this monastery in 1482. 2nd. This venerable pile is hallowed by its connection with the two immortal Dominican monks and painters who long occupied cells here, Fra Angelica and Fra Bartolommeo.

In the cloisters here are fine frescoes by Fra Giovanni, Angelico da Fiesole. Christ on the cross, with St. Domnico near by. Over the door, under the portico, St. Peter, with his finger on his mouth, indicative of the silence of the order. Over the door of the refectory, a Pieta. Over another entrance, Christ as a pilgrim, welcomed by two Dominican monks, beautiful, expressive, lovely. In the chapel house, Christ crucified between two thieves, with a number of saints standing near, all by Fra Angelica. Upper floor, where are the deserted cells of the Dominican monks, are numerous frescoes and paintings by Fra Angelica and Fra Bartolommeo. A bronze bust of Savonnarola. The last cell on the left possesses a peculiar interest as being the one occupied by the prophet-priest, Savonnarola. Cell No. 13 is sanctified by his portrait, by Fra Bartolommeo, and his crucifix, plain and simple as the soul of its former possessor, also his autographs and a painting representing his diabolical taking off. Another cell is that of St. Antonio, Bishop of Florence, who also was one of the order. The library, the first public library in Italy, contains many illuminated books of the 10th, 11th and 12th centuries. Many of these are so beautifully executed with the pen, as to appear printed; all on parchment. Another cell, that of Cosimo, when visiting the monastery, is ornamented with frescoes by Fra Angelica, among these, the adoration of the Magi, a beautiful painting; also his portrait and other mementoes of this greatest of the Medici. A long line of cells, the former homes of pious monks line, either side of the passage, each with the little window opening out on the open space. And this as if furnishing too much light and air, and consequently pleasure or comfort, though not more than fifteen inches square and closed with a wooden shutter, has in the middle of the shutter still another, not more than eight inches square. Over the head of each bed is a small fresco, a crucifixion, a Madonna, or some saint, done by their pious, divinely-gifted, sweet-natured brother, Fra Angelica. That these small cells, the life-long homes of these simple-minded, pious monks were doubly endeared to them by these lovely little frescoes and paintings, is most certain. They are lovely yet and even to a passing stranger, mementoes of love and devotion. And strange to say, time with its effacing finger for more than 400 years, has scarcely dimmed their luster. Many of these frescoes and paintings here by Fra Bartolommeo and Fra Angelica possess a charm, not only for their incomparable perfection and beauty, but in their freshness, pointing to departed genius, which, though absent, can never die. The skillful hands and loving hearts that conceived and wrought them have for near half a thousand years lost their cunning and warm emotion, yet these immortal embodiments of their spirits live on and on, speaking trumpet-tongued from the long, dimly-remembered past, and children's children, shall long yet visit them as holy shrines. But not only have these loving brothers, Savonnarola, Fra Bartolommeo and Fra Angelica, with their pious, devoted companions and brothers, gone, all gone, but the very order itself has perished—been suppressed, and

    The cells are all silent, deserted, alone,
    The monks have departed, the painters are gone,
    Thrice-sacred San Marco, though all lonely now,
    Cicero was not more eloquent than thou.

SAN CROCE.

This immense structure in the Lombardo-Gothic style, built in the thirteenth century, is one of the most interesting churches in Florence. In front is an open piazza, in the middle of which is a colossal statue of Florence's greatest poet, Dante. The interior nave and aisles are 489 feet in length and 65 feet to the flat ceiling, which is supported by fourteen massive columns. Interior, tomb of Michael Angelo, whose dust reposes here. Monument to Dante, who died in exile at Ravena. Statue of Alferi. The marble pulpit, highly decorated with silver and precious stones, is said to be the finest in Italy. Five reliefs, representing the Franciscan order, the Stigmata. The death of Saint Francis. Statuettes of Faith, Hope and Charity, Fortitude and Justice. Many beautiful frescoes and paintings by the old masters make this old church quite a picture gallery.

Dec. 14th.—The afternoon being clear and the weather mild as early autumn, we drove to the surpassingly lovely suburbs of Florence, over grounds that have been rendered historical by the battles of a thousand years, and classical by the writers of almost every age and country, and rendered ever dear to lovers of art, science and letters, by being the homes of great men, among them Galileo. Passing out over the Arno over a solid stone bridge that had witnessed the march of mailed knights as they passed over it on their way to retake the Holy Sepulchre, we issued from the city through the Porta Romana, which had withstood the fierce assaults of Gaul and Spaniard, when, turning to the right, we drove along the old stone wall of the same period, ascending the hill to the Bellosguardo, from which point we had a fine view of the city. From here we continued our drive through a highly-picturesque country to an old monastery upon a lofty eminence, some three miles from the city. This old cloister resembles an old ruined fortress of Antediluvian times. It was built in 1366, and though it has battled long and well against storm and time, like the order it represents, it is falling to decay, and after having witnessed the long struggle man has made for his intellectual and religious freedom, without, I fear, having greatly contributed to either, has melted away before the noonday splendor of the nineteenth century. We were kindly received by one of the few remaining monks now here, who looked as though he might have assisted at its foundation, and who kindly showed us over the old church, the open court surrounded by long lines of vacant, mouldy cells, where through centuries many generations of these monks have lived in these close, dark, solitary cells, thinking to secure heaven by making earth a hell. The chapel has a beautiful marble pavement and side stalls, or pews, of beautifully-carved hard wood. A good painting, Death of Saint Bruno, hung over the altar; other paintings and frescoes, old and faded, ornamented the walls. We descended from the chapel to the crypt by old worn stone steps, where are monuments of priests, many of them four and five hundred years old. The stained windows are by Giovanni.

THE UFFIZI.

Dec. 16th.—Visited the Uffizi Picture Gallery, one of the most valuable collections of art in Europe. Arabesque portraits of kings, emperors and distinguished persons adorn the arched ceiling over the stairway. Entering the long corridor we find the wall covered with wood, metal and canvas paintings by the old masters. These paintings, though not without great merit in many instances, are principally valuable as illustrating the gradual, slow, but constantly progressive change from the old, or Byzantine, to the new or classical style of painting. The oldest of these paintings, a Madonna and Child, is by Rico in 1050, and of course Byzantine in style. It possesses much interest in being one of the oldest paintings extant. It antedates oil painting, is in *distemper*, that is, size is used instead of oil, and yet, though upwards of 800 years old, retains its colors well, so much so that it gives strong suspicion of having been retouched, if so, this is not stated in the catalogue as is generally done. We are thus left to infer that the colors are those of the artist. It is on wood, to which fact, perhaps, it owes its preservation. I am not aware of any painting so old as this on canvas, indeed, nearly all of the very old paintings are on wood or metal or fresco, the latter term applied to those paintings in which the colors are laid on the still moist plaster of walls or ceilings. The next two are by Cimabue and give us the first departure from the old style which, continued by his great pupil and his school, developed the Renaissance style. This entire revolution is fully given in these paintings in this hall, and is the result of the labors of Giotto and his school. Another important historical fact given here, and which serves to increase our admiration for the wonderful genius of the immortal Giotto, is that many of his ideal conceptions of figures have constituted the models which all subsequent painters have adopted. For instance, his "Head of Christ" is retained as the model, only given with an increase of beauty and dignity by Leonardo de Vinci in his Last Supper, and the St. John of Giotto has an effeminate appearance which has been retained by all subsequent painters to the present day.

A point then here given, and a most important historical fact, but little known, is that the portraits of Christ and Saint John are the *inventions* of this great master of the thirteenth century, and were entirely unknown to any previous painter, both are entirely *ideal*, and the creations of Giotto, and if more like those they represent than like Moses or Mahomet, it is entirely an accident. They certainly differ greatly from all those given from times nearer Christ, as seen in all the Byzantine Greco-religious or Church style of all the older mosaics and frescos. And the same, only to a less extent, may be said of his Madonnas.

Entering the first room, we meet with many paintings of superior excellence to those met with in the long corridor first entered. We shall, however, only stop to notice one of these, and this not more on account of its superior excellence than from the fact that it introduces us to a great artist and the most distinctly Florentine of the time, Fra Giovanni, called and known in the art world as Fra Angelica, from the beauty of his angels. Having once met with this extraordinary painter, we never lose his characteristics, recognizing at a glance a painting by this master by the distinctive beauty of his angels, (and almost all his paintings have angels, if not, all have angelic faces) never so successfully imitated as to deceive us into attributing it to Fra Angelico. I do not now recall but two other painters in which the individual style is so clearly marked as to enable one, not a connoisseur, to immediately determine the author, Rembrandt and Raphael. Perhaps Murillo might with less certainty be added to this list. This painting was done in 1433, for the Guild of Florentine Merchants. It is in three pieces. On the center tablet is a Madonna and Child, life-size, while around them are a multi- of angels of ideal beauty, playing on different musical instruments. St. John the Baptist, St. Mark and Peter are on the side pieces or doors. In the shading the colors are so softly blended as to give an indescribable harmonious beauty to the figures and to transfer them from the plane of mortals. In what colors did Fra Angelica dip his pencil? From where did he borrow these tints? Surely not from earth!

Another large and carefully-finished picture, representing the Virgin and St. Anne with the Child and St. John, with other figures, is by Fra Bartolommeo, a brother Franciscan monk of San Marco. The interest of this historical collection is very great as showing the advance and attainments of the art. *Oil* has here, and now taken the place of *distemper*, while perspective, which great masters had been for 200 years laboring to discover, is now a well-known science. The improved knowledge of anatomy had also aided in making these figures more natural, while chiara-oscura is now under established rules.

Through this collection in the corridor, and the first room, we are brought down to, and introduced to the great masters of the fifteenth and sixteenth centuries, in which all the mysteries of the art being fully known, and the classical or Renaissance style being fully established, the greatest men known to the art are working on those immortal works that adorn every picture gallery in Europe. But it is in Italy, and more especially here in Florence, the nursery of art, that the halls are filled with their most choice works. We now enter the room known as the *Tribune*, where we meet with a collection of these works together with the best gems of ancient sculpture, nowhere else met with to the same extent and beauty. We will first notice the statuary, as this first attracts our attention on entering the room. First, and occupying the center of the room, is the world-renowned marble statue, the Venus de Medici. This beautiful production of the Greek chisel is thought by many good judges to be the best marble statue of Venus extant. It has only one rival, the Venus de Milo, in the Louvre. A comparison between these two wonderful works of art is hardly just to either, as they represent quite different styles of beautiful women, both perfect in their style, and a choice, like that between brunettes and blondes, is a mere matter of taste. Both are Greek works possibly by Praxiteles or his school. Aside from their wonderful perfection and beauty there is, however, a comparison that must be made by everyone seeing these statues, and may readily be decided in favor of either without any disparagement of the other. The Venus de Medici is the statue of a nude female of rather small size, rather petite, and gives the ideal perfection of the beauty and grace of the human form divine, a surpassingly beautiful woman, yet a woman, and as woman, the more beautiful because she is nothing else, only woman, with the idea woman so perfectly and beautifully given that could we in thought, increase this perfection and beauty to infinity, the idea would still remain and be, woman, whereas the Venus de Milo is the draped colossal statue of a wondrously-beautiful woman, with a something added which unmistakably makes her more than a woman, a queen, a goddess, and with all her perfection and beauty as a goddess she is placed a little beyond the grasp of our knowledge and affections, while we involuntarily cling to that which we do know which embraces and fills the measure of, our affections the *only*-woman, as found in the Venus de Medici. We admire the one as a goddess, the other as a woman, and as the woman is nearest us, we admire her most.

Another gem of Greek sculpture, and thought by some to be the best that has descended to us from the ancients, is the Dancing Faun. Scarcely less admirable is the Knife-grinder, a stolid, brutal-looking Scythian, whetting his knife to flay Marsyas ; also the Apollino, a youthful Apollo, very fine !

PAINTINGS.

The first of these is the Madonna with the Child and St. John standing near by with a small red-crested bird, known as the Madonna Del Cardinello, by Raphael. St. John is a fine boy with all the beauty of youthful life, richly dressed, is no doubt a portrait from some fine-looking, gaily-dressed son of an Italian nobleman. A female portrait, by Raphael, also another female portrait, long attributed to Raphael during his Florentine period, is of great beauty, and may well have been by Raphael.

A Venus, by Titian. This has been much admired, and is certainly admirable for the perfection of the flesh tints, but fails to impress me favorably. I do not like Titian's type of females. There is a gorgeousness of beauty, a gushing appearance I do not like. All his Venuses in particular are wanting in that soft, mild, delicate beauty we might expect to meet in the goddess of love. A Madonna with St. John and

St. Francis, by A. Del Sarto, a beautiful painting. Adoration of the Magi, by Dürer. Holy Family, by Michael Angelo. Pope Julius, by Raphael. Holy Family, by Paul Veronese. Adoration of the Magi, by Leonardo de Vinci. Madonna and Child, with angels, by Botticelli.

In the Hall of the ancient masters, are fine works by Fra Angelica, Lorenze de Credi. Madonna and Child, by Lippi. An Annunciation, by Leonardo de Vinci. Holy Family, by Luca Signorelli. A Landscape, by Salvator Rosa. Holy Family, by Rembrandt. Landscape, by Jacob Van Ruysdale. Venus and Adonis, by Rubens. Madonna, by Van Dyck. Entombment, by Roger Von der Weyden.

The cabinet of jems contains many curiosities of much interest. Among them a vessel of Lapis Lazula with two bas reliefs in gold and jasper ground. A vase of jasper with lid and the figure of a woman in gold, adorned with diamonds.

In the room of Venetian painters there are many works by their greatest painters. Among them portrait of the Duchess and Duke öf Urbino, by Titian, one of his best works. Titian's Flora, much admired.

Passing by the multitudes of other fine paintings and curiosities and gems and medals and bronzes of great beauty and excellence, we enter the Saloon of Niobe, containing the group of Niobe and her children in the act of being slain by Apollo and Diana. This beautiful group of seven sons and seven daughters of the demi-goddess queen, who had incurred the displeasure of heaven by preferring herself to the goddess Latona, are being slain in the presence of their mother who endeavors in vain to protect the youngest of her daughters who has fled to her for protection. The arrows shot from unseen bows by invisible hands from above, flash into view on their unerring mission. One by one the terror-stricken children, pierced by these arrows, fall in the presence of their agonized mother, who, with the lofty grandeur of a queen, is looking upward towards the source from which they come, with an indescribable agony that complains not, upbraids not, nor asks for mercy. No more expressive group was ever made by human hands. It is a poem or myth beautifully told in stone. And is that providential destruction of a family, as we see in epidemics, personified. It is one of the finest of the Greek works. Most likely belonged to the Temple of Apollo, and is by the hand of Phidias or Praxiteles. No other age than that of Pericles could have produced it. Let no one visiting Florence fail to see and study it.

THE CATHEDRAL (ITALIAN DUOMO).

This beautiful building of the mixed Gotho-Italian style was commenced in the thirteenth century on a plan by the great architect and painter, Giotto, and partly completed in the fifteenth century, some 200 years having been employed in its partial completion. It is highly ornamented externally by variegated marble so artistically arranged as to appear as a vast mosaic. It has been built at an incredible cost of time and labor, and is in fact not yet completed, although the work has been, and is now, going on for more than 600 years. A large body of men are now employed on the west end, not in repairing, but in finishing it according to the original plan, and in correspondence with the other exterior parts of the building. In conversation with the superintendent of this work he informed me that if nothing happened and the full force of workmen, some twenty or thirty, could be kept on the work, he expected to complete it in ten years, that is, in 1894. In one-third of the time in America we have built a thousand cities, conquered a wilderness and established a mighty nation of fifty millions of people, and since its foundations were laid Europe has passed from the gloom and ignorance of the early middle ages to the light and civilization produced by 600 years of progress. The vast time this work has gone on, ever nearing, but never attaining, completion, has given rise in Florence to a most significant proverb, that an enterprise, like the Cathedral, will never be completed. The Florentines have, however, for excuse, that it is not only an immense, but an elaborate structure, that necessarily requires much time and labor for its completion. The Cathedral is 500 feet long, 140 feet wide and 300 feet to the top of the dome, all of which is adorned by elaborate frescoes by Giovanni Vasari. And while the interior presents a much less ornate appearance than the exterior, there are some frescoes and paintings of much merit. Among the paintings is an equestrian likeness of Sir John Hawkswood, of England, a freebooter, or soldier, of fortune, who, leaving England at the downfall of his party, wandered over to Italy, where, with his band of bold English adventurers, he roved over the land, fighting for that party that payed the best. At first he was employed against the Florentines, whose experience with his prowess soon taught them the value of his services, and with true political sagacity they opened negotiations with Sir John which secured his services for, instead of against, the city, when he soon, by his valor and good fortune, won for the city the greatest benefits over those for whom he had just been fighting. And Sir John, as a tower of strength, continued in good faith with his invincible band of adventurers, in the service of Florence until his death, which was suitably observed and bemoaned as a public calamity, which indeed it was to the Florentines. His body was wrapped in cloth and carried in great state to the Cathedral and buried with all the religious pomp and ceremony becoming a Christian hero, and his portrait placed here as might have been that of a saint. Another equestrian painting in the Cathedral is that of a captain, also a freebooter, who fought with great valor and success for the Florentines. The monument of the architect of the Cathedral, the great painter

Giotto, is in the church, and near it that of Pierre Farnese, a soldier of fortune, who fought for pay on the side of the Florentines, and who died of the plague in 1363. Other monuments are of bishops and distinguished churchmen. Bishops and freebooters are alike honored here; perhaps the latter were equally pious, and certainly were much the most useful. The richly-stained windows are of the fifteenth century.

This old Cathedral has witnessed some fearful scenes of blood during the stormy times that have swept over and through Florence since its first occupancy. In 1747 the two Medici were attacked in the Cathedral by armed confederates. One of them was slain, and the other, wounded by a priest, fled to the sacristy.

The beautiful variegated marble of the exterior was obtained from Siena, Carrara, Prato, Lorenze and other quarries. The beauty and grandeur of the structure well fulfill the swelling instructions given the architect by the, at that time, wealthy and powerful city of Florence, to "build the finest structure that human art could conceive or the wealth of the world afford." The vanity of such inflated ideas is shown in the fact that the wealth and glory of the city faded long ere its completion.

The Campanille, or Bell Tower, stands separated from the Cathedral, and is an immense pile some fifty feet square and 300 feet high, and is ascended by 420 stone steps. It was designed by the same architect, Giotto, in 1334. It is elaborately ornamented with statues and bas reliefs, and is the most beautiful structure of the kind in the world. We ascended to its lofty parapet, from which we had a fine view of Florence and its suburbs and adjacent beautiful country extending to points bounded only by the horizon.

NAPLES.

Jan. 7th.—The city of Naples, situated on the beautiful Gulf of Naples, is the largest city in Italy; contains 500,000 inhabitants. It is in the centre of a highly-volcanic region where the uncertain earth trembles with a chronic ague, and the beautiful coast is lined with the ruins of ancient palaces, villas and temples, whose unsteady foundations, alarmed at earthquake shocks, have exchanged places with their roofs, while Vesuvius, towering 4,000 feet above the city, yawns destruction on all the cities of the plain, adding to the uncertain terrors, or heightening the charm of this strange region, where storm-scared and earthquake-riven towns are often two and three thousand years old, while adjoining mountains, that look as though a part of the everlasting hills, are only two or three hundred years old. Here, in this enchanted district, as if in very sport, the entire order of things is reversed, cities are being built for a thousand years, while mountains are formed full-grown, finished and rounded off, in a single day. Monte Nuovo, only a short distance from Naples, stood forth, fully formed, one morning, where the day before had been a level plain.

Took carriage and drove around the bay to the west of Naples through the Grotto di Posilipo, to Pozzuola. On the hill through which this grotto passes, was Virgil's villa, where he composed his immortal work, the Æneid—and here is his tomb, where he was buried, having died at Brundusium, B. C. 19. Visited on our way the Dog Grotto, and Salfatora, a cavern out of which hisses hot steam and stifling sulphurous smoke, passing over the amphitheater-like depression, which is the crater of an extinct volcano, the ground sounds hollow, cavernous beneath our feet, while the caverns and fissures from which issue jets of steam or smoke, with stifling sulphur and carbonic-acid gasses, show this spot on which we now stand only a half-latent volcano, liable at any moment to uncover the yawning terrors of a boiling volcanic cavern, whose destructive furies are only half concealed by an uncertain crust of trembling earth.

The town of Pozzuola, now of but little importance, was long.the principal seaport of the Gulf of Naples. St. Paul landed here after his shipwreck, from whence, after remaining a week, he continued his trip to Rome, along the Via Apia. At this point, in time beyond memory, there was constructed a bridge to the opposite point of the gulf. Many of the pillars are still seen, rising above the water. Visited the remarkable ruins of the temple of Serapis· (Serapium) built by some unknown Greek or Etruscan colony in unknown times. It was long almost entirely hidden with gravel and ashes by some volcanic eruption, but this has lately been removed. It consisted of a square enclosed by forty-eight immense marble and granite columns, with many adjoining small chambers. The portico rested on four Corinthian columns. Three of these bearing a rich frieze, still remain. In the center of the court stood a circular temple, surrounded by Corinthian pillars. The interior was approached by four flights of steps. In the center of the inner temple was found the statue of Serapis, now in the Naples museum. This temple, built by some ancient Greek colony, perhaps many centuries before the founding of Rome, had fallen into decay, and was repaired by Marcus Aurelius, at which time most probably the fine Corinthian columns with friezes were added. Of course, when built, it was on the hill, high above the sea. At some subsequent time, unknown, it was sunk by some convulsion below the sea level, where it remained as a ruin, rising out of the sea for many centuries; during this time of submergence, the marble columns were perforated for some six or eight feet near their middle, the lower eight feet being protected by a volcanic deposit of lava, by a small shell-fish, giving them a honey-combed appearance. Subsequently they were again elevated, lifted up bodily, floor, temple, pillars all, some thirty feet, and yet these columns are now standing erect and just as they were placed by the unknown people who first erected them, unknown, whether Etruscan or Greek. and who worshipped at these shrines, whose god has been in disfavor for at least 1,500 years. Silent witness, this old temple, of a high civilization not indigenous, but invited here by the loveliness of its clime and beauty of its smiling bay, whose waters, stirred by aromatic breezes, flashed upon coral beaches of transcendent beauty, lining this amphitheater of hills, at a time when northern Italy, Germany, France and England were shrouded in that primeval darkness that has everywhere invested primitive man. Another ruin farther along the range of hills, is the temple of Neptune, consisting of pillars rising out of the sea. Another, the temple of the Nymphs, that has only lately been despoiled of some of its remaining columns and sculptures. Farther on are the ruins of Cicero's Academy, or palatial villa where he composed his Academia and De Fato, hallowed in its memories, but it, like the surrounding temples and palaces and villas, has given way, melted down by the corroding tooth of 2,000 years, or rent from its foundations to parapet by the fearful earthquake-shocks to which this whole coast-line has been subjected for near 1,800 years, and that have frightened the everlasting hills, casting them from their unsteady foundations. Near these ruins is the Roman amphitheater, somewhat better preserved, but in mouldering dislocated ruins. The groans of its dying gladiators, with the roar of its wild beasts and the shouts of its gay spectators, that died with the passing breeze, appear now scarcely more ephemeral than its massive walls and time-defying granite columns. Close by is another volcanic cavern, emitting hot sulphurous vapors, the fitting breath of volcanic fires that roll in lava billows, upon which set the unsteady hills. Towering above this, is Monte Nuovo, a lofty cone-shaped hill, with an extinct crater on its summit, which was upheaved in a single night, Sept. 30, 1538. Olive trees and vineyards extend high up its sides, in all things looking much like the surrounding hills, many of which, with their everlasting granite bases, clapped their glad hands at creation's dawn.

Between this hill and the Boga Hotel Della Regina, the hillsides are almost composed of ruins of villas and palaces of times antedating, and immediately subsequent to, the Christian era, and still more ancient temples. Among the latter are the temple of Diana and temple of Venus, once splendid temples, but which have long since yielded to the fearful earthquake-shock, with rising hills and falling rock, and are ruins all. Near this point is the Villa Bouli, where in A. D. 59, the devoted son planned the murder of his loving mother, Agrippina, who had tenderly planned the murder of her much-loved son, Nero. How fearfully must the times have been, wrenched from all moral anchorage when such things were possible.

At this point is the villa of Julius Cæsar, who was wont to retire from the din of Rome and for a season live here, at a time when the name of Cæsar filled the world, and where his sister, Octavia, resided after the death of her second husband, Marc Antony. Near this villa, we ascended Cape Mirino, a bold, projecting rock, crowned by a ruined castle, from the casemates of which we had a most enchanting view of the city of Naples, Pozzuola, with the silvery bays of Naples and Gaita, stretching out to the foot of Vesuvius, which, clothed in living terrors, towers to the clouds. This volcano is now in a state of semi-activity, great clouds of smoke and ashes are issuing from its snow-capped crater, while ever and anon the earth is felt to quiver at detonations from its half exploded magazines.

From this point we turned and drove back to Naples. Having spent the entire day in this wondrously-interesting drive along the margin of the bay, around the semi-circle of hills that form this classical amphitheater of hills, the entire sides of which were formerly lined by splendid palaces adorned with, and surrounded by, all the splendor that oppulent Rome could produce in her prime. Emperors, orators, poets, statesmen, heroes, alike loving to retire to this Elyseum where the heat of a southern clime with its semi-tropical verdure was tempered by the aromatic breezes from spice-laden isles beyond the smiling bay of Naples, and where through all historic times nature had been as uniformly stable as lovely. All is changed now, and all these splendid structures have been for more than a thousand years riven to atoms, torn from their foundation, crumbled to shapeless ruins, by volcanic forces, that, after forming much of this romantic coast, had slept for thousands of years in the deep, dark, silent, cavernous depths of Vesuvius. But which in the first century of the Christian era, aroused from their slumbers, rent the everlasting hills as though they had been fragile things of clay, sunk the mountains into plains, and lifted the plains into mountains, crumbling cities, temples, palaces, towns, all, as in very wantonness of might, laughing to scorn alike the mightiest works of man, and most stable things of nature.

Looking at these ruins now before me, I can but think that history has made a mistake in its chronology, as these ruins look to be antediluvian, and were co-existent with the hills of which they form an undistinguishable part. But then these hills themselves are in some instances of quite recent origin—were made long since Cæsar's villa, while perhaps some of these ruined temples reach back in their origin to times anterior to Jason's expedition in quest of the Golden Fleece, at which time this region was settled by Æolians or Etruscans from Asia

Minor, as this settlement is not only prehistoric but may antedate Jason's expedition by many thousands of years. Certain it is that at some unknown remote period southern Italy was settled by a branch of the Aryan family, which coming into Europe from some point in Asia, either as conquerors driving out the primitive inhabitants, or themselves driven before some more powerful tribes, settled around the Mediterranean Sea, not Greeks, because not of, or from, Greece, but cognate peoples.

Returning to Naples, we find 500,000 people crowded into six square miles, within a space three miles long by two wide, giving a compact mass of unpleasing houses crowded together without order, with narrow, crooked, alley-like streets, here called via, crowded with a multitudinous mass of impecunious macaroni eaters. They have, however, a cheerful disposition, which no penury, no misfortune seems capable of depressing, a cheerfulness which makes us half forget their troublesome faults. It is gratifying to know that under the new regime, begging and beggers, which have almost disappeared from northern and middle Italy, are also rapidly disappearing here, and could some system of labor be devised whereby the unfortunate over-crowded poor could be given employment at which they could earn an honest living, these Neapolitans with their cheerful natures and better instincts would soon mount a higher plane whereby the name Neapolitan would no longer carry reproach.

There is almost nothing that is indigenous in Naples, the work of man, that is valuable. Almost everything here worth seeing is and always has been exotic, and if a Virgil wrote here it was only because he did so before falling under the influence of this soft, enervating climate, which here invites only to repose, dissipating all the manly virtues. Consequently Naples, notwithstanding her superior advantages, has no history of her own, no indigenous warlike navies ever issued from her ports on expeditions of conquest or glory. Etruscans, Greeks, Romans, Galls, Vandals, Goths, Spaniards and Normans have alike been masters here, and have alike fallen under the enervating influence of its soft climate, and have not only failed to infuse into the native population a manly energy, but have lost their own.

THE MUSEUM—MUSEO NAZIONALO.

No one visiting Naples—and none should come to Italy without doing so—will fail to spend much time in the National Museum where are gathered art treasures of priceless value, to be found at no other place. First, on account of its striking appearance as well as its great worth, we will notice the Farnese Bull, the work of the Greek sculptor Appolonius, which though greatly mutilated when found, has been skillfully repaired by perhaps the only modern artist who was worthy to mend a work by Appolonius—Michael Angelo.

In this remarkable group we have an entire myth scarcely less intelligibly given than in a written poem. The sons of Antiope are avenging upon Dirce the wrongs she had done their mother by tying her to the horns of a wild bull, which they have seized upon the brow of a rugged precipice and which they hold with the strength of Hercules while they secure her to a rope passed around the horns of the wild animal. The bull as well as the two young men are typical of more than animal strength. Their mother Antiope stands in the background in an attitude as though imploring her sons to be merciful. No more wonderful work of the Greek chisel has come down to us. Near by this is the Farnese Hercules found like the former in the Thermae of Caracalla at Rome, and like the former a Greek work. Like the Farnese Bull, it is a poem, and represents a myth in which is given one of the labors of Hercules, which was to bring to Greece the golden apples from the gardens of the Hesperides and which could only be obtained by killing the ever-watchful dragon. After searching in vain over most of the world for the gardens, he found Atlas supporting the world upon his shoulders, and engaged him to get the apples. Hercules, in the meantime, holding the world for him. When Atlas returned with the apples, being tired of holding the world, he thought of taking the apples on to Greece and letting Hercules continue to hold the world, which indeed he could not let go without help. To this Hercules assented, provided Atlas would hold it while he adjusted the pad upon his shoulders. To this Atlas agreed, laid down the apples and took the world, but Hercules, being relieved, took up the apples and carried them to Greece, leaving Atlas as he found him with the world upon his shoulders, which in turn he could not let go without assistance. The statue represents Hercules leaning on his club, holding in his left hand behind him the much-prized apples. There is a quaint roguish smile in the appearance of the hero, significant of the trick he has played upon his friend Atlas. In the centre of another room is the marble statue of Serapis, found in the ruined temple of Serapeum, and many fine busts of Greek philosophers, poets and heroes, among them an inimitable bust of the old blind poet, Homer; all Greek works. Another room is filled with finds in Pompeii, hundreds of bronze and iron domestic utensils, stoves, pans, spoons, lamps, etc. In a large case are surgical instruments found in the house of the surgeon—probes, bistouries, surgical needles, speculae, forceps, etc. In another case are the contents of a grocery and confectionery shop, figs, walnuts, grapes and various fruits and seeds, perfectly preserved, with pound-cakes, jelly-cakes, split open and a layer of jelly placed between the slices, just as at the present day. Muffin and other cake-rings and patterns, just such as we have at present.

POMPEII, OR THE CITY OF THE DEAD.

An ancient Oscan city, founded at an unknown period, perhaps 1500 years before Christ, and when it became a Roman town, in the fourth century, was a prosperous city with a large commerce, and though of Greek origin and civilization, at the beginning of the Christian era, had become thoroughly Romanized. In A. D. 63 it was nearly destroyed by a fearful earthquake, which threw down most of the houses, perhaps all the taller ones, and much injured the walls of all, as seen in their repairs. So much was the destruction that it had to be rebuilt. This, through the assistance of imperial Rome, at this time mistress of the world, was soon accomplished, insomuch that within a few years it was fully restored with life and business as gay and active as before its destruction, and what is almost certain, really finer than before the calamity. Looking now at this singular occurrence, what at the time was a great calamity to many, appears indeed a most fortunate accident, as the newly-built city was to become embalmed, if not *for*, at least serving to instruct, all future times, as without this preceding earthquake and destruction of the old city, while it would alike have been embalmed with its art treasures, it would not have so perfectly presented us with the social condition, art culture, and manner of living in a Roman city at the beginning of the Christian era, or 1,800 years ago. As it is the city presents us with the conditions essentially of a new city, giving everything not as it *had* been, but as it actually *was* in A. D. 79. This restoration of the city was hardly completed, as while the private houses, residences, admitting no delay, had all been occupied for years, some of the larger public buildings were in a state of restoration. In some cases the columns prepared and on the ground but not yet raised, in others the walls and columns up but the roof not yet on, or the frescoing of the walls not yet finished. In this state, the embodiment of the time, the whole city, as if intended for a Belle Arte Museum for future times, was, on the 24th of August, A. D. 79, buried beneath a shower of ashes from the overhanging volcano, Mount Vesuvius. This destruction was as overwhelming and universal as sudden and unexpected, for, though warned of the dangerous character of the neighboring mount by the destructive earthquake of only sixteen years previous, that this warning should not have been understood, forgotten or neglected, by these gay, prosperous and luxury-loving people, was most natural when it is known that from time immemorial Vesuvius had given no indications of volcanic activity. Vineyards and olive trees extended up its sides to near its summit, while cattle grazed, and had done so for hundreds of years, upon the flat, grass-covered meadows on its summit. At the time of its destruction the city contained some 30,000 inhabitants. Only about one-third of the town has been excavated and this gives evidence of having been densely peopled, the entire ground having been covered with buildings and their courts, and narrow streets, twenty feet wide, well paved with flat blocks of lava. These pavements are old, of course, not having been disturbed by the previous earthquake by which the houses were thrown down, and are cut into deep ruts by the wagons and carriages and carts that had passed over them for centuries. Like all walled cities, the streets were not only narrow but tortuous, crooked, short.

The walls are still standing around the entire city, but are entirely (except where exposed by excavations) covered to a depth of many feet with ashes. We ascend a flight of steps and enter the city through the Porta Marino, or sea gate, at one time immediately on or near the wharf, now removed a mile from the bay. Passing under an archway we came out in the open city. Nothing can be more strange. Nearly all the houses are only one or only a part of a story high, all the upper portion having been thrown down or pressed in with the roof, by the weight of ashes—nothing but bare walls with narow, crooked streets between them. The unexcavated parts of the city rise fifteen or twenty feet above the tops of the houses in the excavated portions, as a smooth plain, giving no indications of houses beneath the surface upon, which cattle have grazed for centuries. Looking over beyond this elevated plain, beyond what we afterwards learned was the wall of the city, the surface suddenly becomes depressed, presenting an extended evel plain some thirty or forty feet lower than the surface of the town. At first we were disposed to account for this phenomenal condition of the surface-level by supposing the ashes, like snow, had drifted, or that they had fallen much heavier here than there, and felt regret that the city had not been situated farther over on the plain where the ashes appeared to have fallen not near so deep. The first theory, however, that of drifting of the material, was at once dissipated by observing the character of the material which is scoria, ashes, cinders and stones, some of the latter as large as cannon balls, that had crushed down through roof and ceiling to the solid pavement below. A fearful hail-storm this. The next theory, that it was unfortunate that the city was not situated further over on the lower plain, was corrected by learning that all this lower surface, upon which cattle were now grazing, or was under cultivation, was at that time the open sea, the gulf of Naples, extending quite up to the walls of the city, and was filled up by a like fall of ashes and stones to that which covered the city. Doubtless the bottom of the bay, extending between the city and the present water line, has also been elevated by subsequent volcanic forces.

Under the care of an intelligent government guide, we went over the city along its well-worn paved streets which give frequent proofs that a city election was near at hand, by paintings on the pavements and side walls urging the claims of their candidate, just as printed placards announce such facts at the present day. The houses are generally small and divided up into a number of small apartments. The numerous shops opened directly onto the streets, but the dwelling houses had neither doors nor windows on the sides next the streets, but presented long, dark, blind walls to the streets, the houses opening into an open court, which is entered from the street by a passage. These houses, although the rooms (the bed and family rooms in particular) are small, very small, had many or all the conveniences of modern houses. Leaden pipes are seen, with stop-cocks for turning on or off the water, which was brought to the city from some distant source, just as we have at the present day. In the open court of the houses was a small water-tank with vases for flowers around, and flower-beds bordering it. There was a large sitting-room or parlor in the house next the open court, and this with some of the smaller rooms had been furnished gaudily, extravagantly. In the houses of the wealthy, the walls of the rooms were in most cases decorated with frescoes, in many instances highly finished and beautiful. Indeed there is every proof that these luxurious Pompeians were a highly-cultivated, artistic people. Many of these frescoes would do credit to the finest halls in New York or St. Louis. Often the character, calling or taste of the owner is easily determined by these frescoes. One house we entered belonged, unquestionably, to a sporting gentleman, whose tastes were much as an English gentleman of the present day, fond of fishing, and the chase. Here on the wall was a beautiful fresco, a pack of hounds attacking a wild boar; there a stag pursued by hounds and hunter; again, several kinds of game just brought in by the successful hunter; then he is seen going out hunting with dogs, footmen and game-bag; here again, are fish and an angler in the act of pulling one out of the brook. Another house belonged to a tragic poet who is reading Sophocles to actors on the stage. Another house belonged to a wine merchant, Here are five empty wine jars sitting on a table and evidently holding different kinds of wine, beneath is a wine cellar, etc. Another house is a bakery. Here are kneading troughs, there the ovens in which the bread was baked and could be baked now. Another house is a miller's. Here are the mill-stones and hoppers in which the corn was ground, and could be ground to-day. These curious mills were to me exceedingly interesting, as being the models of the mills, with their stones and hoppers, used in the country when I was a boy. Here is a large theatre with its long rows of stone seats rising one above the other. Here, a temple to Mercury, with an altar in the middle in marble, with reliefs; on the front, victims; on the side sacrificial utensil; on back, oak garlands. A temple of Jupiter unfinished. Pantheon—the walls decorated with frescoes, beautiful in its ruins, but unfinished at time of the catastrophe. House of Meleager—a beautiful edifice with fountains, porticoes, frescoes in yellow. House of the Faun—so-called from the bronze statuette of a dancing faun found here. It belonged to a gentleman of great wealth and culture, is the finest house in Pompeii, is 202 feet long and 125 feet broad. It contains many beautiful frescoes and mosaics. At the entrance in mosaic is the greeting, "Have." Other mosaics represent doves near a casket. Its roof was supported by twenty-eight marble Ionic columns, on its walls was a beautiful fresco, Battle of Alexander; at the back is a garden enclosed by fifty-four Doric columns. The Stadium Therma, or warm baths, with a sudatorium or sweating room, a splendid establishment containing a great number of cold and warm baths, with neat little bathing rooms furnished with shelves for the clothes, towels, etc. The amphitheatre is at the far end of the town, has seats for 20,000 spectators, dens for the wild animals and a large area for fighting them, or for the combats of gladiators. The floors of all the houses are paved, many of them beautifully tesselated, and not a few have elaborate mosaics. The streets are named as in a modern city. The work of removing the lava and ashes from the remaining two-thirds of the city is progressing slowly. It is calculated that at the present rate the entire city will be excavated in seventy years. What will be revealed in the yet uncovered portions is, of course, impossible to say, many art treasures will doubtless be found. It is thought that the most important parts of the city have been cleared, but this is entirely conjecture, as we are as profoundly ignorant of the other parts as we were of the part cleared. All particulars of this long-lost city are, and have long been, unknown. Only as they are revealed by removing the ashes do we learn anything concerning them. It is generally supposed that nearly all the inhabitants escaped, only some eighty skeletons having been found, but this does not prove that they were saved, as they may have fled to some other part of the city, that part farthest from the flaming mountain, for greater safety and there been overwhelmed *en masse*. This can only be determined when the entire city is excavated, if indeed then, as they may have fled to the ships or beyond the walls and then perished.

VESUVIUS.

Jan. 13th., 1885.—The weather during our stay of eight days at Naples had been rainy, cold, disagreeable, except two or three days, which we had devoted to visiting the surrounding district. On Tuesday the 13th, although the weather was unsettled, threatening, stormy, in company with Mrs. .I and her lovely nieces, we set out for the ascent of Vesuvius, at present in a state of semi-eruption. Great volumes of smoke, forming an inverted cone of angry, turbulent, billowy darkness, stand over the mountain during the day, which illuminated at night look like a city in conflagration, lighting up land and sea with a lurid glare. The ascent is made by carriage some ten miles to, and up, the mountain, as far as the railroad depot. This took three and a half hours hard driving. At this point we took a car which is drawn almost perpendicularly upwards, at an angle of 65°, making an ascent of 1300 feet in 900 yards, the length of the road. Then we climb up the cone 200 yards to the crater. It is thought to be rather a bold undertaking with an eruption threatening at any moment in good weather, but almost hazardous on a stormy day, such as this proved to be. Storm-threatening clouds flit across the heavens, which, with fitful gusts of wind and occasional smothered sunbeams, gave a still more wild and weird appearance to the fantastically rugged scene around us. From the foot of the mountain quite up to the railroad depot, vast masses of lava, in strangely distorted winding ridges, covered the sides of the mountain. These lava masses, which have been thrown from the crater at a comparatively recent eruption, still preserve their rugged outlines in terrific grandeur. The vast masses of liquid lava, in running down the sides of the mountain, had cooled, becoming semi-solid, then stiffening into plastic, then hard stone. In this process they had rolled into all conceivable shapes, evidencing the cyclonic fury of the forces engaged in their shaping. Here mountain-piles of huge snakes, hydra-headed and distorted in their coils, with here and there giants that had petrified in their struggles to free themselves from these folds, now monstrous vultures mixed up with winged lions or uncouth monsters of the deep, gave present evidence of titanic forces, at the struggle of which all nature had been convulsed. The wind had increased to a furious gale, while darkening storm-clouds veiled the heavens, and cast a shadowy gloom on the depths deep below. When half way up the railroad and hanging apparently midway between heaven and earth, suspended only by a wire rope, the clouds lifted and the sun shone as a bright flash through the opening, lighting up the vast landscape with almost a painful vividness, revealing a scene grandly beautiful. Far off in the distance flashed the sun-lit amphitheatre of hills that engirdle the bay. The islands of Capri and Ischia shone as fairy gardens in a crystal lake, while on this side the bright coast-line appeared as far as Vallo. The city of Naples was at our feet, almost directly beneath us, while the gulf of Naples, lashed to fury by the storm-wind, flashed as a sea of boiling liquid-silver glory. It was only a moment, when the storm-cloud reached us in all its fury, just as we had commenced the steep climb up the cone, and with a force seemingly aggravated by the dangers of our situation. On we struggled through the deep snow, and yet deeper volcanic ashes, along a narrow ridge over which the wind, as if delighting in our helplessness, threatened, at every moment, to hurl us to the vast depths below. As we approached the crater, the blinding storm of hail and snow, with the thick gathering clouds, through which we walked, had so increased the darkness that we groped our way at noon-day not without difficulty. We were now in the midst of tangible volcanic action, walking over a thin crust of new-made lava which overlays a vaulted roof of unknown, but no great thickness, which alone separated us from the burning caldron beneath. Through a hundred fissures in this crust issued, with a hissing noise, as the breath of hydra-headed monsters, stifling, hot, sulphurous vapors, while here and there were larger openings or chimneys from the red-hot mouths of which issued sparks and flames. We stood now on half-liquid, half-cooled lava, vomited from these small craters only three days before, when the mountain was so active that the railroad authorities refused us permission to make the ascent ;

and so active now was the volcanic forces that one of these furnaces, which we had passed fifteen minutes before, as we returned had fallen in, half filling it with red-hot cinders. The wreaths of sulphurous smoke, lifted by the storm and whirled into fantastic forms of stifling vapors, added to by the wild, lurid glare of the open craters around us, heightened by the cavernous howlings of the storm, in symphony with the deep-toned bellowings beneath us, awed even our stolid guides, who advanced with hesitancy and turned back with manifest delight. We hastened to the railroad, that looked as though the cars had been hung on to the moon to await us, and, with feelings of relief, again returned to Naples. Our descent from the top of the cone was much easier than our ascent, and made in much less time ; perhaps this time was somewhat shortened by the knowledge of the dread dangers behind us.

ROME.

The Eternal City, whose name was long the synonym of the world, and in whose history, for half a thousand years, was written that of all nations, and whose ruins are redolent of the mightiest achievements and greatest triumphs of civilization over the untaught savage tribes of men, long the light of the world, which at her fall was shrouded in cimmerian darkness, a darkness of the soul, to be again dispelled only, by the smothered light of ages, emitted by disturbance of her ashes.

Here, some two hundred years after the time when Homer sang the exploits of gods and heroes, a city was founded by a few freebooters, on one of the seven lava hills that guard the Tiber. This soon possessed the others, then the adjacent country, and then the world, which, like the sun, it lighted and governed. Here was builded palaces, temples, amphitheatres and other mighty works, not alone the wonder of the age, but whose very ruins awe and inspire the world, and from whose broken columns, time-defying arches and mouldering walls flashed the Renaissance evolving into the glory of the present wondrous nineteenth century. Hallowed mother! whose tears, like our affections, are immortal, and whose mighty deeds were carved too deeply on the world's history ever to be effaced. But, though long the world's Niobe, she is so no longer, as she again wears a civic crown only, and from her reanimated dust has sprung a united Italy that is coming forth to assist in the conquest of the world, not now by the force of arms but by the arts of peace. Already the dark places in Africa have flashed her coming light.

In approaching Rome from Naples, we cross the wide expanse of the Campagna de Roma, once the granary of Rome, which now is, and for a thousand years has been, a vast uncultivated paludal waste, the fitting home of death-bearing malaria. This entire plain was at one time in the world's history a part of the sea from which it was redeemed by floods of lava ejected from the adjacent hills, the extinct craters now forming beautiful lakes upon these summits as Lacus Albana. This lava being impervious, retains, when uncultivated and undrained, the surface-water, forming it into a vast half-marshy district during the wet season, which drying up in the hot season, the rotting, rank vegetation causes the destructive fevers from which the wretched inhabitants of the Campagna are compelled to flee, hastening to the hills upon the approach of autumn. This condition, the result of neglect, caused by destructive invasions of Goths and Vandals, and aggravated and continued by Church grants to religious orders, we may hope will now be repaired under the new regime of united Italy, of which, once more, Rome is the capital. Across this dreary waste, and nearly parallel with the road, is seen a long line of stately, imposing ruins, the aqueduct of ancient Rome. These stately arches, extending many miles, supported or formed on their surface a trough along which the stream of water ran, and as the trough had to be level, only a slight and continuous decline, the arches are of different heights according to the surface-level of the ground over which the line passed, some twenty, thirty, forty or fifty feet in height. Most of these massive arches are intact at the present time, having battled successfully against the storms of 2,000 years, while here and there a broken arch, that has yielded most likely to an earthquake shock, gives evidence alike of what Rome has been and now is. No ruins in Rome or elsewhere, not even excepting the Colosseum, impressed me more than this long line of massive arches.

Now the Eternal City breaks upon the vision, and, with the golden rays of a setting sun lighting up its ruined towers and lofty spires, fills the soul with emotion, for who could approach Rome without emotion? In the distance, towering far above all others, lifting its dome to the clouds, is seen the grandest temple ever erected by human hands, San Pietro (St. Peter's), reflecting the genius of ages. The present cathedral is said to be on the site of a basilica church, built in the time of Constantine in A. D. 340, and upon one of the spots where St. Peter was crucified. But as we are shown several different places here in Rome where reliable legends assure us St. Peter was crucified, there may be some mistake here. But we are glad to know that this does not affect the grandeur of the cathedral, the building of which required 100 years, and absorbed much of the income of eighteen different pontiffs, costing $60,000,000, which was equal to $100,000,000 at the present day. The first architect was Bramonte, but he died before the work was fairly commenced, then Raphael, San Gallo, Michael Angelo and others.

We approach St. Peter's Cathedral through a piazza in the

centre of which is an immense Egyptian obelisk, 130 feet in height, of one solid block of granite. On either side of this obelisk at the distance of 200 or 300 feet is a beautiful fountain sending forth crystal jets some thirty or forty feet in height. On either side of these fountains are semicircular colonnades of four rows of beautiful marble columns, seventy feet high. At the farther side of this piazza we mount three flights of marble steps to the open portico, 80 feet wide and 468 feet long, supported by lofty marble columns. Five high portals open from the vestibule into the church. This vestibule is paved with variegated marble and covered with a gilt vault eighty feet above the pavement, and is farther adorned with pillars, pilasters, mosaics and bas reliefs, with equestrian statues at either end, one of Constantine, the other Charlemagne. Over the vestibule is a bas relief, Christ giving the keys to St. Peter. The church is 615 feet long by 450 feet wide. The dome to the summit of the lantern is 403 feet above the pavement. and is supported by four columns or buttresses, each 234 feet in circumference. There are twenty-nine altars in the church and many of the side rooms are as large as an ordinary church. The vast floor and walls are paved with variegated marble. Many statues of popes and saints fill the niches. Among the statues is one of St. Peter, in bronze, seated on a throne. This bronze statue of the tutelar saint of the Church is held in great veneration by the devotees of this temple, so much so that its projecting bronze foot has the toes kissed off by human lips. Now sceptics say that this bronze statue, held in so much reverence, is not, and never was, the statue of St. Peter or any other Saint or Christian, but the statue of a heathen god, Jupiter, while the great bronze door to the church would certainly better suit the temple of Jupiter than of Christ, as it contains elaborate heathen myths, among them the Rape of Europa. We ascended the lofty dome, 400 feet above the pavement, from which we had a fine view of Rome and surrounding campagna as far as the snow-clad hills.

Visited the church of St. Pietro in Vinculo (St. Peter in chains) in which are preserved the chain with which St. Peter was bound when in prison here. Said chain was preserved by the wife of Valentinian and given to Pope Leo I. The interior of the church is a basilica with twenty antique Doric columns, and contains the monuments of many distinguished painters and learned men. In mosaic, St. Peter with the keys and chains. Several marble statues; among them the famous statue of Moses by Michael Angelo. This statue, so much admired, is rendered ridiculous by horns. Two horns, several inches long, on his head, are to me utterly revolting, so much so that the other attributes or perfections of this statue, utterly fail to redeem it. Moses here looks much more like a Hindoo god than a Jewish lawgiver. But this blundering is not the fault of Michael Angelo, but the error of the translators of Exodus, chap. xxxiv : 35.

Church of St. Maria Majiore, a name signifying that this is the largest of the many churches here in Rome dedicated to the Virgin. It is one of the oldest churches in Christendom, and owes its origin to a visitation of the Virgin, who appeared to the patrician Johannes and Pope Liberius (only in their dreams however) and commanded them to build to her a church on that spot where on the morning of the 5th of August they should find snow. The church is ornamented with many beautiful mosaics of the thirteenth century. The lofty roof is supported by forty-two Corinthian columns. In front of the high altar is a porphyry sarcophagus that contains, or did once contain, the body of St. Matthew (?). There are here also ten porphyry columns and five boards from the manger of the infant Christ(?). Over the altar which is gorgeously decorated with lapis lazula and agate is an ancient and miraculous picture of the Virgin, painted by St. Luke(?).

Piazza de S. Giovani in Laterano, is, next to St. Peter's, the most important church in Rome. In the centre of the piazza is the largest Egyptian obelisk in Rome, and there are fifteen or eighteen of these beautiful obelisks here, brought here when Rome was the mistress of the world and Egypt was one of her provinces, and consequently her wondrous works of art were but the spoils of the conqueror, and brought to Rome to adorn the only city in the world worthy of them. This obelisk, not only the largest in Rome but said to be the largest in the world, is of red granite, and, like all obelisks, of one solid piece. It was brought by Constantius from Thebes, in Egypt, where it had been erected by Thothmes III., one of Moses' Pharaohs, 1,600 years B. C., 3,500 years ago. On the opposite side is an edifice containing the *Scala Santa*, or holy stairs, once belonging to the palace of Pontius Pilate, and the very marble steps upon which the Savior trod (?). They were brought here from Pilate's palace in Jerusalem some few hundred years after the destruction of Jerusalem. At the top of the steps is the *sancta sanctorum* which it is permitted to reach only by ascending the steps on the knees. At almost all times of the day a number of devout men and women may be seen crawling up these steps on their knees, kissing the steps and repeating their prayers or counting their beads. Absolution from all sins is obtained by making the ascent; or, if desired, by counting beads and saying enough prayers, an immunity or receipt against purgatory for a thousand years may be obtained. We saw two or three men and as many women making this painful ascent, kissing the steps—no, not the marble steps supposed to have been sanctified by the feet of the Savior, for these were covered with wooden boards, but kissing these planks; rather a diluted grace one might suppose. It is but just to say that all those we saw were of the poor and most ignorant class; but better people, I am told, are sometimes found making this ascent. It is said that Luther once started on this pious task, but, after getting half way, up arose to his feet and walked down repeating "The just shall live by faith."

The church is a basilica, first built in the time of Constantine. It was overthrown by an earthquake, and rebuilt in its present form in the ninth century, and consequently is 1,000 years old. The nave, 420 feet long, is divided from the aisles by lofty marble pillars, and the walls and ceiling gorgeously decorated with mosaics, frescoes, paintings of apostles, saints popes and martyrs. In the baptistery on the piazza is the fountain, a marble basin, in which we are told Constantine was baptized by Pope Sylvester, in 324. It is believed, however, that this is mythical, and that Constantine was not baptized here or elsewhere, if so, only on his death-bed. The Museum Gregorianum contains many statues and other antique works of much interest, and would fully repay careful study. Among these are a statue of Poseidon, found at Porto, a marble statue of Sophocles, by Praxiteles, one of the finest statues in existence, a sarcophagus with the Calydonian Hunt in bas relief, on its sides ancient Christian inscriptions, miracle of Jonah, mosaics and frescoes.

VATICAN PALACE.

This is the largest palace in the world, and said to be the finest, and yet with all its gorgeous splendor it is an awkward and unsightly structure. Visiting the museum in a carriage, we cross through the piazza under the colonnade, driving around, behind, and several hundred yards beyond, St. Peter's Cathedral. We get out of the carriage and walk several hundreds of yards farther along the palace wall and beyond the garden gate, when we enter by way of the noble stairway, and ascend to the hall of the Greek cross. This stairway is elaborately ornamented with bronze balustrades, entablatures, bas reliefs and columns of marble, granite and porphyry. The door-way through which we enter the hall is of red granite, with red granite statues of Telemus on either side. There are three beautiful antique mosaics inlaid in the floor or pavement. They represent Minerva armed with the helmet and ægis and four genii, Bacchus distributing wine, baskets of grapes, flowers, etc. On either side is a colossal Egyptian Sphinx of much interest. Two colossal sarcophagi made out of single blocks of red porphyry, with bas and alto reliefs of fine workmanship. These sarcophagi rest each on four immense marble lions. One of them, we are told, once contained the remains of the daughter of Constantine the Great. The bas reliefs are pagan but like many other pagan ideas and works have been interpreted into Christian symbols. In a niche in this hall is the Cnidian Venus, a Greek work of much beauty. The next room, the rotunda, is ornamented with stucco work; the roof is supported by fluted columns of marble. The niches contain small statues of Greek workmanship. In the centre of the pavement floor is one of the largest and most beautiful of ancient mosaics, representing combats between Centaurs Nereids, Tritons, and sea monsters, with beautiful flower borders. Here also is an immense antique porphyry vase forty-two feet in circumference and more than 2,000 years old. It was found in the baths of Titus. On each side of the entrance are busts of Hermes, found at Hadrian's Villa. At the side of the hall a colossal Greek statue of Jupiter Tonens, worthy the statue of a god, and a colossal statue of Hadrian's favorite, Antinous, a work of great beauty, perhaps the finest male statue that has descended to us from antiquity. A beautiful statue of Ceres holding ears of wheat in her hand. A colossal bronze statue of Hercules holding in his right hand a club upon which he is resting, in his left hand the golden apples taken from the garden of the Hesperides. The skin of the Nemean lion is thrown gracefully over his shoulders. This is thought to be a Greek work. Pius IX. purchased it for the sum of $54,000. A statue of Juno Regina, called the Barberino Juno, found in the baths of Olympia, is quite as beautiful as the most renowned of the Greek Venuses—is a great work. A colossal statue of Claudius as Jupiter, said to be the best likeness extant of this Emperor. Many other statues of great beauty and of the best period of Greek art adorn this hall.

HALL OF THE MUSES.

This is a splendid octagonal hall with dome supported by ten columns of Carrara marble, the capitals are ancient Corinthian found in Hadrian's Villa. Frescoes of the Muses on ceiling. Oil paintings in the corners represent Homer, Virgil, Calliope and Tasso. The mosaics in the pavement are from Pompeii and Hadrian's Villa. Statues of Hermes, Diogenes, Sophocles, Mercury, Persephone and Ceres.

Hall of animals in mosaics found at Palestrina, and a vast collection of animals in marble; a griffin in alabaster, an eagle fighting with a monkey, a stag attacked by a dog or wolf, goose killing a snake, and a great quantity of other animals, in which plastic marble is made as expressive as oil paintings.

HALL OF THE STATUES.

We can only mention a few of the vast number of fine statues. A Cupid, by Praxiteles; a bas relief of offerings to Esculapius; Hygea, etc.; Penelope seated; Amazon; Apollo.

The hall of busts contains a great many busts and statues by Greek artists—Esculapius, Faun by Praxiteles, Domitia, wife of Domitian; two large candelabra of white marble, etc.

Hall of masks contains dancing girls in marble—Apotheosis of Hadrian; Venus leaving the bath; infant Hercules strangling a serpent—a fine Greek work—etc. Cabinet of Laocoon contains this wondrous group, the work of the Rhodian sculptor, Agesander, and his two sons. It represents Laocoon, priest of Neptune, in the act of sacrificing on the sea-shore near Troy, attacked together with his two sons by a monstrous hydra-headed serpent which envelopes all three in its folds, while it sinks its deadly fangs in their sides. The work is an unrivalled production of Greek art. There are many other statues and groups here of great merit, but we forget all in contemplating the Laocoon group.

CABINET OF APOLLO.

This room contains the celebrated statue, the Apollo Belvidere. The god is represented as having just discharged an arrow, perhaps at the children of Niobe. A more beautiful statue of the human form divine, or of gods', was never made in marble, if we except two or three Greek Venuses. The hall of Meleager contains a masterpiece of Greek art, the world-renowned fabulous hunter, Meleager, with his dog. Meleager is bearing the head of the Calydonian Boar, which has long laid waste the lands and destroyed everyone sent to hunt it, and which he has just killed.

Another vestibule contains, among other sculpture, the Belvidere Torso, so much admired by Raphael, Michael Angelo and others. It is a mutilated statue of Hercules, by Apollonius, son of Nestor, the Athenian. I failed, as I had always done in plaster casts of this statue, to see any particular beauty in this mutilated statue. We spent days among this great collection that constitutes the world's museum of sculpture. Indeed were we to add to it the Farnese Bull, and Hercules from the Naples museum, and the Venus de Medici and the Niobe Group from Florence, the Venus de Milo from the Louvre, with the Freize of the Pantheon from Athens, now in the British museum, known as the Elgin Marbles, we would have all that is truly great, grand, beautiful, sublime of the sculpture of the world. And if the chisel of Phidias ever produced better, as it is thought it did, it is perhaps as well that such works have not come down to us, as it would be impossible for modern art or culture, no matter how gifted or cultivated, to appreciate them.

VATICAN PICTURE GALLERIES.

As all things are esteemed by comparison, it is just possible that after having examined the vast collection of incomparable sculpture just referred to, we may at first feel some disappointment on passing into the picture gallery. But while the pictures in this gallery, of the highest merit, are but few, these by their excellence fully compensate for the absence of the many of less merit. We shall, however, notice only a few of these.

The Bologna School..—This is the first saloon we enter. The Virgin and Child, by Francia. The Last Communion of St. Jerome, by Domenichino, is a grand and glorious work, and would do credit to Leonardo da Vinci. It has a curious history illustrating the darkness and ignorance of the cloister and Church in regard to works of art, causing the destruction, by neglect or by whitewashing over the finest works of the fifteenth century. These works are even now being revealed after being lost for centuries. This work was painted for the monastery at the stipulated price of $65. Many years afterwards the great French painter, Poussin, was employed by these monks to paint for them an altar piece, and was offered this picture, which was found covered with dust in an obscure closet of the monastery, as old canvas upon which to paint his piece. Poussin, to his immortal credit, at the sight of the picture, not only refused to commit such a vandalism, but tore up his lucrative contract, declaring that he was unable to produce such a work. Under Napoleon I., this painting with other treasures, was carried off to France, where, so greatly was it esteemed, that it was valued at $5,000. St. Jerome is represented as an exceedingly old man, wasted to a mere skeleton by long vigils and fasting, unable to support himself, half-reclining, half-kneeling, he is receiving this, his last sacrament, from the hands of a bishop of the Greek Church, assisted by deacons. A noble Roman lady, an early convert to Christianity, St. Paula, is kneeling by his side weeping and in the act of kissing the holy man's hand. A lion, his constant desert companion, is lying near his feet, while an Arab, wearing his turban, stands sorrowfully looking on, and at a little distance above, hosts of angels hover in the air. The scene is laid on the altar steps at Bethlehem, in Judea. A Crucifixion, by Guido Reni, a fine picture, by a great artist. The Acts of St. Nicholas, by Fra Angelico. The figures in this allegorical painting are in miniature, very beautiful. It is in the last act, when the Saint is in glory surrounded by angels, the divine gift of this gentle monk, Fra Angelico, appears to best advantage. Indeed so meek, gentle, and lovely were his life and character, that he seems to have lived among the angelic hosts he so much delights to paint.

Sixtus IV.—This painting was formerly a fresco on one of the walls of the old Vatican Library, and was removed by order of Pope Leo XII. to canvas, without the least damage. How is this done? It is now a painting on canvas. I have seen several frescoes that have been thus transferred. It really looks like transferring a shadow after the substance has faded. And I have asked several painters how it was done without receiving an explanation.

THE ROMAN SCHOOL.

The Mysteries, by Raphael. This is said to be his earliest painting and done when he was only 19 years of age. It has much merit and certainly forecasts his subsequent triumphs in the unequaled excellence of his Madonnas.

The Theological Virtues, by Raphael. The three virtues, Faith, Hope and Charity, are charmingly given in perhaps the only manner they could be given on canvas, as three beautiful young women, and though a work of his younger years, if the virtues are as lovely as these women, then all men should be ready to adopt them. I heartily accepted all three.

The Transfiguration, by Raphael. This is the crowning glory of the Vatican, as indeed it would be of any picture gallery, a grand and glorious painting in oil, made in the prime, as well as last, period of Raphael's life. This wondrous painting, like a glorious setting sun, after having through the day painted hill and dale in gorgeous beauty, kissing buds to flowers and flowers to golden fruit, at its setting lights earth and heaven with a glory so transcendently lovely that we almost forget his path of triumph through the day—awes us into sublimest reverence. It has been pronounced by eminent judges the finest painting in the world, and certainly has but one rival, his Sistine Madonna, in the Dresden gallery. The painting was made for the Cathedral in France, by order of Cardinal Julio di Medici, who, afterwards, on becoming pope, refused to let it be removed. Raphael received $1,650 for the painting, which although an unprecedented sum at the time, represents but a small fraction of what it would now bring. The picture is divided into two parts, one of which, in mid air, high above a mountain top, is Christ ascending in graceful, easy motion, his body enveloped by a graceful mantle. On either side are Moses and Elias, enveloped also in loose, flowing mantles. These three figures so clearly indicate breath, motion, that we almost believe we can see them ascending into the opening heavens. They are not on clouds, but appear to rise on the buoyant air. Beneath, on the top of the mountain, lie prostrate the three apostles, St. Peter in the middle, with St. John on one side, St. James on the other. All are hiding their faces with their hands, as though dazzled by the divine light emitted from the body of the ascending Christ. Off to one side under some trees, by a fearful anachronism which, however, does not mar the effect, are seen St. Julian and other more modern saints kneeling in adoration. At the foot of the mountain is a group, among which is one possessed by a devil, and others with various diseases, imploring the apostles to cure them. The apostles, nine in number, in different groups, show by their emotion their perplexity. One of the apostles is excitedly relating their perplexity to one newly arrived, who, by his indifference is shown to be Judas. The beautiful young woman kneeling is Raphael's enamorata, Beatrice Fornarina. The apostles indicate that he who could have cast out devils and heal the sick is on the Mount, not yet understanding that he had ascended into heaven, not having yet received the power to cast out devils. This great painting, scarcely finished at the time of his death, was carried in the funeral procession.

The Madonna de Foligno, by Raphael, is another of this artist's best works, and with the one just mentioned and St. Jerome's last communion, would enrich any gallery. Raphael was induced to paint this work for the convent at Foligno, by Sigismund, secretary of Julius II., and for many years it was so piously guarded, that it could but seldom be seen by visitors, was indeed held in this convent among these simple-hearted, pious nuns, who saw in the sweet, lovely countenance of this Madonna a ready answer to their prayers, as a fetich, an idol or object of worship. It was carried by Napoleon to Paris, but returned with other spoils in 1815. In the upper part of the picture the Madonna is seated on the clouds with the Child on her knee; she is gracefully clothed in a sky-blue mantle, and surrounded by a glory, with a multitude of angels hovering around. Below are saints. In the distance is the city of Foligna, over which a bomb or thunderbolt is seen to fall in a graceful parabolic curve on the convent, without, however, doing it damage. It is one of those beautiful pictures we are loth to leave, and on looking at our watch, we found we had lingered here much longer than we had supposed.

Coronation of the Virgin, painted by Raphael in fresco. It has been cleverly transferred to canvas.

The Spanish school has a few good paintings, a St. Catherine, of Alexandria, by Bartolomeo Stefano Murillo, is doubtless a good work, but were it by some obscure author instead of the great Spanish painter Murillo, I doubt whether it would attract special attention. There are several other paintings by Murillo, but none of them equal to other paintings by this author we have seen.

The Venetian school is well represented. A St. Sebastian, by Titian, is a beautiful picture by this great master of colors. That is, it would be fine if St. Sebastian were left out. Every painter here in Italy, except Fra Angelico and Raphael, seems to have had a mania for painting St. Sebastian and sticking as many arrows in his carcass as possible, consequently St. Sebastians, bristling with arrows, meet us in every public gallery, pursue us to the churches and stare at us in frescoes from side walls of chapels and convent cells. It is always, no matter how artistic, a most abominable, disgusting, unnatural picture, and could only have had its monstrous creation in the diseased imagination of some cloistered monk. St. Helena, by Paul Veronese, is a fine picture of a beautiful Empress. This is the Empress saint, who, in a *dream*, had the spot indicated where the True Cross was buried. Consequently we are glad to make her acquaintance, as we are especially indebted to her for the discovery of this valuable relic.

THE VATICAN FRESCOES.

We enter the Apostolic Palace at the extremity of the long colonnade to the right of St. Peter's Cathedral, mounting to the bronze gate by a long flight of travertine steps; two angels are placed on the architrave. Passing through several halls adorned with mosaics and costly sculpture, bronzes and paintings, we mount other flights of steps, pass through other rooms of paintings and frescoes, when, mounting other steps, some 300 in all, we enter into the Sistine Chapel, into the stupendous, awful presence of the greatest triumph of human genius —Michael Angelo's frescoes. This great hall, ceiling and sides, is adorned by, covered with, these immortal productions of, perhaps, the most remarkably gifted man of his or any other age. These frescoes constitute a study that might engage us for years—have, indeed, been so studied by thousands; but, like the starry heavens above, awe, entrance us without inspiring even the most gifted with the hope of being able to successfully imitate them. This great man, whose Moses and David had placed him as the greatest sculptor, as had his able defence of Florence against the combined armies of Spain and Germany shown him to be the greatest engineer of the world, had, by his wondrous battle-piece painted for the city of Florence, attracted the attention of the strong-minded, self-willed, art-fostering, splendor-loving Pope Julien II., by whom he was ordered to Rome to paint this chapel. In vain Michael Angelo pleaded that he was not a painter—especially not a *fresco* painter, and therefore unequal to the work. Fortunately, however, Pope Julien was inexorable, and as Popes in that day had to be obeyed, Michael Angelo went back to Florence, studied better the manner of mixing paints and preparing the walls for frescoes, and doggedly, sullenly, returned to Rome to perform this wondrous work which occupied most of the remaining period of his life. But then he could not have been more usefully engaged, as he here accomplished work that gives him a bright immortality, and has been, and is, and is to be for ages yet to come, the delight, wonder and instruction of all men.

In this stupendous work we scarcely know which most to admire, the almost superhuman brain that conceived, invented and blended into a wondrous whole, the strangely cunning hand that executed, or the human endurance that performed the mechanical labor of such a work. This work, while not more beautiful, perhaps not so beautiful as that in the next room, the Loggia of Raphael, impresses us quite differently. Raphael's Loggia wins us by the harmony, the symmetry of its easy, graceful beauty, much as we are impressed by a surpassingly beautiful, smiling landscape; the quiet loveliness of a transparent lake, lighted by the silver sheen of a rising moon, or the light, floating clouds of a summer sky, tinted by the golden glories of a setting sun, while this fills us with feelings of awe, as the very nature of the work breathes, speaks, thunders the titanic struggle of heart and brain of him who wrought it, the breath of volcanic forges, the earthquake shock that levels mountains, raises valleys, overwhelms cities—the darkening storm king that laughs at the puny works of man, swallowing whole navies as if in very sport, the thunderbolts of Jove, in his battle with the giants, that shake earth, air and heaven, are seen, heard and felt in the presence of this mighty work of human brain and hands. God the Almighty, Christ, angels, prophets, sybils, saints and sinners, men and devils, snakes, vultures and sea-monsters appear in awful grandeur, or rave and storm in fearful fury as in the birth of worlds; the driving away of darkness and creation of light, the fall of man, the wreck of matter. We are lashed and storm-tossed with more than cyclonic fury until the brain reels and the heart beats with fiery whirlpool's force—would gladly no longer see it and close our eyes. The picture is only turned in upon the brain, to burn with greater force. Would we flee its presence and forget it? Let him do so who can.

The whole ceiling and three sides of the wall are covered

with figures embracing the Old Testament history, together with heathen mythology, gods and demi-gods, giants and heroes mixed up with patriarchs, priests, sybils and prophets, a vast surging mass, where all is motion—no rest is seen in even the most tranquil pictures, the motion is everywhere, tangible, vivid.

Turn now to the fourth wall upon our right; this is the Last Judgment, and the crowning glory of this great work. Upon the right of the throne are those saved, or to be saved, climbing, pressing, hurrying up, some quite at the top, seated, with happy, serene, smiling faces? No, not quite so; there was no placid, happy nature in the storm-tossed soul of Michael Angelo, and consequently could not be in his pictures—no, not even in heaven. In the midst of the upper part of the scene stands the half-pleading, half-despairing Virgin, while standing near her left hand is Christ, with an angry, threatening mien, as, with Divine wrath, He drives the damned over the battlements of heaven, from whence, in their headlong plunge, with writhing torture and dismay in every look, they are chased, scourged and driven by frightful devils into the nethermost hell. But even here they are not hidden from the angry glances of an offended, angry Christ, from whose divine wrath men and devils, even in hell, are, with horror, struggling to flee away, and, with movements tangible and voices audible, are hiding behind and calling the trembling, smoking, burning mountains to fall upon and cover them from the consuming wrath of an angry Christ.

Well, this is wondrous strange! Who but Michael Angelo would have, could have, successfully thus portrayed the meek and lowly Jesus! Perhaps the hint was given the painter in the thought that some very meek and humble men had made violent, stormy popes. Possibly, too, the knowledge of this peculiarity in his own history made the painting the more tolerant, if, indeed, not positively pleasing, to Paul III., whose metamorphosis in this respect was quite notable. But the great painter, whose storm-tossed soul had now long been chafed beyond endurance, grew even more stormy in his ceiling painting. Julien II., who now was old and childish, was naturally anxious to see the great work before he died, had the scaffolding taken down ere the work was quite finished in order that he might the better see it, regardless of the inconvenience this caused Michael Angelo's storm-darkening soul. This art-loving Pope beheld the wondrous work with great joy and in the presence of a great assembly of notables, solemnly pronounced it good and blessed it. Pope Julien II. died and had been succeeded by other Popes to Paul III., who, without the culture or taste of Julien II., found fault with the nude figures and, through his secretary, Cardinal Cerena, constantly annoyed Michael Angelo by insisting upon his clothing his figures. To all these annoyances Michael Angelo replied that when nature improved in this respect he might do so. The work went on, partaking more and more of the stormy nature of the fretted painter's mind. At last, after many years and when the painter had grown old, it was completed and the scaffolding removed, when lo! in the right hand corner of hell, with long asses' ears, was the officious cardinal, who, in great distress and alarm at finding himself in hell, and thus characterized, fled to the Pope, begging him to have the painter remove him from such a place and such company. The Pope, amused at his secretary's distress, asked him "where Michael Angelo had placed him?" "In hell, please your holiness, in hell?" Well, the Pope told him he regretted the place he was in; had he been in purgatory he would willingly have removed him, but as he was in hell he must stay there, as he had no power over hell; and there the officious cardinal is to the present day.

At the bottom of the picture is the river Styx, across which old Charon, with grim visage, is busy rowing lost souls. He has just arrived with a boat-load on the opposite shore, where his passengers, frightened at the dismal caverns, lighted up with a lurid, sulphurous glare, and into which they are to enter, vainly wish to linger in the boat; but it is a busy day and the ferrymen has no time to waste—has seized an oar and is driving the affrighted inmates over the bow of the boat, where devils seize them and drag them into the dismal caverns. Well, I am sure that the painter has satisfied the most callous, who look on the picture, that hell is a good place *to stay away from*.

The Capitoline Hill, in the ruins of which are mouldering tablets that concern much of the world's history. Upon this hill was the ancient Capitol and Temple of Jupiter, in which sat enthroned the authority and power, not alone of Rome, but the world. But now for a thousand years this Temple of Rome's mighty god, Jupiter, like the power of Rome itself, has been shattered to fragments, mouldering ruins, in whose heaps no image of temple is seen. A small church now stands upon the ruins of the Temple of Jupiter. Even the Tarpean Rock down which prisoners were once cast, has had its high wall gnawed down by the tooth of time, and its base so lifted by the gathered debris of ages, that it could no longer be used for this purpose. We ascend the hill either by a flight of broad steps or by carriage way, to the great square upon the summit, where there is a statue of Marcus Aurelius, the finest equestrian statue in the world. During the time of the residence of the Popes at Avignon, the population of Rome had become so reduced that the Capitoline Hill was a grazing field for sheep and goats. Some wolves are kept in a cave near the summit; wolves of course have always been sacred animals at Rome since a she-wolf was foster-mother to the founder of the city. Deep down in the tufa rock, beneath the debris of the

Capitol, was a cavern in which former prisoners of State were kept, among whom was St. Paul. We descended to the bottom of this ancient prison by a long flight of steps, a dark, gloomy, dismal vault, where no ray of light penetrated, to the cell which we were assured was the one once occupied by St. Paul and St. Peter, and had pointed out the small pool where St. Paul baptized the jailor and his household. Now while not hurt with credulity, and taking most things related by guides *cum grano salis*, we know of no reason why St. Paul may not have been here, and as it is quite pleasant to believe these things, we were prepared to believe anything told us concerning St. Paul. On the spot where the Temple of Jupiter once stood, is now the Church of St. Maria in Aracoeli. It was while sitting upon the steps of this church, observing a procession of bare-footed friars, that Gibbon conceived the idea of writing the "Decline and Fall of the Roman Empire." In this church is seen the Sante Bambino, which is held as the principal treasure of the church, and is shown as the Infant Jesus, and rented out to the Romans when sick. One foot or leg is shorter than the other, and we are gravely told by the church custodian, a priest, showing it, that a sick Roman lady having procured the Bambino (child), determined to keep it, and had another made like it which she sent back to the church, and the fraud was not detected until in the night a loud noise with some one kicking at the door was heard. On opening the door, behold! it was the Bambino who had left the house where he had been fraudulently kept, and came back to his church. His much kicking at the door had shortened his leg. This thing is sent out to administer to the sick and afflicted, here in Rome, in great state, and when it passes in its carriage along the street the people kneel—and yet we are sending missionaries to China!

The Capitoline Museum contains an extensive collection of

ancient art treasures, statues of gods, goddesses, heroes and emperors, sarcophagi, etc. The room of the Dying Gladiator, contains this beautiful statue. A dying gladiator, with a wound in his side, his sands of life fast running to their finish, is sitting on his shield, supporting himself with his hand on the ground, where he is soon to fall, with thoughts on his far-off home, with visions of wife and children, as cradled in the great world they are unsteadily swinging, before him. His head is dizzy now, his pulses faint, his last battle fought, the last sounds of the applauding crowd have died away as the world recedes from sight and his spirit hastens back to the forest-fireside to hover around loved ones. It is a wonderfully expressive, pathetic statue. Other fine statues, Antinous, Alexander the Great, a Satyr by Praxiteles (Hawthorn's Marble Faun,) a girl protecting some doves, Satyr in *Rosso Antico*, Socrates, Diogenes, Hippocrates, and multitudes of other statues. In another room is a beautiful mosaic on the wall, Doves at a Fountain. In another room is the beautiful Capitoline Venus, by Praxiteles. No one visiting Rome should fail to see this beautiful statue. Cupid and Psyche. All Greek works of great beauty. It were idle to attempt an enumeration of even the most beautiful of this wonderful collection, which of itself would well repay a visit to Rome. We must not, however, omit to mention the lightning-scarred historic she-wolf, in bronze, nursing Romulus and Remus, erected by pious Rome in B. C. 296, in grateful remembrance of the kindly care this animal gave the founders of the city.

PALATINE HILL.

Across a depression, once a marsh, is the Palatine Hill, upon which the imperial palaces once stood. The palace of Cæsar and Nero's golden palace are all ruins now, and it is only of late that excavations have revealed the foundations of these mighty edifices whose possessors governed the world. Between these hills was the Forum, the most historic spot on earth. It was here all popular assemblies met, here was determined the fate of nations—of the world. It was here Cicero delivered those classic orations, the delight and instruction of all subsequent time, and it was here, after the assassination of Cæsar, that Mark Antony delivered his marvelous oration that so stirred the assembled Roman people that they voted divine honors to the murdered Cæsar, and drove his assassins into exile. But this place, so hallowed by memories, so adorned by art, like Rome and the world itself, was obscured by the destruction of the Roman Empire, then lost beneath the accumulated debris of ages, and it is only during the present century that its outlines are again produced, and this has been done by removing forty feet of debris, as this was the height to which the surface level between the Capitoline and Palatine Hills had been raised by the wear and tear of more than a thousand years of ruin and neglect. The Forum was an open court, 612 feet long and 117 feet wide, enclosed by beautiful palaces, temples, etc., and adorned with the most beautiful marble columns, statues, etc. In these excavations many works of great value, now in the Capitoline Museum, have been found, which, thanks to the accumulated debris which hid them, escaped the Christian Vandalism which has done more to destroy ancient Rome and the immortal works of art collected here, than Goth, Frank and Vandal invasions ever did. And if we condemn the Moslems for heating their baths by burning the books of the Alexandrine library, what must we think of those who wantonly mutilated the finest works of human genius because they reminded them of the religion that built up Rome and made her the mistress and light of the world, or of popes, priests, nobility and people who broke up the most beautiful columns, or tore down artistic temples to erect uncouth churches, feudal castles or prop falling convent walls, or broke up the most beautiful friezes of temples, statues of gods and heroes, the most beautiful productions of human genius, to feed the lime-kilns and form mortar for the building of blind walls and stables, and yet this was engaged in by popes, nobles, priests and people for more than half a thousand years. Let us then instead of indulging in vain regrets at the absence of so much we should meet with here, and at the almost sacrilegious desecration we everywhere meet with, rather rejoice that indolence, conflagration, ignorance, riots, earthquake shock, falling castles and Tiber inundations, by concealing from view through a thousand years of benighted vandalism, have left us so much.

THE COLOSSEUM.

Not far from the Forum, in the centre of Rome, stands the mighty ruins of the world's wonder, the Colosseum, 1,400 feet in circumference and 150 feet in height, erected by Titus, A. D. 70–80, after the conquest of Jerusalem, and by the labor of the captive Jews, a vast multitude of whom, as was the custom, were brought back with the captor as spoils of war, and employed here on public works.

This amphitheatre, unparalleled in its magnitude, would accommodate 100,000 spectators, was four stories high, including the three known orders of architecture, and must have been, when perfect, as shown now in the portion standing, of great beauty. The first story is Doric and thirty feet high, the second is Ionic, forty feet high, the third story Corinthian, forty feet high, and the fourth or upper story also Corinthian, forty-four feet high.

It was, as all the world knows, used for the sports in which this warlike people most delighted, gladiatorial combats, in which champion captives fought to the death, combats between gladiators and wild beasts, in which lions, tigers, and other fierce and savage beasts, turned loose from their dens under the lower benches of the amphitheatre, sprang upon the gladiator, who, armed with spear or sword and shield, joined in deadly combat, as others of his comrades had with their fellow-captives. Often the monstrous lion or tiger instantly killed one or many gladiators and tore them to pieces amidst the wild plaudits of the assembled tens of thousands of delighted men and women, but not unfrequently the lion or tiger or other wild beast was slain by the man. We may suppose either result was equally acceptable to the crowd of human beasts that watched the combat. At the opening or dedication of this amphitheatre in A. D. 80, which lasted 100 days, 5,000 animals were killed; all the killing or fighting, however, was not done by men, as frequently several or many fierce lions and tigers, with elephants or other animals, were turned loose into the arena where they joined in mortal combat with all the destructive fury of their untamed natures, reproducing, greatly to the delight of the citizens, here in the heart of Rome all the wild terrors of an African forest or Indian jungle. During the persecutions of the Christians under Nero and other emperors, many Christians constituted the human victims offered up in these savage sports. In the early part of the fifth century gladiatorial combats were forbidden as abhorrent to the precepts of Christianity, but combats with wild beasts were continued until the sixth century, when, from many and overwhelming disasters, Rome was tottering to its fall, these shows ceased, and the Colosseum like Rome herself fell into decay, a decay over which the shrouded ghosts of night spread their black wings through the long dark night of ages, during which this *indestructible structure* that trembled only as the world trembled at the earthquake shock, and that laughed at the fierce thunderbolt, at storms and flood, and bid defiance to the corroding tooth of time, was itself destroyed.

The outlines of this structure with its beautiful exterior columns, its endless rows of benches, its floor and ground plan with the caves in which the wild beasts were kept, are very clearly seen and traced, although not a third is left standing, and even this has had much of its finer stone removed for the construction of less-sacred edifices. It should be seen and studied by daylight, but is most beautiful as seen by the softer, kindlier rays of the full-orbed moon, as this beautiful soul-stirring, massive ruin, like a city belle, blushes to be seen in her faded complexion and tattered garments by the strong light of day. I loved—and who would not—to sit among these mighty ruins and read the history of eighteen hundred years, as stereotyped in their battle-scarred, time-worn masses that had witnessed this march of ages, and, but for the vandalism of benighted man, might have witnessed the funeral dirges of time itself.

Near the Colosseum is the Triumphal Arch of Titus, one of the most beautiful things time and vandalism has left in Rome, and much the most beautiful triumphal arch in the world. It was erected to Titus, conqueror of Jerusalem. On its beautiful frieze is a sacrificial procession with Titus mounted on a triumphal car driven by *Roma*, with a mighty multitude of captive Jews. The contents of the Holy of Holies, the table of the shew-bread and the seven-branched golden candlestick were carried in the procession. We may with difficulty imagine what a revelation and shock this must have been to the captive Jews who had ever been taught to believe these things, stored away within the innermost sanctuary of their temple, were under Divine protection, now irreverently seized and carried along as spoils of war, and placed as offerings to Rome's god in his temple, the Temple of Jupiter on the Capitoline Hill.

Visited St. Paul's outside the walls of the city, and the Three Fountains, two miles farther out of the city. We passed out of the city through the Porta St. Paolo, the most picturesque gate of the city, consisting of a double gateway, the outer one by Theodoric, the inner by Claudius, flanked by towers. Some half mile out on the road we passed the small chapel of Saints Peter and Paul, built, we are told, on the spot where these two saints parted on their way to martyrdom. Over the arch of the chapel is a Latin inscription, giving their brave but tender words at parting. Paul said to Peter, "Peace be with thee, foundation of the Church, shepherd of the flock of Christ." And Peter said to Paul, "Go in peace, preacher of glad-tidings and guide to the salvation of the just." Some half mile farther on is the church of St. Paul. This is the handsomest church in or about Rome. Before the Reformation it was under the protection of England, was lately burned down and the new church first opened by Pio Nono in 1854. It is a basilica with the wide nave divided from the aisles by forty lofty, massive, graceful Corinthian columns of marble on either side. I stepped the vast length of the nave, 132 yards, and 74 yards in breadth across the nave and aisles. The interior is a marble palace, from the polished surface of walls, pillars, altars and pavement of which flashed the mirrored image of the interior of the church. The grand triumphal arch is a relic of the old church, and the Byzantine mosaic, Christ and the Twenty-four Elders, is one of the oldest of these church mosaics, being of the fifth century. Fine marble statues of St. Peter and St. Paul adorn the sides, while portraits of all the popes, beginning at St. Peter, form a continuous mosaic around the church above the columns. The gorgeous altar is supported by four pillars of oriental alabaster, translucent, given for this church, strange to say, by Mehemet Ali, Pasha of Egypt. A marble chapel beneath the altar, reached by a marble staircase, in which a lamp is kept constantly burning, contains the bodies of the martyrs, Saints Paul and Timothy. The resplendent malachite altars at the ends of the transept were given by the Czar of

Russia. A costly and elaborate alabaster candelabra sheds by night its soft light upon the beautifully-painted windows. The mosaics on the beautiful façade facing the Tiber are not more elaborate than beautiful. As seen from the ground they appear as beautiful as fresco paintings. They represent Christ with Saints Peter and Paul, with four prophets, also symbolic scenes from the New Testament. The entire structure is most beautiful, and the most Christian-like basilica church in all the world. Leaving this church and continuing out on the road, we arrived at the *Tre Fontane*, Three Fountains, which sprung up at the place where St. Paul was beheaded. When the severed head fell to the ground it made three leaps, and at each place where it touched the ground a fountain sprung up which continues to the present day(?).

SAN PIETRO IN MONTORIO.

Feb. 2nd.—The weather having greatly moderated, being spring-like, we made a pleasant drive to the church of St. Pietro in Montorio and the villa Pamphili Doria. Passing out at the Porta Settimiana, we ascended the hill along the via Garibaldi to the church, which is situated on a lofty eminence commanding a fine view of the city and the Tiber as it winds through the city and adjacent campagna. Rome is seen as on a map at our feet, its palaces, lofty spires and towers rising from almost every square. Towering high above, and in majestic grandeur, far surpassing all others with its cloud-piercing dome, is St. Peter's Cathedral. The immense magnitude of this structure can scarcely be appreciated when in or near it, because we have only itself to compare it to, but from here it is seen in all its greatness, and, by comparing it to the city, we readily see that it is an important factor, if to it other churches dwindle to cabins. The long line of walls enclosing the city with their several gates, twelve or fifteen in number, are beautifully seen from this point. These walls were built by Aurelian, and though added to and strengthened at different times, are substantially the same that have surrounded the city for 1,800 years. They are some thirty feet high and of great thickness, and must have been a most formidable obstruction against attacking Gaul, Vandal, Goth, Lombard and Spaniard, and yet by all of these stormed and the city taken.

This church of St. Pietro was erected by Ferdinand and Isabella of Spain, and is yet, I believe, under the control of Spain. In the court of the monastery over one of the spots on which the cross upon which St. Peter was crucified stood, is a small round temple with sixteen Doric marble columns, in which is a bas relief with St. Peter hanging to a cross, head downwards—we are told here that the saint preferred this position. But what is even more convincing and even touching, is a small hole or well in the pavement, into which the blood of St. Peter ran, coloring the sand which it continues to do to the present day. To satisfy us of this fact the kind-hearted monk who was showing us these things, passed down a small tin tube which brought up a spoonful or more of the blood-stained sand, which we accepted as proof positive and took the sand to show to anyone who should doubt the thing, not forgetting to reward him for his attentions. Over this small well, very properly, a lamp is kept burning. In the church are some good paintings, and the tomb of the unhappy, unfortunate, beautiful Beatrice Cenci, whose tragic taking-off has filled the world with her name, as has her portrait with the glamor of her great beauty. Who does not recall her divinely-beautiful, sweet, sad, face?

Ascending the hill, we pass the Pauline Fountain, built out of the ruins of the temple of Minerva and supplied with water brought thirty-five miles by the Aqua Trajana, built 1,800 years ago. Beyond this are the beautiful grounds of the villa

Pamphili. Nothing can exceed the beauty of these grounds, with their statuary, lakes, fountains and gardens and trimmed hedges. A *columbaria*, but recently discovered and consequently in a good state of preservation, gives additional interest to the place. The walls of this columbaria are pierced with numerous small niches or appertures, in each of which is a small terra cotta urn with ashes and bones, just as they were placed here 2,000 years ago. Numerous frescoes cover the walls, and with colors still quite fresh.

VILLA BORGHESE.

This beautiful villa and grounds are situated a mile outside the city walls. After driving through the extensive grounds highly ornamented with grottoes, antique statues, old ruins with Doric columns and broken arches, we come to the Casino. It has long belonged to the Borghese family and formerly contained the finest art museum in Europe, which was purchased by Napoleon I., whose beautiful sister married Prince Borghese and whose full-sized statue as a reclining Venus in Carrara marble, by Canova, is one of the most beautiful statues of modern times.

VATICAN PALACE FRESCOES.

Raphael's Stanze.—These wondrous frescoes adorn four rooms of the palace that were used for the consistories and papal congregations. Leo X., had caused several of them to be frescoed by distinguished painters, but the art-loving Pope, Julius II., who was not less remarkable for his supreme taste in the fine arts than for his great ability as head of the Church, ordered Raphael, whose reputation had now spread throughout Italy, from Florence to Rome, to complete the frescoes, but after Raphael had made his first fresco, so far did it surpass those of the other great masters that Julius ordered all the frescoes erased, that Raphael might paint them anew. This order was rigidly enforced except in a few instances. Raphael had them spare a work of his former preceptor, Perugino. At this time Pope Julius had summoned to Rome the great artists of the world, so that at the same time there were at work in and upon the Vatican palace, Michael Angelo, Leonardo da Vinci and Raphael, while Bramante, no less distinguished as an architect, was at work upon St. Peter's. Here, in 1508, in the twenty-fifth year of his age, this greatest of the world's great painters commenced his wondrous task of ornamenting these four great halls, a work on which he was almost constantly engaged for twelve years, or up to the time of his untimely death, at 37 years of age, in 1520, killed by overwork. It would be difficult to overestimate the loss the world sustained in the early death of this immortal genius, whose inspirations were in beautiful harmony with the purity and gentleness of his short life. In him the Roman school attained its chief glory, and all Rome was appalled by his death and attended *en masse* his funeral, which was conducted in all the pomp and glory the Pope and Church could give a Prince. His remains were carried to and deposited in the most fitting mausoleum even his artistic genius could have conceived—the Pantheon. His last great work, upon which he was engaged at the time of his death, The transfiguration, was carried as a fitting banner in the funeral procession.

The great frescoes in the Stanze are known as the Disputation, the School at Athens, the Jurisprudence, the Parnassus, the Expulsion of Attila, the Liberation of St. Peter from Prison, the Fire in the Borgia Palace, with many other smaller works. There are hundreds of figures painted in these great frescoes, and yet none not perfect.

The Ghetto.—This, the Jewish quarters of the city, is a low, flat surface near the banks of the Tiber, and subject to inundation. Was so named as meaning the dispersed. In this crowded ill-ventilated place, this unfortunate people were compelled to live, deprived of nearly every means of living, and subjected to every humiliation and extortion that the diabolical ingenuity of their Christian tormentors could devise. They were not permitted to own property or do business in any other part of the city, and even in this the narrow streets were closed by gates. They were forbidden to be out of doors after sunset; were compelled to wear yellow hats and veils; to furnish the money to buy the prizes offered at the races of the Carnival, at which they were not permitted to be present; were compelled to assemble once a week to listen to a sermon from a priest, in which their sacred laws and ceremonies were villified, and for this they were compelled to pay the preacher; forced to complete their tile of brick without either straw or clay; for a thousand years subjected to a slavery, compared to which the 400 years of their fathers' slavery in Egypt were a holiday, and yet they lived and made money. The history of this unfortunate people is the most remarkable of any of the human race, and their torments and persecutions by a Church whose patron saint was, and is, a very Jew, is the most incomprehensible aberration of the human mind. Well, a day of deliverance came, and united Italy knows no distinction as citizens between a Jew and a Christian. So mote it be!

THE COLUMBARIA.

The Catacombs are situated around, not in or under, Rome, as has been stated. Those we visited were out on the Via Appia. In company with our archæological guide, Prof. Forbes, we passed out of the old walls of the city through the *Porta Appia*, where Horatius, after his victory—in which all three of the Curatii and two of the Horatii were slain—returning as the proud victor, and only survivor, of the six champions who had joined, that day, in deadly combat, met here his sister, who, on seeing on him the garlands she had woven for her affianced, now one of the dead Curatii, bewailed the death of her betrothed, blaming her brother for killing him. This unexpected reception so enraged the victor, that he marred his glory by killing his sister. A monument was reared upon the spot where she fell. The brutal brother, on account of the great victory he had gained for Rome, was not beheaded. Yet pious Rome could not permit so great a crime to go unpunished, and he was made to *pass under the yoke*. Crossing the brook Almo, we pass the little round church of St. Giovano in Oleo, St. John in oil, built upon the spot where we are informed St. John was thrown into a caldron of boiling oil and came out uninjured. Near this church is a lofty concrete tomb B. C. 242. Near this is the columbaria of Cæsar's officers and household. These columbaria (especially this one) have an interest only second to the Catacombs. And that those who have not seen the latter may be the better enabled to understand these structures, we shall describe them here. A columbaria, like the Catacombs, is a burial place, and like them, underground chambers in which the urns containing the sacred ashes, after the body had been cremated, were placed in niches shaped like a dove's nest, hence the name columbaria. They consist, sometimes, of a single room, say twenty or thirty feet high or deep, dug out of the solid, but soft, tufa rock, lava, and twenty to thirty feet square, with pigeon-holes in the sides to hold the urns containing the ashes after cremation of the body. These urns were closed with a well-fitting moveable lid—sometimes the lid, or top, was fastened on the urn—then it was pierced with a small aperture through which was poured warm sacred aromatic oil upon the revered ashes below. Most commonly only one urn is in a pigeon-hole, but not unfrequently two are placed in the same niche. A lamp was now placed by the urn. This was kept burning by the sexton or priest, whose business it was to watch over these sacred urns, and to keep the lamp filled and burning, for perhaps hundreds of years.

This columbaria of Cæsar's officers and household, in order to increase its capacity, had left in the center a solid portion, or square pillar, the sides of which, like those of the main chambers, were pierced with numerous small apertures containing funeral urns. By means of this construction, and its great size, this columbaria had its capacity so greatly extended that it contained, perhaps, thousands of urns. All these were marked by small marble slabs, inserted in the wall below the niche, with the name of those whose ashes were in the niche inscribed upon it. Sometimes the age or social condition of the person was named.

These urns, where they had not been disturbed, contained the ashes just as they did when placed here 2,000 years ago. Some beautiful and significant frescoes are on the walls. I notice that of a beautifully-executed peacock, emblem of immortality, while two doves, emblems of innocence and purity, with other like significant emblems, were on another wall. The same emblems of less beautiful workmanship constantly recur in the Catacombs. By all these we learn, if indeed we did not know the facts otherwise, that these pagans believed in the immortality of the soul, and that many of the rites and ceremonies associated with our religion are but borrowed from them; for instance, doves, so intimately associated with our religious ideas, were associated with these tombs, while the lamps kept constantly burning on tombs in chapels, here in Christian Rome, are borrowed or continued from the funeral lamps in these *columbaria*. But what gives this *columbaria* of Cæsar's household especial interest, and in the presence of which I felt the same awe and reverence felt in the Catacombs, is the names of persons mentioned by St. Paul as Christian converts belonging to Cæsar's household. Now as these names are very uncommon among the Romans, some of them found nowhere else than in the writings of St. Paul and here, it is almost positively certain that these urns contain the ashes of those mentioned so fervently by Paul, and are fellow-Christians belonging to the flock of this apostle, and among the first converts to Christianity in Rome. These ashes were placed here because they were buried by their pagan friends, relatives and fellow-servants of Cæsar's family, and in accordance with pagan rites, their bodies were burned and their ashes placed here with that of their friends, and not buried in the Catacombs as would have been the case had they received Christian burial. We find the reverse of this beautifully-affectionate thought and act in the Catacombs, where we now and then find among the earliest Christian tombs those of a pagan, doubtless, though not of the same faith, a brother or friend, and buried here by his Christian family or friends instead of having his body cremated and his ashes placed in the *columbaria*, as would have been done had he received pagan burial. But 1,500 years and more have left but little distinction between the ashes placed here and the bodies of their friends laid away in their winding-sheets in the Catacombs. All alike, long since, in most cases, are common dust.

Near the gate is the triumphal arch of Drusus in a good state of preservation. We now come to the Porta Appia opening out through the Aurelian walls onto the great highway, the Via Appia. A Byzantine fresco painting of the Madonna, sixth century, is under the arch of the wall at this place. Passing out of the walls and descending the Hill of Mars, we pass a number of once-splendid tombs, now heaps of rubbish. We are fairly out of the city on the great Appian Way.

THE VIA APPIA.

This great highway, which gives us an excellent idea of Roman military roads, found everywhere in Europe, as well as the greatness of this wondrous people, is best described by Procopius in the sixth century. "It leads from Rome to

Capua." (Afterwards extended to Brundusium, a seaport town on the Gulf of Naples.) "Its breadth is sufficient for two chariots to pass each other." (It is about twenty feet in width.) "In constructing this great work Appius caused the materials to be brought from a great distance so as to have all the stones hard and of the nature of mill-stones, such as are not found in this part of the country. Having ordered this material to be smoothed and polished, the stones were cut in corresponding angles so as to bite together in jointures without the intervention of copper or other material to bind them, and in this manner they were so firmly united that on looking at them we would say they had not been put together by art but had grown so upon the spot. And notwithstanding the wearing of so many ages," (then 900 years, having been constructed by Appius Claudius in B. C. 312) "being traversed daily by a multitude of vehicles and all sorts of cattle, they still remain unmoved, nor can the least trace of ruin or waste be observed upon these stones, neither do they appear to have lost any of their beautiful polish." And we may add that now, after an additional wear and tear and waste of neglect of thirteen additional centuries, this road is in many places in a good state of preservation. We drove out upon it eight or nine miles in carriages. This road has well been named, The Road of the Tombs, from the long line of once-splendid tombs, now in ruins, that line either side of the road, constituting a double line of tombs and mausoleums stretching out through the campagna eight or ten miles from the city.

After passing the ruins of many tombs and mausoleums, we came to

THE CATACOMBS OF ST. CALIXTUS.

These ancient burial-places of the early Christians are dark, narrow passages, hewn in the solid tufa rock or lava, some twenty feet in height and four to six wide, with the sides and floor at right angles to the roof. From these main passages there are others running off at right angles, and these are again sometimes crossed by others, forming a complicated labyrinth of cross passages.

This tufa is a very durable rock, hardening on exposure. Many of the buildings of Rome were of this material. The whole length of these subterranean passages around Rome, would, it is said, if placed in a straight line, be upwards of 500 miles, and as they were the burial places of Christians for centuries, they contained more corpses than the city ever had inhabitants at any one time. There are some sixty of these catacombs around, not under, Rome. There are no catacombs in or under the city, as has been stated. The Christians first begun to form them and bury their dead here in the latter part of the second century, and continued to do so for six or eight centuries, and after Christianity became the recognized religion of the empire, pagans were sometimes buried here, as shown by inscriptions and frescoes. These pagan frescoes are generally better executed and of a different style than those of the Christians.

The catacombs of St. Calixtus are entered from a pagan tomb that looks like a small temple with Corinthian columns. This tomb doubtless belonged to some wealthy pagan family, who, on becoming Christians, gave it to their brethren. We descended from this tomb, which stands near the Via Appia, into the long, narrow passages of the catacomb, which occasionally opens out into a chamber, where was buried some bishop or saint, or some family of wealth or distinction. The walls on either side are honeycombed with niches or vaults, one above another, sometimes being as many as six or eight tiers, with one or two feet of the stone wall left between them. Some departments are exclusively for children, the niches being only two or three feet long, and not more than six or eight inches high. These horizontal vaults are of sufficient depth and width to admit the body, which was enclosed only in its winding sheet, or shroud—no coffin of any kind being used. After the body was deposited, the aperture was carefully closed with a marble slab, which was securely plastered in, so that these vaults were sealed air tight, and the name of the person cut upon the slab enclosing the niche, and, as in the columbaria, a lamp was often placed in the niche, and as most of these early Christians were poor, for economical purposes, these slabs were often taken from pagan temples or tombs with other inscriptions upon them. But these bodies, thus carefully and affectionately laid away in the rock everlasting to await the resurrection, found in most cases quite a different one from that promised. First the Vandals and Goths who had been converted to Christianity, in their irruption into Rome, deeming all these bodies those of saints and martyrs, broke open the vaults and carried the bones back with them, where they were prized higher than gold—especially if the name of some well-known saint or martyr was attached to them by the vender—and sold to the churches of Transalpine Gaul, or to the pious, who placed these holy relics in their family burial-grounds to sanctify it. And again Holy Mother Church here in Rome, removed thousands of these bodies and placed them under the altars of their churches for the same purpose. One church here in Rome tilted twenty-seven wagon-loads in a pit beneath its altar. In this way, as the bodies of saints and martyrs had an especial cash value to the vender, the list was made to embrace many names unknown to heaven, and as these catacombs were the common burial-ground of Christian Rome, whose Christian public, to say the least, was no better then than now, it happened that the bones of many a publican and sinner found themselves suddenly transformed into those of a saint. But if these semi-barbarians and the Church were cheated by the trick, the devil most probably was not. Many others of these vaults were opened and their contents disturbed in quest of trinkets or other valuables, and others by that idle curiosity, which though rampant at the present day, has not been confined to it. So great has been this disturbance that but few of these vaults readily accessible are still closed or contain bones. We saw no bones. In one of the larger chambers we entered in this catacomb was deposited the body of St. Cecilia, after her martyrdom in A. D. 220. In 820, or 600 years after her burial by Pope Urban, it was removed by Pope Pascal I. to consecrate by its presence the church of St. Cecilia, where a beautiful statue of this saint is found. We are told that when this tomb was opened her body was found fresh and perfect as when it was first laid in the tomb, and clad in rich garments mixed with gold, with a roll of linen clothes stained with blood, found at her feet, and that this statue in the church of St. Cecilia was made by the sculptor from her corpse as it then appeared. This a beautiful and touching tale and deserves to be true, but as it has all human experience and reason against it, and only interested legends to establish it, we must be excused for receiving it with a slight feeling of doubt. But the body of this saint was to be again disturbed. And when in 1599 the Church was restored, the body was found by Cardinal Sprandrali (a most veritable witness) just as when it had been placed there more than 700 years before, or 1300 years after her burial, and we must suppose it still exists without change. But what is of real interest here in connection with this saint, is these frescoes on the wall above her tomb—a portrait of St. Cecilia—and on her right, Christ with a nimbus, on the left Pope Urban in full pontifical dress. Here we observe in the nimbus or glory that surrounds the head of Christ, a cross. But as this fresco is Byzantine in style, and known to be not earlier than the seventh century, it gives no support to the worship of the cross or its emblematic importance, as all this is the invention of times long subsequent to the martyrdom of this incorruptible saint. In all the early Christian frescoes and paintings in this catacomb and elsewhere, the symbol of the cross never appears. In all their efforts to illustrate in these symbols their faith, the sign of the cross never appears—absolutely never. There is not, I believe, in all Italy or elsewhere, the sign of the cross in connection with Christian rites and ceremonies of an earlier date than the fourth century, showing conclusively that this whole *cross question* is an invention of later times. How could it have been otherwise? and how could these early Christians in the simplicity of their faith have looked upon the cross otherwise than with horror, reminding them of the wickedness of the Jews in putting Jesus to this cruel and ignominious death? The facts are as I state them, be the conclusions what they may. Farther on is the burial-chamber of a family, doubtless of wealth and influence. On its walls are rude, but intensely-interesting and highly-instructive frescoes—The Baptism of Christ in Jordan by John, in which Christ is standing in the water while the saint is pouring water on His head; Jonah being swallowed and again thrown up by a monstrous half-serpent-like fish. This is unmistakably intended to show their belief in the resurrection of the body. Moses striking the rock, intended to symbolize the living waters that were given his flock by the blood of Christ; the woman at the well of Samaria; the paralytic man taking up his bed and walking with it on his shoulder—the bedstead is an iron one with a spring mattress; doves, as we had seen in the pagan columbaria, emblems here, as there, of purity and innocence; two pigeons, and the good shepherd with a lamb on his shoulder—this is the earliest and most constant symbol of these early Christians met with in these frescoes and paintings. These frescoes in this chamber are purely Christian, and by a

Christian artist of the second or third century, and though rude are a thousand times more touching, life-like, and instructive than if by a skilled Greek or Byzantine artist. 1st, because though rude they are Christian, by an unskilled native artist, and without conventionalism, are efforts to paint nature as it is, which lead to the brilliant triumph of the Renaissance. 2nd, because in these constantly recurring efforts of untaught, native Christian artists, we have given the religious belief of these early Christians—endeavoring, learning, to symbolize their faith and hopes. The doves, the peacocks, Jonah and the fish, Moses striking the rock, the Good Shepherd and sheep, all symbolizing the Christian faith, and 3rd, the absence of the cross—teaching by its absence, that these early Christians had not yet learned to venerate it.

THE FORMATION AND USES OF THE CATACOMBS.

It has been thought and often stated that these early catacombs were quarries, from which stone was obtained for building purposes. Nothing could be more manifestly false. Why should anyone have pushed a stone-quarry along these long, dark, narrow passages, when they could have obtained the same stone with greatly less cost and labor from the front. That stone of this kind was obtained for building purposes from the readily-accessible quarries around Rome is shown by the condition of these quarries. It is quite likely that even the stone taken from these catacombs may have been sold for building purposes, thereby assisting to defray the expenses. It is true these catacombs sometimes commence at an old stone-quarry, but this was for economy. They were made for no other purpose than that for which they were used, the burial of the dead, and were constructed by an engineer at the least cost of time and labor, hence the narrow passages, just wide enough to admit a funeral procession to pass with the corpse, with an occasional large chamber or space in which some bishop, saint, or otherwise distinguished or rich person was buried, and which were used on occasions as chapels, and where doubtless a few of the pious were often gathered, during times of great persecution, for prayer and exhortation, these being greatly protected here by the sanctity of burial places in the Roman laws. These cells and passages are dimly lighted from above by an occasional shaft sunk for this purpose. Immediately under or near these shafts, which are generally over a larger space or chamber, it is light enough to read by daylight, along the passages between them it is quite dark, so that we had to grope our way with lighted candles and torches.

Another error more general is, that these catacombs were secret hiding-places, known only to the Christians, who fled to them as hiding-places in great numbers. Nothing is farther from the truth. They were it is true, obscure, out-of-the-way, quiet, secluded places, and that far secret, but known to all Rome quite as well as to the Christians themselves. How could it have been otherwise, when the mountains of stone removed in their excavation had to be placed outside by a people who had no means of hiding this debris, had it been possible otherwise? And then the daily funeral processions necessary to deposit these hundreds of thousands of corpses during two or three centuries of persecution forced a knowledge of their existence upon, not only the Roman authorities, but the entire Roman people. As stated, what really protected them was the sanctity of burial-places, protected by the Roman laws, which held all such places inviolable, inalienable, and while doubtless an individual or a few noted individuals most marked for slaughter did occasionally, during times of great danger, take shelter in these labyrinths until the more immediate danger had passed, being supported with bread and water by some of the faithful, that any considerable number at any one time could have done so, is simply impossible.

Another error promulgated concerning these catacombs is in regard to the number of martyrs they contained. This error has been published more from design than ignorance. That they did contain some who died *for* the faith is unquestionable, but the multitude buried here died *in* but not *for* the faith once delivered to the saints. But it answered a purpose in "Books of Martyrs" and homilies, as the timid were more impressed by swelling the numbers, and perhaps made more devout, in an age of ignorance, by these frightful pictures of the seas of blood that had purified and watered the Church, and that too by those who had filled every Christian land with spies and informers, and many a dark and dismal dungeon with helpless, innocent Christian men and women, accused of heresy, that is, of doubting some Church dogma, while the God-inspired spirit of inquiry and the inalienable heritage of freedom of thought was crushed by the torture of fire and the rack, or drowned in a sea of innocent Christian blood. Even here in Italy many more Christians have been murdered by Christians than all the pagan emperors ever slaughtered. I saw the word martyr on a tomb in this catacomb only once, and our archæological guide, who has explored these catacombs extensively and examined them carefully says it occurs only some thirty times, and while this is no proof that only this number died for, or on account of their religion, it indicates very clearly that martyrdom did not belong to the multitude buried here, an indication clearly confirmed by abundant evidence. Yet there were martyrs, and in some instances their dust lies here, and many a vacant niche is consecrated by their former presence, together with thousands of others who would readily have suffered death for their faith, men and women who died that the world might be the better through the triumph of their *faith*, and it was bettered by their sublime sacrifice, as their blood like a mighty river broke down—swept away—masses of error, that, reared in times of ignorance supported by fraud and craft, had imposed upon the lives and consciences of men for centuries. Perhaps this mighty work could not have been done so certainly in any other manner as by the blood of these noble men and women, as while their death for, did not prove the *truth* of their religion, it did prove their sublime sincerity, a heroism that awed, subdued, conquered the world.

In walking in these narrow passages with a wall of human dust from departed ages on either side, I felt as did Moses in the presence of the burning bush, 'that the place whereon I stood was holy ground.' After visiting other portions of this catacomb and examining many frescoes and inscriptions, we emerged from this region of sepulchres by an old flight of stairs at a point remote from where we entered, and continued our route along the via Appia, passing the deserted church of S. Urbano, with Corinthian marble pillars, the Villa of Herodes Atticus and a great number of other ruined temples and tombs, among them the tomb of the two Horatii and the three Curatii who fell in mortal combat here, as the champions of the Roman and Latin armies, continuing our route as far as the nine mile stone to the Appian Forum and *Three Taverns*, at which point the brethren in Rome having heard of Paul's coming came out to meet him. See Acts xxviii.

The day, Jan. 22nd, 1885, was very cold and disagreeable, ice being frequently present on the pools of water by the roadside, while large icicles hung under the dripping walls, the ground was frozen in the shade, and yet the vegetation was not killed, grass green, oranges hanging on the trees, and some of the more hardy garden vegetables still growing in the gardens, apparently none the worse for this freezing weather, I do not know how this is. I am sure such weather would destroy grass and all garden vegetables in St. Louis.

PISA.

Feb. 13th, 1885.—Left the Eternal City at 2 P. M., and after a pleasant run of eight hours arrived at the long-since-finished city of Pisa, which still stands in her wedding robes, but robes so tattered and torn from the wear of 600 years without repair that they might be mistaken for working garments. But Pisa works not, and her dress is the more interesting from the fact that it presents us the full dress suit of mediæval times. The great world around her has moved on, and fashions changed, but Pisa changes not. Here we parted with our pleasant and accomplished St. Louis friends, who had accompanied us in all our wanderings through the classic scenes of Italy.

Pisa is situated on the Arno, six miles from its entrance into the Mediterranean, and is practically a seaport town. It has now only 26,000 inhabitants, but in the days of its glory had many times this number, with a history dating back to the third century B. C., at which time it was an important Roman colony. But it was not until the eleventh and twelfth centuries it obtained its greatest commercial importance, and attained its greatest splendor in the twelfth and thirteenth centuries, rivaling Venice and Genoa in the daring of her exploits at sea, and with her strong fleet of war vessels driving back the conquering hordes of Saracens that threatened the conquest of Europe. In the middle of the thirteenth century she unfortunately engaged in a disastrous war with her great naval rival, Genoa, and after many years of fierce and destructive combats at sea, finally in 1288, sustained an overwhelming defeat by the Genoese, in which she lost her fleet and liberty, and from the disastrous consequences of which she never recovered—and in 1406, like a female slave, was thrown upon the market and sold to her former rival, Florence.

Feb. 18th.—We visited the Cathedral, Leaning Tower, Baptistery and Campo Santo, the four only objects in Pisa of any particular interest. But these constitute Pisa a point of wondrous interest to the tourist, who sees in these ghostly spectres that stand out from the shadowy light of the Middle Ages the image of what Pisa was when her embattled hosts withstood the Moslem power, and also the embodied crystalized plastic art of the close of the Dark, and early dawn of the Middle, Ages, eleventh to thirteenth centuries.

The Cathedral (Duomo), erected in 1163, is among the largest and finest churches in Italy. It is a basilica, 312 feet long, 110 feet wide, with a transept near the far end constituting a Latin cross, with a lofty dome over the center of the cross. It is built of white marble with just enough black marble placed in the wall surface to break the monotony of a plain white wall. The handsome façade is ornamented with columns, arches and open galleries. The interior has four rows of lofty columns and two aisles on either side of the nave—this latter is paved—beautifully tesselated with variegated marble, which produces a most pleasing appearance. The sides and ceiling are ornamented with frescoes. There are twelve altars of a later construction, and said to have been built by Michael Angelo. Near the high altar which is elaborate and very fine is a Madonna by Reni, and St. Agnes, by A. del Sarto. The choir has finely-carved stalls, a large mosaic of the twelfth century, Christ with Mary and St. John on either side. Over the arch of the choir are mosaics of angels and saints. From the lofty ceiling in the nave, hangs a lamp suspended by a rod more than a hundred feet in length, the swinging of which suggested to Galileo the idea of measuring time by the pendulum. This immortal genius, who was a good Catholic, being in attendance at church, and his attention not entirely absorbed by the service, observed that this great bronze chandelier, which had been set swinging by the sexton, continued to pass through a certain arch in a given time, conceived the happy thought that if a pendulum could be kept passing over a given segment in a given time by machinery, it would correctly measure time. Hence, the clock, the pendulum, with all its benefits and uses. Surely there never was a lamp more prolific in results ; and in observing it, suspended by a rod 150 feet in length, moved by the least vibration, I felt satisfied that no chandelier ever presented conditions more suggestive of such a thought.

THE BAPTISTERY.

The Baptistery, also entirely of marble, is a beautiful structure, circular, terminating in a lofty dome 190 feet above the pavement. It is 100 feet in diameter, and is surrounded by a gallery with marble columns, with a beautiful marble font in the center, elaborately decorated. A highly-artistic pulpit, by Pirono, is supported by seven columns. The echo in this building is the finest I have heard—truly astonishing. A note sounded is repeated again and again, echoed back in a different key each time ; first clearly, from the lower half, then from the upper gallery, and lastly from the lofty dome, until it is difficult to believe, and must be repeated, to satisfy that the last is the echo of the first sound. Let none visiting the baptistery fail to observe this beautiful phenomenon.

THE CAMPANILE.

The famous Leaning Tower at Pisa, long mentioned as one of the wonders of the world, is indeed a wondrous structure, built also of marble, 179 feet high, and leans so much as to be thirteen feet out of the perpendicular. To look at it we naturally wonder how it stands, and yet it has stood just as it now stands since its first erection, in the twelfth century, unmoved by the battles and storms of 700 years. That it leaned in this manner before its completion is proven in the fact that the upper story is leaned in the opposite direction, evidently to balance the false position of the lower stories. So much is this the case that were the column below straightened, this would fall off. Why did they not stop the work, when, by the foundation giving away, it leaned in this manner? Well, simply because it was built in this oblique manner intentionally; and it certainly accomplishes the object of the builder, in giving it a greatly increased interest. As a straight column it never would have rivaled the incomparable campanile of Giotto, at Florence. As a leaning tower it possesses an interest peculiarly its own. It is composed of eight stories, each ornamented with rows of light Corinthian pillars running around the tower. It is ascended by stone steps winding around on the inside, to the top, where are several large bells, the largest of which weighs six tons, and is placed on the upper side to assist in balancing what seems to be the tottering structure. I ascended to the top—290 stone steps. The leaning state of the tower was so marked in the obliquity of the steps, that I felt uncomfortable and hardly enjoyed the grand view of the city, plain, the winding Arno and distant mountains, obtained from its lofty summit, lest the crazy thing would fall, which it certainly threatens to do at any moment. Galileo took advantage of the obliquity of this tower in making his calculations regarding the law of gravitation.

CAMPO SANTO.

The Campo Santo was first consecrated in the twelfth century, by Archbishop Ubaldo, who, after the conquest of the Holy Land by the Moslems, caused fifty-three ship-loads of holy earth to be brought from Mount Calvary and deposited here, in order that the Christian dead might repose in holy ground. It is 411 feet long and 171 feet wide, being an open court in shape of an oblong square. Externally there are arcades resting on forty-four pilasters; internally an open hall with open round windows opening upon a green quadrangle. There are three small chapels opening into the covered way, which, as a wide portico, runs around the entire interior. The marble slabs composing the pavement of this portico are tombstones—the entire pavement is made up of tombstones—every square foot representing corpses. The strange, unique frescoes on the walls constitute perhaps the greatest charm of this very strange place, where we are brought directly in contact with the crude materialistic notions of the Christians, or the Church, during the Middle Ages, concerning the soul and its hereafter. These are beautiful or frightful according as the artist wishes to portray the states or conditions of the soul, as taught by the Church at that day.

On the north wall is a large fresco of an equestrian group, who, in high, gladsome spirits are going out to the chase, when they came suddenly on three open coffins, each containing a corpse in different stages of decomposition, with hideous snakes crawling over them. This is to remind us of the transitory nature of pleasure, the uncertainty of life and the certainty of death. The grouping of the party, the surprise of the horses and the different manner in which each individual is affected is admirable.

To the right of this, is the angel of death, with his scythe mowing down indiscriminately rich and poor, young and old, kings and beggars, and a rich harvest he is making. On one side of death are a party in rich attire, good-livers, who are horrified at the approach of death, and fain would get out of the way; on the other, a group of the poor, the disconsolate, the lame, halt and blind, who, dissatisfied with their lot here, are quite ready to take their chances in the hereafter; these welcome the angel with outstretched arms and with feelings of evident delight. Farther on is the last judgment; above is Christ with the Virgin on His right hand, both seated on thrones and wearing crowns; on either side opposite their feet are six apostles; on the right, are a large group of the saved, whose countenances express their happiness; on the left, a terrified crowd chased by devils, who catch at them as they are pitched over the battlements of the upper world, some falling headmost, others seized and dragged down, or driven before frightful devils; on the right, coffins opening and the bodies coming forth to judgment; others just dying, with their souls as small dolls, escaping from their mouths—the last breath. These in some instances are pointed to the right by angels, in others seized and dragged to the left by monstrous devils. One tomb-stone is being lifted, and a bishop with mitre on is coming forth, who thinking his place is to the right, is starting for that point, when an angel seizes him by the head and points him to the left, where an angry-looking devil is anxiously waiting to get and bear him company to other quarters. The look of disgust, disappointment and terror shown in the face of this bishop, who had expected to go to heaven as a bishop, in finding himself turned into hell as a man, is truly ludicrous. They should have had more respect for the bishop; well, perhaps they did, but this was so intimately associated with the man, that when the devil got the latter, the former had to keep it company. So much for being found in bad company.

GENOA.

Genoa is picturesquely situated upon a semi-circular ridge of hills that rise several hundred feet above the bay, and is the most important commercial city in Italy. The city has 150,000 inhabitants, and after the fall of the Roman Empire, long stood as the guardian and bulwark against the marauding expeditions of the Saracens, protecting by her powerful fleets the more defenseless cities of this part of Italy.

The town has always been fortified, and now, since the erection of fifteen or twenty formidable modern forts upon the higher hills overlooking the harbor, is a very Sebastopol. The crescent-shaped harbor has light-houses upon its projecting promontories at its entrance. These, with their bright calcium lights high in the air, with the long line of gas lights that run along the semi-circular hills, city lights, together with the numerous lights from lanterns hung to the masts of the ships in the harbor, present at night, as I am now writing, a most beautiful, weird appearance. With an intelligent guide we drove over the city, passing the Cathedral S. Lorenzo, built in the eleventh century, S. Ambrosio, Palazzo Ducale, and on to the Campo Santo, continuing our drive to the Palazzo Rossa, a very paradise upon the mountain side high above the city. From this lovely situation we had a fine view of the city, with its churches, palaces and fine palatial houses running around and over the semi-circle of hills upon which the city is built, together with the beautiful harbor crowded with schooners, ships and steamers, from almost every nation. The evidence of industry and thrift everywhere present, with the absence of the swarms of lazy beggars that infest Southern Italy, of itself greatly increases the pleasure derived in visiting this beautiful historic city. We visited, as will all Americans, the beautiful Piazza Aqua Verde, in which is a colossal statue of Columbus, a Genoese. At the foot of the statue is the goddess of the world he discovered, America, then a primeval wilderness, the habitation of savage beasts, and yet more savage men, now the abode of 50,000,000 of civilized, cultivated men, with its wilderness changed to a garden and its desolate places into crowded cities. Allegorical figures are around the base, appropriately symbolizing the America of to-day, religion, strength, wisdom and geography.

MILAN.

Feb. 18th.—Left Genoa at 10:30 A. M., and arrived at Milan —94 miles—at 3 P. M., and put up at the Hotel de Lione.

Milan is much the finest city in all Italy, with a population of 250,000 inhabitants. The houses are well-built, streets wide and clean, with the general appearance of thrift. The men are larger than in Southern Italy, well becoming the descendants of the conquerors of the world, while the women are handsome, charmingly so, large, dark, lustrous eyes, heavy eyebrows with long eyelashes, giving them a charm peculiarly Italian, and if their remote Sabine grandmothers were as *taking* I wonder not that the Romans *took* them.

The Carnival struck us at Rome, followed us to Pisa, from there to Genoa, and now we are in its midst here at Milan, which we are told is the last point at which this church revel takes place. But this is *Ash Wednesday!* the first day of Lent, and with Catholics considered most holy; well, but these pleasure-loving Milanese could not help this, they were entitled to their Carnival and if Ash Wednesday came on too soon for it, it was no fault of theirs. The fault was manifestly in the Carnival not coming around sooner, or in the Ash Wednesday coming around too soon, consequently the day—not the Milanese—must give way. Well, the pope was equal to the difficulty, and by a bull or otherwise, declared the day off, and the Ash Wednesday, not the Carnival, gave way. Consequently on this first day of Lent, Ash Wednesday to the contrary notwithstanding, we are in the midst of Carnival, feasting, drinking, yelling, blowing horns, with masquerade balls, etc., etc. But still another difficulty presents itself, the fourth day, on which their grand parade and high revel was to take place, was rainy, insomuch that the parade could not take place; well, this again was no fault of the Milanese, the clerk of the weather had blundered, consequently the high revel took place on Sunday, first Sunday in Lent, feasting, revelling, dancing, and merry-making. Well as he whose business it was to look after the weather, had neglected to do so, the pope very properly came to the aid of these devout Christians and declared Sunday off, and like Rip with his drinks, did not count the first five days of Lent, Ash Wednesday and Sunday included. But after all, while it really looked strange, I do not know that there was anything wrong—the whole matter, the fixing of the time of Lent, Lent itself with the distinction between Sunday and any other day are entirely church regulations and appointments, why not the head of the Church declare them off and on; and here in Italy they have someone to do this.

The cathedral dedicated to Maria is justly the pride of all true Milanese, for while · not the eighth wonder of the world, and hardly a wonder at all, except that we might wonder that any people should be so foolish as to waste money as much of this has been wasted, yet it is a most beautiful structure, and is, with only two exceptions, the largest church in the world, and while not so large or costly as St. Peter's it is much more beautiful, is 477 feet in length, is 183 feet wide and 155 feet in height. The dome over the centre of the transept is 220, and the tower 360 feet above the pavement. The entire structure is of marble and so elaborately carved and ornamented as to present a beautiful lace-work. There are on its exterior alone 2,000 marble statues which adorn the doorways, the windows, recesses, niches and walls, many of these statues of apostles, saints, angels, Cupids, gods and heroes, are in bas or alto reliefs. The interior is scarcely less elaborately adorned. The vast pavement or floor is of variegated marble with figures as elaborate, delicate and beautiful as a highly-wrought carpet. The church is in the shape of a Latin cross, with double aisles, divided by fifty-two marble pillars 100 feet high, which support the roof. Each of these pillars is twelve feet in diameter and connected above by beautiful sharply-pointed Gothic arches. The choir is Gothic in style. The lofty Gothic windows, with their beautiful stained glass, are strikingly beautiful. Many statues, tombs and paintings, with eight or ten altars adorn the interior. In front of one of these altars I noticed a small picture, or piece of silver, some two inches wide and six inches long, which the devotees, as they passed, kissed, when high enough, and when not—as with many women—passed their fingers over it and crossed themselves. I regretted I could not learn the history of this image, and on noticing it I could not divine its nature, but suppose it had, in some way, some very sacred association, possibly the piece of money miraculously obtained from the fish's mouth, as it looked like some old Roman coin, or a silver beetle—the *fetich* of some saint.

The tower is ascended by 512 steps, 194 inside and 318 outside Unfortunately the morning we ascended it was a little hazy, so much so that distant objects were indistinct. Far off was the long line of snow-capped Alps indistinctly outlined, rendering it impossible to distinguish Mount Blanc or Jungfrau, both of which are distinctly visible from this point on a clear day. The city of Milan, however, and a wide range of the plain of Lombardy, were beautifully shown. After mounting to the roof we walked over its flat surface 200 feet above the pavement, covered with marble statues and pinnacles. One of these statues is that of Napoleon, by Canova. This roof has been, not inaptly, called the Flower Garden.

Visited the *Brera*, or *Picture Gallery*, containing 600 pictures, many of them of much, and a few of very great, merit. Among the latter, and the gem of the collection, is Raphael's Sposalizio or Nuptials of the Virgin. Near this is a much-admired work, the head of Christ, by Leonardo da Vinci. Other works of much merit are St. Jerome, by Titian; Madonna, by Bellini; portraits by Mengs, Rembrandt, Van Dyck; Madonna and Saints, by Dominichino; Dead Monk, by Velasquez.

The Gallerie Vittoria Emanuel, connecting the cathedral square with the square of the stairs, where are placed the statues of Leonardo da Vinci and his pupils, is a beautiful glass covered passage, the finest of its kind in Europe.

Visited St. Maria delle Grazie, an old abbey church of the 13th century, built by Bramante. It contains some fine tombs, monuments and frescoes. In an adjoining small refectory is the wondrous fresco of Leonardo da Vinci, The Last Supper. Perhaps no other work of art ever received so much attention as this marvelous fresco. Unfortunately 400 years of corroding time, with neglect and vandalism—the ignorant monks cut a doorway through it and have dealt harshly with it, leaving it in ruins. But, like the Colosseum at Rome, it impresses us, perhaps, none the less favorably even in its ruins, as in this we have what it now is, while the excited imagination is stimulated to fill up from the immeasurable void what it may have been, returning from the dreary waste with the consciousness that its restoration is impossible—but even this serves to increase our curiosity by investing it with greater mystery—a want ever increasing, never satisfied, insatiable. No painting has ever been so often copied or engraved, so widely diffused, so universally known. Where could a person be found who is unacquainted with Leonardo da Vinci's Last Supper? But even the earliest and best copies are inferior to the original, even in its ruins, as all others, though highly-gifted, have utterly failed to impress the *motive*, the shock produced by the words "One of you shall betray me," as it affected the different apostles, and shown in their features, only in the original. Some six or eight artists were engaged in copying it, aided by several early copies to enable them to fill the gaps time has made in the original, and it is said that many highly-gifted artists, after coming here to copy it, and after studying it for days, have left in despair, fearing to even attempt so impossible a work. While no praise of this wondrous fresco—the nearest embodiment of the unattainable ideal—in the soul of the greatest of geniuses—can perhaps be overwrought, or scarcely considered extravagant, is it not quite possible that the religious sentiment, so intimately associated with the occurrence or facts expressed in this picture, has much to do in so impressing all Christians; and is it not possible that a great Mohammedan painter, did such exist, might place it far below many of Raphael's paintings, or his Vatican frescoes?

Visited the old church of St. Ambrosia, founded by St. Ambrose in the fourth century, on the ruins of a temple of Bacchus, and one of the oldest churches in Christendom. Its antiquity impresses us not more in its time-worn appearance than in its antique shape. After passing down several steps, we pass through a gateway opening into an open court, surrounded by a wide corridor, containing early Christian inscriptions and sarcophagi with bas reliefs, some of these from the old temple, and 2,000 years old. The church is a basilica supported by granite columns, so old that, though of granite, they are much corroded and injured by time. They most likely also belonged to the old temple of Bacchus. The gates of the church we are informed are the same that St. Ambrose closed against the wicked emperor Theodosius, in 399. The interior contains many old and faded frescoes and mosaics of the fifth, sixth, and ninth centuries. In one side of the nave is a coiled brazen serpent mounted upon a post, which we are assured is the identical brazen serpent that Moses lifted up in the wilderness more than 3,000 years ago. If so it is the oldest serpent in the world—the devil only excepted. I believe the history of his serpentship is a little misty, mythical, but it is here nevertheless. There are several other old churches here in Milan quite worth seeing, and, like all the old churches in art-loving Italy, containing many frescoes and mosaics, monuments, sarcophagi and statues, many of them of artistic or historical importance.

LAKE COMO.

March.—Left Milan for Lake Como, distant thirty miles, at 2 P. M. At Como took steamer for Belagio, a beautiful point on Lake Como, where the lake divides into the arms which run to Como and Lecco. The day was clear and beautiful and the trip on the steamer from Como to Belagio, fifteen miles, one of surpassing loveliness. This lake is a sheet of crystal water, enclosed by rough, ragged, volcanic mountains, rising on either side to a height of from 4,000 to 8,000 feet. The weather had been cold and rainy, and all the higher points of these mountains were covered with snow, which on the north sides, and in places not exposed to the sun, extends down the hill-sides to within a few hundred feet of the lake, greatly increasing the wild beauty of this Alpine region. The waters are clear blue or green as the depth varies, the lake having in some places so great a depth as 2,000 feet. These mountains rise directly from the lake, the lake in fact being only the depressions between the mountains filled with water, which has risen until it has found an outlet in a considerable river forming one of the numerous tributaries of the Po. These placid waters, being surrounded by the encircling mountains, are seldom disturbed by more than a passing breeze. The nights here at Belagio have continued clear and the sky in this Alpine region truly beautiful—bright, blue, serene, bespangled with gold, each star shone as a diamond in an ebony setting. Quite charmed with this Alpine sky, we remained until late at night on the open piazza of our hotel, which overhangs the lake, admiring this wondrous gold-spangled vault above us, while each star was reflected from the water as from a mirror.

Took steamer for Colico, at the upper end of the lake some ten or twelve miles distant, at which point the mountain stream Adda enters the lake, from which its waters again flow at the lower end of Lake Lecco. Beyond Colico the course of the river is traced by a long gap in the mountains—the entire region is of volcanic origin—the bare volcanic rocks rising on either side in rugged grandeur. But the most curious and interesting feature of these steep and almost inaccessible mountains is the triumph of man over nature, in forcing from those rugged, rock-ribbed and forbidding cliffs, not a scanty subsistence for a few inhabitants, as we see in other even more promising districts, but an abundant and profitable supply for the most densely peopled district on the globe. Nowhere else, not even in the richest valley, is it possible to support so dense an agricultural population as is found here on these, by nature, sterile hill-sides. Almost a continuous line of villages, towns and clusters of houses, line the base of these mountains on either side of the lake, from Como to Colico, a distance of thirty miles, while the mountain-sides, to their precipitous summits, are dotted over with farm-houses and villages of perhaps from 500 to 1000 inhabitants, with churches almost innumerable. At one view I counted twenty churches, not in a city, but in villages in clusters, or now and then situated on an almost inaccessible rock, two or three thousand feet above the lake. Surely, if we are to judge the piety of a people by the number of their churches, these must constitute a multitudinous swarm of saints. Now how have these sterile hill-sides been made so fertile ? All their fertility is of man's creation. In the first place they are terraced often from near the lake to a height of 3,000 feet. These terraces run along the hill-sides, seemingly, as seen from the lake, are only long, wide steps for ascending the mountain. But in fact they are long lines of stone walls, six and ten feet high, with intervening terraces or flat surfaces, ten or twenty feet wide, according to the steepness of the hill-side. On these terraces are grape-vines and mulberry shrubs; the shrubs making supports for the vines, and furnishing the food for millions of silk-worms—the product of which supports and gives employment to this dense population, this district being the very heart of the silk-producing section of Italy, while higher up the mountains, where it is too cold for vines and silk-culture, olive-orchards furnish employment to a number of inhabitants. Still above these olive-groves, chestnut and walnut trees continue the profitable culture to the very summit of these hills. Millions of cubic yards of masonry are in the terrace walls, and the very earth upon the flat surfaces in which the trees grow is often carried and deposited there from other points, in baskets. All this is possible in this country, where labor is abundant and cheap, but very strange to an American. Why, to terrace and treat in this way the Missouri River hills would cost more money, than all the wine and silk of Italy would pay for in, perhaps, a thousand years.

March 11th.—Took steamer for Lecco, which is at the terminus of the other branch of the lake, eight or ten miles from Belagio. This branch of the lake lies in a sterile, precipitous, rocky Alpine gorge, and by exposure to a cold wind from the snow-clad Alps, is rendered so sterile that no effort of man has been able to redeem it to but a limited extent, and being but illy adapted to the vine and not at all to silk-culture, has long since attained its farthest possible culture, giving unmistakable evidence that one or two thousand years ago this district contained quite as many inhabitants as could possibly wring from reluctant nature a scanty support. All the farmhouses and clusters of houses are old, very old, in many cases not less than 1,000 or 1,800 years old. The very tiles, though indestructible, are rotten and covered with a brown lichen or moss, giving them much the same appearance as the brown, moss-covered, sterile hills above and around them, and of which they seem to form a part. These are tenanted, as they have been for a thousand years, by those who, like their remote ancestors, eke out a precarious existence upon the product of the few walnut and chestnut trees that these hills support. These people live in the same houses their ancestors lived in 1,000 years ago—no more, perhaps less. What has become of all the children that have grown up here in the last thousand years? Doubtless the solution to this question, though sad, is an easy one. From age to age, inexorable necessity has driven these sons and daughters from the rock-bound, but none the less loved, homes of their infancy, to seek subsistence elsewhere, leaving only such as would supplement the death-rate of fathers and mothers. That this has been so—that these mountain-born poor have been driven, not by election, but inevitable necessity, from their hearth-stones, is as certain as the rock-bound history of their native hills.

March 12th.—This is the fortieth anniversary of our wedding. How very few of those who knew and loved us then are living now! Alas what havoc time makes in forty years. In forty years more perhaps none of all earth's inhabitants will know that we ever lived. We have spent five days at this, the most beautiful of all Italian lakes. Left March 13th for Verona.

VERONA.

March 14th.—This is a gala day here. Bright flags wave along the streets, while military companies in their brightest uniforms, with bands of music are parading in the streets. It is the natal day of the king and also of the unification of Italy.

Verona, situated in northern Italy, near the Austrian line, has a population of 60,000, and is strongly fortified. It is an old city, having been founded by the Rhœtians. It became a Roman city B. C. 100, and is, next to Milan, the most important city in northern Italy. It is immortalized by Shakespear, whose Romeo and Juliet lived, loved and died here.

March 15th.—Took carriage and drove over the city, visiting its churches and most important points, among them the tomb of Juliet which is visited by all English-speaking people with much the same reverence a pilgrim feels in visiting the shrine of a saint. It is a small red granite sarcophagus in the open court of an old monastery, and was covered or half-filled with flowers, the offerings of the multitudes of visitors here. Now it is possible it is not a sarcophagus, but a bath-tub, and may have never contained the corpse of Juliet or anyone else, and yet, as it represents her tomb, it possesses a far higher interest than the costly tombs of kings or queens. How wonderful the work of genius. Here the immortal Bard of Avon has embalmed a love between two young hearts, that will outlive this granite urn, yea more lasting than even the everlasting pyramids of Egypt, as while these perish, love is immortal, and shall outlive the great globe itself, and when it dies earth and heaven would exist in vain. The house in which Juliet lived is still shown here, and perhaps will be, as long as a house exists in Verona, as such places live as long as persons wish to see them.

The old Roman amphitheatre, built in the third century, is I believe the only one of these structures in a good state of preservation, and used for fetes and shows at the present day. It is 550 feet in circumference and the wall 100 feet high. On the inside, rows of marble benches run around the wall, rising quite to its summit, and capable of seating 20,000 people. From the top of the walls we obtain a fine view of the town and adjacent country.

The old church of S. Zeno Magiore, built in the eleventh century, contains many fragments of ruins, broken columns, friezes from pagan temples and urns. One of porphyry, twenty-five feet in circumference, belonging to an old heathen temple, is 2,000 years old. There are many old paintings and frescoes, one by Giotto.

In the public garden are antique grottoes, perhaps used as temples by the Romans, and a number of large cypress trees known to be 500 years old.

MUNICH.

Munich is situated at a greater elevation (2,000 feet) above the sea than any other capital in Europe, and is, as we found on our arrival, correspondingly cold. Winter still lingered here, with snow on the north sides of the house-tops, and the street gulleys full of snow and ice. This, after leaving the warm, bright skys of sunny Italy, gave a chilly, hyperborean appearance to the place, which was scarcely dissipated by our three-weeks stay. I am sure Munich should not be visited before May or June. Were I traveling here again I would spend February in Naples, March in Rome, April and May in northern Italy and June in Munich and southern Germany. It is the capital of Bavaria and has a population of 170,000, and next to Dresden is the most important art city in Germany, in modern painting perhaps the most important in Europe. It has for its river the " Isar, rolling rapidly," but as it was in April we most frequented its banks, not dark as winter, but bright as summer, was its flow. The Isar is spanned by several bridges. The most interesting one is the Maximilian's Brücke, which spans the Isar at the island, and the Maximilianeum. The most interesting street is the Maximilian's Strasse, on which is a beautiful platz, containing some fine statues, and surrounded by public buildings and palatial houses. This and other squares contain many beautiful monuments and statues of Bavarian kings, heroes and statesmen and others in marble and bronze. Among these are the statues of Max Joseph, Maximilian, Lewis I., Gen. Deray, Schelling the metaphysician, Frankhofer the optician, Liebeg the chemist, Gluck the composer.

There are two picture galleries, the old and new Pinakothek, which contain a large collection of paintings, many of them of much merit. As all the most important are by painters whose works have been met with and mentioned, we shall not now mention even the most important of these, excepting the two girls counting their money, received by the sale of their fruit; two beggar boys eating grapes and melons; old woman combing boy's head while he is eating bread, by *Murillo.* These are the gems of the gallery and are truly great works, and that they are taken from life, and faithfully and accurately represent the persons, class and scenes of that day in Madrid where they were painted, no one seeing these beautiful works of art can doubt.

The Glyptothek (repository of sculpture) contains an immense collection of ancient sculptures, many of them of great beauty, forming a most valuable school for the study of ancient sculpture, as well as constituting a most delightful and profitable place to the tourist.

The damp, cold weather had rendered our stay here much more prosy than it would otherwise have been—and this was increased by the state of our health. Wife had another attack of hepatic colic—the first since leaving Carlsbad. This hastened our departure. We left May 8th for Carlsbad, and after remaining some five weeks, with wife's health much improved, we left for Nuremberg, May 16th, at 4 P. M., where we arrived at 11 P. M.

NUREMBERG.

Nuremberg is a quaint old German city of 100,000 inhabitants, in which we have a mediæval city preserved more perfectly than in any other of all the cities of Europe. But this being a German city, we have not alone a mediæval city, but a German city of the fifteenth century, in a beauty and perfection found nowhere else in Germany. Indeed within the walls the pleasing picturesque peculiarities of German architecture of the Middle Ages have been preserved almost as unchanged as have those of a Roman city, of the first century of our era, by the lava beds that covered Pompeii. Here within this old city we are brought in direct contact with the German civilization of 400 years ago, and are enabled to read in its stereotyped forms that witnessed the introduction of printing and the Renaissance of arts and science, what Germany then was without its forms being changed by changes that remoulded Europe. Consequently the most interesting thing to be seen in Nuremberg, is Nuremberg itself. Its quaint, old-fashioned houses, with their bow windows, quaint devices, high, steep gables, and red tiled roofs, how queer! Not alone the body, but the very soul of Teutonic mediæval times is in them, and we readily feel that we are listening to their expressions of incredulity, as the vague reports of the discovery of a new world are being circulated through these, then isolated, parts of the world, while its fortifications tell us that they were constructed when the bow, the lance and battle-axe, with coats of mailed armour were being replaced by the crude, short-ranged match and flint-lock musket, and were constructed to meet a want made necessary by times in which, practically, might made right, when all things belonged to him who could take them, and consequently when the persons and property of cities could only be made secure by such means as bid defiance alike to roving bands of freebooters, and invading armies. And against all of these perhaps no town in Europe had made such sure defence as Nuremberg.

First around the old town, of perhaps 30,000 or 40,000 inhabitants, a deep ditch thirty feet wide and twenty feet deep, was dug, and this lined with heavy perpendicular walls of solid masonry. On the inside of this ditch was erected, quite around the city, a solid stone wall of great thickness and thirty feet high, with, every hundred yards, a tower of different height and shape, rising thirty or fifty feet above the walls. The ditch and wall, some three or four miles in length, entirely enclosed the city, with strong gates at convenient distances, approached by a draw-bridge.   Before the invention of gunpowder and heavy cannon, 10,000 determined men—and these old Teutons were determined men—could have defended the city against an army as numerous as that with which Xerxes invaded Greece.

May 17th.—Drove around the walls of the city, visited the old castle, a former stronghold that protected rulers against the Nurembergers, as the city walls protected these against outside invaders. Visited many of the most noted houses and places— the statue of Palm, a Nuremberg patriot, who fell a victim to the remorseless despotism of Napoleon I.; also the statue and house of Dürer, the greatest of the German painters. Watches were first made here, and from their flattened, egg-like shape were long called Nuremberg eggs.

FRANKFORT ON THE MAIN.

May 20th.—Left Nuremberg at 9 A. M. for Frankfort on the Main, where we arrived at 5 P. M. Put up at the Hotel Swan, a hotel with accommodations inversely as the charges, prices high, fare mean. Our route was along the constantly-enlarging Main, which at the quaint old German town of Wurtzburg has become a navigable river, adown the beautiful, fruitful valley of which we continued to Frankfort, near its junction with the Rhine, and really within its vine-clad valley.

Frankfort, with a population of 140,000, is one of the most wealthy and oldest cities of Germany. In 790 Charlemagne held a convocation of bishops here and made it one of his royal residences. It is situated on either side of the Main, which is spanned by four or five bridges, some of which are 700 years old. It has the appearance of a modern city, with most of its objects of interest belonging to modern times. Visited most of these, among them the monument of Gutenberg, with its three statues of the printers, Faust, Gutenberg and Shaffer; a statue of Luther on the spot in the cathedral square, where he preached a sermon on his way to Worms ; the Romer, a quaint old building of the sixteenth century; the great shopping street, the Zeil; the Ariadneum, containing a most beautiful work in marble, Ariadne seated on a panther, by Dannecker; the Art Institute, a beautiful Renaissance structure situated on the left bank of the river, containing a collection of art works, paintings, etc., of which the Frankforters are justly proud; several excellent paintings by the Hobeins, elder and younger; a number by Rembrandt, Rubens, Hals, Tenniers and Van Dyck, of the Dutch and Flemish schools. The Italian school is poorly represented by P. Veronese, Bellini and Reni.

WIESBADEN.

May 23d.—This is one of the most popular watering places in Europe, some 60,000 persons visiting it annually. It is resorted to not more perhaps on account of its healing waters than its mild, equitable climate and the loveliness of its surroundings. It is a fashionable resort, where the wealthy and aristocratic classes delight to loiter away the spring or summer. It is an old watering place, known to the Romans, who built baths here prior to the beginning of the Christian era. The ruins of these baths, and also an old Roman fort, are found here at the present time, and as in this curious, searching age all things that have an antiquarian appearance are interesting in proportion to their approach to antediluvian times, these time-scarred ruins are perhaps of more interest and value than when useful. For a thousand years after the fall of the Western Roman Empire, Wiesbaden and its baths continued a source of strife between the Teutons, who possessed them by right of territory, and the rapacious Gaul who wanted them. During these fierce struggles, which lasted through the dark and early middle ages, this section changed hands repeatedly, Wiesbaden being several times burned and sacked by contending or conquering hordes. It was long the paradise of gamblers, and thousands of fortunes have been lost here. After a long and fierce struggle here between morality and sin, virtue finally triumphed over the gambling tables, modern civilization over barbarism, and in 1873 these gambling hells were closed, and the palatial halls turned over to the municipality.

Most of these beautiful improvements were made by the gambling company, who were licensed by the State, and so enormous were their ill-gotten gains, that after the property had passed into the possession of the Prussian Government, in consideration of their license being extended two years, they paid 3,000,000 of marks. The city paid 100,000 marks for the Curhaus and 47,000 marks for the furniture, but these sums represent but a small fraction of that which has been expended in embellishing this beautiful place, in rendering this one of the most enchantingly beautiful spots on earth.

The Colonnades consist of two long building porticoes, each 500 feet in length, open on the sides facing each other, supported by long rows of lofty marble columns. There are bazars containing almost everything that could tempt visitors to buy that which they do not need. These Colonnades are separated some 100 yards. The open plat or court between them is a most delicately beautiful tapestry garden, with two splendid fountains. Nothing of its kind can surpass the beauty of this miniature garden, with its fountains and adjacent colonnades. All these buildings and flowers are within a large park, with numerous ponds, fountains and flower-beds, and all re-embowered with a great variety of beautiful trees and shrubs, so that one can walk for miles along its graveled walks at noonday without being exposed to the rays of the sun. The number of different kinds of trees collected here is truly astonishing. If the intention had been to exhibit in these grounds most of the known trees of Europe, they could scarcely have collected a greater variety. Many of these trees are as beautiful as rare. Hundreds of hawthorn trees are interspersed with elms, beech, flowering chestnut, linden, oak, maple, willow, ash, sycamore, and other trees both native and exotic. The hawthorn is in full blossom and is the gem of the park, its only rival being the flowering horse-chestnut. Running all the length of the park, lining the sides of Wilhelm Strasse, is an avenue, some thirty feet wide, lined on either side with rows of old sycamore trees. At the farther end of this avenue, and just beyond the colonnades, is the covered way of 350 yards leading to the Kochbrunnen. Here a band plays from six to eight o'clock in the morning, at which time a great concourse of people collect to drink the waters and join in social converse between glasses.

We generally left our pension at 7:30 A. M., walked to the springs either through the park or along the Wilhelm Strasse, a distance of over a mile, drank two or three glasses of the hot, slightly salt water, and returned home and breakfasted at 9 o'clock, having walked two or three miles. The water is not unpleasant to the taste, being a little like weak broth. The drinking of these waters together with the use of the hot, warm baths are especially serviceable in rheumatism and gout. The old gouty Kaiser Wilhelm comes here annually to drink and bathe in these gout-dispelling waters. Well, if he would board at our pension he might dispense with drinking the waters, as our light, scanty fare would prove specific for gout, and yet in despite its scanty fare, the house is full, mostly English. I do not know why this is so, except that the house is kept by old English maids, and most English-speaking people find it difficult to speak the guttural of the Teuton, whose lips are of less service in talking than his throat. And then perhaps the light fare assists the waters in relieving the plethora produced by too much 'alf and 'alf indulged in by the average beef eating Englishman.

The museum of Antiquities contains some 1,200 specimens, many of them of great interest, consisting of relics of prehistoric man, primitive tools, weapons, ornaments of horn, stone, bones, shells, pottery, found mostly in caves.

May 29th.—Drove out with some English ladies to Sonnenberg and Rombeck. At the village of Sonnenberg is an old fort in ruins and watch tower built in the twelfth century. The old fort is on an eminence in the midst of a narrow valley, strongly built, and must have been well nigh impregnable. Though storm-battered by assaulting armies of the middle ages, and over grown with ivy, it is yet strong, fit emblem even now of the Teutonic ghost of olden times. From the high, rocky ridge beyond Sonnenberg we have a fine view of the most beautiful part of the Rhine valley—a long stretch of the river is seen as a silver thread winding through the vine-clad valley, bordered on either side by castellated hills, the whole country being checkered over with towns and villages, making a landscape of surpassing loveliness.

June 4th.—With our English friends, made an excursion to Niederwald, the Denkmal or National Monument. We took cars some four miles to the river, when taking steamer we ran up the Rhine eight or ten miles. Nothing can surpass the beauty of this portion of the Rhine, with its shores lined with towns, its wide extended plain a continuous orchard and vineyard, and the hill-tops dotted with ruined castles or modern villas.

We ascended the mountain by railroad. This road is about a mile long, is of a grade of 30°, being only a little less steep than the one by which we ascended Mt. Vesuvius, but of different construction. The cars on the Vesuvius road were drawn up the almost perpendicular side of the mountain by means of an endless chain, here they ascend by means of cogs placed on a wheel which works in notches in a central rail. On the top of the mountain is the splendid monument overlooking the majestic Rhine, at a point opposite to " Bingen on the Rhine," which was constructed at a cost of $250,000, in commemoration of the splendid triumph of the Germans in the Franco-German War. On the summit is a collossal bronze female figure, richly clothed, representing Germania. On the sides are beautiful bronze alto reliefs, representing Kaiser Wilhelm surrounded by the kings and princes of Germany, together with the most distinguished generals and statesmen and persons of Germany. Another side represents German soldiers leaving home. Another side represents their glad return after their glorious triumphs. It is a beautiful work of art, well calculated to gladen the soul of a Teuton or depress that of a Frenchman. On the corners are beautiful allegorical representations of peace and war. We returned to Wiesbaden about sun-down. The excursion was, perhaps, the most delightful of all those we have made in Europe.

June 5th.—This is the evening for the exhibition of fireworks, and though hardly well enough to be out in the night air, the evening was so beautiful, mild, balmy, with a cloudless sky, and the occasion offered so much to be seen only here—as the Wiesbaden exhibition of fire-works is supposed to excell all others in the world, that we yielded to the temptation, went out, and certainly were well paid for the fatigue and exposure to the night air, which fortunately resulted in no mischief.

The exhibition was in the park at the Cursaal, on the margin of the large pond, in the middle of which is the great fountain previously mentioned. Numerous colored lights lighted up the lake and adjacent parts with strange, weird, changing lights. Now the jet of water was a vast fountain of crimson, while the adjacent trees were clothed in silver, every leaf being beautiful filigree work. Now the color changed and a vast column of liquid silver arose in the middle of the pond, while the trees glowed in crimson and purple. Now commenced a fierce bombardment on the different sides, or all around the lake. Thousands of bright rockets flashed through the air exploding with terrific noise, while the whole air was filled with falling golden stars. Whole swarms of serpents waged a hideous and terrific battle in mid-air, and with a hissing noise charged and chased each other. Now a grand and wondrously beautiful performance of Blondin walking the rope across the chasm at Niagara. This was the representation of a man in, or of fire, walking on a fiery wheel on a rope of fire, rolling the flaming wheel of fire on which he stood, with his feet, running across, now backwards, forwards, swaying to either side as though he would fall, balancing with a long flaming pole of fire. This wonderful feat lasted perhaps fifteen or twenty minutes until the gauze-like, fiery image was consumed, gradually fading away.

June 6th.—Left Wiesbaden for the far-famed town of Heidelberg, where we arrived after a four hours run, and put up at the Pension Anglais. The road lay along the Rhine valley, passing through the quaint old German town of Darmstadt, where we made a short halt. Darmstadt is the capital of the Grand Duchy of Hessen, and contains some 50,000 inhabitants. Most of the way is through a densely-populated country, highly cultivated, with numerous towns and villages, with not a few ruined castles crowning the summits of the hills.

HEIDELBERG.

June 7th.—This is a university town—indeed owes all its importance to its world-renowned university, which, however, is not now of so much importance as formerly. The city, of 25,000 inhabitants, is situated on the west bank of the Neckar, (a small mountain river) some two or three miles from its junction with the Rhine. The town is built along the river in a narrow defile between mountains, some five or six hundred feet in height.

June 8th.—Took carriage and with an old Heidelberger, an Anglo-German lady, drove to and around the Schloss ruins, the Schloss Hotel, over the high ridge beyond. From the top of this ridge we had a magnificent view of the town and the valleys of the Neckar and Rhine. Descended into the valley some miles above the town and drove down along a beautiful carriage-way, through the rather pretentious Karlsthor, which separates Heidelberg from the village of Schlierback. This entirely useless and not very artistic gate owes its origin to the rather singular fact that the Heidelbergers found an excess of money in the treasury and not knowing what to do with it built this gate. Modern city treasurers are careful to let no like misfortune happen in these days.

The old castle, which is to the tourist one of the principal attractions of Heidelberg, is the largest, and perhaps the most interesting, ruin in Germany. It was first built in the thirteenth century, and to the old castle was added others by successive rulers, until with walls, terraces, towers, gardens, groves and shaded walks, it must have been a very fairy-land, and even now in its ruins, is impressive, grand, beautiful. This wondrous castle with its time-defying granite walls, ten to twenty feet thick, the glory and pride of electors, dukes, kings and emperors, was with the town of Heidelberg stormed, battered and partially destroyed during the Thirty Years' War, and the tower partially blown up. Again the French with a Vandal army took and blew it up, or rather blew parts of it down, as the walls in their massiveness were proof even against gunpowder. Again, after its partial reparation, lightning struck it, exploded its well-filled magazine of powder, and blew down a portion, lifting one-half bodily and removing it some twenty feet, where it settled down as a divided granite mountain, weighing thousands of tons. On the north side the old walls of the palace are still standing, storm-scarred, time-worn and ivy-covered, but in a tolerable good state of preservation, and evidencing the former splendor of the structure. Old linden trees that have witnessed the storms of centuries form a dense shade to a lovely graveled walk through the old court and gardens. Ivy-covered walls and massive rocks, old linden and poplars, covered to their summits with ivy, give to these ruins a sombre beauty, scarcely anywhere else met with to so great an extent.

We passed under the Triumphal Arch, erected by Elector Frederick V. in honor of his wife Elizabeth, of England, daughter of James I., who died here in 1615. Underneath the castle are deep cellars, in one of which is the great wine tun, which holds 285,000 bottles. It is the largest tun in the world, and unlike the palace above it has survived the Vandalism of wars and the earthquake shocks of exploding magazines, and stands now fast where it was first set up, in a deep vault twenty-five feet high. It was first filled November 10th, 1752, and has been subsequently only twice filled, and has now been empty 120 years. We passed through these dark, gloomy subterranean vaults, under arches and by pillars that looked as though they had been built to support a world, so massive were they in construction. Saw deeper still the darker and more gloomy donjon-keep, where many a hapless victim of tyranny has suffered cruel wrong for crimes never committed. With how many moans of helpless prisoners are these granite walls stereotyped. I could almost fancy they had embodied themselves in living, tangible forms that might yet be seen. Well, oppressor and oppressed have long since met at a Supreme

Court, where the royal robes and glittering cohorts of dukes and kings protect not against the accusations of their once helpless victims. We passed through the botanical garden to the concert platz, where we partook of ices and coffee while listening to a splendid brass band. We then passed to the elevated parapet next the river, from which we had a fine view of the city with its churches, the lofty spires of which were far below us, the bright flashing silver stream of the Neckar, the wide extended fertile valley of the Rhine, with the long, low range of mountains in the distance, the bright hill-sides of the streams, the long expanse of the Adenwald's thick, wild forest, which extended until lost in the darker foliage of the Black Forest; altogether a landscape view that for extent and beauty is scarcely surpassed in any section of the world. Passed off this to an adjoining grove, where seated on a bench in a thick cluster of chestnut trees we listened to the song of blackbirds— a thrush that sings much like our mocking-bird—also the softer note of the nightingale, until the sun had sunk behind the high tower-crowned hills of Heidelberg, leaving all around wrapped in the soft silvery shade of early twilight. We were all alone, the children with their nurse-maids that had been playing around us had gone home. Here and there a visitor to the ruins passed by returning to the city. When we descended along a quiet path that ran along, and under the projecting ivy-clad ruins, down the hill to the city. Well, all this was somewhat saddened by the reflection that we were old and alone in the world, and that we could not have visited this place when heart and brain were young and more impressible.

Attended the surgical clinic at the university, witnessed several clever operations by distinguished professors. Attended in the evening lectures at the university. Heard Prof. Fisher, the lecturer on Political Economy. He speaks fluently and is a man of much ability. The university is a large unpretentious one-story building, old and dingy. The lecture rooms are small, not well lighted, and furnished with seats placed on the floor without being elevated, all on the same plane, looking much like the furnishing of an old-fashioned country church or school-house. Each bench was capable of holding six or eight students, and had a plain plank nailed on the back for writing purposes, with another some six or eight inches below this for holding books, slates, etc. This apparatus of each bench is used by those occupying the bench behind it. Nothing could be more rudimentary or ill-adapted to the comfort of the pupils. The lecturer occupies a raised platform with a railing and desk in front, much like the pulpit in a country meeting-house.

There were present at Prof. Fisher's lecture forty or fifty young men, from eighteen to twenty-five years of age, a few older, most of them thoughtful, attentive students, many of them with their note-books taking notes.

There is another large class of students here, those particularly mentioned by Mark Twain as "Club Men." Each club is distinguished by its cap. I noticed among these, white caps with red bands, green caps and yellow caps. These caps form or belong to separate clubs, with little or no fellowship with caps of another color. These cap men are seen riding in twos and fours in fine two-horse carriages through and around the city, are met at the concerts, club-rooms, restaurants, beer-gardens, cafés, etc. At the castle restaurant there was near us a table of white caps with red bands. Not far off another table of red caps with white bands. Still another table was occupied by green caps, and another table was surrounded by yellow caps, all drinking wine, beer, and coffee, and smoking pipes, cigars, or cigarettes, and each table had several large dogs standing or lying around, and to which were given bread, cheese or cake, and I believe in some cases beer. Almost every one of these cap-club men had scars or fresh wounds on his face. Many had their faces covered with plasters; some had as many as eight or ten wounds upon their face. One spare-built lad I noticed had an ugly scar some two inches in length where his cheek had been laid open, doubtless to the bone. All the members of a table politely raised their caps when a member of another cap passed, but had no farther communication with him in public, even though a blood relation.

Now who and what are these cap men? They are not really *students*. True they have matriculated and figure on the university lists from year to year as students, but do not attend lectures. I failed to see one of them at any of the lectures either medical or literary, and those I saw in attendance upon the lectures were singularly free from scars or wounds—had indeed no right to either, as these badges of honor are for club men.

These young men whom Mark Twain found with so much leisure on their hands, are not here for the purpose of study, do not attend the lectures, but are the sons of aristocrats and men of money, who come here to spend some years of university life in attendance at clubs, gambling, drinking, riding, boating and dueling. Those who do not make shipwreck go up with their badges of honor, scars, to Berlin, Vienna or Bonn. But greatly the larger number, I fear, and certainly many, are wrecked, fall by the wayside, succumb to a two or four years' life of dissipation with wine and dueling. These scars are badges of honor, marking them as heroes, and are evidently passports to society, to promotion, but even for this purpose and with this reward are too often obtained at too dear a cost by the wreck of health and contraction of habits of dissipation that forbid future usefulness.

Why is this relic of barbarism still preserved, retained, fostered or even tolerated at Heidelberg? Why do the public authorities, or public opinion permit this savage relic of the Feudal or Dark Ages to exist here, to the destruction of multitudes of young men, who if better trained might make valuable citizens. For be it known the fault is not in these young men, but with those who foster a custom that encourages, or forces them to spend two or three years of their youth in habits, if not utterly destructive to their future welfare, at least utterly useless, in fighting duels or be branded as cowards. The only possible excuse that could be given for the retention of this savage and destructive custom is that it inures them to danger, and by making them expert, fearless swordsmen, furnishes a class of young men, representing the best families, those having the greatest interest in the State, ready trained and fearless of danger, to defend their country in times of need. But this excuse, that might have had force at the time the custom originated, when the lives of a community, a city or whole country might depend upon the personal prowess of a few well-trained, fearless, strong men, no longer exists, now that standing armies of well-trained officers and men are ever ready to defend the State against any foreign invader, while a paid police secures the individual against personal violence, and the enforcement of wise and humane laws throughout the civilized world, gives ample security to even the weakest in the protection of their persons and property, while the improvement in the military art has rendered mere brute courage, or individual prowess of but little or no avail. True, the *esprit de corps* of an army is of great moment, but it is as a multitude, as an organization it is so, personal, daring, only securing the destruction of the individual, and possibly endangering his fellows, not his enemies. Witness the Arab hordes, driven off, routed, slaughtered, murdered, by a small army of well-disciplined Englishmen, much their inferiors in personal strength, or endurance, in bravery as individuals, but invincible as an organized army.

It is a scandal and disgrace to the nation or people who permit or foster such wanton, self-destructive barbarism, and shows that these Teutonic peoples, notwithstanding their high accomplishment in many things, are really only half-civilized, still retaining much of the Vandal, wild boar instincts of their savage ancestors.

Met at the Medical Clinic, Dr. ———, of Chicago, an accomplished gentleman who is here on a visit to his family, who are here for the education of the children; and, really, if Americans must be educated abroad, which I do not admit—I know of no place in Germany preferable to this. The town is neat, clean and healthy, the inhabitants moral, sober, peaceable, intelligent, and the means of obtaining an education unsurpassed by any city in the world.

The town is Protestant; 13,000 Protestants, 9,000 Catholics. Luther preached here and the doctrines of the Reformation early found credit in this section. One of the largest, oldest and finest of the Catholic churches divided so equally by one portion professing the new doctrine that a feud arose concerning the ownership of the church. The reformers claiming it by virtue of their numbers, the Catholics claiming it because it was a Catholic church. The excitement grew into a bitter and bloody strife, when the happy expedient was adopted of building a partition wall across the church. This continued several generations, the demon of discord, not dead, but slumbering, when one of the electors, himself a Catholic, proposed to the Protestants to give up their half and he would build them a new church. This they refused to do, perhaps suspecting his sincerity, when enraged at their obstinacy, he had the Protestants expelled, the church and the partition wall pulled down. This resulted in a fresh outbreak of the feud with increased intensity, insomuch that the Emperor had the partition wall again rebuilt, and here it stands at the present day. The mass and mitre on one side, wine and bread on the other. Well, perhaps the devil will hardly see the wall, finding rich booty on both sides.

BADEN-BADEN.

June 10th.—Left Heidelberg for Baden-Baden, where we arrived after a run of two hours over a rather interesting, level country ; put up at Hotel zum Hirst, a most excellent hotel, with warm mineral baths in the house, and a fountain of the hot water for drinking, at the door. The rather small town of Baden-Baden is situated on the right bank of the small mountain brook Oos, consists of 12,000 inhabitants. At the upper end of the town, on a spur of the mountain is a grand old feudal castle, with groves, walks, fountains, etc. It was built after the destruction by the French, of the old Schloss, the ruins of which in beauty and grandeur, crown the rocky crest of a lofty mountain overlooking the town and valley of the Oos. The hot springs are also on the right side of the Oos, high up on the hill side just under the schloss. But with the exception of Frederickshall, a princely bathing establishment, are but little used at this point. The main body of hot water being carried across the town and, under the Oos to the beautiful and level grounds, or the left bank of the brook, at which place is the palatial Conversationhaus and the Trinkensalle, together with the theater and highly ornamented parks and bazars, with their fine wares to tempt visitors.

These springs, like those of Wiesbaden, were known to the Romans, and have been the resort of invalids through all ages. The waters have in fact little or no medicinal property, being only hot water containing a little, a very little, common salt, and are in fact not near so valuable as would be the water of the Sweet Spring at Brownsville, Mo., if the waters of this spring were drank hot. They are supposed to be especially beneficial in catarrh of the stomach, mucous membranes of throat and bronchi, gout and rheumatism, rather a full list, and as nearly all these complaints affect most the wealthy, privileged classes, good livers, it is with them a favorite resort. Like Wiesbaden, it was also long the resort of gamblers, a gambling company licensed by the State, owned it and made most of the costly improvements here with the accursed gains from their tables. Here many a princely fortune has been squandered and many a proud family reduced to poverty and want. Here many a new fledged hero of fortune has met the tiger and become his victim, not a stone in its costly edifices, but should have melted at the anguish these gambling tables have caused. But thanks to a higher civilization, these gambling dens have been closed ; let us hope, forever.

It it a beautiful place where art and nature have combined to make a very Eden, and perhaps no place on earth is more lovely and better calculated to inspire a love for this world, than the west bank of the Oos from Lisltanthal, to a point opposite the Hirst hotel, together with the charms added by the adjacent shaded nooks, pleasant walks, drives and surrounding scenery.

June 16th.—Took carriage and drove to the Alte schloss, an old fortress castle of the third century. It through all the dark and middle ages belonged to the Margarates, or rulers of this country, up to the time of its destruction by the French in 1689, during which time it was a palatial stronghold or castle, but for 200 years it has remained in ruins, but even in its ruins is grand, imposing, indicating what it must have been when the proud, old feudal lords, with their mailed knights and retainers inhabited it. It is a thousand feet above the town and so directly over it, that it hangs from the porphyry brow of the rock-crested mountain top, as if watching with its ghost of other days the changed scenes below. And, though not perhaps a mile from our hotel and accessible by the finest carriage road in the world, we were an hour or more in reaching it in the carriage. The castle was of immense extent, sufficiently large, I would suppose, to hold a thousand soldiers with dukes and their families, half a score. It was built upon and against the precipitous bluff, so that in many places its walls were the cliff-rock, in other places I noticed the walls were eight and ten feet thick. Foot passengers mount to the ruins by winding stone steps, in many places cut in the rock. I suppose the lower perpendicular wall is a hundred feet high, with a farther descent of hundreds of feet, almost perpendicular rocks, with the other sides rendered so inaccessible as to be impregnable to all but the modern means of warfare—gunpowder and artillery. Indeed without these it is no wonder it battled successfully for 1,200 years against the storms of time and those more destructive still, human foes.

The view from its lofty parapets is very fine, extending along the winding, picturesque valleys of the Oos and Rhine as far as vision extends. We took refreshments at the café kept, here and returned by a more circuitous rout along the dimly, darkly, wooded hillside to our hotel, having passed a most delightful morning. Next day with our friends drove out five miles through the densely wooded portion of the Black Forest, to Yager Haus, a beautiful sylvan retreat, where long a royal hunting club held its headquarters. Many a high revel has been held here, but now it is only a pleasant resort, with neat café. The view from this point is also very fine, the vast expanse of the Rhine valley, with here and there a flash of the silver stream, stretches away to andbeyond Strasburg, we could from here distinctly see the dome of the Strasburg cathedral.

On the way to the Yager Haus we passed some children—ittle girls—gathering ripe huckelberries, (whortleberries) growing on low bushes, just as we have seen them at home when we were children. We stopped the carriage to gather some, and bought a pint or more from a little girl who had a quart mug nearly full, we gave her ten pfennings, two and a half cents, which was twice as much as she expected, and for which she would gladly have given us the contents of the mug. We only permitted her to give us half, and gave her an additional ten pfennings, in all five cents. It was truly pleasant and worth far more than the berries, to see how her face brightened, she had perhaps seldom had so much money, and felt rich, indeed almost burdened with treasure. Well, after all, riches are only relative, and I remember when a child, I too would have felt that this was a large sum. We had the berries for supper, and thus far returned back in life many years.

FREYBURG.

June 19th.—Left Baden-Baden for Freyburg, where we arrived after a run of three hours, and stopped at the pension Utz. This pension was not excellent but we were induced to stop at it, as we were induced at some others, not the best, on account of its being the resort of English-speaking tourists, among them a very pleasant Irish family with whom we were acquainted. The road from Baden here is through the Black Forest, along the Rhine valley which is highly cultivated, while the hills and adjacent highlands are clothed in a primeval pine forest, the dark foliage of which throw their sombre, melancholy shadows across the winding river.

Freyburg is a manufacturing town of 36,000 inhabitants, mostly Catholics, and is situated in the midst of the Black Forest, on a small mountain stream, the Dreisam, in an amphitheatre of pine clad hills. It is an old German town. Many of the old houses, with their high gabled roofs and dormer windows, date back through the middle ages. Some of the modern houses are very fine. It is the seat of a university, many of whose professors have a European reputation. There are some 800 students here, many of them medical, with a large hospital, to which the great reputation of the medical professors in the university bring patients from a distance, giving it clinical advantages greatly beyond what might be expected from so small a town. It is a pleasant place to spend a few days. Its cathedral dates back to the thirteenth century, and is a large Gothic structure of some considerable beauty. It is ornamented inside and out with hundreds of statues cut out of old red sandstone, of Christ, Madonnas, apostles and saints, male and female, numerous bas and alto reliefs, sometimes rudely carved, and many of them strickingly archaic. These are mixed up, interspersed with numerous images of animals, many of them nondescript, but really not more so than many of the saints. But even this very archaic character really heightens their beauty, as it gives the life expression of a people just emerging from the night of the dark ages.

The semi-barbaric customs of the university clubs are in full force here. The students, as at Heidelberg, are divided into red, white and yellow caps, and most of them have their faces badly scarred from dueling. These scars, like the Mohawk's scalps, are regarded as badges of honor, constitute their possessors heroes. Cultivated or learned such people may be, refined they certainly are not, retaining to the latter part of the nineteenth century savage customs not tolerated in enlightened England, France or America.

The twenty-first of the present month was the seventieth anniversary of the *Red Caps*, and was celebrated much after the style of their barbaric ancestors. The principal event was the drinking and singing feast at the hall during the evening which, being invited, I attended. Long tables, four in number, extending the length of the hall, each table accommodating twenty-five or thirty guests, all members of the club and wearing red caps. Each plate was furnished with a glass. Six or eight officers sat at the end of the tables. These were furnished with long swords which were laid on the table in front of them. With these swords the exercises were announced by striking with them three loud raps upon the table, when all drank and sang a song, or sung a song and drank, or the band played some patriotic air or love song, when all drank. A few clever speeches were made at the conclusion of each, loud clanging of the swords announced another drink. Some of those present had been members of the club in their university days. These had on the red cap, and each of them, besides drinking with the others, of all the regular and irregular drinks, had in addition, to drink a mug of beer for each year he had been a member, and as many of these were men of middle age and a few old men, it necessitated, in some cases the drinking of twenty or thirty glasses in addition to the regular drinks. At the conclusion of each song and drink the glasses were brought down on the table with a loud and rather rhythmical sound. The entertainment, while partaking so much of barbaric Teutonic times, was really not otherwise objectionable, but quite enjoyable. The singing being excellent, the speeches good, and the behavior of the young men much more orderly and much less boisterous than would have been on a like occasion in America. These red caps being so accustomed to full potations of beer, that even the enormous quantity of forty or fifty glasses that the old members had to drink, had but little effect upon them.

June 23rd.—Drove out with some English ladies to Hotel Sternen, a post station fourteen miles from Freyburg. The road leads through the Schwaberthorn, running up the beautiful fertile and highly cultivated valley of the Dreisam. For the first eight or ten miles the valley is broad, with fine crops of hay, rye and wheat. I never saw better crops than here, no not even in the Mississippi valley. The valley is at first two or three miles broad, bordered by lofty hills, which in some places are cultivated quite to their summits, others too steep or rocky for cultivation are covered by dense forests of dark pines, interspersed in some places with the lighter colored but equally dense birch and linden. Several old ruins are seen on the rocky crests, while numerous villages dot the valley or hill-sides. Many quaint old German barn-like structures, containing the family, together with the horses, cattle, hogs, poultry, dogs, farm implements, wagons, carts, ploughs, hoes, rakes and store of winter wood are seen along the road-side. Twelve miles out the valley suddenly contracts and we enter a narrow gorge, called the Hellenpass or vale of hell; walls of ragged granite rise on either side hundreds of feet in perpendicular frowning buttresses, overhanging, in some places the road. At the narrowest part of this gorge, where the walls some 200 feet overhead are only separated a hundred yards, is the Hirschensprung, upon a lofty projecting point of which is the statue or wooden image of a stag with immence branching horns. At this point legend informs us, a monstrous stag of a size and strength only known to days of yore, when Woden and his followers were wont to visit this forest, hard pressed by a Teutonic king and his pack of dogs, also of monstrous size and strength, leaped the chasm and alighted on the rocky cliff beyond. It is so pleasant to believe these old legends; that I never permit myself to doubt them. While musing on the feat of this old Teutonic stag and comparing it with a like statue and similar feat of a hard pressed stag at Carlsbad, we scarcely doubted the truth of both legends, but then stags and dogs as well as men have degenerated since that day.

We drove along the wild gorge until the very considerable stream of the Freidsam became a small branch, still wild as its mountain home, to the post station, Hotel Sternen (star), where we took dinner, and after resting an hour, returned to the city at 8 o'clock P. M., having been absent seven hours. The drive was most enjoyable and the road, one of the finest in the world, was first built by the Austrian Government in 1770. Shortly after its construction, the princess Maria Antoinette, drove along it on her way to France, to wed the Dauphin, afterwards Louis XVI. Unfortunate princess, it was her last view of fatherland, a fatal trip, big with ghastly horrors. She and her husband were imprisoned, insulted by the blood-thirsty, hooting mob and beheaded by the Jacobins. How strange! I have here in the room where I am writing this, just after returning from this ride, a fine steel engraving of this lovely woman, princess, queen and her family in prison, guarded by brutal, drunken soldiers, and from which she went to the scaffold a few days afterward. How strange are the vicissitudes of life, from the palace to the gaol, to the scaffold where her headless body was scoffed at by an insane rabble. But far be it from me to suppose this rabble had no cause of complaint against its besotted rulers, and if the innocent suffered with the guilty, it was what too often happens. The French people had been so wronged, insulted, robbed, trodden down, oppressed by kings and priests, that we cannot wonder at their excesses when once in power. This drive was in the very heart of the Black Forest, with its wild forest-clad hills and dales, seemingly big with unseen dangers, from robbers, goblins, headless giants and wild beasts, but really containing only peaceful, industrious, honest men and women and playful fair-haired children.

It was in the midst of hay-making, and a few men with troops of brawny peasant-women were busy in the meadows. These peasant-women in this Black Forest have a peculiar build—a breadth of shoulders, waist and hips I have nowhere else seen, nor do I believe such exist anywhere else. They are in fact a different style or race of women from all others, *sui generis*. Almost all of these women are peculiarly formed—not deformed, but on the contrary made to be the mothers of a race of giants. And while the mountain peasant men are large, well-formed, I wonder that they are not larger than they are—indeed, why they are not giants. It must be that the almost constant devastating wars in which these people have been engaged, either in self-defence or for conquest, by calling for the largest, tallest men to supply the wants of their armies, have kept down the standard of these, while the female has retained the characteristics of their grandmother. This like condition, and as the result of the cause suggested, is notably the case in Italy, where the women as a class are larger and better proportioned than the men, and it is a fact well known that the destructive wars of Napoleon I., who called out by conscription or otherwise, the tallest Frenchmen to constitute, fill up, his armies, has reduced the military standard from five feet ten inches to five feet eight inches, reducing the average height of Frenchmen two inches. The same laws that apply to other animals, and even vegetables, apply to man, he forms no exception, by virtue of his position as man.

Now if by a process of selection, either natural or artificial, only the largest and tallest of these mountaineers were married with the most brawny of these peasant women, a race of giants might be produced, in which Maximilians, the ancient German eight feet tall, and who could pull a cart that an ox could not move, and who, by his Herculean exploits, so won upon the Roman army that they made this ignorant barbarian Emperor, would be common with this people.

Visited the large, well-apportioned city hospital; attended interesting clinics of learned professors; witnessed several important operations. The great ability of some of these professors with the ample clinical material at their disposals, constitutes Freyburg an important point for medical education. A large number of attentive medical students were in attendance at the clinics. None of their faces were scarred. They did not belong to the cap men, their attendance here meant business.

June 26th—Arose early in the morning and ascended the Schlossberg, returning to breakfast—a walk of three or four miles. From the top of the Berg we had an extended view of the valley, and so densely populated is the country that from where I sat I could count seventeen towns of from two to six thousand inhabitants each. The town was spread out as a map nearly immediately beneath me. I could almost have counted the houses. The old Clock Tower, a quaint structure; the Munster, with its lofty turrets, that have looked down upon the stirring scenes of struggling hosts for a thousand years; the quaint old houses with their sharp gables, dormer windows, red-tiled roofs, and time-worn walls, from which issued many a bold crusader to do battle against the Turk for the possession of the holy sepulchre; old churches and quaint moss-covered structures, at whose portals the tooth of time had been busy for half a thousand years; all were distinctly seen as in a picture, all being tinted by the golden rays of an early June morning, that reflected every light and shadow of these old structures with great beauty and distinctness. I remained here quite alone an hour or more, only disturbed by an occasional early visitor to the Berg, viewing the historical panorama spread out before me, and whose strange interesting ruins mixed in fantastic forms with the realities of other days, until mediæval manners and customs stood out in full dress from their quaint niches and battle-scarred turrets.

BASLE.

At 8 o'clock A. M., took leave of our kind-hearted Irish friends, and took the train for *Bale*, (English) Basle, (French) Basel,

(German), an important town in Switzerland, where we arrived after a run of five hours, and stopped at the Hotel Trois Rois —Three Kings, an excellent hotel standing immediately on the left bank of the Rhine, from the waters of which, like the palaces on the Grand Canal in Venice, it seems to arise, as its river wall is the walled bank of the Rhine. Took carriage and drove over the city, visiting the Munster, an old cathedral, the lofty, time-worn parapets of which stand out as beacon-lights from the gleam of the dark ages, and whose storm-battered walls of old red sandstone have witnessed the rise and fall of empires. Many of the houses are 600 and 800 years old, bringing us by and with their queer old fashioned construction in contact with the mediæval ages. Customs here as well as the houses have scarcely felt the impress of the nineteenth century.

FALLS OF THE RHINE.

June 27th.—Left Basle at 10:30 A. M. for Neuhausen, or Falls of the Rhine, sixty-one miles, where we arrived at 1:30 P. M.

The weather was warm, the cars somewhat crowded, the train moved slowly, rendering the trip rather tedious and uncomfortable. The road was most of the way along, or near, the rapidly flowing Rhine, which here is bordered on either side by lofty spurs of the Black Forest. The valley is in part very fertile and all the way highly cultivated, presenting with its little farms with stone walls or trimmed hedges the appearance of beautiful landscape gardening, which the topography of the country renders highly picturesque. The whole country is so densely populated that four or five towns and villages are sometimes in sight at the same time. The hill-sides, where not too steep and rocky, are planted in vines to their summits, while the dark pine forests covering those not cultivated give to them that dark, sombre appearance peculiar to the Black Forest.

The rapidly flowing river grows ever quicker as it hurries on, until at Shaufhausen, some two miles above the falls, the *vis a fronte* of the falling waters is seen in its becoming more narrow, with a marked fall in its surface, while the waters, dragged on with an irresistible force, are lashed to foam long before reaching Neuhausen.

Above this boiling mass of waters, some half a mile above the main fall, on a projecting rock, hangs the old Schloss, a monastery of the fourteenth century, but long since deserted by the monks. But the spirit of meekness of the order lingers in its deserted halls, as if in communion with the wild spirit of the waters, whose angry turbulence it would still. From the old monastery hall, steps descend into a cavernous vault deep below. In this cavern passing a spring of fresh water, we step out onto a piazza quite against the surging billows, the wild rush and roar of which are grand, sublime, awe-inspiring. The rock trembles at the shock, the head grows dizzy and the heart faint at the immediate presence of this stupendous force of nature. The Schloss is now used as a museum and picture gallery. Many beautiful works in carved wood and inlaid tables, cabinets, etc., of Swiss workmanship, are kept for sale here. Some excellent modern paintings, with a few old paintings of but little merit are in the halls. It is approached from Neuhausen by a railroad bridge which spans the angry flood at this point.

Upon inquiry, whether man or beast had ever passed over these falls and lived, I was told that several bold swimmers and many animals had been caught by the draw of the waters at and above this point, and were dashed to death against the hidden boulders or drowned in the billows, only one instance was known of any animal having passed over the falls alive, and this was an old, vicious and worthless dog, whose owner determined to destroy him, and threw him in the rapids above the

Schloss, where he passed over the falls without injury, swam ashore and returned home to torment his owner.

We stopped at the palatial Hotel Schweizerhof, which is situated directly in front of the falls, on the crest of a hill 220 feet above the river. We sat for hours upon the spacious piazza, where we had taken dinner, listening to the deafening roar, and watching the rushing maddened waters as, lashed to foam and spray, they plunged over boulders, and dashed against torn granite columns in their onward leap and thundering fall into the boiling caldron, deep below. Late in the evening we descended the hill along a graveled, shady, winding path to the edge of the water, where resting upon a bench beneath a fragrant and wide spreading linden, with the eddying currents of the angry whirlpool at our feet, and clouds of spray above and around us, we remained long at the very foot of the cataract, watching the changing colors of its iridescent sea foam, and ever changing clouds of spray that, wreathed in fantastic forms, hung like winged spirits around us, and formed rainbow colonnades above the foaming caldron mass of falling waters, whose deafening thunders shook the solid earth beneath our feet; while nature, as if in symphony with the maddened spirit of the river, returned in audible echo from caverned hill-side and distant mountain top the trembling sound.

The moon was in its full, and just as the sun was setting behind the western hills its broad-faced disc was coming up above the long line of distant Alpine mountains that lift their snow-capped summits above the eastern vale, with its rays falling full upon the winding river, turning its foaming waters into a stream of molten silver, and its spray into clouds of sparkling silver lace.

'Tis midnight, the great bell upon Shaufhausen's cathedral has just tolled twelve, and the sentinel from the lofty parapets of Munoth's Watch Tower cried, "All is well." The lights have gone out and all human voices are hushed or drowned by the deafening roar of these noisy waters. The full-orbed moon hangs now directly over the falls, giving, by its soft rays, a more weird appearance to the wreaths of spray that hang like spectres of the night above the foaming waters. Silent, alone I sat upon the lofty balcony of our room, watching the changing sheen of this molten silver glory, and listening to its ceaseless, deafening thunders, that startle even the dull ear of night, until oppressed by the tangible, audible spirit that was over and round about me, in very helplessness I cried to the Rhine god, to hush these ceaseless, weary wailings. Why I asked, disturb thou the slumbers of men? Know you not that man is of more importance, mightier far than thou? When from the midst of the foaming waters came a voice; saying,

"Since time began, through ages all
   Hushed have been my thunders never,
While nations rise and kingdoms fall
   Wailing, I flow on forever.

" My palace hall is ocean's wall,
   Its floor is strewn with dead men's bones,
With crystals, pearls and gems, and all
   Its structures are of precious stones.

" Proud cities perish, temples fall,
   Mortals' works are stable never;
To crumbling ruins perish all,
   I live from, and to, forever.

" The might of man lasts but a day,
   His aid nor care ask I never,
When he and his have passed away,
   Murmur on shall I forever.

" The first of Night and Chaos born
   With trident I rule the ocean,
My spirit builds the cloud and storm,
   Changing forms and modes of motion.

> "Cloud-driving Jove his bolts of war
> That startle earth, air and heaven,
> Borrows from my o'erflowing store,
> In Vulcan's forge newly riven.
>
> "My name is Neptune, god of sea,
> Of this and every river,
> All nymphs and sea-gods own my sway
> From Ganges to Guadalquivir."

Enchanted with this place, its flower-gardens, its cool shaded walks, its fragrant bowers, embossed with woodbines, honeysuckles and climbing roses, its forest glens where nightingales, forgetful that it was day, filled the groves with sweetest song, with its picturesque landscape of hill and dale, dark pine-covered mountain-tops, cultivated hill-sides and vine-clad valleys, we were loth to leave, and lingered here yet another day, basking in the Arcadian loveliness of this earthly Eden, where

> Swift as our thoughts the days come on to stay,
> But fanned by gentle breezes, made, poets say,
> By angels' wings, pass quite as soon away.

ZÜRICH.

June 29th.—Left for Zürich, where we arrived after a run of two hours. After dinner drove over the city. Visited the academy, hospital, cemetery, etc. From the eminence above the town we had a fine view of the city, lake and distant snow-capped Alps. Zürich is principally distinguished for its silk manufactories. Left Zürich in the evening for Lucerne. Arrived at 5 P. M. and put up at the Pension Hotel New Schweitzerhof, located high up on the hill-side overlooking the city and lake of Lucerne, with the lofty storm-engendering Pilatus to the right, and the Rigi on the left, with a long snow-clad range of Alps in front, forming a panorama wild rugged, grand and beautiful.

LUCERNE.

Lucerne, the capital of the canton of Lucerne, is an old town of 20,000 inhabitants, situated on either side of the clear, bold lake river Reuss, which issues from the lake at this point in a rapid current. The city is rendered picturesque both by its construction and its old walls and watch-towers, one of which is in the middle of the Reuss, placed here as a point of defense, also by its quaint old covered bridges, three or four hundred years old, and which with the new iron bridge serve to connect the two parts of the town. These bridges are ornamented with paintings of the Middle Ages. One of these Kaltenbruck contains 150 paintings, illustrating ecclesiastical and historical subjects. The other is ornamented with quaint old paintings, reminding us of the Campo Santo at Pisa, called the "Dance of Death." An object of far more beauty, and one of which the Lucerners are justly proud, and which no tourist will fail to see, is the colossal statue of a couchant lion cut on the face of a sandstone cliff. This beautiful work of art is intended to commemorate the brave and desperate resistance the Swiss guards made against the attack upon the palace at Versailles, which this mere handful of Swiss guards defended against a thousand times their number, and would have successfully defended Louis XVI., the queen and royal family, but for the cowardice or ill-conceived advice of his counsellors. In this fearfully unequal combat they stood as a living iron wall against the fierce assaults of the enraged and ever-increasing mob. As their comrades fell, the lines closed in to prevent a breach. The palace hall was full of their dead and dying, and its floor shoe-deep in blood, but not a man was dismayed or faltered in his duty to God and the king. Already the mob were driven out, and in despair, when the guards were ordered to desist, and lay down their arms, in the vain hope that the assailants would withdraw. But, as might have been expected, the mob were only maddened by the withdrawal of resistance, broke into the palace, put the remainder of the now defenceless guards to death, and took the unfortunate king and queen prisoners. The lion is resting his paws on the French flag, in his dying moments attempting to defend it. A large wound in his side is represented, showing that the defence only ceased with life. At this point also are the beautiful, interesting and instructive Glacier Mills, which we shall refer to in describing the Rigi.

But it is not Lucerne itself, so much as its surroundings, that constitutes this place an important point to the tourist. These are indeed beautiful, grand, imposing, as we are here in the heart of Switzerland, with its crystal lakes and wild, snow-clad mountains and fields of glacier ice. First we have here the beautiful Lake Lucerne, which, with its connecting lakes extends into four cantons, and is perhaps the prettiest lake in Switzerland, with its rugged mountains rising in the distance to the region of perpetual snows, and which are brought into panoramic view by ascending the two more immediately accessible mountain heights that tower over Lucerne, the Rigi and Pilatus.

RIGI KULM.

The Rigi is ascended by means of a railroad, to reach which we take steamer at Lucerne and run across the lake to Visnau, situated at the foot of the mountain. The road runs up the side of the mountain to its loftiest summit. This road is constructed with a third rail running through the middle, in which runs a cog-wheel, dips through tunnels, spans, by means of gossamer bridges, yawning chasms and hugs the cliffs on the edge of frightful precipices overhanging the unmeasured depths below. But so solid is its construction, and so careful the management that we feel assured, while the enchanting scenery so captivates us that we forget all danger and find ourselves placidly contemplating the quiet lake thousands of feet directly under us, and calculating the time required to reach it should the wheels miss the rail only a few inches.

July 4th, 1885.—We had been some time at Lucerne, and had determined to spend this, our national birthday and night, on the Rigi. The morning had been dark and stormy, and our kind host and hostess warned us against going, as we would be unable to see anything on account of the mists and fog which not seldom obscure the vision on these mountain heights, and pointed us to Pilatus, whose top and sides were covered with threatening mists and darkening storm-clouds, from whose depths issued deep-toned bellowing thunders, in confirmation of their prophecy. But not having the respect for Pilatus as a weather-guage for all this section, known to and felt by all true Swiss, in despite these warnings, we left our pension, determined to spend the night of the 4th in or above the clouds, and, as usual, fortune favored the brave, and we arrived at the Hotel Rigi Kulm an hour before sunset. Scarcely were we half-way up the mountain, when the clouds cleared away before a brisk northwest wind, and we had a serene, cloudless sky with a glorious sunset. Watched from these lofty heights the god of day as he mantled himself in a golden glory and sank behind the far-off snow-crested Alps, casting back an Alpine afterglow, that, as illuminated shadows from his royal robes, lighted up hill and dale with a soft silver light, known only to these Alpine regions. His setting well became the glory of a god.

We entered the hotel and drank at supper a glass of sparkling Swiss champagne in remembrance of fatherland, and a health to those we had left behind us. At half past three o'clock, we were aroused by the sound of the Swiss horn that rang through hall and corridors with much the soft musical cadence that did the long cracked tin horn with which the stage driver announced his coming into the village when I was a boy. We were quickly dressed and out on the parapet, the brow of an almost perpendicular cliff that towered a mile above the vale below, to witness the sun lift his magnified disc from behind the distant serrated snow-capped Alps, lighting up with a sea of golden glory this vast range of snow-crowned Alps. Grandest among these mountain giants were Jungfrau, Finesterhorn and Titlis, that glowed in their silver mantles of eternal virgin snow, while the vast fields of glacier ice sparkled as seas of liquid silver. Far as vision could extend in a cloudless sky, Alps arose around, beyond and above Alps in a white, serrated line around us, embracing the far off Jura Alps, whose lofty summits were seen to pierce the very heavens as they blended with the distant horizon. The scene was impressive, grand, awe-inspiring, overwhelming us with the magnitude of this snow-mantled range of mountains, while the rarified air, aided by our lofty position, gave an extent to vision that seemed to embrace half the great globe. We stood here 6,000 feet above the sea, watching this gorgeous, ever changing scene, the home of mountain terrors, until the sun was an hour high. Enchanted by this glorious vision, we stood on the parapet from whence the lakes and cities and farms of the valley were dwindled into ponds, clusters of play-houses and tiny gardens, when the scene below us changed, and such a change! At first the lake seemed lifted up to near where we stood, and covered with transparent sheets of granulated ice, looking like frost-work on a window-pane, and this was so earnest, real, that I called the attention of several persons near us, who saw it much as we did—now spectre form spread their immense snowy wings and rose up near us, changing form, now stopping, now springing up in surging billows, until towns and lakes and farms disappeared in a thick fog, which hid all below us in a mantle of night, which rolled in fleecy clouds at our very feet, while all was clear, bright, serene above and around us.

After breakfast, we started out over the summit; saw a number of chamois and other Alpine animals that were kept in a small menagerie here. Viewed with glasses and marked out as if on a map, the distant mountain peaks.

The Rigi Kulm, like nearly all these Swiss mountains, when not covered with perpetual snow, is clothed to its summit with green verdure. Even far above the timber line, these beautiful mountains are covered with rich pastures. Thousands of sheep and fat cattle pasture upon the sides and very summit of the Rigi. We noticed droves of small, agile Jersey cows and calves around the Rigi hotel, 6,000 feet above the sea. Not only are these lofty peaks and mountain sides clothed in richest grasses, but thousands of bright flowers make them very flower gardens. This peculiarity, nowhere else to the same extent met with, gives to the mountains of Switzerland, much of their irresistible charm. How different from the dreary, monotonous, sombre appearance of the hills of Scotland, where from base to summit they are clothed in the dreariness of peat bogs, whose eternal sterility corresponds with their forbidding, gloomy appearance.

A peculiarity of the Rigi that I have scarcely seen mentioned, is the entire mass of the mountain, as seen in its perpendicular walls of from two to four thousand feet, in its projecting peaks, in the sides of the tunnel and railroad cuts, is composed of cobble-stones and water-worn pebbles, cemented together with lime and clay. Millions of tons of these smooth water-worn pebbles and boulders are here piled up into a mighty mountain mass 6,000 feet high. Where did they come from, and how were they made, and by what almighty force were they piled up here? ' The stones out of which they were made must have been brought here and polished by some stupendous force or forces acting through measureless ages. Strange to say, the mills in which some of these stones might have been manufactured, exist here in number and perfection, found nowhere else. On the surface of a hard granite rock at Lucerne, some thirty of these mills of various sizes and perfection are seen. Many of them are like hominy mortars, some as small as druggist mortars, others of great size; one twenty-five feet wide and thirty feet deep. All of these have one or more cobble-stones lying at their bottom. These stones vary in size, from a cannon-ball to that of a flour barrel.

That these stones and the mills bear in some way the relation of cause and effect, that is, that these stones have been rounded in the mills and at the same time have made the mills, there can be no doubt, but how? Glacier action has been invoked to account for this. But millions of years, with millions of such mills would scarcely suffice to account for, or make the amount of artificially rounded stones found here. And then how were they piled up into this mountain? Certainly glaciers could not have done this as their action is to smoothe down, not to heap up. In fact, glacier action in manufacturing these stones, like the Darwinian theory of "Natural selection and survival of the fittest" having formed the present genera and species of animals and plants, is accepted because it to some extent accounts for *how* these things *may* have been produced without proving that they were thus formed.

PILATUS.

The other mountain, Pilatus, is a bold, torn, rugged mountain, almost isolated from the Alpine chain. It stands as a sentinel to watch and guard, to catch and to intensify, a laboratory to manufacture the storms of this entire section, and serves as a barometer, or storm-gauge for the people who consult this mountain for their weather chart.

Pilatus is 7,000 feet at its summit above the sea, and yet is not covered with perpetual snow, though snow falls upon it every few days during the summer, snow covered its sides and top yesterday, July 3rd. A hotel is situated near its summit, standing at the base of almost inaccessible torn granite columns that rise as needles, 200 or 300 feet above its rugged crest. At the base of these is a deep lake, through whose sluggish ill-omened waters the plummet falls to the cavernous depths far below. Tradition informs us that Pontius Pilate, when driven out of Judea, mad at life's history and in remorse for the part he had enacted in the scourging and death of Christ, came here and drowned himself in this lake. And we are assured by reliable visitors to these forbidding heights, that of dark, stormy nights, his unquiet spirit disturbs its waters, while strange wailings are heard and strange phantom lights are seen to play upon its unquiet waters. Certain it is, this mountain has a bad name and no peasant passes its dark shadows, even in midday, without crossing himself.

It is said to be the home of the cloud-compelling Jove, who, mad at the misfortunes of his favorite Greece, and disgusted by the frequent visits of the bold mountain-climber, left Mount Olympus two thousand years ago, and builded here his throne, and here forms clouds and storms surcharged with thunderbolts newly riven, and drives them against the affrighted giants of this entire Alpine region. Many conjectures have been made why all the storms of this part of Switzerland originate in or around the granite riven crest of Pilatus, but none have been deemed satisfactory by the inhabitants except that which makes it the throne of the storm god, or the home of the evil spirit of Pontius Pilate. It is not so great a favorite with the tourist as the Rigi, not alone on account of the difficulty of ascent, but also, because, though 1,000 feet higher than the Rigi, we seldom obtain so good a view, as it is most generally more or less clothed with mists or clouds. When, however, these are not present, the view is truly grand, well repaying the toil of its ascent.

THE BRUNER PASS.

July 7th.—Left Lucerne at 10 A. M., for Interlaken. The first twelve miles to Alpnach is by boat across Lake Lucerne. From Alpnach to Brienz, twenty-five miles is by diligence, from Brienz to Interlaken by steamers.

The route by steamer across Lake Lucerne is rendered interesting, both by the beauty of the lake and high, perpendicular, picturesque wall of scarred granite or scarcely less abrupt walls of cobble stones, that by diligence from Lake Lucerne to Brienz is so highly interesting as to cause us to forget the fatigue, and become oblivious to all save its surpassingly beautiful scenery—deep chasms, beautiful, wild mountain glens, flashing water falls and lofty Alpine peaks covered with eternal snows. From the summit of this pass is seen a silver stream of water issuing from beneath, or between the overhanging rock, which falls a thousand feet or more into a deep chasm, unlighted by the rays of even a noon-day sun. Yet, though a large stream of water, the mountain trembles not at its fall, as long ere it reaches its lowest depth it is dissolved into clouds of silver spray, light and lovely as the gossamer veil that hides the face of the blushing bride at the altar, and like the unseen clouds that too often hang around the bridal altar, are seen not by the curious world, but gathered to themselves, flow on and on to the gathering again of broken ties in the far off lake, whose gathered waters tell not of the storms through which they have passed. Four thousand feet below us is seen the sheen of Lake Brienz.

This lake is of a light soapstone color, caused by the snow and ice just melted from and beneath glaciers, with a great quantity of air entangled in its waters, and this milky color of the lake is continued in the river, flowing from it along the west side of the Interlaken valley to Lake Thun. At Brienz we take steamer for Interlaken, passing within sight of the beautiful waterfall of Geisback, thought to be the most beautiful waterfall in all Switzerland. A hotel is situated on the lofty, almost inaccessible mountain top, and the cataract lighted up of nights by a calcium light. Some of the passengers landed here to visit this, but we were satiated with wild scenery, and continued on to Interlaken, putting up at the fine Hotel Beaurivage.

INTERLAKEN.

Interlaken is a narrow valley enclosed between high mountains on either side, and lies between lakes Brienz and Thun. It was evidently at one time a continued lake which has been filled at this point by debris brought by the river Oos, from the mountains above.

The valley contains some 4,000 square miles, is very fertile, or is made so by the cunning industry of man, who is forced to wring from reluctant nature treasures which she does not possess. It is densely populated and contains several small towns and villages, the principal one of which is Interlaken, situated on the river and in front of a wide gap in the mountain foot range, that permits a fine view of the loftier snow clad mountains beyond, grandest among these are Jungfrau, Silverhorn, Breithorn and Wetterhorn. The town is only of importance to tourists as a central point from which to visit these Alpine giants, and consists mostly of hotels and pensions and shops for the sale of numerous articles to tourists, such as b(itiful carved wooden objects—Alpine sticks, poles, canes, cl mois hoin canes, etc., etc.

GRINDENWALD.

July 10th.—Took carriage, and in company with our Scotch riends, drove to Grindenwald at the foot of Jungfrau, which rises nearly 14,000 feet above the sea, and flanked by Silverhorn and Schneehorn all covered with mantles of eternal snow, some of whose crystal flakes may have witnessed man's first transgression or blushed at his vain attempt to build the Tower of Babel. At the very foot of these, near the smaller glacier, is situated the hotel. Here we took horses, wife remaining at the hotel, and rode over a wild, broken path to the foot of the great glacier, a wall of ice hundreds of feet high; entered a grotto that has been cut several hundred yards into this blue hyaline mass. It is impossible to imagine anything wilder, grander than this vast sea of ice, rapidly melting in the rays of a July sun; a river rushes from beneath it, while lofty, irregular spectre-like masses, weighing many tons, hang in startling grandeur along and above its perpendicular walls. These ice masses becoming detached by melting are seen toppling over, falling with a thundering sound into the gorge deep below. This glacier is from some unknown cause, now slowly receding, and has been for years. I noticed in the worn, scraped granite rock walls of this gorge indisputable evidences that this great glacier at the foot of Jungfrau, had, in comparatively recent times, extended over the ground on which we were standing, reaching down and filling up the deep gorge some half mile below.

This I pointed out to our company, who thought I must be mistaken, but on returning to our hotel at Interlaken and mentioning the fact to our landlord, who is an old and highly intelligent and cultivated Swiss gentleman, he said I was correct, that when he accompanied Agassiz to this glacier forty years before, they walked over this ice gorge at the point I had indicated, that it had been receding for many years, and should this continue Interlaken would loose much of its charm to tourists. But this he did not expect, as from some unknown cause glaciers for many years contracted, and then from like unknown causes they rapidly expanded. This must be the result of a series of cold or warm seasons. While I was pleased to have my scientific observation thus readily confirmed, I was surprised that it had been so recent, as I thought most likely it had been centuries since this change had taken place.

The air at this place, notwithstanding it was midsummer, was chilly, wintry. After returning to the hotel and taking lunch we returned late in the evening to Interlaken, having had a delightful drive through a wild mountain gorge of twelve miles out and return, twenty-four miles.

LAUTERBRUNNEN.

July 11th.—Took carriage and drove to Lauterbrunnen, Staubach, eight miles. The road leads up through a wild chasm lined on either side by precipitous walls of granite or limestone and silt, that rise four and five thousand feet above the mountain torrent, and in some places directly overhanging the road. Great granite masses, weighing in some instances hundreds of tons, lie scattered in wild grandeur throughout the gorge. These great granite masses have been detached from these overhanging walls by earthquake shocks and have fallen to their present places with a force that must have shook the great globe to its center. Nothing can be grander or wilder than this chasm, with its time-worn, lightning scarred and earthquake riven walls, that mount to the very clouds, and may have been erected as barriers by the gods against the giants in their wars with this fierce earth-born race, or their mother Ge, who fought with her children, may have built them for the giants to scale heaven. In either case, with what almighty force these walls have been prepared may be seen in the distorted, twisted, vertical layers of rock that have been bent and wreathed as willow twigs. At the upper end of the lower valley is Lauterbrunnen (all springs) and Staubach (Dustbrook) —here we are again at the foot of Jungfrau and Breithorn, but the view of these, owing to projecting cliffs, is not so good as at Grinwald. The principal attraction of Lauterbrunnen, besides its cool air and wild, rugged scenery is the Staubach, a waterfall, where a considerable stream of water falls over and down a perpendicular granite wall, 960 feet. It is called dust stream from the fact that at its first appearance on the brow of the cliff it is seen as a cloud of dust, powder, smoke or spray, having been already lashed into spray by its previous plunge from some more distant height, and this appearance as a cloud of bright smoke or dust it maintains to the foot of the rock, a bright cloud of silver smoke or lace swayed to and fro by the wind, now disappearing, now as a bright mist, wreathed in fantastic forms, and flashing in the sunbeams as a bridal veil of glass lace. We sat long at the foot of this cataract watching this weird bridal veil, made for water nymphs, whose airy forms were scarce concealed as they blushing drew this mist-veil around them, nor until the evening shades were throwing their spectral shadows across the gorge did we return to the hotel where we had left our carriage, took coffee and drove back along this cool Alpine gorge to Interlaken, all alone, our Scotch friends having left for Paris. These lofty mountains, like the Rigi, are clothed even to their summits with green grasses and bright flowers; hundreds of cattle, sheep and goats find rich pastures here, while far up their steep sides, as far as and even above the timber line, houses are seen; one of these not less than 6,000 feet above the sea is seen from this gorge hanging upon the brow of a seemingly inaccessible mountain top. These houses are the summer home of herders, who go upon the mountains with their flocks after the melting of the snow in May, and remain with their herds until driven down by the fall of snow in October. Where many of these houses are the snow falls sixteen to twenty feet deep in winter. How dreary must be the lives of these goat-herders during the short summers, separated from all mankind, surrounded only by their herds, utterly ignorant of all that is going on in the great world below them, they live the lives of hermits until the kindly snows drive them back to the society of men. And yet so wonderfully are we constituted, that, though the most gregarious of all animals, more so than even the bee or the ant, we are readily adapted to circumstances, substituting the society of our dogs and goats for that of men. Who can say that the lonely mountain herders and chamois hunters are not happy?

Our kind-hearted, gentlemanly host was, as before remarked, a man of much intelligence. I now found him a man of great moral, social and political worth. In a general conversation I remarked that drunkenness was greater in Switzerland than with any other people. At first his national pride was naturally touched, and thinking only of the reforms introduced he was much tempted to, if not deny, at least to extenuate it, when I referred him to the report of the Swiss legislature (of which I found he was a member), when he frankly admitted the truth of the report, and stated the reason of the former prevalence of drunkenness, with the remedies applied. Formerly, as I knew, wines and liquors of all kinds were admitted from France and Italy, duty free, while no hindrance was put upon the manufacture, by the farmer, of cheap liquors from barley, potatoes, etc., whereby not only was it rendered throughout the rural districts quite possible to get drunk on a few cents, but much of the food produce of the country, was distilled, causing drunkenness, idleness, crime, poverty. With great difficulty the legislature was induced to pass laws against home distilleries and place a high duty on imported liquors, by which the masses were made more temperate by necessity. This great moral change had been brought about through the aid of temperance societies established in every town and village, and these I learned from this gentleman were established upon a wiser plan than any I had ever known. All temperance societies as such, signing pledges not to drink, are failures, and then these could not have been established at all in many of the rural districts. In the place of these, taking advantage of and improving the almost universal taste and fondness of the Swiss for music and singing, they established social clubs, singing societies, in every neighborhood. These societies were at once popular among the young people, as membership in them served not only for the culture, but gave at once social recognition, and not to be a member, either from not joining or from expulsion, was everywhere considered as constituting the young person as unworthy of social recognition, and this in despite of wealth or family. These societies abjured wine-drinking, and any member getting intoxicated was immediately expelled, and after a second offense was not only deprived of his certificate of membership, but all the other Societies were notified of the fact. He then became a pariah, an outcast from society, one with the mark of Cain upon him, with whom it was dishonorable to associate. Thus these societies, including all the young people, not only served as schools for instruction, badges of social position, but at the same time enforced sobriety with a certainty nothing else could have done. The result was magical. It sent up to the legislature sober temperance men, who passed the laws referred to, which acting upon the ignorant masses by necessity, and upon all the better classes by social and moral suasion, were rapidly making Switzerland the most temperate of the countries of Europe. Our host himself was, as I learned, President of these societies in his canton and an able temperance advocate.

FROM INTERLAKEN TO BERNE.

July 15th.—Left Interlaken at 1:30 o'clock for Berne. Took railroad to a point on Lake Thun, two miles, where we took steamer for the town of Thun, situated beyond the lake on the river Aar. This river, after forming lake Brienz, runs across the isthmus of Interlaken into Lake Thun, from there to Berne, and after receiving the river from Lake Neuchatel, empties into the Rhine a short distance above Basle. Thun is situated on this river just after it leaves the lake, at which point we took cars to Berne, where we arrived at 7 o'clock P. M.

Lake Thun is one of those beautiful sheets of water that give so much interest to the scenery of Switzerland, and is unsurpassed for the quiet beauty and often picturesque grandeur of its landscape views, and lake shore, by any other like body of water in the world. At first the lake retains the milky appearance, though not so marked as in Lake Brienz. Soon it becomes a bright blue color, reflecting from its transparent waters every passing shadow. The portion of the lake next Interlaken is bordered by mountains, wild and Alpine in character, rising from 4,000 to 6,000 feet above the lake, and often with perpendicular walls of 1,000 feet, with wild rugged peaks rising to the region of perpetual snow. Gradually as we approach the lower end of the lake the mountains become undulating, high hills, cultivated to their very summits, and so densely populated that the houses constitute almost a continuous village. The steamer touched at several points on either side of the lake. Beautiful villages with ornamental hotels or pensions indicated the great multitudes of visitors to these regions during the summer months, though I learn that it is a delightful residence even in winter. These hotels and pensions were not confined to the towns but nestled among the vine-clad hills, with long shady avenues, and pleasant graveled walks, overhung by the wide-spreading branches of lime trees, constitute very Edens, where one of a cultivated, contented mind might spend a season with as much pleasure and quiet happiness as in any place on earth.

BERNE.

The road from Thun to Berne is down the narrow valley of the Aar, and uninteresting—soil poor and scenery uninviting. Arrived at Berne, capital of canton Berne, and also of Switzerland. Put up at the very excellent Hotel Bellevue, situated near, but a hundred feet above, the Aar. It was only a few days before their annual International Shooting Feast, and all the city was gaily decorated for the occasion. Many thousands of streamers and flags waved over the city. Every hall and public building was gaily decorated, reminding us much of San Francisco two years ago when the Knights Templar met there, or of Copenhagen last year during the session of the International Medical Congress.

Berne is a mediæval city of some 40,000 inhabitants. Many of its features have stood through the storms of time, unchanged. It stands upon an elevation almost surrounded by the Aar, which flows as a rapid mountain torrent 100 feet below the city. Its site was evidently selected on account of its easy defense against attack, and consequently even in this, points back through the Dark Ages, when only might made right, when inability to defend only secured attack. The Aar is spanned by several bridges connecting the two parts of the town. One of these is the iron railroad bridge. Another a beautiful iron bridge with three arches, the principal one 100 feet above the river. The objects of especial interest are first the old Clock Tower, a quaint old structure, with a clock much like that of Strasburg. A curious and massive mechanism moves at each hour, at the time of striking, numerous figures. We were, however, disappointed in this performance, for, while ingenious, it was, we thought, rather tame, and not near so fine as the clock at Prague. Visited the Cathedral, an immense and splendid Gothic structure 500 years old. Visited the museum, which I shall not attempt to describe, though its collections are to the Archælogical student, or lover of natural history, of very great importance. Saw and bought a photograph of the faithful and intelligent old St. Bernard dog, Barry, who though only a dog, did in his day more good, and made for himself a brighter immortality, than most men. It is said that this noble and sagacious animal, whose history I would here relate did not the world know it, saved the lives of some seventy persons, who must have perished but for his self-denial and devotion to duty.

Visited the Graben, containing bears, which, like the wolf to the ancient Romans are sacred animals with all true Swiss, especially here in Berne—the city Berne receiving its name from this rather uncouth and awkward animal. A bear is on the Swiss banner, bears on the coats of arms, bears ornament the fountains, bears in the houses, bears on the walls, in the bedrooms, bears in the shops, bears in wood, in ivory, in gold, in marble, in bronze, indeed bears everywhere. Visited the Corn Hall, an immense structure with store house, cellars, intended, and formerly used to store corn and wine during seasons of plenty, for and against seasons of famine, reminding us of Joseph in Egypt. But this, as Joseph's storehouses, was before the time of railroads, which by making it possible to feed a people from a distant province, make famine, want, an impossibility, and though no longer used or needed they speak trumpet-tongued of other days, ere man had so far triumphed over time and space by steam and the telegraph as to bring the ends of the earth together, and by outrunning the sunbeam in its flight, is enabled to prevent, by anticipating, the wants of men. Took carriage and drove over and around the city. At 1:30 o'clock took cars for Freyburg where we arrived at 7 P. M., put up at Hotel Grand National.

FREYBURG.

July 17th.—Freyburg is an unimportant town of the middle ages, built upon a projecting high point, with the mountain torrent Saane running in a deep gorge nearly around the town and more than 100 feet below it. The torrent is spanned by a suspension bridge 900 feet long. Another suspension bridge spans a yawning chasm 350 feet above the stream. It is a fortified town surrounded with its walls of the early middle ages, and in every nook and corner of this non-progressive town, the ghost of other days spreads its wings at noon-day. Attended the old cathedral to witness the monthly performance on its grand old organ, one of the finest in the world. The cathedral was dimly lighted with a single small oil lamp, intended, I suppose, by shutting out all other senses, the better to leave that of hearing the more acute. The music I must suppose was grand, but I am compelled to confess that I failed to *see* it to the extent of gushing ; possibly I was not in a good mood for doing so ; could not see satisfactorily ; was not sure that I was secure from ghosts in the gloom ; certain it was that I was not "moved by the concord of sweet sounds" as I was at a much less pretentious musical performance during high mass at the Lateran in Rome.

LAUSANNE.

July 18th.—Left Freyburg at 11 A. M., and arrived in Lausanne at 1:30 P. M. Much of this route is along and over a cultivated district, with the latter part of it affording the most enchantingly beautiful landscape pictures in the world. We pass through several long tunnels, after passing through the last, the lovely Lake of Geneva, Lac Leman flashes upon us in a panoramic vision of enchanting loveliness.

Sunday, July 19th, 1885.—Lausanne is a Calvinistic town of 30,000 inhabitants, and not worth visiting, if one has any other place to which he might go. We put up at Hotel Gibbon, as doubtless thousands before us have done, for no other reason than that here Gibbon concluded his immortal work, "The Decline and Fall of the Roman Empire," in 1778, a work that has been more read, praised and abused than almost any other work of man, and from the mere fact that it was written here will give to Lausanne a place in the world's history when much that its people now most pride in shall have been forgotten.

Well, we expected to find here some memento, some immortelle to the memory of this man, but found not a trace, not even the name Gibbon carved on tree, bench or stone, nothing whatever to indicate that such a person ever lived or wrote here or elsewhere. We were shown the tree under which it is said he was wont to sit, no name carved upon its bark or bench; we were also permitted to inspect the two little rooms in which he lived while here—again no trace of the event. Wise, however, as serpents in all things that make for pelf, they have named the hotel Gibbon. This catches the tourist or visitor and does bigotry no violence.

The old cathedal, an old Gothic structure, is situated upon the lofty crest of the hill overlooking the city and the Lake Geneva, and is reached from the Gibbon Hotel by ascending some 200 stone steps placed at different points of the hill. It being Sunday morning, we wished to attend service in this venerable pile, big with historical incidents, not the least of which was the famous disputation between Calvin and a Catholic priest, which after a fierce struggle, not without loss of life, resulted in the Catholics being driven out, dispossessed of their church, and the Calvinists being installed instead. And what did these people gain by the fearful struggles this commotion caused? Only a change of masters, and, I am constrained to believe, a change for the worse.

The morning was warm, the route circuitous, the ascent steep and tiresome, and although we had left the hotel early it was perhaps nearly 11 o'clock before we, quite fatigued, reached this old cathedral, at whose turrets the tooth of time had gnawed in vain for more than half a thousand years. We approached it with feelings of awe and reverence begotten by a knowledge of the great things it had witnessed. Though time for church we noticed the doors were closed, and as we approached to enter the church two young women placed as sentinels or guards on the outside came forward to meet us, as was their duty, informed us that services had commenced and therefore we could not enter. What! not enter the house of God, because, forsooth, as strangers in a strange place and not knowing the difficulties of the ascent, we had been so unfortunate as to arrive at the church doors a few minutes late? The house of God closed because services had commenced or were about to begin? And were only those fortunate enough to be present at the beginning of the discourse fit to be saved, while strangers and those belated were turned into hell? Well, if this be Protestantism, and it seems to be here in Lausanne, give us Catholicism. In all our journeys through so-called benighted, priest-ridden Austria and Italy we have seen nothing to compare to this. Everywhere the doors of Catholic churches, like gospel gates, stand open wide day and night. At all hours and everywhere these churches are what they profess to be, houses of God, where the soul-burdened man, woman or child, though a wayfarer and stranger, may enter their sacred walls to ask from indulgent heaven consolations earth has not given.

Being denied admission to the church, we returned to the hotel, ordered our baggage sent to the steamer, and felt a positive relief when, an hour after leaving the cathedral walls, we left on the steamer for Geneva.

GENEVA.

Left Lausanne at 11 A. M. for Geneva, where we arrived at 12 P. M. and put up at Pension Picard, a most excellent pension. We found a number of very pleasant Americans here, among them Dr. Stevens, author of the "History of Methodism," and "Life of Madame De Stael," with his family.

Geneva is an old city of 50,000 inhabitants, much of it finely built. The old part of the city is mediæval, with steep tile roofs and narrow, winding streets.

July 21st.—Visited the cathedral, whose Gothic worn walls and turrets have witnessed the retiring clouds and darkness that shrouded Europe in her long night of gloom, caught the first twilight of the middle ages, as the returning crusader diffused through the songs of the troubadour, the dim light brought from other lands, saw the aurora dawn of the Renaissance, and with proud defiance of storms and time, stands yet in its prime as a witness and promoter of the glorious light of the present day. More than 800 years have come and gone since first its altars were erected, and its deep-toned bell summoned its worshipers or tolled the funeral knell. Alas, what multitudinous hosts who once worshiped here have been forgotten, time out of memory. How many blushing brides have stood before its altar who have been followed by their children's children to the lonely grave, where more than half a thousand years ago time's finger wrote,

"To dull forgetfulness a prey."

For more than half a thousand years, this old cathedral was Roman Catholic, but in the sixteenth century its congregation became Protestant. No saints, no madonnas, no high altar, no statues of Apostles are seen; all is as plain as the spiritual tastes of its congregations require or demand. In walking along its sombre aisles, I could but think the ghosts of these things looked out at me from the walls and made moan from the empty niches.

The chair in which Calvin sat when in the pulpit is still seen here. It is as straight-backed and unelastic as Calvin could have been, and I fancied I saw a striking likeness between this old chair and its former occupant. Why not? Does any one suppose there is a stone in this old pile but is redolent with his thunders that shook Europe with a moral earthquake, whose vibrations will be felt with ever increased and increasing force to the end of time? Visited also Calvin's old house in which he lived during most of the time of his ministry here, but little or nothing is found here to remind us of the former presence of this great man. The building is now used by the Board of Health and the rooms for charity clinics. We visited not his grave, for the reason, if no other, that the exact spot where rests his dust is not certainly known, and we dislike doubt in anything that concerns Calvin, who had none. Whatever may have been his faults, doubt was not one of them. When he came to die, he enjoined it upon his friends that no monument should be erected to his memory, and in very kindness and veneration they observed his request so literally that no stone was placed to mark the spot, and, like Moses, "where he was buried, no man knoweth to the present day." This I was told here by those who ought to know. I have seen it contradicted, but have the best of reasons for believing his grave is unknown, though guides, doubtless, could be found in Geneva who would point it out to the curious tourist for money.

July 22nd.—Took steamer, and in company with some very pleasant American friends left for a trip around the lake, but principally to Chilon, an old mediæval castle-prison, whose strong prison wall confined many a hapless victim, who on entering them, passed through only on his way to heaven, among these the illustrious, the noble Bonivard. We descended deep down into its gloomy donjon keep, saw the rock and iron ring to which he was chained for many fearful years, traced the deep path worn in the rock by his naked feet as he walked forward and backward the length of his chain. This castle-prison with its horrid woes, like the Bridge of Sighs at Venice had sunk into dim remembrance. The echos of the dying groans of its hapless victims had almost ceased to reverberate through its dark, damp, dismal cells, until reanimated by the genius of Byron, whose poem " Prisoner of Chilon," will live and stir the souls of men against cruel wrong, when its massive rock-built and time-defying walls have crumbled to decay. Yea, when the vast depths, "a thousand feet or more," through which the plummet sinks near its walls, shall, like its moat, have become dry land. We carried along with us and read, as shall yet a thousand generations of children's children do, this immortal poem, which echoed back from the gloomy walls, seemed the spirit of its victims.

> "Chilon, thy prison is a holy place
> And thy sad floor an altar, for 'twas trod
> Until his very steps have left a trace,
> Worn as if the cold pavement were a sod
> By Bonivard ; may none those marks efface,
> For they appeal from tyranny to God."

We climbed up and looked out of the small, doubly iron-barred window upon the only cheerful spot he could see.

> "And then there was a little isle
> Which in my very face did smile,
> The only one in view,"

which is a beautiful little island on the opposite side and upper end of the lake, about a mile off, and looks from the castle much like a large tub sitting in a garden lake. It was walled around, and planted with three elms, the only ones for which there is room, by an English lady a hundred years ago. These three trees are upon it now, and appear from the castle much like three large orange trees in a garden tub, setting in an artificial lake of crystal water. Nothing can be more peaceable or lovely than the view from here, these old prison walls alone remind us "like the smiling prospect of Ceylon," that "only man is vile." But thanks to the spirit of the age and changed conditions, even these old prison walls are wont to wreath themselves in smiles, which half conceal the wrong they have witnessed in other days; and why should they not, since captor and captive, oppressor and the oppressed have long since met on common ground? How sad it is to feel and know that life as short as man's should be spent in oppressing his fellow man! When shall the new gospel of the universal Fatherhood of God, and the universal brotherhood of man—that man is only less divine than his Author—make us really love and treat with brotherly kindness all our race?

July 24th.—Took steamer and went to Coppet, a pleasant run by steamer, of an hour from Geneva. This old chateau, and former Swiss home of the great financier Necker and his wonderfully gifted daughter, Madame De Stael, is, and will long be a holy place to all those who worship at the shrine of genius. The chateau is in a good state of preservation, and still in the possession of Madame De Stael's descendants. Her granddaughter lives here now, but we were sorry to find her absent from home at the time of our visit. We were politely shown through the principal rooms, once occupied by Madame De Stael and her literary friends, among them Lord Byron. The large library saloon has its book-cases, with their well-filled shelves of valuable treasures, much as she left them, with the costly tables, chairs, cabinets, old piano and many other things much as when last she fondly saw them. We saw a glass box of curious workmanship and filled with keepsakes, little mementos, souvenirs of loved ones, just as she had with loving hands arranged them, pictures and engravings hung upon the walls of the room, doubtless just as she had placed them. How touchingly lovely! To me these mementos were more eloquent than Tully, her spirit breathed, burned, in everything in these walls. To those who love all that is intellectual, grand and great in woman, Madame De Stael will appear truly sublime. With a soul too proud to bow to earth's despot and ruler, Napoleon, to whom the kings of the earth were bowing the supple hinges of the knee to ask for thrones, she refused to do him honor, and dared to withstand the tyrant on the throne, and in her incomparably brilliant conversations in her saloons, with the force of the red-hot thunderbolts of Jove, threw nightly the ghost of the murdered liberty of France in his face, at his feet, until the affrighted tyrant, appalled by the danger of the ghastly corpses, stooped to banish her by edict from her much-loved France. This fearless woman was mightier with the pen than even the conqueror of Europe was with the swords of half a million men.

The mausoleum of father and daughter is enclosed by a high wall in a silent grove near the garden. It was erected by her father and enclosed with this wall, pierced only by a door. He was buried here, and at her death Madame De Stael was laid by her idolized father, and according to his will the entrance was walled in, and all the world shut out forever. Since then this holy ground has never been tread upon by stranger's feet. Lovingly united in death, as they had been through a stormy life, they await here the last trump. Let all the world hope that "now that life's fitful fever's o'er, they sleep well." Is there a man or woman who could retrace our steps through this long to be remembered day without emotion? We dropped a tear as an immortelle to her memory, and late in the evening with no wish, no capacity, to see more, returned to Geneva.

Immediately opposite, across the lake, nestled away among romantic old trees far up on the side of the hill that overlooks Lake Leman, is the beautiful villa, occupied by Lord Byron while here. Down near the edge of the lake stands his boathouse in which his boatman lived. Byron had just then parted from his wife and been driven out of England by public opinion which his proud soul, though more keenly feeling the pang of the disgrace than any other man could have done, was too proud to conciliate. Frenzied at the thought, and mad at life's history, it is said that of dark and stormy nights when the Bees blew the maddened waves against the affrighted shores with a fury and a roar that startled the inmates of adjoining church yards from their coffined slumbers and whitened the shore line with shrouded ghosts, who, thinking the last trump had sounded, were anxiously expecting earth and sea to give up their dead, Byron would call up his boatman, order his boat, hoist sail and drive with frenzied fury through the white-capped waves that had no terrors such as racked the storm-tossed soul of him who dared their fury.

The affrighted boatman, though a Swiss, a bold swimmer and unused to fear, conscious of the danger, a danger greater than mortal man or fiend infernal was wont to meet, counted his beads on such occasions; and when contrary to all human expectations, he again reached shore returned pious, deep, sincere thanks for his unexpected providential deliverance and with trembling awe looked upon his master, who was disappointed in his wish of being drowned, as possibly being his Satanic majesty himself embodied in human form. Daily this pious boatman, after saying his morning prayers, swore by all the saints in the calendar to run away, to fly from this terrible danger and perhaps from the service of his old enemy, the devil, who his catachism had taught him to fear even when in a safer place than on Lake Leman, in such nights.

July 25th.—Took carriage and drove through the suburbs of Geneva and around the picturesque and highly improved lower or western portion of Lake Leman, passed by many palatial villas that adorn the hillsides, among these the summer residence of Baron Rothschild. From one of these lofty points we had a splendid view of Mount Blanc, that near Chamois, fifty miles off, lifts its eternal snow-capped summit to the very heavens. It is a splendid sight as seen through our glasses even from here, so massive that it confounds distance, appearing close by us, and so brilliant, as clothed in its mantel of virgin snow it sparkles and flashes in a noonday sun that we feel almost pained by the glare.

July 27th.—Left Geneva at 7 A. M. in diligence for Chamoinex, fifty-three miles distant. The road passes at first through the beautiful and densely populated environs of the city and three miles out passes the intersecting line, France-Savoy, soon reaching the valley of the Arne, a wild, muddy, mountain torrent, up which we continue to near its source at Chamoinex. Some thirty-five miles out from Geneva we reach a considerable town St. Martin, where we obtain a fine view of the Mount Blanc range of snow-clad mountains. And so great is the magnitude of Mount Blanc, that distance is apparently annihilated, it appearing to hang almost directly over us, while in fact it is ten miles to its base and twenty-five miles to the point at which we are looking, its summit. The valley up which we pass is but a deep gorge between lofty, perpendicular walls, rising thousands of feet above the river Arne, which has in many places at some time occupied the entire valley, leaving nothing but rounded stones and pebbles, rendering all efforts at its reclamation utterly fruitless.

At other points it widens out into a valley half a mile or more in width. These points are very fertile by nature or have been rendered so by the industry of man and are highly cultivated and densely populated, so much so, that scarcely a square rood is unoccupied, the houses presenting an almost continuous village; and even the mountain slopes in many places are cultivated to points far above the timber-line, while the neat little Swiss cottages are seen even upon the ofty summits.

At one point where the valley is lined on either side by wild, precipitous walls of granite, cistose and mica, slate, rising to the very clouds, we come upon a mighty battle-field where was fought the greatest battle that earth or heaven ever witnessed. We have seen in the gorge, between Interlaken and Lauterbrunnen the field where the vanguards of the two contending hosts first met, and fought desperately for choice of position, while the main battle, a battle that decided the status of earth and heaven, of gods and men, was fought here. And had we no other proof or knowledge of this great event than that given in its rock-leaved pages here, we still might trace the stages of this fearful struggle and mark the advancing or declining fortunes of the contending hosts.

But fortunately we are not left alone to this rock record, either for the nationality of the forces engaged, the causes producing the war or its results and consequences.

The sacred historian Moses, in his chapters devoted to the world's early history, without entering into the particulars, as these were foreign to his purpose, with a clearness and fullness of meaning known only to inspiration, gives us the names of the parties and the causes leading to this unpleasantness in these expressive words, "There were giants upon the earth in those days and the sons of God beheld the daughters of men and saw that they were fair." Heathen mythology gives us the particulars by and through which we are enabled here on the battle-field to trace the varying fortunes of the day.

This discovery of the gods referred to by Moses, resulted in the cultivation of too close an acquaintance, whereby numerous demigods were produced upon the earth. This very naturally aroused the jealousy of the giants who determined to destroy the gods by storming heaven. Thus was the beauty of woman the cause of the first war as certainly as was the beauty of Helen the cause of the siege and destruction of

Troy. War being declared, the forces of earth were gathered upon this battled-scarred plain. And where could they have selected a better point than this, where the summits of the cloud-piercing Alps lift the earth to heaven?

The battle must have been a long, fierce and bloody one, in which the gods drove back the impetuous, determined, assaulting giants, by tearing off great granite blocks from these mountain summits and hurling them at the attacking party as they attempted to scale these perpendicular walls of thousands of feet in their furious efforts to reach and storm the battlements of heaven.

Many of these blocks are as large as a Swiss cottage, while some of them are as large as the Milan cathedral. Thousands of these missiles of the gods lie piled, heaped up in and across the valley, some of them having been thrown from a height of more than a mile and to a distance of a mile from the base of the parapet, against which the giants had placed their scaling-ladders.

The contest was at length decided against our ancestors, of whom Hercules was but a degenerate scion, not from any superiority of strength or valor upon the part of the gods, but by mere advantage of position. Had the result of this contest been different, as from the valor of our remote ancestors it deserved to have been, we, the lords of creation, instead of being confined to earth as at present, might have been in full possession of heaven. But this change of position, while it might have gained us many and great advantages, as wives and daughters were left at home during these assaults, might have lost us woman. If so, I gladly accept the result.

This road, which has been built with incredible expense, runs nearly all the way up the narrow valley, but occasionally when this is contracted to a mere chasm cleft through the mountain through which the river rushes with the roar of a cataract, leaving no room for a road, it mounts to a lofty height along the precipitous wall that overhangs the river, only separated from the precipice by a few feet, which is occupied by a low stone wall two feet high. At these points we look down from the top of the diligence, or out of the windows over this low wall down the yawning chasm a thousand feet and more upon the angry river, whose wild roar fails to reach our dizzy height.

The diligence is drawn by five horses and these are changed six or seven times, so that each trip requires no less than thirty or thirty-five horses. Greatly fatigued we reached Chamoinex at half past four P. M., and stopped at hotel de l'Union, a very good hotel, except that the semi-barbarians are unacquainted with any Christian language. Only French is spoken. The hotel is situated immediately at the foot of the Mont Blanc group. A beautiful cascade is in front of our window, it is a bright, clear stream from melted snow and ice, which leaps down the almost perpendicular side of the mountain 6,000 feet, breaking into silver spray. In the early morning it is only a silver line, in the afternoon, when the vertical rays of a July sun have kissed the fields of snow and ice that rise a mile and more above and beyond the point at which it is first seen, it becomes quite a torrent. The river Arne, which flows immediately under our window, observes the same daily peculiarity.

MONT BLANC.

Took carriage and drove down the valley some two miles, to a point opposite the glacier Mer de Glace, where we left the carriage and, accompanied by our guide, ascended the foot of Mont Blanc, some 2,000 feet above the valley. The road is a wild mountain path, overshadowed by trees and great granite blocks which have been detached from the sides of Mont Blanc and driven by former glaciers and piled up in

MONT BLANC. 265

wild grandeur along the sharp ridge. Under the protecting shade of these we often stopped to rest, when after traveling two or three miles, we reached the foot of the glacier, the ice wall of blue, crystal, sparkling beauty, that rose from 100 to 1,000 feet in front and above us, and half a mile to two miles wide, and from eight to ten miles long, containing ice enough to fill all the ice-houses in the world. Near the foot of this glacier wife rested, while I with the guide ascended half a mile or more along its precipitous wall, where hung hundreds of feet above us thousands of icicles as large as church steeples. Many of these were constantly falling with a thundering sound into the cavernous vault below. The wildness, majesty and beauty of this ice-field cannot be described—must be seen to be appreciated. Late in the evening we returned from this ice gorge to our hotel.

A MULE RIDE.

July 29th.—Engaged a mule and guide for the ascent of the Brevent, a lofty rock peak overhanging the valley west of the village of Chamoinex. The ascent is very laborious even with a good mule, and requires four hours. We had made arrangements with the factotum of the hotel to procure us a good mule, and guide who spoke English or German, all of which he failed to do as we found when too late to remedy it. The guide was a stupid Frenchman, who scarcely knew any of his mother-tongue and not a word of German or English, while the mule was an old draft animal that possessed in an eminent degree all the vices. stubbornness, laziness, mulishness, devilishness, without any of the virtues, steadiness of foot and sagacity, of the beast known as *mule*. The road a mere bridal path, difficult and dangerous, zigzags up a depression in the side of the mountain where every 100, fifty or ten feet we are compelled to turn short to the other side. The stubborn, stupid, lazy beast was dragged around one end at a time with difficulty, and not until his head was quite over the perpendicular wall of twenty or 100 feet. At one point the path was defective and falling away on the perpendicular side, and after, with much difficulty dragging one end of the mule around, the other with his hind legs remained on the point of the path that was giving away, I sprang off on the upper side, fully expecting, and really hoping to see the stupid beast go over the precipice into the chasm a hundred feet below. The guide, however, who was really as worthless as the mule, took in the situation, and by seizing the bridle extricated the beast. The sun shone against this mountain side intensely hot, and after much toil and fatigue with walking much of the time, at 11 o'clock we reached *Place Bel Achat* a small inn hanging like a bird's nest upon the brow of the mountain 7,000 feet above the sea. Here we took coffee, rested and proceeded on our way to the dome, one and a half hours farther, and 2,000 feet higher up the mountain, the bridle-path becoming ever more difficult and dangerous, running now on the narrow backbone of the ridge, only as wide as the path with, on either hand, nearly perpendicular sides to the valley thousands of feet below, and to add to the difficulty and danger, the mule had become more and more mulish, until now it would often stop, and no amount of beating or kicking would move it an inch, until the guide took hold of the bridle and started it again, when, like some infernal machine, it ran or moved until it stopped again, which, I noticed, was nearly always at just such points as were least desirable for prolonged parleys, as I could not alight on either side without standing on the brink, or falling over the sides to the valley below. After two more hours, near 1 P. M., I reached the dome, which is only thirty or forty feet square, with precipitous walls overhanging the town of Chamoinex, 7,000 feet below.

Here I met with several persons, one an English lady from

our hotel who had preceded me on foot, and had been here long enough to lunch and rest. This point is a giddy one, not only from its great perpendicular height, 9,000 feet above the sea, but also from the very small space we have to stand upon. There is no snow upon the summit, nor is this even called a snow mountain, or one covered with perpetual snow, notwithstanding the fact that we are here 2,000 feet above the vast glaciers and perpetual snow fields across the valley. The reason for this is the same that prevents the Aiguille being covered with perpetual snows, though some of these around us are nearly as high as Mont Blanc. There is no surface on either for snows to gather or lie upon. In the depressions on the side of the mountain, where snow can accumulate, thousands of feet below where I am standing, the snow and ice are six to ten feet deep, or even much more than this. At one point, we passed over one of these snow patches in which the mule sank to his knees in snow.

THE BREVENT.

The view from this lofty point is wild, rugged, grand, imposing, awe-inspiring. Almost immediately below me on one side is the valley of the Arne with its numerous towns and villages, with beautiful cultivated fields and groves, looking like so many gardens, the fields not appearing larger than the squares in a garden, while the avenues lined with trees resemble garden walks lined with hedges or currant bushes, with a smaller and wilder valley gorge on the opposite side of this mountain, unsoftened in outline by snow deposits. Nature in and beyond the narrow valley gorge, is wild and forbidding as at creation's dawn. In front is the Mont Blanc group, while around me the lofty, rugged, storm riven Aiguilles, or needles, stand out against the clear sky in startling grandeur and wild beauty, while the monarch of Alpine and European mountains, Mont Blanc, is seen to better advantage from this point than from its dome itself. As on the latter the great height and vast distance is such that things are but imperfectly seen, while comparison is lost by the magnitude of the mountain, which of itself embraces, or includes, almost the entire field of human vision. Here at Chamoinex we stand at the very foot of this mountain pile, with its vast field of virgin snow, the accumulation of æons of ages, stretching up in sublime beauty to the very heavens, three miles above the sea. So bright and clear does it arise against the blue sky that it is difficult to believe that we could not see a man standing upon its very dome, and yet with the aid of strong opera glasses we could not see a house, perhaps not even St. Paul's Cathedral. The distance appears only a few miles and yet it is twenty-five or thirty miles to its summit. A party of two gentlemen and three guides had left our hotel the evening before, to make the ascent. They had remained all night at a little hut built behind or below some projecting rocks, the *Grande Mulets*, situated far up on its sides, from which point they had started at daylight. At 10 o'clock we looked at them through a powerful telescope when they were seen distinctly, all five in a single line, they were toiling over the Camel Hump near the dome or summit, and while distinctly seen and counted through the telescope, they looked much like five flies crawling over a large glass globe. Two hours afterwards the firing of the cannon at the signal station here in Chamoinex, announced that they had reached the top. They returned to Chamoinex that night. Next day two Russian ladies, accompanied by strong guides to assist them, indeed to almost carry them if necessary, started off for the ascent, staying that night, as is the custom, at the Grande Mulets. Next morning the telescope showed one woman with the guides. The other, having broken down remained at the Grande Mulets. Whether this woman ever reached the summit I did not learn. Very few women have ever been able to climb this mountain, indeed, but comparatively few men can do so, even with the aid of strong guides.

THE AIGUILLES DU DRU.

Yesterday two strong athletic, sunburnt, young Frenchmen came into Chamoinex with their guides, having come over Mont Blanc from the other, or Italian, side. This evening they left with their guides, selected here, three bold, hardy Alpine climbers and chamois hunters, inured to toil and peril, to undertake the perilous ascent of the Aiguille du Dru, a bold, rocky needle, or torn granite spear, rising 12,000 feet in the air, as steep and as difficult to climb as would be a church steeple of the same height, and only the same amount of interest could attach itself to the accomplishment of the feat as would be obtained in climbing a bean pole of the same height. Their lives are placed in the most imminent peril, as well as those of their guides, with no possible good in view, only a foolhardy desire or ambition to do what no one but a fool would wish to do. This Aiguille has never been successfully climbed but once, though several fools have lost their lives in the attempt, while the boldest and most experienced of the guides here look upon the attempt as but little better than suicide. Of course these men place their lives in their profession, and will attempt any possible or impossible feat in their line, that men or devils dare attempt, and would feel disgraced if any one wanted their assistance to help them climb all the impossible Aiguilles, or inaccessible mountain peaks in the entire Alpine range, and should offer to pay sufficiently for the risk, should they refuse. I noticed as these men with their guides, the latter natives, left on their perilous venture, the most experienced guides shook their heads ominously, the attempt being tabooed as a foolhardy one that would almost certainly result in failure, and most likely in loss of life. Compared with the difficulty and danger of the undertaking, the ascent of

Mont Blanc is considered as mere child's play. All five of the men had each a strong pole some six feet long, armed at one end with a sharp, strong, steel spike, at the other with a case-hardened, steel pickax and hook for cutting holes in the granite column and catching on to projecting crags. They had also a long, strong rope, capable of holding all five of the men. This rope is to be thrown over projecting crags, and then the men pull themselves up by it, or otherwise used as occasion or possibility may suggest. All five men, tourists and guides, are fearless, strong athletes, inured to toil and fearless of consequences, capable of doing what man can do. I await anxiously the result.

July 30th.—Took carriage and drove up the valley to the Mer de Glace, known as the *Glacier des Bois*, a vast sea of ice, two or three miles wide and ten or fifteen long. At this point the Chamoinex valley terminates, also the river Arne, mostly formed by the large streams that come from this ice field. The great highway along which we had traveled from Geneva, now enters a wild, mountain gorge, and continues to Martigny. We drove through this gorge where the scenery is wild and beautiful, to a degree seldom equalled even in these Alpine gorges. Returned to our hotel as the light of day was being replaced by the "Alpine glow," or after day glow.

THE ALPINE GLOW.

This Alpine Glow, which long after sunset lights up the snow fields and sky almost as light as day, comes on after the sun has long entirely disappeared from the loftiest mountain tops. It is doubtless the dispersion or emission of rays of light that have been absorbed by the vast fields of deep snow and ice during the day. It is a beautiful phenomena, and not the least strange and beautiful of these Alpine wonders.

Lac Leman, vain would be any efforts of mine to paint thy loveliness, which even the pen of a Byron, Rosseau and

Madame de Stael have failed to delineate. When and where undisturbed by the Bees, as is almost nowhere and never the case, its waters, as are all the lakes of Switzerland, fed by torrents of melted ice and snow, are of a milky white appearance, caused by included particles of air, but when ruffled by the wind, or as seen from the steamer, are of a deep indigo blue, and when lashed to fury by the violence of the Bees, as has been the case all of to-day, with white crested waves breaking over mole and pier, its waters become of even a deeper indigo tinge. This indigo color of its waters, ascribed by Sir Humphrey Davy to the presence of iodine, gives the lake a peculiar charm, which with its beaurivage stretching out to the long range of Jura Alps bordering its right bank, bespangled with villas, cottages, groves and sweet garden fields, constitute it a diamond mirror set in a frame of rubies and gold, a very Eden, more lovely far than the gardens of the Hesperides, with their blossoms of silver and apples of gold, or the Vale of Shinar, with its lilies that spring in eternal beauty.

FROM GENEVA TO ENGLAND VIA PARIS.

Aug. 4th.—Left for Paris at 8 o'clock P. M., where we arrived at 8 o'clock next morning, a run of twelve hours, and put up at Hotel Londres et New York, which, however, did not correspond with its large name.

Aug. 5th.—As we were only passing through Paris, en route to England, it was not our purpose now to stop long enough to visit its world renowned treasures of art, but to do this on our return here this Fall and Winter which we expect to do, and remain many weeks or months. However, Paris is of too much interest to the tourist to be passed through as we might do with some other places. We accordingly took carriage and devoted a day or two to driving over the city and its immediate environs, visiting its palaces, parks, monuments, driving through the principle boulevards, etc., whereby we obtained much valuable information, as well as deriving an incalculable amount of pleasure, as there is no city in the world that possesses so many of these, or any perhaps so beautiful, there being in the world but one Paris.

FROM PARIS TO LONDON.

Aug. 6th.—Left Paris for London via Calais and Dover at 11 A. M., arriving in London at 7 P. M., a run of only eight hours between the cities.

The road passes over highly cultivated plains, but of no especial interest until we reach the historical, highly fortified seaport town of Calais. This important city, so long in the possession of the English, was permanently lost to them during the reign of Mary, who deemed this loss the greatest misfortune of her life, and on her death-bed said that if her heart were examined Calais would be found written upon it. Poor woman, this feeling which does so much credit to her true English heart and soul, and which was participated in by most, if not all Englishmen of her day, was really like many other occurrences in human life, or the history of nations, "a blessing in disguise." Here we took steamer across the channel to Dover, a distance of twenty-five miles, which is made in one hour and fifteen minutes, which is certainly a most remarkable speed.

The channel, often so stormy, was as smooth as a lake, and the passage a most delightful one. The weather was a little hazy, so that the white chalk cliffs of Dover were not seen to advantage. At Dover we took railroad to London. After a long residence of fifteen months among peoples speaking a strange tongue, it was really delightful to be on the soil of our ancestors and among a people of a like language, religion, laws and customs with ourselves. It was the first time we had ever been upon the soil of old England, and we felt a pleasurable emotion that can only be surpassed by standing again upon our own native land. God grant that these two mighty nations so closely united by so much that constitutes one people, may long continue to cultivate the closest ties of peace and friendship, the only rivalry between them being which may do the greatest good.

Arriving in London we put up at the large hotel at the station—Charing Cross Hotel—where we remained two days, and as our object now was not to remain in London, but to visit England, Scotland and Ireland during the warm season, leaving London until our return late in the fall, as at Paris, we took carriage and drove over the city, seeing only its outlines of palaces, parks, public buildings, etc., when after having obtained a general outline of this world's center—

Aug. 8th.—We took the cars on the Midland railroad for England and Scotland, making our first halt at Rowsley, put up at the neat, small, old-fashioned hotel the Peacock, in mid England, a building of the sixteenth century, and 150 miles out from London. Unfortunately the small hotel was crowded and we were compelled to take the only vacant room in the building. It was Saturday evening and our object in stopping here was to see the celebrated castles Hadden Hall and Chatsworth. Next day being Sunday, and as in puritanical England halls and parks are not open on this day, we were compelled, if we would see them, to remain over until Monday. Unfortunately the weather was cold, rainy, disagreeable, and our large garret room without a fire-place, and the only accessible fire was in the smoking-room. I had a fire made up in this, but as ill luck would have it, the waiting maid of one of the lady guests had to eat here, and as she employed most of her time in eating, we were compelled to remain out of it, most of the seemingly endless, long, wet, dreary, rainy, cold lonesome, puritanical Sabbath, which it really seemed, would never end. Altogether here Juno's bird only showed us its feet, and I heartily wished the peacock and the maid in Africa. But all days, even the dullest and most disagreeable of all, a cold, rainy Sunday in England, at the overcrowded Peacock hotel, will end if we live long enough to see it. Night came at last.

Monday, Aug. 10th.—The gloomy Sunday had passed and with it the rain; weather beautiful, bright. Took carriage and drove first to Hadden, situated some two miles from Rowsley, on the beautiful Wye, and a very typical and English baronial mansion it is. It dates back to the eleventh century, was the property of Sir John Vernon, and from him to his daughter Dorothy Vernon, who eloped and married Sir John Manners. It has been the residence of England's kings and queens, who on hunting or other expeditions have often visited here, whose lordly owners were scarcely less proud or powerful than themselves. From Sir John Manners it descended to the dukes of Rutland, who, though no longer living here, still keep it up, and have a keeper to show it to strangers, tens of thousands of whom visit it annually. While not the oldest baronial castle in England, it is the oldest one in a tolerable state of preservation—all the others of like date being ruins, only ruins, but this, although falling to decay, might readily be fitted up as a lordly residence. It is really interesting and instructive to learn, through the testimony of this old castle, the advance in comfort, convenience and luxury of living modern times have brought. Its old wooden tables and chairs, the long, rude, old oaken table in the dining-room, at which lords and ladies were wont to sit at great feasts, and where, with their flowing bowls of ale, many a plumed knight told of feats of daring in Palestine or in France, when at the battle of Agincourt, the French chivalry went down before the

English battle-axe or cross-bow, while attending troubadours sang the exploits of heroes in rescuing their imprisoned lady-loves—this table is such as only the poorer classes of working-men would use at the present day.

The great dancing hall, fine in its day, lined with solid oak plank, with some rude wood carvings, with no ceiling only the naked rafters and roof, such as might be seen in a Dutch barn or woodshed, was in its day a grand hall where on festive occasions were assembled the beauty and chivalry, even including royalty. It was on one of these occasions of high revel, when this hall was filled with knights and ladies, that Sir John's daughter, the fair Dorothy Vernon, silently left the hall, slipped out of the back door and, stepping softly down a flight of stone steps, joined Sir John Manners, who, with his retinue, was awaiting her in the yard below. The door through which she passed and the stone steps, are shown the visitor. How hallowed become such memories! And how stronger than bars and bolts was the flame Cupid had kindled in the heart of lovely, innocent, foolish, giddy, flashing Dorothy. Alas! how many hopes and fears have moved the souls of her children's children since that eventful night. Hark! sounds of alarm! Now are hurrying human feet to and fro. To horse, mailed warriors and retainers full four score, arm, mount and hasten in pursuit; but in vain, the bird is secure in its flight. Dorothy and the knight of her choice have passed by the church upon whose holy altars the candles were burning and where they halted long enough for the mitred priest who awaited them to pronounce them man and wife and give them a benediction, and now they are safe in their new castle home, whose strong walls forbid assault. The changes the finger of time has wrought in this old castle since that night is shown in the stone steps now nearly worn away by passing footsteps, which for more than half a thousand years have pressed them, while the great fire-places in the hall with their antique garniture have long stood as silent mementoes of the past. And the wide hearthstone and great jams of the kitchen, with their great bars, and spits, and hooks, and revolving gridirons, upon which was roasted many a boar's head and noble stag, for noble or royal guests, have for ages forgotten their uses, and anything approximating them in primitive rudeness could only now be found in some negro cabin in the Southern States of a then unknown world.

But then when these old halls were new, most of England was a forest. London was a small town of ill-constructed houses, with narrow, unpaved, unlighted streets ; and the printing press and mariner's compass were unknown. Indeed the long, dark night that shrouded Europe after the light of the world had been extinguished by the fall of the Roman Empire had not withdrawn its curtains. That strange movement the Crusades was stirring Europe for the rescue of Jerusalem from the Moslems, a movement that precipitated Europe upon Asia, and Richard Cœur de Lion was marshalling his mailed warriors for this emprise. In these halls, then new, many a mailed knight quaffed his ale, and in presence of his lady fair, swore to rescue the sepulchre, though he had to kill half the Turks then living, and after their return, many a strange minstrel halted here to sing the songs of the troubadours. We noticed in the dining-hall the date 1545. Old, faded tapestries hang on the walls. The bed-rooms, as are the halls, are dimly lighted. A mirror in one of these rooms belonged to queen Elizabeth. Of course we all beheld ourselves in this glass that had reflected the image of good queen Bess. We ascended the castle tower from where we had a fine view of the lordly manor. The crests of these two lordly families were the Boar's head and the Peacock, which are still present in the wood carvings, also in the garden where two cypress trees are trimmed, the one representing a boar's head the other a peacock. The little Peacock hotel at Rowsley also represents the house of Vernon, as this was once an appendage of Hadden Hall.

CHATSWORTH.

From Hadden Hall we drove by Bakewell to Chatsworth, a royal domain given by William the Conqueror to his natural son Percival, and now the property of the noble house of Cavendish, now rendered immortal by the foul murder of its late owner, Lord Frederick Cavendish, Lord Lieutenant of Ireland, by misguided Irish patriots, in Phœnix park, near Dublin. The grave of the noble lord is in the little family church yard. No tomb, no stone, marks the spot. The fresh grave was covered by fresh flowers, immortelles, placed here by the loving hands of wife and children. The castle is in perfect preservation. Indeed the family live here two or three months in the year, as was wont to do the late lord. The remainder of the year is spent either on another royal domain or in London. It is a splendid structure with some of the finest statuary and paintings in England. A Hebe by Canova, and a Venus by Thorwaldsen, are among the finest works of the modern chisel, indeed require the practiced eye of a connoisseur to see that they are only less fine than like works of the Greek Praxiteles. An attendant shows visitors through the palatial rooms, with their rich furniture, becoming royalty. We next visited the extensive gardens. Nothing in Europe excels the beauty of the landscape or extensive plan of these gardens and lawns. All that taste and wealth can do to make these naturally lovely, has been done to render them surpassingly beautiful. In the park, as we approach the castle, we pass a tower or keep, surrounded by a moat with a small drawbridge, where was long confined the unfortunate Mary Queen of Scotland, who was sent from here to the tower in

London, where she was beheaded by order of her cousin Elizabeth.

We noticed in the pasture a flock of sheep singularly marked with black and white spots, ring-streaked and striped. These, we were told, were a special breed of sheep belonging to this manor, and were very properly called Jacob's sheep, and most likely were the direct descendants of those with which Jacob tricked his father-in-law, and that they had been on these grounds for five or six hundred years.

Returned to Rowsley, and took cars for Manchester, a dingy, smoky manufacturing town of 400,000 inhabitants, where we arrived at 5 P. M., and put up at the very neat and excellent temperance hotel, Trevelyan.

EDINBURGH.

Aug. 12th.—Morning dark, cold and rainy—so cold that we had a large coal fire made up in our room. In the evening cleared up and we went out—walked to Princess street, walked to its farther end, passing by the beautiful city gardens. A military band in bright scarlet uniforms were playing in the open grounds.

Edinburgh, the Capital and most important town in Scotland, has 250,000 inhabitants, is a grandly picturesque old city, situated near the Frith of Forth, and was founded by Edwin, king of Northumbria, who erected a strong castle or fort upon the lofty, almost inaccessible rock that rises here on most points with perpendicular walls 300 feet above the plain, having some seven or eight acres of comparatively level ground upon its summit. Upon this was built the castle, palace, and battlements, and from these grew, spread out, the old town of Edinburgh. From its erection to quite recent times, the history of this castle has been intimately associated with—indeed has been—that of Scotland. In a small room 6 x 9 feet

Queen Mary's bed-room, was born James VI., of Scotland, who became James I., of England, where his unfortunate, helpless, beautiful mother was long confined as a prisoner of state. In the afternoon we took a walk, crossing a long bridge which spans a deep ravine separating the old from the new city. Visited the beautiful monument erected to Sir Walter Scott. A fine statue of Sir Walter and also of his favorite dog are here.

We visited many places of interest, among them John Knox's old house, now 300 years old. Visited the old historical castle of Holyrood Palace, first erected in 1128. It has been several times partially destroyed and again restored, and is now, after 700 years, in a good state of preservation, except the royal chapel. The ancient dining and dancing hall, now a picture gallery, is hung around with the portraits of Scotland's kings, queens, heroes and court belles. Queen Mary's apartments contained several mementos of this beautiful queen, At the head of the steps, entering her drawing-room, is shown the blood stains where her private secretary was murdered while clinging to her garments for protection, by her fierce, untamed, half-savage, and altogether brutal nobles. In vain the brave but helpless queen, at the eminent risk of her life, endeavored to protect him. One of the brutal assassins placed a pistol at her breast, others flashed their naked swords in her face, while others ran theirs through the body of their victim while clinging to her dress for protection. This was only three months before the birth of James I., of England, and it is an interesting physiological fact that James, though not a coward, during his whole life could not bear to look upon a drawn sword. Well may blood spilled under conditions so diabolical have left a stain that neither time nor art has been able to remove. Could we examine the souls of these brutal murderers they would present a deeper blood stain than this floor.

Visited the Nelson monument, also the National Burns monument, which to me is of more interest than all others here. This monument is constructed with much artistic taste, and reflects credit upon this highly-cultured people. It contains many relics, souvenirs of the highly-gifted, but unfortunate, national poet.

Aug. 15th.—Visited the National Antiquarian Museum, containing a most excellent collection of stone and bronze implements, antique iron weapons, and instruments of torture, among them the guillotine with which Morton was beheaded in 1581, and after him many others. Its iron blade was rusted from human gore, while its every joint creaked with the groans of its hapless victims. Saw also John Knox's old battered pulpit, and the camp stool which the hysterical, fanatical old maid, Jenny Giddes, threw at the Dean of St. Giles while he was reading the liturgy. For this she should have been treated to the " ducking-stool," but the Dissenters continuing in the ascendancy she was deemed worthy of immortality. For much less offences these sterling old Covenanters have imprisoned, hung or beheaded others who happened to differ with them in articles of faith. Well, after all, what is the use of believing anything if we do not make others think as we do?

Just outside St. Giles Cathedral is a stone with the letters J. K. in brass, which marks the spot where John Knox was buried. Near by is the old Talbooth, or old Parliament House, afterwards a prison, famous as the " Heart of Mid-Lothian." Not far off, in a small irregular piece of ground, is a fine statue of Charles I. I asked an intelligent old Scotchman, who, seeing we were strangers, was kindly pointing out these things to us, why they did not erect a monument over this truly great man? He replied that all parties were not agreed on this, and such an attempt might result in the destruction of the present statue or St. Giles, showing that the lawless spirit that has murdered their kings, imprisoned their queens, and beheaded their noblemen, or hung Dissenters, was not yet dead, only sleeping, perhaps kept so by the dominant conservatism of England.

St. Giles of course was formerly a Catholic cathedral, but after it came into the possession of the Covenanters they removed every relic of what they termed idolatry; the paintings from the walls, the statues from the niches, crucifixes and high altar from their places, leaving it as bare of all ornamentation as a Dutch barn. Its beautiful long rows of columns, its high arches, are out of place, are dissonant with the present forms of worship. No one on entering it need be told that it was built for other forms of worship than that now here. Indeed these good people have about as much use for such a structure as a Highlander has for a knee buckle.

MELROSE ABBEY.

Made an excursion to Melrose Abbey and Abbotsford, one and a quarter hours run from Edinburgh. We reached Melrose Station. Near by is the ruins of Melrose Abbey, rendered classical as well as immortal by the genius of Sir Walter Scott. It is now, and has long been, in ruins, but grand and beautiful even in its ruins, and must have been one of the finest structures in all Scotland. How hardly has time and neglect dealt with this once beautiful structure, so imposing even in its broken arches and fallen columns, impressing us with the sense of awe and reverence we might feel in walking among the broken tombstones of our fathers. It is, I suppose, its very ivy-covered ruins that clothe it with an interest even greater than we feel in more splendid but better preserved cathedrals. We spent an hour musing among its all-silent ruins, and in endeavoring to decipher the corroded inscriptions upon its crumbling arches, around which the ivy clung as if in the vain attempt to prevent their decay.

From here we drove over to Scott's home, Abbotsford,

which has but little to recommend it, other than that it was the home of Scotland's immortal poet and novelist, from whose fertile brain every stone and rafter was coined. It is in the possession of his great-grand-daughter, is not a prepossessing structure, and is badly located, being in a low, flat situation near the river Tweed, which meanders through the meadow some 200 yards in front of the villa. Much of it is copied from old castles and ruined abbeys. I noticed several old stones taken from ivy-covered ruins with quaint inscriptions upon them, some of them hundreds of years old, built in the walls, his library-room and valuable library-chair and writing-table, much as he left them. A long room is filled with armory—guns, pistols, swords, spears, etc., two pistols taken from Napoleon at Waterloo among them, Rob Roy's gun, Montrose's sword, James IV. armor. The keys of the old Talbooth prison at Edinburgh, together with many portraits of kings, emperors and great men, also a great many bric-a-bracs or keepsakes given him by kings and historic persons. Indeed every part of the house contains articles dear to the lovers of this great man. It is to the literary world holy ground, and to none more so than Americans, who are as familiar with the works of Scott as the Scots themselves. We were pained to see that these frugal money-loving, penny-saving, canny Scots were careful to profit by the desire all lovers of their ancestor feel to see any and everything hallowed by association with him. A shilling is levied upon every visitor, some fifty of whom were at the house while we were in it. And I was informed that the Saturday previous 1,200 persons visited this house. This, it is quite safe to say, gives $20,000 collected annually from strangers who turn aside to do homage at the shrine of genius. Would not the same want of veneration and love of money induce these loving descendants to sell his bones to the soap boiler? Having loitered here some hours, late in the evening we drove back to Melrose and took train for Edinburgh.

Aug. 15th.—Left Edinburgh at 10:30 A. M. for Stirling, where we arrived at 2 P. M., and put up at Hotel Royal. After dinner we visited the old castle, which stands upon a projecting promontory, some 300 feet above the valley of the Forth. This was long one of the strongholds of Scotland, and the residence of her kings. James I. and James II. of Scotland were born here. On the esplanade, now used as a parade ground for the garrison here, is a splendid statue of Robert the Bruce, and other statues of distinguished Scotch heroes. Within the grounds is a small chapel built by Mary. Within the castle we were shown the Douglas room, where James I. cowardly, treacherously, murdered his unsuspecting, invited guest, the Earl of Douglas, a most cowardly dastardly deed, such as none but a Stewart could have perpetrated, and had justice prevailed against might, his infamous carcass would have ornamented a rope's end.

From the parapets of this castle we obtain one of the finest views in Scotland. Before us lies the beautiful and fertile valley of the Forth, the most fertile of all Scotland. The railroad from Edinburgh to Stirling runs up this valley, which stretches from the Frith of Forth to near Loch Katrine. At this point three streams or small rivers unite to form the Forth, which is seen as a great serpent winding in a silver stream through the valley. It is a beautiful, winding, crooked stream, bending now in a long curve around some projecting point, now meandering through the meadows, and so fertile is the valley that it is said truly "a crook of the Forth is worth a county in the North."

Sunday.—Visited Greyfriars church, in which Mary, queen of Scotland, was crowned, as was also her son James VI. of Scotland, afterwards James I. of England. Queen Mary's coronation sermon was preached by John Knox, in which in his fearful denunciations of papacy he included and insulted his unfortunate, lovely, helpless queen; and this at a time when her lawless nobles, taking advantage of her helplessness as a woman and the turbulence of the times, were plotting her destruction; and for this, though a thousand times a saint, I would not like him. Her sin with this earnest reformer, Knox, was her religion. She was a Catholic, and therefore to be destroyed. O, that these turbulent nobles had had her grandfather, Henry VII., or her uncle, Henry VIII., to deal with. As it was, they hunted her down, betrayed, insulted, and finally sold her to the English, who *mercifully* ended her life of sorrow by chopping off her head by order of her coussin, *good* queen Bess. But, we are told, she was wicked. This was related of her by those who betrayed and murdered her. I believe it not. In looking upon her portrait, I behold in her beautiful, sweet, sad face a reflex of all the virtues—a face that could not be kissed into a more perfect reflex of heaven by all the cherubs that float around the bright Elysium. Heaven makes no such mistakes as to connect this sweet face with an impure soul. In visiting the castle, we pass through the old cemetery where many of these old covenanters who stood for God and liberty are buried. Peace to their ashes! Upon these old tomb-stones are many quaint inscriptions which carry us back vividly to the times of the Long Parliament. In the evening walked over to the Abbey of Camberkenneth, founded by David I. in 1147. The Abbey, like Melrose Abbey, has long been in ruins, only the tower and gallery remain. The foundations of the entire Abbey, however, are quite distinctly traced. Immediately under the high altar James II. was buried. His tomb mouldered to decay with the Abbey that enclosed it, but has been restored and enclosed with an iron railing by his grateful descendant, Victoria, and thus the resting-place of the dust of the son of a base murderer has been rescued from oblivion by England's queen. From the old Abbey we walked two or three miles to a lofty eminence upon which stood a beautiful monument to Wallace, who occupied these heights which command the valley the evening preceding the battle of Stirling in which the English suffered a disastrous defeat.

On approaching the monument we noticed on the door, which was closed, "Admittance 2d. on all lawful days," which means that it is open on six days in the week, for which two pence is exacted, but on Sundays, which are *unlawful* days, it is *closed*. We stood here a moment to ponder upon the blind and destructive folly of these good people in closing this as well as all other innocent resorts—except churches—on Sundays. No parks, no reading-rooms or pleasure resorts are allowed old or young, on unlawful days, Sundays, which are made Jewish Sabbaths, a Jewish institution for which there is no authority other than that found in Jewish laws and customs, none whatever in the acts or teachings of Christ; and yet are these people Jews or Christians? Do they love the Jews, whose laws and institutions they thus honor above those of Christ? How much better it would be to throw open this historical, pleasant and innocent resort, *free* on "*unlawful* days," charging, if they wish, two pence, or twice this amount, on *lawful* days. How pleasantly, how innocently, how instructively and profitably might the children of the poor of Stirling and vicinity spend the *unlawful* days in visiting this their national monument, and receiving from its impressive presence patriotic inspirations. By closing it on Sundays, or by not throwing open its door on this day *free*, they exclude all those whose struggle for existence forbid their visiting it on any other, and thus shut out the very people who most need patriotic culture. But were the masses allowed this innocent recreation and profitable pleasure the churches might have fewer unwilling attendants.

While musing on these things, I walked slowly towards our hotel in Stirling; when midway, and just after crossing the bridge over the Forth, I passed an unpretentious wooden structure, from behind which came two lads, well dressed and evidently of good families, deeply under the influence of whiskey, half drunk. This was most natural, denied all rational, innocent enjoyment they sought this den of vice. "The devil finds some mischief still, for idle hands to do," and were these good people as wise as devout, they would know that the means they employ for making saints are just those the devil would suggest for preventing the growth of morals—an enforced idleness—and then if we must have a Sabbath it should be Saturday, as there is no authority by precept or example for any other day. Yet with all this we gratefully acknowledge our indebtedness to this grand, great and noble people.

Aug. 17th.—Left Stirling at 10 A. M. for Loch Lomond, via the Trossachs and Loch Katrine. We ascended the Forth to its origin in Loch Ord, a beautiful small lake in a mountain cañon. We wound around Loch Con and through the wild mountain gorge, every foot of which has been made classical by the pen of Scott. In the wildest of this wild region we passed the well of Rob Roy, whose ghost, I doubt not, still lingers here, as it is just the place I would expect it to most delight in. I felt glad I had company, and that it was in midday. I most certainly would not like to be here alone in the night. I got out of the diligence and gathered some beautiful heather in memory of Rob Roy's well. Both the bell and true heather grow here to a perfection and beauty I found no where else and were in full bloom. The road runs through a dry gorge, then skirts a small mountain lake, where Fitz James met Rhoderick Dhu, by the Trossachs to Loch Katrine, where we take steamer for quite the length of its romantic, crystal water.

Shortly after leaving the lower end of the lake the steamer passes the classic isle, Ellen's Isle, where the lady of the lake met Fitz James—a very gem, an embossed pearl, bright as the eyes of its lovely mistress, for whom alone it was a fitting home. The palace had decayed, not a vestige remained, and yet who so dull as to be unable to replace its ivy-stone ? The isle and the crystal water that surrounds it, made classic by the muse of Sir Walter Scott, will live in the hearts of those who love the pure, the beautiful, as long as Ben Venu shall cast his protecting shadows over its silver sheen.

The water supply of the city of Glasgow is obtained from this lake. But though the water is clear and cool, the lake is surrounded by peat bogs which cover the highest mountains to their very summits, and it is found to contain millions of microscopical particles of vegetable matter, consequently not wholesome. Ben Venu stands as a sombre sentinel over Loch Katrine, whose crystal waters, as though in pride, reflect his grim outline. This rough outline of the mountain-sentinel, as reflected from the transparent bosom of the lake, reminds us of a Tartar savage guarding the palace of a fairy queen.

The steamer lands at the Northern extremity of the lake, at Hotel Shannocklochen, a short name for a long hotel, at which point we take diligence for Loch Lomond. The road runs through a wild mountain gorge, skirting a beautiful lake from which descends a stream of water, quite a mountain torrent, to Loch Lomond. Near its junction with the lake it rushes over boulders, breaks into beautiful cascades and leaps over falls. At one of these the water falls twenty-five feet with a wild, picturesque beauty which throws a charm over the Inversnaid Hotel and its picturesque surroundings. Charmed with the beauty of this place and the neatness and comfort of the hotel, we remained here several days. This point, Inversnaid, is crowded with tourists, who are constantly arriving here and departing, some on their way to Loch Katrine, others, like ourselves, in the reverse direction, from Katrine to Glasgow by way of Loch Lomond.

INVERSNAID.

Next morning before breakfast we walked down to the romantic little wharf on the lake shore, some fifty yards from the hotel, and as we were returning to the house we saw standing upon the rocky pinnacle of the mountain that overhangs the hotel a woman, who we supposed one of a party of tourists who had left the hotel at daylight and gone up there, as we had often seen done in Switzerland and Germany. Not doubting that the point was readily accessible, and as it overlooked the lakes, the constant resort of travelers, it never occurred to us that the point was not the common resort of tourists, that in fact it was almost entirely inaccessible and had perhaps almost never been pressed by stranger's feet. How could we have thought so when we had the evidence to the contrary before our eyes, and then I had been all summer accustomed in Switzerland to go, with other tourists, men and women, over mountains much higher, sometimes before breakfast, taking refreshments at a café on its sides or summit.

After breakfast, I started off to make the ascent, but after passing some straw-thatched hovels on the hillside, some half a mile from the hotel, I lost all trace of a path, but as I was without a guide, I supposed I had only missed the road and would certainly meet it again on my farther progress, not doubting but a good road or path led to the top, where we had seen the tourists. With this feeling I pushed on with difficulty and soon came not upon a path but a wide depression or valley in the mountain, over which spread a deep, rough peat bog. I crossed this with great difficulty, leaping over slimy pools from one tuft of peat to another, often sinking half way to the top of my boots in mud and water with the certainty that should I miss the unsteady tuft I might sink out of sight in the treacherous mire. After crossing this hollow and ascending to the summit of what I had supposed the top of the mountain, found that I had another peat bog to cross and another hill to climb, which I did with great labor and difficulty, the entire distance being a miry peat bog; and not until two hours of laborious effort, was I able to reach the rocky projection upon which we had seen the tourists in the morning. And here I saw that the real summit was a mile or more beyond me, but as I had climbed thus far, over not only a difficult, but dangerous, way, where to return was as dangerous as to go on, I determined to go ahead, and then I hoped by doing so, I would fall in with the road or path, as I still did not doubt but such existed, yet I felt the effort was greatly beyond my strength, as I was quite exhausted and felt that it was necessary for me to get into the road, as it would be almost impossible for me to again cross this miry bog, and no one could come to my assistance. In very desperation then I started for the distant summit, feeling that should I fail to reach it, my body would soon sink out of sight—would never be found. In vain I regretted the foolish venture, but as is often the case, these repentings came when too late. To advance or retreat was perhaps equally perilous, but then a forward movement had at least this advantage, that I did not know what was ahead of me, and I might hope for the best, while to retrace my steps, the difficulties and dangers were too well known to permit a hope. Finally, and when nearly dead, I reached the top, a wide, flat, rocky summit, whose forbidding waste had perhaps never been visited, except by an occasional shepherd boy. A few loose stones were piled up as if done to employ a lonesome hour.

I remained here an hour or more in the enjoyment of the beautiful panorama spread out around and below me, which with our fine glasses were brought into great distinctness. Two thousand feet below me on one side of the mountain was Loch Katrine, with its bright flashing waters at its southern extremity, with Ellen's Isle hiding itself behind Ben Venu. On the other side, and almost directly under me, was Loch Lomond, with its upper extremity just above the hotel, terminating abruptly, jutting in against a bold, wild headland, whose frowning rocks were scarcely less inviting than its fields of heather, that our experience had now taught us covered forbidding peat bogs. Towards its southern extremity it extended far away, dividing into a thousand channels, embracing as many little islands, that in the distance looked scarcely larger than so many boats surrounded with bands of silver. These stretched on and on until lost in the protecting shadow of Ben Lomond, the giant of these highland mountains. But the interest of this beautiful view from this lofty summit, only centered, was not embraced, in these bright lakes. The distant view was grand and awe-inspiring from its very sombre, sterile stillness. Around me stretched in the distance heather-covered hill beyond hill, embracing the almost entire extent of the highlands of Scotland. But I looked in vain for what to me would have been a far more pleasant view than all the highlands—a road or path. None was here—no use for one except to me—none other had ever had use for it. In all my dreary, dangerous ascent I had not seen even a sheep-path, nothing for sheep to feed upon, no birds, for the same reason. In all the morning I had only seen now and then a stray sheep that startled at the sight of a man, and had startled from their safe hiding place only two or three frightened grouse that had taken shelter here from the sportsmen on the surrounding hills. I now looked at my watch, and found that

I had been absent from the hotel three hours, and knew that my wife would be alarmed, and yet the perils of the descent were before me. These I found much the same I had encountered in the ascent—except the difficulty of climbing. I plunged down, leaping from one tuft to another, meeting not with a single foot track of man or beast. When about two-thirds of the way down I hailed two young men, natives, who my wife in her alarm had sent out to search for me. Farther on I met a servant from the hotel sent out to search for me. After I had been gone for some time my wife mentioned to the hotel keeper where I had gone, and inquired if there was any danger, when he frightened her by saying I was very imprudent to attempt it, as there was no path, that it was never climbed even by the natives, as it was a treacherous peat bog and nothing to climb it for. But my wife remarked that we had seen persons, which we supposed were tourists from the hotel, upon its top that morning, and among them a woman. He assured her that no one had gone from the hotel, that tourists never ascended it, and that it was utterly impossible for a woman to do so, that it must have been some shepherd-boy she had seen, and that he had never seen even these upon it; that he had never been upon its top, nor conversed with one who had. Not that it was positively inaccessible to a man, but that its ascent would be at least very difficult, and then there was nothing to climb it for. This, of course, had greatly frightened my wife, who had sent out all hands to hunt for, and rescue, me. When I arrived at the hotel I had not a dry thread upon me. My clothes were as wet from prespiration as if I had swam the lake, and I was so much exhausted that I remained in bed the remainder of the day.

GLASGOW.

Left Inversnaid for Glasgow on steamer, passing the whole length of Loch Lomond, a beautiful sheet of water some twenty miles long, and six miles wide at its lower end. Passed Rob Roy's prison—a cave in the rocky wall—passed along the base of Ben Lomond, whose lofty summit towers above the lake as a great sentinel standing here to guard the spirit of the lake. At Balloch we took train for Glasgow, twenty-two miles, where we arrived at 2 P. M.

Glasgow, the most wealthy, populous and important commercial city of Scotland, is a wretched, dirty, smoky place, truly undesirable for, perhaps, any other purpose than money making.

Took steamer Columbia for an excursion down the Clyde and through the Frith. We were on this fine steamer from 7 A. M. to 7 P. M., during which time it made the round trip, 180 miles. During the trip we had a fine view of all this portion of the Highlands, together with the extensive ship building docks and yards of the Clyde, the most extensive in the world.

AYR.

Left Glasgow at 1:30 P. M. for Stranyer, by way of Ayr Arrived at Ayr at 4 P. M., and put up at the Wellington Hotel.

The town of Ayr, rendered immortal by being the home of Burns, has some 20,000 inhabitants, has a fine harbor with docks, and is a thriving city with many neat and some fine residences. In wealth and comfort how changed since the greatest and most unfortunate of rural poets lived here.

Aug. 22nd.—Took carriage and drove to the home of Burns, saw the house in which he was born, which is a low, straw-thatched stone building in a good state of preservation. It was kept as a public inn, but has been bought by the Burns Association and a man and woman placed in attendance. Many interesting relics of the poet are here, many photographs and a number of autographs, original manuscripts, letters, etc. I noticed in one of the glass cases the original manuscript of

Tam O'Shanter, with erasures and corrections. Burns himself always thought this his greatest production, an opinion in which I agree with him, and yet I am fully sensible of the fact, that he wrote many verses greatly superior to any poetry in Tam O'Shanter, but nothing of so much invention. There are numerous small articles kept for sale here. We purchased several souvenirs of the immortal Bard of Ayrshire. A little beyond this house is the Old Kirk of Alloway, where Tam encountered the witches. The old church is roofless and long since in ruins. In the gable hangs the bell as it was in the days of Burns, also the nook in which Old Nick played the fiddle, and the window through which Tam saw the witches dancing, and out of which they flew after him, are still seen. Visited the churchyard where are graves and tombstones with quaint inscriptions, some of them 250 years old. Among these are the graves of Burns' father and mother and younger sister. Saw also the grave of Tam O'Shanter who was a veritable person by the name of Graham. How these graves by their association with the immortal bard hallow this place! In vain the Old Kirk of Alloway will yield stone after stone to the tooth of time, like the poet it is immortal, stereotyped in the memories of men, to be transmitted to children's children to the latest times! From here we were enabled to trace the line of Tam's ride from the Inn where he parted with his friend Sauter Johnny until he crossed the bridge that spans the Bonny Doon. This line was pointed out by an old Scotchman who lives among the tombs, and from his venerable appearance and familiarity with everything connected with Burns and Tam, may have been with them in their visits to this Old Kirk. It may be he touched glasses with Burns, if not, he embodies the very spirit of the times in which Tam lived.

After lingering here for some time, we went to Burns' monument, a beautiful structure, built by the public, and well becoming the memory of this divinely inspired self-taught plowboy. Would to God a discerning public could so far have appreciated this great-souled, unfortunate, neglected, starving man, as to have contributed a tithe of this and other structures erected to his memory to him and his family in his day To the disgrace of his age and country, chill penury was permitted to repress the aspirations of his noble soul, and after a manly but unequal combat, he fell beneath fortune's wheel, his manhood and genius crushed—when driven to strong drink, as is too often the case, he was wrecked ere half his work was done. How vain the pomp of monuments to him who was left to suffer, to starve. Every stone in Old Alloway, every ripple of Bonny Ayr or Doon, shall bear though ages all the wail for this neglect. And yet, though coming too late to benefit him they are intended to honor, as the testimonials of a grateful posterity to his immortal worth, they can but be pleasing to his disembodied spirit, which we can but believe still haunts the banks of the bonny streams where in life he was wont to muse, and whose names and beauties he has stamped in verse that will outlive his marble monument. Near by his monument, in a neat little stone building is the wondrous, sandstone statue of Tam O'Shanter and his boon companion, Sauter Johnny, as they appeared at the ale house on the night of Tam's adventurous ride.

This remarkable work, the best of its kind I ever saw by any sculptor, ancient or modern, is by a young, untaught native artist, who, in his line, was not less gifted than Burns in his, and who unfortunately died young and before he had performed other works. These statues are worthy the chisel of Thorwaldsen or Canova. Indeed I doubt whether either of these justly celebrated sculptors ever produced an ideal work so suggestive. Just beyond this, alongside of a little flower garden, is the old bridge, spanning the Bonny Doon, across which Tam rode on that fearful night, where his nag Meg saved her rider but lost her own grey tail, Tam being saved by the skin of his teeth, and only because the witches could not cross running water. The old bridge, a rude stone structure, is standing yet, in a tolerable state of preservation, but only foot passengers are allowed to cross it. We walked over the Doon on this bridge, as have tens of thousands of others, with feelings of almost idolatrous regard for this place, rendered immortal by Ayr's unfortunate bard, and not entirely without a belief in witches. The Doon is really a beautiful stream and deserving of all the regard the poet had for it. We drove by the ale house where Tam and Johnny drank their ale. Called to see a relation of Burns', an old maiden lady, whose memory is replete with all things concerning Burns.

Visited the old bridge of the Twa Brigs of Ayr, and crossed over it on foot, as, like the bridge of the Doon, foot passengers only are allowed to cross it. Both these bridges are very properly deemed too sacred for ordinary use. How wonder ful the genius that could thus embalm and sanctify these old structures in the memory and hearts of a grateful people. This bridge, as an inscription on its walls informs us, was built in 1252. Its construction is rude, but surprisingly good for the time in which it was built. Let us but think what was the state of Scotland at that day and what this old bridge has seen. It has witnessed mailed knights as they departed to the Holy Land, has withstood the storms of the middle ages, saw the dawn of the Renaissance, and was old when printing was invented. It owes its origin to two old maiden ladies, who bequeathed their entire fortune for its erection. The portraits of these two public benefactors were carved in the rude stone wall that rises above the floor of the bridge, but all likeness in these images has disappeared, either by the ravages of 630 years, or by passing fingers over them.

Previous to the erection of this bridge the Ayr was crossed on stepping-stones, and when swollen by rains was dangerous or impassable. Peace to the memory of these two noble minded, public spirited women! The other of the Twa Brigs has been replaced by a fine new structure since Burns' day.

Aug. 24th.—Left the pleasant city of Ayr, the birth-place of Burns, for Stranyer. Remained all night at the pleasant, home-like hotel George. Left next morning for Lorne, in Ireland. The voyage is made in a good steamer, distance forty miles. The day was calm and beautiful and the channel remarkably smooth. Stopped at the old Fleet Hotel, a filthy den. Preferred not to sleep between dirty sheets, and, not being able to procure clean ones, we paid for a room for a day, though not using it, and left for Belfast, where we arrived at 8 P. M., and put up at the very excellent hotel, Royal Avenue.

BELFAST.

Aug. 26th.—Made an excursion to the Giant's Causeway, a singularly beautiful rocky construction. Tens of thousands (I believe forty thousand have been counted) of columnar masses are seen covering a large area. Some of these are thirty or forty feet high and packed so closely together that even water would not pass between them. They are basaltic crystals and are of a pentagonal, hexagonal and rhomboidal shape. The whole presenting much the appearance of a magnified honeycomb.

These columns run down into and are lost in the water of the channel, and it is said that a similar construction is observable on the opposite English coast, showing that its formation was previous to the formation of the channel that separates Ireland from England. Its regular masonic formation gives it strikingly the appearance of having been made by human hands. So much so is this the case that my wife thinks yet it was so formed, and hence its name, Giant's Causeway, as it was thought that in prehistoric times, mentioned by Moses, " And there were giants on the earth in those days," these giants had constructed this causeway to connect the two islands. It is, however, a natural formation, resulting at the time the earth's surface cooled, by the existence at this point of a mass of liquid basalt, which on cooling formed these beautiful, uniform crystals, and are just such columns as might now be formed were an equal mass of basaltic matter cooled down to a point of solidity. It is, however, a beautiful result, and must always, as now, interest both the ignorant and scientist. We are here certainly and instructively brought into direct resultant connection with a time when our earth revolved in space as a liquid mass, with an intensity of heat beyond conception, compared to which, iron at a white heat would scarcely appear hot.

The coast along which we traveled was the most beautiful we have anywhere seen. The night previous there had been quite a storm on the channel, in which one vessel had gone ashore, and the wind was still quite fresh, so much so that the white-crested waves rolled in long swells, and broke in beauty and grandeur against the foot of the cliff along which we were traveling. After having spent the entire day we returned to Belfast at 9 P. M.

Belfast is an important commercial and manufacturing city of some 200,000 inhabitants. Perhaps, Dublin excepted, it is the most important city in all Ireland, its trade extending to all parts of the world.

We visited the harbor, which is crowded with steamers and merchant ships, presenting quite a business appearance. The imports and exports last year amounted to the great sum of $130,000,000. The city is well built, with many important and really fine buildings, churches, colleges, etc. The streets are wide and clean. On Queen's Square is a lofty monument to Prince Albert. We failed to see any beauty or significance in this structure, unless it is a manifestation of loyalty to the rulers of England, and this perhaps is genuine, as this part of Ireland is in closer sympathy with England than other parts of the island, or, indeed with the other portions of Ireland. The entire city presents the appearance of thrift and industry. It is the most important linen market in the world, not an insignificant portion of its capital and industry being connected with this. Of course we made purchases of Irish linen articles that are manufactured here in a profusion, beauty and perfection quite irresistible to an American.

Aug. 28th.—Left Belfast for Dublin. The route passes through Drogheda. This highly-important town in the history of Ireland possesses now but little to interest the tourist. A part of the old wall with which the town was formerly surrounded, is still standing. Near here was fought the decisive and, by the Irish, forever-to-be-remembered battle of the Boyne, where the desperate valor and personal daring of the ill-disciplined Irish went down before the discipline and valor of the English.

The country between Belfast and Dublin is an extended agricultural district in the highest state of cultivation. The soil is thin and requires careful husbandry. But such is the care and skillful culture that a full yield of barley, wheat, oats, potatoes and rye is obtained. Perhaps the yield is quite as great as with us on our virgin soil. The towns and villages are neat, and the entire country presents an appearance, if not of thrift, certainly not of destitution. The houses are mostly of stone, low one-story, with roofs of straw. The amount of destitution, want, poverty, degredation, starvation, so generally in our country associated with Ireland and the Irish people, most certainly is not seen here—belongs not to all this northern or middle portion of Ireland. Arrived at Dublin at 6 P. M.

DUBLIN.

Dublin, the capital and largest and most important city of Ireland, has but little to interest the tourist. We put up at the large and most excellent Hotel Shelborn, in front of Stevens' Green, one of the principal parks of Dublin. St. Patrick's Cathedral is the most important church. According to legends, this fine Gothic structure dates back to the mythical times of St. Patrick.

As we were here in the heart of a Catholic city—and as with us almost everything connected with St. Patrick is Catholic, we were not a little surprised to find this not a Catholic church. It is a Protestant church and has an interesting history, embracing much of the history of Dublin, indeed of Ireland. A great number of banners belonging to the Knights of St. Patrick, and other insignia, are hanging upon the walls. There are many tombs and monuments to great men in the church. Among these was that to the eccentric, talented Dean Swift, and his strange and unfortunate Mrs. Johnstone, "Stella." How strange and mysterious the relation between those two persons, and how unfortunate! The one died broken-hearted, and the other from softening of the brain, perhaps from grief for her loss, or remorse. Who can tell? The strange relation, connection or association between these two unfortunate persons was a secret, known only to themselves, and can only be given up at the Last Day, and yet all the world wishes that, now that the storms of life are past, they may rest well.

Aug. 30th.—Visited Phœnix Park, rendered famous by the murder here in open daylight of the Lord Lieutenant of Ireland, Lord Cavendish, and his under-secretary, Burke, by misguided Irish patriots. O, Liberty, how many crimes have been committed in thy sacred name! We drove by the spot where their dead bodies were found, in an open ground, on the public highway, in view of every passer-by. It is almost impossible that this deed should have been committed without being seen by one or many persons. The probabilities are that those who saw it were either in sympathy with the murderers or were afraid to inform upon them or even to let it be known that they witnessed it. The spot where they fell is marked by two small holes by the roadside some ten feet apart. Well, fortunately for the best interests of society—of man— "murder will out," and after much delay these misguided men paid the penalty by the forfeiture of their lives. Had these deeds been committed against any power less civilized and conservative than Great Britain it is fearful to think what would have been the consequences. Suppose such a deed had been committed in Cromwell's day ; half of Dublin would have been sacrificed.

Phœnix Park is seven miles in circumference and contains 1,700 acres. It is a beautiful park, with extensive drives, graveled walks, shaded paths, flowery trees, monuments, etc. Wellington's monument is 265 feet high. Thousands of deer of many kinds are grazing as quietly and tamely as so many cattle. We counted 140 in one herd. In early summer, when the hawthorn and chestnut trees are in bloom, this park must be most beautiful.

Although in August, the day was cold, damp, disagreeable, so much so that when we returned to the hotel we were thoroughly chilled, really suffering from cold. We noticed the blackberry bushes in the park full of green fruit and flowers and were told by the carraige driver that these would ripen, yet this was the latter part of August. Strange ! I am quite sure with us fruit would never ripen in such a temperature, with the weather almost cold enough for snow. If fruit ever ripens here with this absence of heat and sunshine it must necessarily be very indifferent, can contain little or no sugar, and yet it may be that these people, unaccustomed to better, and ignorant of the excellence of this same fruit when ripening under more favorable skies, as with us, may think it quite good. I am sure no American would think so. I may mention that harvest is just beginning and much of the grain will not be harvested before the 10th of September, at which time we are sowing wheat for the next year's crop.

Drove over and through Dublin, which really possesses but little of interest to the tourist. Perhaps no city of Europe possesses less. Is this because of the misfortunes of this unfortunate people, who possess a native talent of the highest order and are intellectually capable of doing whatever man can do? Visited the poorer quarter of the city, where we met with an amount of poverty nowhere else seen. Hundreds of badly-clothed women and half naked children are seen with faces unwashed and tangled, unkempt hair, that looked as though it had not been combed since they left their cradles. Here the long misrule and fearful misfortunes of the land are seen in the changes they have wrought upon the people. And the end is not yet.

Aug. 31st.—Left Dublin at 7:15 A. M. for Holyhead. The morning was dark and misty, with a fresh wind blowing from the southeast, presaging storms, and as a gale had been predicted for this or the following day wife was much alarmed lest one should strike us before we reached the opposite shore. The steamers on this line are of the finest class and make the surprising time of 18 miles an hour, crossing the channel, 64 miles, in 3 1-2 hours, which speed would rapidly get us out of danger. I asked the captain about the predicted storm. He thought we would have one and was evidently expecting one at any moment, and as the wind was momentarily increasing, with the air more murky, I noticed my watch not without interest. The previous night had been quite calm and the water was at first quite smooth, but before we reached the opposite shore the sea, in response to the increasing wind, was beginning to be quite rough. We, however, beat the storm, and had a good voyage across the channel.

WALES.

Holyhead, the point of departure and arrival of steamers to and from Dublin, is a busy seaport in Wales. We took the cars at this place for Chester. The road runs along the coast, passing many small towns and villages of more or less interest as bathing places.

This northern coast section of Wales is among the most beautiful of Great Britain, not excepting the Highlands of Scotland. Much of the country is but poorly adapted to agriculture, but the tact, industry and thrift of these hardy Welsh have surmounted seemingly impossible difficulties, and turned places sterile, and by nature uninviting, into fruitful fields and rich pastures. A general appearance of comfort and thrift characterizes the country. Along the coast the many little villages are inhabited principally by sea-faring people or colliers and workers in foundries, as much of this section is underlaid with coal and iron. We arrived at Chester at 3 P. M., and after taking dinner at the Queen's Hotel ordered carriage and drove over the city.

CHESTER.

Chester has a population of some 40,000, is a mediæval city, and in some respects one of the most interesting towns in the kingdom. It is a walled city and retains many of the features of the good olden times with the architecture of the Dark and early Middle Ages. It has possessed more or less interest since the beginning of the Christian era. In A. D. 60 it was possessed and governed by the Roman troops. It partook largely in the civil wars of the Roses, suffered from investure and sieges, from which its high and strong wall, still in a good state of preservation, did not always protect it. And yet so high and strong are these walls that before the introduction of the present improved means of warfare they must have proved formidable barriers against assault. It is situated upon the small river Dee, which runs immediately alongside of its walls.

We visited the old cathedral, first erected in the seventh century. It is a large structure built of old red sandstone, with lofty buttresses and pinnacles, architecture of the times of the Tudors. Inside are many monuments of men distinguished in their day, some now forgotten. Rude, quaintly-carved oak stalls, with numerous niches and decorations in wood and stone. It was long a Catholic cathedral and connected with a religious order. But since the time of Henry VIII., when this order was abolished and its lands confiscated, it has been shorn of most of its internal splendor. The paintings, statues, and, most missed of all, the high altar, have been removed, and though still used as a place of worship, most of it is unprovided with even benches, showing it to be unused, most likely for want of worshipers. It is, even in this half-deserted condition, one of the most interesting cathedrals in Europe. And if Ichabod is written in its vacant places of worship, it only shows, and this it shows clearly, though men will not see it, that its massive structures have better withstood the ravages of time and change of thought than has the religious sentiment among the people. And this I may truly say is not the only cathedral, massive and time-defying, we have visited in which the same fact is forcibly, unmistakably manifested. Talk as we may of our religion and its influence upon the masses, nothing is more certain than that if it ever did really control the thoughts and actions of Europe, it does so no longer. Let us moralize upon this as we may, it is cer tainly true, and this perhaps to an equal extent in Catholic as well as Protestant countries.

We also visited a venerable pile, St. John's church, which was built by Ethelred, king of Mercia in the seventh century. The bell tower, which was standing until recently, is now a mass of shapeless ruins, having yielded to the storms of 1,000 years. Much of the church, however, is in a tolerable good state of preservation. It stands upon the wall of a perpendicular cliff overhanging the Dee, which here washes the foot of the cliff.

BRISTOL AND BIRMINGHAM.

We left Chester for Stratford on Avon, passing through, first Bristol, which is the third largest town in England, with a population of 450,000; next, Birmingham, one of the great, perhaps the greatest, manufacturing cities of the world. Great forests of tall chimneys, from which issue volumes of smoke or livid flames, rendering day obscure and night ghastly, crowd the city, line the road and cover the country for miles in and around this entire Birmingham district. The city owes its importance to its vast iron manufactures. Indeed there is no part of the civilized world where Birmingham wares are not found. Situated in the midst of England's richest coal and iron district, it is a very Vulcan's forge, and nowhere else is her vast wealth and industry seen to better advantage. Much of the power of this mighty nation, whose commerce embraces the earth, originates, receives form, in the forges and workshops of this district. But this enormous and constantly increasing use of iron now going on in England, while quickening her industrial resources, points, I am sure, to exhaustion, if not in the near, certainly in the remote, future. Iron, by its cheapness and abundance has created a want for it not really existing in fact, as it is now employed for many purposes for which wood could be economically used. And while this use of iron appears to answer the very desirable purpose of saving forests, it must sooner or later exhaust the iron supply of England. And iron cannot be grown, while forests can. And then the wasteful manner in which she is using her coals—shipping them to all parts of Europe, at a cost that only pays for the labor—yielding little or nothing for the coal, as coal, points again to exhaustion. And then what will England be when her coal and iron are exhausted? But we may be told this is a very remote future. I do not believe it is as remote as we have been taught to consider it. But granting the truth of the calculations as to its duration, the life of a nation and a race of people, belong to the remote future.

STRATFORD-ON-AVON.

From Birmingham we continued on to Stratford-on-Avon, where we arrived, quite fatigued, at 10 P. M., and put up at the Shakespear Hotel, a filthy place, where dirt and bad accommodations meet a compensation in high prices. We left this hotel next morning and obtained comfortable accommodations at a small inn.

Sept. 1st.—Stratford-on-Avon, the birth-place, home and burial ground of the world's greatest dramatic writer and poet, is a neat, quiet town of three or four thousand inhabitants. Visited the house in which Shakespear was born. It is an unpretentious building and yet has an air of philosophical importance, as though conscious of the merit it had received from its connection with Shakespear. After visiting it I imagined I would have picked it out from the other houses of Stratford as the one that had a claim to this distinguished honor. It is now owned by the public, carefully preserved, and will doubtless last as long as the name and deeds of Shakespear shall bring to Stratford his worshipers. For be it known such places have the peculiar power of self-rejuvenation.

We have seen through Europe many places that were old and in ruins when touched by the immortalizing finger of genius that are new now. Keepers are here to show all matters connected with Shakespear to tourists. We were shown the room in which he was born. It is small, low and roughly-finished, yet quite as good as, and larger than, that in the castle of Edinburgh, in which was born James I. of England. Formerly it did not require as large a room for great men to be born in as at present. In an adjoining room is a desk with his name rudely cut upon it at which he is said to have learned his boyish lessons, and the rude old fireplace at which he was wont to sit when a child while listening to the relation of nursery tales and ghost stories—all are here, and with the exception of the desk, are possibly genuine. The positive assurance we feel of being in the very rooms, and looking at much that witnessed his childish sports and development, brings us into the immediate presence of this immortal genius. How hallowed they are by this association. And as all things connected with Shakespear possess an immediate interest with us, we may state that the house itself is a rude plaster, stone and wooden one, with its entire architecture belonging to the times, and evidences the comfortable but unostentatious circumstances of, a man, neither great and rich, nor mean and poor, of the middle ages. Indeed this house evidences the fact that while Shakespear's father was, if not one of the gentry, doubtless a man of influence, belonging to the great upper middle classes, at whose house we would be most likely to meet with scholars, poets and minstrels, by whom were related many a bold adventure at home and abroad, all of which we can readily see this wondrous child drinking in, magnified, diversified, as it passed through the kaleidoscopic influence of his boyish brain.

Numerous old simple things, such as pipes, knives and trinkets are kept and shown here, as having belonged to

Shakespear, all of which we gladly believe, although we know that the testimony often rested upon dim traditions that might not stand careful scrutiny. But while it is so pleasant to see the knife that Shakespear had when a boy and the pipe he smoked on his visits here from London, who would be so stolid as to even doubt the fact, much less to institute an inquiry as to their genuineness? Thousands of names are written on the tables, walls, doors and ceiling by curious or admiring visitors, and while we had no thought of adding ours, we could well excuse the whim or vanity of those who wrote them, as we were ready to believe all was in veneration for the immortal genius whose association had hallowed them. We were shown the chair in which he was accustomed to sit, and, as had done hundreds of thousands of others, sat down in it. Not as has often been written by prosy critics, with any hope of receiving thereby any portion of his genius, but with a feeling of regard for this old chair from the fact that it* was Shakespear's

Visited the grounds upon which stood the fine house he bought after he retired from the stage, left London and came home to spend the evening of his days with his family, and in which he lived and died. As had the old house some squares off witnessed his birth and childhood with his infant cries embodied in its walls, this had seen him in his prime, and its walls had often echoed the jocund laugh of himself and boon companions, or reverberated back the rythmical music of his voice, as he read to wife and children his immortal productions, at the recital of which good Queen Bess and her court beauties and cavaliers had laughed or wept. How sacred its memories and how a gaping world would lend a quick ear to its recitals, could these things be told. But this new house is not here now, only its sure foundations, which have been cleared of all rubbish, to show clearly the outline and shape of the house, that at the time was the finest in Stratford, for Shakespear was now a rich man. Long after his death this house was bought by an ill-humored, morose, unpoetical man, who lived on the adjoining property, and who was, in the meanness and unsympathetic nature of his soul, so much annoyed by the swarms of strangers from all parts of the world running here and over the grounds and through the house that had now for want of care fallen into decay, that, to stop what to him was a nuisance, he had it pulled down—razed to the ground. But to his utter amazement the crowd seemed only and ever to increase, and he was so much annoyed with this and being constantly, hourly, called upon, rung up to answer some question about the former occupant, and why the home had been destroyed, what he knew about it, etc., that he had a sentinel placed at his own door, and had engaged to have the lot enclosed with a blind wall, when in very rage at the world, which he verily believed had gone mad, and worn out with contending with what he considered its insanity, he died, accursed by all the town, and should he remain in purgatory until posterity forgives him, he will remain as long as the memory of the wrong his vandalism did the world shall remain. Walking over this lot and measuring out the foundations of the house, we were again on sure grounds, there being no doubt about these being the foundations on and above which Shakespear died. We drank from the well, from which he so much delighted to drink, and it is a singular fact that the water of this well remains as it was in Shakespear's day, the purest, best water in all Stratford. In this yard stands the famous mulberry tree which Shakespear planted—no, not the one he planted, but an offshoot from it, the old tree being long since dead. This offshoot is a large old tree, and was full of ripe mulberries at the time of our visit.

There is a new, fine memorial theatre erected to his memory

and called the Shakespear Theatre. A most fitting memorial it is, and must be well-pleasing to his spirit, which we must believe still haunts this place, who in his day, did so much to purify, exalt, enoble the drama. Our own Mary Anderson, since Neilson's death, the greatest of tragediennes, had played here only two nights previous, to a crowded house of the elite of England, many of them having come up with her from London, and with great success, as Rosalind in "As you Like It."

Visited the old parish church which he was accustomed to attend when a boy, and again in later days, and where he lies buried in the chancel. His name is not on the marble slab that covers his grave, but immediately above it in the wall is the world-renowned epitaph, written, it is believed, by himself, and engraven here at the time of his burial.

"Blessed be he who spares these stones,
And cursed be he that moves my bones."

Immediately above this inscription is his bust, and as it is said this was placed here by his daughter, only seven years after his death, we must believe it is a good likeness of the poet. This anathema upon "he who moves my bones," has prevented his grave being disturbed by anyone and prevented his dust being carried to Westminster Abbey, all men feeling a reverential or superstitious fear to enter here, even to do his ashes honor. So great is this belief in the power of the curse, that when, a few years since, a portion of the church foundation gave way, opening his vault, a watchman was employed to guard it, but was hardly needed, as so great was the reverence and so firm the belief in the power of the curse that neither the watchman nor one of the workmen dared even to look in to see what was in the vault, not doubting that should they do so some great and immediate calamity would befall them or perhaps the whole community. And no Stratford man could be found, even though a thief, who would have the temerity to enter this vault, though he knew it contained valuables. Was there ever such a spell associated with an epitaph before?

This church, a large, and for the small town Stratford then was, a very fine one, in the Gothic style of architecture, contained numerous decorations, inscriptions and monuments of distinguished men, but naturally all interest centres on the chancel where Shakespear lies buried. The old graveyard in front of and on the sides of the church, contain many inscriptions and names of individuals running back to Shakespear's day—companions, neighbors and friends of the poet. These tombstones are hid among a grove of fine old trees that surround the church. The beautiful Avon murmurs softly by, near the church, meandering by and around the town of Stratford.

Wife drove out to and through the Chashote park, where Shakespear was accused when a boy of poaching. The tale has but little foundation in fact and yet it is just possible that Shakespear, in the buoyancy of youth, with some other wild young lads, may have gone to these woods poaching, and that this may have had some connection with his leaving Stratford and going down to try his fortune in London. It is more probable, however, that his genius was larger than the very limited field of his native town could furnish with nutriment, and that he went to London to try it upon the stage, for which we must believe, he had instinctive promptings. The farm or manor is owned by and occupied by the descendants of the same person that is said to have prosecuted Shakespear— the Lucys. On the night Mary Anderson played here, at the Shakespear Theatre, deer from this park, the direct descendants of those that it contained in Shakespear's day, were brought in and placed upon the stage, and the Lucy family occupied their box at the theatre. We regretted that we could not visit the house sacred to the memory of the gentle Anna Hathaway, as it was only accessible by walking across a low piece of meadow land, and this was overflowed at the time by the late heavy rains.

We had been several days in Stratford visiting places and scenes sacred to the memory of Avon's bard, when with memory crowded and fancy stimulated with and by these, quite tired I went to bed late on the last night of our stay, but could not sleep soundly, and half waking, found myself repeating Shakespear's plays, and though embodying sayings, many of which are so thoroughly woven into the life and thought of English-speaking people as to constitute a part of our household vocabulary and life philosophy, to my surprise I found none of these referring to or having any relation to Stratford or vicinity while the Aryshire poet, Burns, whose land I was just from and whom I found mixing up in my fancy with Shakespear, has photographed Ayr and its surroundings upon our minds, so much so, that "The Bonny Doon," "The Twa Brigs of Ayr," and the "Old Kirk of Alloway," were scarcely better known after than before I had seen them, while Stratford was an unknown land. Now why is this? Can it be that Burns was a local poet and as such immortalized his native land, its every brook, bridge, loch and mountain, photographing them upon our brains by his wondrous genius, while Shakespear was the poet, not of England, but of the world, of our race, writing the philosophy of the human heart, not that of a special people or locality, but of man, and not for any period, but for *all time.* Stratford people are happy in fancying they find in Shakespear's allusions and sayings Stratford scenes and places, but perhaps none others see thus.

Well, how strange a thing is sleep, which gives us a dual existence, leaves our bodies here and sends out our minds or thoughts in embodied existence to distant places, leaping over time and space, crowding ages into a moment and worlds into a span. Again I slept, but not soundly, forgetting Stratford and Ayr. I now dreamed I was at home and in company with one of our supreme judges, A., whom I had known when we were young men. He was then a young lawyer of much sprightliness, a young Democratic politician and clever stump orator, but really of no startling importance as a lawyer, with only a creditable knowledge of law, but a warm-hearted, genial, good fellow, with many personal friends. After the war, thanks to these qualities, he had the good fortune to be elected circuit judge of one of the interior counties and subsequently, through the activity of personal friends, secured the Democratic nomination and was elected one of the supreme judges and made a very creditable member of the bench. Well, I was in conversation with him and remarked that I had just succeeded in getting my old friend, Dr. ———, of St. Louis, elected circuit judge. At this, Judge A. expressed surprise and said: "Dr. ———! What does he know about law?" "O," I replied, "he does not know any more about law than he does of medicine, but then you know that a knowledge of law is not necessary to make a judge." At this Judge A. laughed heartily, as indeed he would have done had it actually happened.

WARWICK CASTLE.

Sept. 11th.—Made an excursion to Warwick Castle, which is perhaps the best specimen of an old English castle now existing. It was first built by Ethelred, in 915, and is not only in a good state of preservation but is the lovely manor of one of England's proudest noblemen, the residence of the Earl of Warwick and his family. The castle stands on a steep rock which overhangs the Avon, and is said to occupy the site of an old Roman fortification. An old Roman bridge is still standing, spanning the Avon at this point. This bridge was in a good state of preservation until lately, when the new and beautiful bridge was built just above it, on the completion of which the proprietor of the castle had the middle span in the old bridge removed to prevent passage over it, such passage interfering with the grounds and being now no longer necessary. This castle, as all like structures of the Middle Ages, is strongly built, the solid stone wall being no less than nine feet thick. It is approached through a deep defile cut in the solid rock, which renders it still more defensible. Upon the massive walls are several towers for defense. So solid was its construction, and so bravely was it defended that it withstood several protracted sieges. The last was by the Parliamentary forces, who, unable to take it, were compelled to raise the siege. It yet presents evidences of this siege. Numerous iron hooks, upon which were hung bales of wool to break the force of battering-rams, are still seen. We were politely shown over the castle, which contains many reminiscences of former times; old swords, guns, armor and portraits of distinguished men, among these Charles I. on horseback, and Henry VIII., by Holbein. A large room contains cross-bows, armour, etc. Among the most notable of these is the breast-plate of a former owner, Giant Guy. This breast-plate alone weighs fifty pounds, while his sword shown here is eight feet long. This giant was of great renown in his day, and slew other giants, wild boars, and monsters which had previously infested this district, for all of which his memory was long held in great veneration. Now of course these recitals of these deeds are mythical. But the shield and sword are here. Who owned them? They are many hundreds of years old and must have been used by some one. The tower said to have been defended by this giant is known as Guy's Tower. From this lofty parapet it is said the giant threw great stones weighing hundreds of pounds.

OXFORD.

Sept. 3rd.—Left Stratford for Oxford, where we arrived at 2 P. M., and put up at the Hotel Mitre.

Oxford is a university town, and owes all its importance to its world-renowned university and Bodleian Library. We took carriage and drove over the town, and around its college grounds and buildings. There are twenty-six colleges, most of which we visited during the afternoon. Next day was spent in visiting and examining the Bodleian Library, perhaps the most important collection of books in the world, consisting of 450,000 volumes and 30,000 manuscripts. But its real value is not in the number of its books, as this is greatly exceeded by the British Museum, which contains 1,500,000 volumes, and the National Library of Paris, which has 2,000,000 volumes, while several other libraries in Europe have upwards of half a million volumes, but these books are more select than any other, consisting for the most part of standard works. There is no department of knowledge but is contained fully in this library. We noticed in cases and kept under glass, many books of times antedating printing. Many of these were illuminated, finely ornamented, all with the pen, and yet this and the letters of the book so finely executed that it was difficult to believe they were not printed. Some of these books are six or seven hundreds of years old.

The university was founded by Alfred the Great, and has, with various vicissitudes, lived on and through the changes of government, dynasties and forms of religions, through the Dark and all the Middle Ages, even to the present day, constituting, if not the most, at least one of the most, important seats of learning in the world, and furnishing more men great in literature and science than any similiar institution. Indeed, it would be quite impossible to over-estimate the importance of Oxford in the development of modern civilization and learning in Europe.

We visited, with much interest, Lincoln College, the first stage upon which appeared the dawning earnest religious convictions and labors of John Wesley. In the small room adjoining the chapel is the pulpit in which he preached. To-day tens of thousands of pulpits throughout the world are ringing with the interpretations of Scripture and religious thought and feeling given to the world by the earnest, thoughtful, sincere, pious young graduate who occupied it then. In the library of this college is a Wycklif Bible, and in the hall is Wesley's bust, and near the chapel the room in which he studied. This college was founded in 1427.

Visited Christ's College. In this the sons of royalty and those of the higher nobility are educated. Consequently it has quite an aristocratic air. Saw the rooms occupied by the Prince of Wales during his student life. They are now, I believe, occupied by his sons. In this college hangs " Old Tom," the big bell of Oxford, weighing 17,000 pounds. Examined the Great Hall of this college, which is among the finest in England. The walls are hung with portraits of men of world-wide reputation—great poets, orators, statesmen and warriors. We examined them with the more interest as they are known almost as well in America as in England—Chaucer, Spencer, Milton, Dryden, Johnson, Goldsmith, Pope, Addison, Bacon, Newton, Shakespear, belonging to us equally with the English. Indeed, so identified with our literature are the names of the persons whose portraits adorn this hall, that I felt much more at home among them than I would be among our own celebrities in a like hall in Washington City. From here we visited and walked along " Addison's Walk," a beautiful shaded avenue of old oaks and sycamores, that were large trees when the immortal poet and essayist walked and mused beneath them. How mightier than these things is the genius that hallows them! After again visiting the Bodleian Library and examining more minutely the old manuscripts and illuminated volumes on vellum, we left Oxford at 2 P. M. and ran down to London, stopping at Charing Cross Hotel. The country between Oxford and London is fertile, highly-cultivated and populous, many towns and villages dotting the way. In approaching London the road for many miles is along the Thames. After a few days we obtained rooms and board at 74 Guilford St., Russell Square.

LONDON.

London is the largest city in the world, containing within its metropolitan district, which embraces the city proper and its immediate suburbs, more than 5,000,000 inhabitants, and within this district are 6,600 miles of improved streets. Were these streets placed in a straight line they would reach from London to San Francisco, or more than one-fourth the distance around the world. These streets are lighted by more than one million gas lamps. There are in the city 3,000 merchant tailors, 300,000 domestic servants, 90,000 paupers, 1,400 churches, 2,000 charities, distributing more than $20,000,000 annually, and more than 100,000 grown persons who are without religion, belong to no church, and who were almost never in one. There are 600,000 children on the school register, most of these, however, almost never saw or were in a school-room.

To feed this mighty multitude requires annually 2,000,000 quarters of wheat, 325,000,000 pounds of meat, 500,000,000 pounds of fish and 8,000,000 poultry, and 200,000,000 gallons of porter are consumed to wash it down. It is estimated that $1,000,000,000 are expended annually. The daily supply of water is 150,000,000 gallons, and 8,000,000 tons of coal are consumed annually. There are 20,000 public cabs on the streets. Many of the public buildings cost from one to twenty millions of dollars each. Twenty thousand vessels enter the port of London annually, and the exports amount to $500,000,000.

From these figures it is readily seen that we have here a world-centre whose throbbings are felt to the ends of the earth, and there is no place where her lines are not gone out, and the sun in his flight never catches a point where her influence is not seen and felt, and to the civilized world the influence of her commerce is scarcely less failing or less necessary than the tides to the ocean.

BRITISH MUSEUM.

This museum building occupies nearly an entire square, is three stories high with a row of Ionic columns running along its entire front. We will enter first the library, which is the second largest in the world, containing 1,600,000 volumes. But this number, enormous as it is, is easily said and written, but to give us some better idea of this wonderful collection of books, let us suppose the reading of them had commenced at the birth of Christ, with reading a book each day, the library would not be read half through in A. D. 2,000. In other words, it would require 4,382 years. Besides these books there are many thousands of manuscripts. Contained in cases are books illustrating the history of book-making for the last 1,000 or 1,200 years. Among these is a Syriac version of the Bible, and one of the oldest Bible manuscripts of the fifth century. These cases also contain a great many autographs of distinguished persons, foreign and English. Among these we notice those of Luther, Cranmer, Erasmus, Watson, John Knox, Sir Walter Raleigh, Penn, (founder of Pennsylvania), Michael Angelo, Galileo, Sir Isaac Newton, Descartes, Swift, Addison, Lord Byron, Edward IV., Richard III., Henry VII., Henry VIII., Anna Boleyn, Jane Grey, Queen Mary, Queen Elizabeth, Mary Queen of Scots,

Georges I., II. and III., Charles V. of Spain, and many others.

One room contains Roman antiquities found in England. Three others are devoted to Greek and Roman antiquities, busts, statues, etc. The Elgin Room contains the Elgin Marbles, frieze and cornice of the Parthenon at Athens. To have removed them from this old temple and cradle or nursery of the arts seems a sacrilege at which Byron eloquently protests. They are by the chisel of Phidias, of unequaled beauty, and cost $350,000. The Helenic Room contains marble sculptures from every part of Greece. Among them fragments of the Mausoleum from Halicarnassus, built by Artemisia as the tomb of her husband Mausoleus—hence the name mausoleum—in B. C. 352. Also many other marble statues, bas and alto reliefs, showing quite instructively Greek art. The Assyrian Room contains many fragments, marbles and other stones, bricks, pottery, etc., containing cuneiform inscriptions from ancient Syrian cities, from B. C. 2,200 to the overthrow of the kingdom. These give broken accounts of Merodach I., king of Babylon, B. C. 1,800, others of the time of Sennacherib and Sardanapalus. These fortunate finds of Bayard and a Frenchman, and fortunate discoveries of the way to decipher these long lost cuneiform characters have brought to light some at least curious, if not instructive, facts. The Assyrian books consisted in plates or rolls of thin clay cakes or bricks, upon which the history or matter was written and the clay then burned hard. These books were evidently in great number, forming large libraries, containing doubtless much of the early history of nations, of which we now know but little. I noticed among these a small tablet, being the receipt by the treasurer for moneys. And again, I saw on tablets 2,000 B. C., a history of the creation of man, and an account of Noah's flood almost just as Moses gives them.

Three great halls are filled with Egyptian antiquities, and contain if not the most extensive collections in Europe, at least one of these. Some of these statues and stones are 6,000 years old, and yet at the time of the oldest of them it is proven by these impressive and disinterested witnesses that Egyptian civilization and art was in an high state of development, indeed, had attained its zenith, a point at which, like the Chinese civilization, it stopped, crystalized, remaining for thousands of years either stationary or in a slow decline. The causes of the sudden arrest in the progress of the people, who had developed their own civilization is, and most likely always will be, a mystery. Could it have been some disastrous invasion and introduction of some unfavorable new governmental influence? Or was it the ascendency of some idea or influence inimical to change? I must suspect this latter! It is most likely that about the time of the building of the pyramids of Cheops, 4,000 B. C., which seems to have been the period of Egypt's highest development, the priesthood obtained control of the State, and lest their influence, or that of their gods, should suffer by change, arrested all further progress as innovations upon the sanctity of religion, and by pains and penalties dwarfed the national mind and stereotyped things as they then were; and as without progress there must be decay, the arts and science slowly declined. In the unknown vast periods of time in which this self-taught people were developing the high state of culture at which we first meet them, we are carried back to a period of time in the existence of our race truly astonishing. Many thousands of years were doubtless employed in this development; previous to the building of the pyramids, 6,000 years ago. But as it is impossible to believe that the first of this race commenced this development, we must suppose that many thousands of years elapsed before their remote ancestors first emerged from the **savage state.**

The more we learn of this interesting people the more are we convinced of our loss in not knowing more. Why is it that we are unable to trace back their hieroglyphical history no farther than near the time of the pyramid-builders, at which time it is positively certain that a high state of civilization of arts and science have existed for many ages? This must be, in part, that advances in these had long been going on before this people, with whom everything was original, indigenous, discovered the art that embalms the thought—discovered how to transmit to posterity, even by picture-writing, their thoughts, and until they had done this, of course, all beyond was void.

That Egypt was the cradle of arts, of civilization, and that her people did invent or discover for themselves everything which they possessed, is now no longer a matter of doubt. In this strange land, by this people, at some remote period in the world's history, a period possibly remote beyond anything that has been suggested, was kindled and set up an intellectual light at which Greece and other nations lighted their first torches. Consequently their progress must have been inconceivably slow, necessarily so, while those who borrowed the tools they had invented, as Greece, may have sprang forward with great rapidity.

After obtaining control of the State, and crushing the liberties of the people, which appears to have been about the time of the discovery of picture-writing, the Hierarchy seem to have suppressed all writings or books, other than those concerning religion, consequently while we have now in our possession as much as hundreds of volumes of Egyptian writings, they are comparatively worthless in throwing light upon the great questions that deeply interest us, as they are all in some manner connected or relating to their religious forms and ceremonies—their Liturgy, the *Book* of the *Dead*. And we are the more readily inclined to this opinion from the well-known ecclesiastical tendency in this direction, two most notable examples of which are but too well known from the disaster they entailed. When in this same land of Egypt the Mohammedans obtained possession, the Caliph on being asked what should be done with the Alexandrian Library, replied, that if the books concerned the Koran they should be burned, as the Koran was all-sufficient and needed no exposition or proofs, and if they were not in accordance with the Koran they must be burned as heretical. The books were accordingly burned as being worthless or injurious. Again during the history of our religion an *index expurgatorus* was established, almost equally destructive, as it prevented the publication of all books not deemed religious, or in accordance with the then interpretations of the dominant religious beliefs. This was almost as fatal as the Mohammedan or the ancient Egyptian edict, as it not only prevented progress, but led to the destruction of much that had been known and written. With these facts we have no difficulty in supposing that the further advance in Egypt, and the absence of much of its history of important events, is the result of Hierarchical influence, an influence which was most likely the cause of the downfall of themselves, their religion, and the destruction of their temples and their gods.

This strange people, unlike all others, as though conscious that their thoughts, ideas, improvements, should serve as a basis only for the improvement of others, built their structures, pyramids, arches, sphinxes, all, to last forever. The Greeks, the instructors of Europe, built for ornament, beauty of form being the cardinal idea; the Romans, like ourselves, constructed for usefulness, combining beauty of form only as an adjunct. And thus having in all things, as the leading idea, duration, and farther influenced by their religious opinions, they labored to render their bodies also immortal. And in this they certainly succeeded, and these if undisturbed in their rock-bound catacombs might have lasted as long as have and will their pyramids, or forever.

An immense hall in this building is devoted to mummies sarcophagi, coffins, etc. Some of these mummies are yet in their coffins, others are in their bandages or winding sheets, in still other cases the bandages have been removed so far as to expose the face, the feet and hands. There are hundreds of these mummies, besides the mummies of their sacred animals, as cats, monkeys, crocodiles, etc. There are mummies of old men and women, young persons and infants, including the great and the poor as shown, as would such distinction be shown at the present day, by the fine bandages, coffins and sarcophagi in the one case and the rude accompaniments in the other. Most of these mummies are in quite a good state of preservation, though desiccated and blackened. But so well are their features preserved, that in some instances, they might doubtless be recognized by their friends and relations, were such living, but these also have been dead and forgotten for three and four thousand years. Nation, tongue and people, all have passed away, and the language and writing forgotten for thousands of years, and not until the accidental discovery of the Rosetta Stone could these be deciphered. This important find, the Rosetta Stone was discovered by the French during their military operations in Egypt in 1802, and through the genius of Champollion was made to give up the secret of ages. It was shipped to Paris, but on its way was captured by the English, and is now here set up in the passway of this hall. It is a tablet of black porphyry, dressed only on its upper face, is about forty inches long by thirty wide, with inscription in three languages, first, Hieroglyphic, second, Demotic and third, Greek. Hence called the trilingqual stone.

This embalming and preservation of the body by these

ancient Egyptians, about which so much wonder has been expressed was not diffcult of discovery or practice, and bodies could alike be rendered incorruptible at the present day were we foolish enough to desire it, or did our religion, as theirs, require it, and was after this manner:

The brain was first removed through the nostrils, and the calvarium filled with hot bitumen and aromatics. The other viscera were then removed and cavities filled in like manner. The body was then perfectly encased in linen bandages saturated with aromatic bitumen; over this was poured bitumen and another encasement of bandages, and sometimes as many as four or five folds of bituminous bandages surrounded the body and limbs. By this it was entirely protected from air and moisture. The body thus protected was now placed in a wooden coffin containing in hieroglyphics, on the inside of the coffin, the social condition of the deceased, with lengthy quotations from the Book of the Dead, giving ample instructions how to conduct themselves at the tribunal before which they were to be judged according to deeds done in this world. This coffin after being sealed air tight, was placed within a massive, granite sarcophagus, which was cemented with some indestructible cement, made thrice air tight, or thus thrice protected from air and moisture, the sarcophagi were securely placed, in most cases, in niches cut in the walls of the everlasting hills and these niches again closed. The result has been as we see here, these bodies have been perfectly preserved, and now after four or five thousand years retain many of their peculiarities of feature.

In a jar were some hands and feet that had been cut off to show their perfect preservation and looked much like those seen in a dissecting room, except these were more dried and blackened.

But how vain all this effort to render immortal that which it is better it were mortal! Who would have their body preserved as a mockery and a show, when all that rendered it lovely, the quickening mind, has ceased to bear it company, to protect it, to render it loved or hated, and when all who knew and loved us have with their entire nation, tongue and kindred long since passed away, have ceased to love or hate.

Could this curious people, who, with this wondrous care and ingenuity, labored to render their bodies immortal, have known that thousands of years afterwards these bodies would have been thus removed thousands of miles from their native land to be curious shows and jests of a nation and people who then had no existence, they would, methinks, scarcely have thought success in this direction desirable.

Great numbers of statues of men and gods, monstrous winged bulls, great winged lions with men's heads, sphinxes, great stone beetles and multitudes of other Egyptian curiosities are placed in this room. Some of these statues are of the Fifth Dynasty, and consequently six thousand years old. We saw three wooden statues more than five thousand years old.

I saw here on the walls illuminated papyrus and frescoes, from the long forgotten ruined palaces and temples of Karnak, upper Egypt, with their three colors, red, black and yellow, so bright, and the design so well executed, that it was difficult to believe they had been done five thousand years ago, instead of last year, and were by a people whose civilization had passed away for thousands of years, leaving behind them these footprints in the sands of time, instead of the works of some strange people still existing.

But leaving this great hall with its works that seem to embody ugliness, repugnance, in their idea of eternal duration, and to these qualities we may also add uselessness, as we cannot suppose the time will ever again come when these will serve as models, we enter other rooms containing great quantities of beautiful and really useful antiquities—useful, if for no other reason, than that a "thing of beauty is a joy forever."

Rooms of Etruscan Vases.—These vases are in some instances as old as many of the Egyptian curiosities, perhaps three and four thousand years, and may be even older than this, as in their workmanship they dawn the awakening Greek mind, or the mind of the unknown ancestors of this wonderfully artistic people. And running through their developmental culture to its highest attainments in the age of Pericles, 450 to 300 B.C., brings us down through its decadence and absorption in the all-conquering Roman Empire.

These vases, of which there is a great collection, are arranged in and, should be studied in, their historic order. Beginning with the crude or archaic, we find a gradual improvement in the design and execution. At first the crude figures of men and animals are in black on a red ground, then more perfect and beautiful artistic figures, until the most perfect art period, when we have men and women with mythological characters, games, battles, seiges, etc., in red on a black ground—a complete transformation or transposition having taken place with the advance of the art, until the black figure on a red ground in the archaic age has changed to a red figure on a black ground in the most perfect. And these are indeed beautiful, perhaps beyond successful imitation, and would to-day adorn the saloons of any palace, where in fact we have often seen them.

Other rooms contain medals, coins, ornaments, jewels, glass and majolica wares. Other rooms contain great quantities of Anglo-Saxon antiquities, while still others contain mediæval articles, arms, armor, cross-bows, guns, swords, spears, pistols, ivory carvings. But it would be as tiresome as difficult to give even an outline of things here. We shall leave this world-collection here, near Russell Square, and run down to South Kensington.

The South Kensington Museum is only a continuation of the British Museum. We shall only notice here the Natural History Museum. The building for this single department is a beautiful romanesque structure, three stories high, and 675 feet long, with wings 200 and 300 feet long. The main hall is 700 feet long, 170 feet wide and 72 feet high. This hall opens out on either side into the great central room, which is the main entrance to the building.

To the right, the entrance hall, 300 feet long, is occupied through its central space with skeletons of great animals, many of these now extinct. First is the entire skeleton of a whale, sixty feet long. Next is the entire skeleton of a mastodon found in Benton county, Mo., U. S. A., and a skeleton of the extinct Irish stag. This last is a noble animal, and, of course, extinct, as there would be no possibility of its existing in Ireland now, or indeed for the last thousand years, except in reserves. Then the head and tusk of an enormous mastodon found here in the valley of the Thames. The tusks of this enormous animal, that once inhabited England, are eight inches in diameter and ten feet long. Next the head of an enormous hippopotamus that also once lived in the valley of the Thames. Also the skeleton complete of the one and two horned rhinoceros of England, and the skeleton in plaster cast of an extinct enormous armadillo found in South America. For comparison, the complete skeleton of the present armadillo is placed by the side of this. On either side of this great hall are cases containing parts of skeletons of different animals. The first case on the right contains skulls and other bones, with flint and bone instruments, of the men who lived in caves in England and France, cotemporaneous with the great cave bear, mastodon, hippopotamus.

Several fragmentary skeletons of these men are seen in these cases. These human remains show a small brain cavity, and a man of rather under size, showing that wherever giants may have lived, our forefathers of the caves were not of them, but rather under size and of low intellect. Their crude and very imperfect instruments of flint and bone must have made their struggles for existence against the cave bear, sabre-toothed tiger, hippopotamus, rhinoceros, and other animals with which they had to contend, a very precarious, and in many individual instances an unsuccessful one. Indeed, it is positively certain that a successful struggle against such animals, with such arms, would have been an impossibility without that force, of which even the rudest men can avail themselves, the strength of aggregation, or acting in multitude, and the use of fire. The almighty importance of these two forces, the latter only available to man, gives him power and dominion over all the beasts of field and forest.

In a case here is the fossilized human skeleton found in South America. This is, I believe, with one exception, the only instance or specimen of fossilized man yet found. But it gives no evidence as to man's great antiquity, as it is in a recent limestone formation, a formation even now going on at the same and other places. It may be many thousand years old, or only a few hundred. In all probability it is long subsequent to the bones found in these caves and shown in adjoining cases. It is the skeleton of a man of medium size, with body, pelvis, ribs and lower limbs almost entire ; with the bones held in position by the limestone rock with which they are firmly encrusted, and looking much as we find trilobites in the limestone rock of the quarries.

Now, while these interesting and instructive remains of human bones and instruments and implements prove positively, what can no longer be disputed, that man and these now long since extinct animals were cotemporaneous, and establish beyond rational doubt the great antiquity of man, unfortunately, we have no possible means of determining what this antiquity really is, whether it extends back for hundreds of thousands of years, or only tens of thousands of years. Certain it is, it was at a time when the climate and topography of England and France, were quite different from what they now are. But when that was, and what these changes have been, and how produced, are mysteries unsolved, and may remain forever undetermined.

But these seemingly silent records of bygone epochs are not without instructive cosmical lessons. First, they teach us, contrary to popular belief, which peoples the earth with giants, that our very remote cave ancestors were not even so large or strong as their posterity. And a curious, but instructive fact here comes to our knowledge, that, while many, perhaps most, other animals have degenerated, man has actually improved, ever improved, physically and mentally. In the fossil remains, or preserved skeletons of other animals now extinct, as the elephant, tiger, bear, kangaroo, stag, etc., the present species are dwarfed, all having been represented by ancestors of greatly larger size, in some instances of twice or three times the size.

These huge mammalian animals, nearest to man, have disappeared, doubtless, when, and as, the changing or changed conditions of their environments became unsuited to their existence, leaving behind them a dwarfed posterity better adapted to the changed condition; while man has suffered no such change, because he could do what no other animal had the power to do—could adapt himself, through the instrumentality of fire and artificial clothing, to the changed conditions, being perhaps quite as large and strong as, and living longer than, his remote cave ancestors, while his intellectual development has rendered him even more superior, in point of fact, to his cave ancestors, than these were to the cave bears with which they contended for the possession of domicile. What would these cave men, with their flint and bone instruments, do in a like struggle with their posterity, with cannon and breech-loaders?

The belief of all nations in man's origin from a race of demi-gods, giants and heroes, of greatly superior strength and moral and intellectual prowess or attainments, finds here, as indeed we know otherwise, positive disproof. The ancestors of all men were ignorant savages, with no superior physical or mental endowments.

The great hall to the left, also 300 feet in length, is filled with beautifully prepared stuffed birds and animals. A collection that for variety and extent is unrivaled by any like collection in the world, containing a full assortment of all and every rare animal and bird.

Great numbers of birds, almost as natural as life, are so arranged as to give to the observer an idea of the animals' entire life, habits and habitats. Here are multitudes of swimming birds and waders, auks, pelicans, black and white swan, ducks, cranes, and the curious ornithorhynchus from Australia, a bird with the body of an otter and the bill of a duck. Also birds of prey, eagles, hawks, vultures, with climbing birds, pheasants, etc. Of animals, bears, wolves, tigers, lions, seals deer, antelopes and others.

Returning to the central room, we mount a broad flight of steps at the top of which is a fine marble-seated statue of the greatest of philosophical naturalists, Darwin, who sits in meditation grand, majestic, as the presiding genius of animated nature. The long galleries are filled with beautiful specimens of birds with their nests, eggs or young with artistically arranged grasses, brooks, rocky crevices, illustrating their habits and habitats. These are all under glasses. All is so naturally arranged that these birds appear as if in their homes.

The great halls are filled with anatomical preparations. A splendid anthropological collection, consisting of typical male and female human skeletons, then crania of all the races, families and casts of men now inhabiting the globe. Europe, Asia, Africa, North and South America, and Oceanica, are here represented by numerous crania. The study of these skulls points out the progressive and non-progressive peoples quite as clearly as the world's history could do.

Near by, adjoining, is a room containing an immense collection, illustrating the anthropoid or monkey families. There are a number of perfect typical skeletons of various species of Simia, then a very great number of crania. These crania have been collected from all parts of the world inhabited by monkeys, male and female crania of almost every variety of the monkey family, running down to the Lemurs.

First there are skeletons male and female of the most anthropoid monkey, gorillas, chimpanzees and ourang-outangs. Some of these are nearly as man-like as some of the crania of the lower orders of humanity. Indeed in two or three young chimpanzees, particularly the cranium of a female chimpanzee remarkable during life for its intelligence and good qualities, this resemblance was so strong as to render it difficult to say that it was not the head of a low order of the human species. But this very close resemblance to the human cranium was only seen in the younger animals; in the older ones the shape departs farther from the human skull. This is dependent upon two causes, race or generic laws and the necessity for the development through use dependent upon their food for strong masticatory muscles which constantly cause a more prognathous head.

The third story contains minerals and geological collections, precious stones, rare crystals, etc., with a great number and variety of aerolites, one of these weighing two or three tons. These are so arranged, often with explanatory notes, as to throw as much light upon their cosmic history, origin, formation and appearance upon our planet as possible. But I must say, after examining these specimens, studying them with their explanatory notes attached, I felt that I knew less about the subject than before, as all this had unsettled my previous, pretty-well-defined views, without confirming me in others. There was, however, one thing I did learn positively by this study, and this was that nothing certain was known on this interesting subject, and this I really regretted to learn, as I had thought there was much which we might accept as established.

COLONIAL EXHIBITION, 1885.

Adjoining the South Kensington Museum are the Colonial Exhibition buildings, covering many acres. And as this Exhibition was at this time, we visited its rooms. Nothing perhaps ever transpired that showed to better effect the wealth and glory and majesty and might and dominion of the British Empire, the equal of which in area or wealth or power does not and never did exist on the earth, not excepting the Roman Empire in the days of the Antonines. Asia, Europe, Africa, America and Oceanica vied with each other in exhibiting the wealth of their products and the endless variety of their curiosities.

Costly shawls and silks and cotton textures, with curious works, wares and goods from India, with native workmen with their looms and in their shops plying their cunning handicraft, much of it, as well as the workmen themselves, is unlike anything to which European eyes are accustomed. From Canada and contiguous provinces, agricultural, horticultural, forest and fishery products. Indians with their furs, paints, bark canoes and war, fishing and hunting implements. Africa with her diamond fields and rivers of gold dust, with her forests swarming with elephants, lions, hyenas, boaconstrictors, chased by or chasing her native Hottentots, Zulus and Caffirs, in the chase, in the field, in the huts, giving the life habits of the land. Australia, with her mountains of bricks of gold, (made in imitation) with figures, giving the hundreds of millions of gold, with her forests and wretched inhabitants in their lonely stick or bark shelters; great kangaroos, with wombats and other strange birds and animals, lurking in the forests or haunting brooks and rocks, together with the costly or valuable or monstrous woods of her forests, or products of fields, pastures, looms and work-shops. Many long halls and great rooms covering acres of ground, are filled with these products, costing millions of pounds stirling, gathered from the ends of the earth, and from a belt that encircled the globe, were here. Here we have an India jungle, composed of trees curiously matted and twined together, with an undergrowth of bamboos, canes and grasses, where the sun's rays never penetrate, and in the midst of these are great elephants, breaking, crushing their way by means of their great weight and strength. Near by are fierce Bengal tigers, couchant, ready to spring on some unfortunate traveler, or devouring their quivering prey. Overhead, entwined or hanging from the limbs, are great serpents, while monkeys chatter or gambol among the higher branches. We step from this across the hall to find ourselves in the midst of a Hottentot village with its naked fetich worshippers. Again, further on, we find ourselves in the midst of an Australian forest, with its lonely bark shelter, with an uncouth, half-naked man and woman making their solitary meal off a few acorns, ground nuts or roasted kangaroo. Within the near distance a brook or spring, about which strange, uncouth, slimy serpents, or still stranger, half-bird, half-beast creatures, crawl or leap. How strange much of this! We wonder if such scenes are really on this earth, or whether we have not been transported to some other planet, or if we are not in a troubled dream where distorted fancies conjure up things not in earth or heaven. Bewildered with sight-seeing, we hail a cab and return to our hotel, when for a whole week we are nightly devoured in our dreams by Bengal tigers, snapped at by bristling hyenas, trodden under foot by elephants, or struggling to free ourselves from the folds of pythons, more hideous than the one that destroyed Laocoon and his sons. Or worse still, we are starving with some wretched native in his lonely, comfortless, cheerless bark shelter, which, as if in mockery, he claims as his home.

SMITHFIELD AND ITS MARTYRS.

Oct. 3rd.—Visited the historic grounds, Smithfield, formerly the tournament grounds, and site where witches and martyrs were burned. In the days of chivalry, many a mailed knight broke here a lance in mock defence of his king and lady love. And where, among other royal persons, King Edward III. and Richard II. in plates of mail, with viziers down and poised lances, in headlong tilt showed to admiring lords and ladies how battles were lost and won. And here the bold, daring Watt Tyler was killed by the Lord Mayor in 1381.

But these deeds of glory, chivalry, important as they may have been at the time, have passed forever away with the improved means of warfare, and may well be forgotten, while the deeds of cruelty and horror Smithfield has witnessed, may well live as warnings to erring humanity. It was here the victims of that strange, fanatical movement, born of ignorance and superstition, witches, were burned. And here another crime, perhaps more offensive to God and men—religious martyrs were burned. Here was day darkened and night rendered lurid by the sickly, ghastly sight of men and women consumed in the flames for conscience's sake. Here the

Church, the dominant belief of the times, both Catholic and Protestant in turn, endeavored to stamp out the inalienable birthright of man, freedom of thought, by burning those who chose to offend man rather than God, who dared to die rather than offend against conscience.

Here Wm. Longbeard, the first reformer, was beheaded in 1196, and in 1305, Sir Wm. Wallace, after being drawn through the streets by horses, was hung, and while still alive drawn and quartered. After this the Church becoming more refined in cruelty, preferred stamping out freedom of thought, the sanctity of conscience by the purifying process of fire, but these fires while consuming the body, only gave new growth, increased strength to freedom of thought. Here Henry VIII., in 1539, had Forest burned for denying the king's supremacy in religion. Here was also burned Joan Butcher, Maid of Kent, for having some doubts concerning the Church dogma of the incarnation. Annie, the beautiful and innocent daughter of Sir Wm. Askew, was first tortured on the rack, broken on the wheel and then burned for doubting transubstantiation. During the reign of Bloody Mary, stimulated by the dark, cruel, bigoted Philip of Spain, whom she had unfortunately married, these fires of religious persecution were kept burning with remorseless, pitiless fury. During her short and bloody reign, 170 martyrs were burned here. With the death of this hysterical, dropsical, bigoted queen, the fires of Smithfield were extinguished forever. These grounds are now in the business center of London, and covered by the costly buildings of the fish and meat markets, where are seen seventy-five acres of butcher's meat.

BUNHILL FIELDS CEMETERY.

This Campo Santo of the Dissenters, is the former burial grounds of those who for, differing in their religious belief from the Established Church, were denied burial in consecrated or holy ground, and were buried here with outsiders. In this, however, bigotry and intolerance, as is often the case, defeated their own ends, as the name and deeds of those who slumber here and in the grounds adjacent have made this holy ground that will be visited by children's children, while their virtues will be retold and their lives and deeds shall improve, instruct and ennoble mankind to the last period of recorded time. As this ground is now within the city, it is closed to further burials. At the time of its closure to interments, 140,000 had been buried here. Among these are the tombs of Dr. Watts, the sacred poet, whose hymns are sung in tens of thousands of churches by millions of worshippers. The tomb of Daniel De Foe, author of Robinson Crusoe, a book, although much less extravagantly praised and much less pretentious than Paradise's Lost, has, I have no doubt, been read by a thousand times more persons, and certainly with a thousand times more interest, and perhaps with equal profit. Not far from this tomb is that of John Bunyan, author of Pilgrim's Progress, a book that with its exalted purity of the English language, the loftiness of its sustained allegory under the circumstances in which it was produced, has a thousand times more of the miraculous than all the miraculous acts of saints, monkish legends, ever recorded and certainly more to excite our wonder and admiration, and may in many respects fairly be placed with Robinson Crusoe, both works of imagination, the one fiction placed on facts, the other facts placed upon fiction, both exciting our intensest emotion, and both will be read as long as the English language exists. The tomb of the earnest, devout allegorist was erected by his congregation, and though of marble, his name and work will outlast it. The other, De Foe's tomb, a granite shaft, was erected, as stated on the pedestal, by the printer and newspaper boys and girls of Europe and America. A most fitting source and tribute, as perhaps more boys and girls have voluntarily and with delight read this than any other book ever published. There are here also the tombs of many others—names not born to die.

Across the street is the church built and occupied by John Wesley. We attended service here, and since the morning curtains were first hung out a more lovely Sabbath morning never dawned upon the world. All nature seemed to be in harmony with the gentleness, the loveliness of the spirits of those who formerly resided' and whose dust still reposes, here. The church is much as he left it, the pulpit the same. The chapel adjoining contains his writing-desk and chair. The adjoining parsonage contains many souvenirs of the Wesley family.

In a little yard behind the church are the tombs of John and his brother Charles Wesley, also the tombs of Richard Watson, author of Watson's Theological Dictionary and Watson's Institutes, and of Drs. Adam Clark and Benson, the Bible commentators. In the front yard, near the gate, is the tomb of Susannah Wesley, mother of John and Charles. a noble woman whose many excellent qualities of head and heart were scarceless less marked than those of her immortal sons.

George Whitefield preached here in Bunhill Fields and at Moorsfield. often in the open air, and it is said to congregations of twenty and thirty thousand, and with such power and effect that the most stolid and hardened men wept as children.

This place was called by the bigots of the age, " the fanatical burying place." But many of those buried here will live in song and story when those who in their pride so considered them shall have been forgotten. For though fanaticism will not outlive bigotry, granting these men and women were such, born of the same spirit both will have a like duration, are indeed often readily convertible states, with this difference, however, that while fanaticism misdirected may and often has and will yet do great wrong, it has done and will yet do much good, while the soul of bigotry is of evil and that continually.

THE TABERNACLE SPURGEON.

Sept. 13, 1885.—Attended service at the Tabernacle, built in the classic style and accommodating 7,000 persons. The erection of this building was found to be necessary in order to accommodate the vast crowds that this modern Whitefield had attracted to listen to his discourses, a crowd that had long greatly exceeded the capacity of any church at the disposal of his followers.

Of the great pulpit orators who, for the last quarter of a century, have attracted most attention there are four, Spurgeon and Parker, of London, and Henry Ward Beecher and Talmage, of New York. Of these four, while most unlike in most things, there are no two more alike in some most vital points than Spurgeon and Beecher. Both are men of sound, logical minds, profound thinkers, and both have outgrown the narrow limits prescribed by their respective churches. Beecher's advance has alarmed religionists from its too liberal interpretation of Scripture and adaption of the most advanced philosophical thought, while Spurgeon's advanced, enlarged, more liberal views only alarmed the more orthodox or Calvinistic portion of the Baptist Church. This great Free Communion Baptist preacher, unable or unwilling to believe that only those who had been baptized by immersion were truly disciples of Christ, threw open the doors of the Church to all who professed Christ, inviting all such to meet him and his at the communion table.

We were fortunate enough, notwithstanding the vast crowd, to obtain favorable seats near to, and in front of, the elevated platform and pulpit. The preacher, Dr. Spurgeon, after a short but most sensible and impressive prayer, gave out a hymn which was sung by the choir on the platform in front of and around the pulpit, the audience joining in the singing. The preacher gave out the hymn, reading an entire verse of four lines at a time.

There was an impressive beauty in his voice and manner that added much to the excellence of the poetry or even the sentiment of the hymn. After the singing, the preacher read a chapter in the Old Testament, Isaiah 50, which he thought contained much of the essence and promise of the New, fortelling the coming and the death of Christ. He read with a distinctness and elegance of diction I perhaps never heard equaled, and which certainly added greatly to the solemn grandeur and beauty of the chapter. He read only a few lines or words at a time, then commented upon them with great ability, eloquence and learning. His reasoning was remarkably clear, logical, and, granting the chapter really referred to, and meant, what he supposed it did, entirely convincing. He occupied some thirty minutes in reading and commenting upon this chapter, and none could have wished the time less. After this came another hymn and then the sermon. He took for his text, the 14th verse of the 6th chapter of Paul to the Gallatians, "God forbid that I should glory, save in the cross of our Lord Jesus Christ." With an ability, finished elocution and clear, logical reasoning I have never known equaled, he expounded his text for some fifty minutes. Besides his easy, finished eloquence and clear, logical reasoning, that which impresses one the most, is his child-like sincerity and manly earnestness and unquestionable, undivided faith, with an unpretentious but earnest desire to convince that entirely hid the man in the subject. The preacher was nowhere, nothing, Christ was all in all, and man's salvation that which of all things most concerned earth and heaven. No one could listen to him without being fully satisfied of his earnestness, of his truthfulness in what he professed, that he really believed what he preached and preached only what he believed, and that with him religion was an actual fact, admitting the clearest solution and most positive demonstration. This of itself gives a power to his sermons, which, enforced with remarkable logical eloquence, devoid of all verbosity or unmeaning, rhetorical flights, is well calculated to carry conviction, while his enthusiasm is in beautiful harmony with the importance of his subject, never outrunning or lagging behind the interest or feelings of his audience, who throughout the discourse were not permitted by the introduction of extraneous matter to wander from the text.

What did it concern him or his audience that Comte had taught a new gospel of positivism, or that Herbert Spencer worshipped the Unknowable, or Darwin taught the descent of man from monkeys? To him the only positivism was man's need of salvation and the fullness of atonement in the blood of Christ, while the Unknowable of Spencer was the unknown God whom Paul found the Athenians ignorantly worshipping, and whom like Paul, he was declaring unto the people to be the Christ; and let Darwin teach what he might as to the origin of man, he taught with the Bible that man had fallen through sin and might again live through the atonement of Christ, and with him Christ was all, everything, embracing all philosophies that were true and all truths that were philosophical.

If all this was not positively stated in the discourse, it was included and only not stated because included and the beauty and harmony of the discourse would have been marred and its usefulness lessened by attempts to show that the whole includes all the parts.

It is impossible that such a man can be listened to with indifference, even were his subject of much less importance than he deemed it. We could no longer wonder that he required a house covering acres to preach in, or that his swelling thoughts and soul had broken over the narrow limits placed by Close Communionists.

In appearance, Dr. Spurgeon is a typical Englishman, about five feet ten and one-half inches in height, with a fine head, thick, short neck, broad, square shoulders and full chest—altogether a fine physique, a heavy-set, square-built, burly son of old John Bull. We readily see in the man one possessed of an iron will and dominated by convictions of right and wrong.

After this it may seem out of place to offer criticisms, and yet I could but feel that his discourse presented objectionable points. We thought the speaker fell into some errors from his mind running too much in a groove or rut. Throughout his discourse he gave too much stress to the word *cross*, which to his mind of course never presented itself as a straight line with a cross-bar or transept, nor as a sign, but a fact embodying the meritorious life, suffering and death of Christ—the atonement, and not in any sense as a sign or object of adoration, and yet his discourse might readily give other impressions. Indeed, so far as the emphasis or stress upon the word *cross* was concerned, it might have been used at high mass. Now in this we must believe he even misinterpreted his author, Paul, who almost certainly did not even use the word cross in this connection or in this passage. The word cross most probably having been added as a gloss or as a forgery. Certain it is that the early Christians attached no symbolical meaning to this word, looking upon the cross only with horror and not until after the abolition by edict of punishment or death upon the cross within the Roman Empire, which was not until the fourth century, did the cross become an object of especial favor or an object of adoration—and it was not until the sixth century that the emblem of the cross became the image of the cross. This is certainly shown in the early tombs of the Christians, the catacombs, where the cross never appears upon, or in connection with, their burial places during the first, second or third centuries, whereas had it been considered of the importance it afterwards attained and that the preacher here gave it, it would have ornamented, or been present at, every tomb.

We must say, also, that notwithstanding the certainty he felt in the prophet's allusions to Christ, we find no possible reason for believing that there is any reference whatever to Christ in this solemn, poetical chapter. See Isaiah 50. But even this did not in the least detract from the impressive, instructive beauty of the discourse.

WESTMINSTER ABBEY.

Sept. 14, 1885.—Visited Westminster Abbey, a noble structure, hallowed as being either the burial-place, or containing the monuments, of many of England's most illustrious dead. It stands upon the site of an old church, erected by the Saxon king Sebert, in 616. This was destroyed by the Danes and rebuilt by king Edgar, in 985. The Abbey was endowed by Edward the Confessor, in 1049. The Abbey was built in its present form, by Henry III. and his son Edmund I. in 1250, consequently it is upwards of 600 years old. It is a very Temple of Fame, and so regarded by all true Englishmen. To be buried within its sacred walls, sacred from memories and by association, or to have a monument here is deemed the greatest mark of respect that can be paid the dead. The church is in the form of a Latin cross with some indifferent mosaics and the windows are beautified with stained glass.

While this world-renowned Abbey is justly esteemed as the most distinguished Temple of Fame in the world, containing the tombs of more truly great men than any other like structure in the world, it also contains many unworthy of such distinction, which should not be here, indeed mar the purpose for which it should be held sacred, such as the tombs or monuments of utterly worthless lords or rich men, whose titles or wealth alone have secured them notice here and, still worse even than these worthless characters, a number of children's monuments are here and some of these the children of rich men only, or of those who possessed or could obtain, by means of their titles or money, favor at court. This is to be deplored, and greatly mars the effect otherwise produced. Even the children of kings who have no historic value should not be here any more than the children of beggars. Every unhistoric tomb, whether child or adult, found here impresses the visitor unfavorably as a kind of desecration. The children Edward V. and his brother, the duke of York, the unfortunate children of Edward IV. foully murdered by their godless uncle, Richard III. are, though but children, very properly buried here, for though but children, they have a deep historic interest. We saw in the tower the place where the bones of these children, who were strangled and buried under the staircase, were found. Shakespear has made their sad, wicked, taking-off immortal, and all the world will be pleased to meet with some fitting tribute to their memory in this place.

To give some idea of the vast interest that centers in this Temple of Fame we will mention a few of the tombs and monuments we noticed here:

William Pitt, Lord Chatham, Beaconsfield, Palmerston, Mansfield, Warren Hastings, Richard Cobden, Wilberforce, Sir Isaac Newton, Charles Darwin, Charles James Fox, James Mackintosh, Lord Holland, Zacharay Macaulay, Wordsworth, Congreve, Buckland, Major Andre (shot as a spy by Washington), *Earl Stanhope, Dr. Isaac Watts, John Wesley, Dr. Bell, Bishop Thornwell, Grote, Camden, Garrick, Addison, Babington Macaulay, Thackeray, Handel, Campbell, Goldsmith, Gay, Thompson, Burns, Shakespear,*

Southey, Mason, Gray, Milton, Spencer, Butler, Ben Jonson, Chaucer, Cowley, Longfellow, Dryden, Old Parr (152 years old), *Lord John Russell, Edward Bulwer Lytton, Sir George Villiers, etc.*

A flight of twelve marble steps conducts us into the elegant chapel of Henry VII. A great number of beautiful statues and figures adorn this chapel. The pomp of stone decoration of the ceiling is truly astonishing. It is difficult to believe it is stone and not of wood, so airy and elaborate is it. Here is a monument to the unfortunate, beautiful Mary Queen of Scots, beheaded by order of her counsin, Queen Elizabeth. A vault contains the remains of Charles II. William III. Queens Mary and Annie. A metal monument to Henry VII. and his wife Elizabeth, of York. Monument to Edward VI. Near by is buried Elizabeth Claypole, daughter of Cromwell. Monuments of Queens Mary and Elizabeth, who are buried here. Here is also the sarcophagus containing the bones of the two children of Edward IV.

Chapel of St. Edward the Confessor contains the monuments of Henry III., Queen Eleanor, Henry V., Henry VII. The saddle, helmet and shield used by King Henry VII. at the battle of Agincourt are shown here. Tombs of Edward III., Richard II. The old and new coronation chairs are seen here. The famous Scotland sconce stone is placed in this coronation chair. The chair with the stone was used by Edward I. in 1257, and every English monarch from that day to the present time, including her majesty Victoria, have been crowned in this chair in which is placed the Scots' sconce stone. This stone belonged to the chair of the ancient kings of Scotland, and connected with it is a legend or prophecy that those crowned upon and possessing it will rule over Scotland, and so strong is custom, habit or superstition, that no monarch of England would dare or would venture or would be permitted to be crowned without this old stone in the chair.

The momuments of Knight Templars, with the figures of the ten knights who accompanied King Edmon to the Holy Land. A monument to Gen. Wolfe, who fell at Quebec in our Colonial wars; also the monuments of Sir John Franklin and James T. Simpson are here We visited the *Jerusalem Chamber*, lined with cedar from Lebanon; in this room is a long table, at which was made King Jame's translation of the Bible, also the New translation.

WINDSOR CASTLE.

Sept. 15th.—Visited this immense structure, one of the residences of her Majesty Queen Victoria, situated some twenty-five miles from London.

William the Conqueror first erected a castle here, which was added to by Henry I., Henry II., Edward III., George IV., and almost every other monarch since William the Conqueror, until it is said to be the largest and finest royal residence in the world, but while it is of great size and may have cost more money than any other palace, it certainly is not handsome, not near so beautiful as others we have seen in Europe, in Denmark, Germany, and other countries, while perhaps not at all like the Pitti palace in Florence, it reminds me much of this, to me, uncouth, structure. The castle covering many acres, consists of two courts, the upper and lower wards. The tower, a strong fortress with great houses, all surrounded by massive, high walls, stands upon a high eminence where was built the first fortress or stronghold, by William the Conqueror. We could not enter St. George's, it being closed from some cause, possibly as being her majesty's chapel was too sacred for the vulgar to enter. We passed through the corridors of the Albert chapel, an old monastery, founded by Henry II., but the main chapel of this was also closed. We were, however, politely shown through the State apartments of the castle, the rooms are of Gothic architecture and handsomely decorated, on the walls are hundreds of full-sized portraits of royal persons, many of these are by the old Flemish and Dutch masters. One room contains exclusively portraits by Van Dyck and is called the Van Dyck room. The grand reception room is finely decorated in the Rococo style and is hung with tapestries representing Jason and Media. Another, the Rubens' room, contains portraits only, by Rubens, some ten or twelve in number.

The beautiful terrace gives a fine view of the immediate surroundings, but the finest view is obtained from the lofty parapets of the Round Tower.

EATON COLLEGE.

Eaton College, one of the best known colleges in England, principally attended by the sons of the privileged classes, is situated within the town of Windsor, about a mile from the castle. We visited it, passed through its beautiful Gothic church with its finely carved oak stalls and beautiful stained windows. It contains many monuments and inscriptions to illustrious dead, and is 500 years old.

All this college and grounds are sacred to the muse of Gray, whose Ode upon Eaton College will be read by children's children when its classic walls shall have crumbled to decay.

We took carriage here and drove to Stoke Poges, whose neat little country church-yard has been made classic ground by one who sleeps here and whose beautiful Elegy will outlast the hillocks of which he sang.

The old church is in a good state of preservation and embossed by old trees, while a thick mantle of ivy clings to its walls to their roof. Many of the tombs and tomb-stones are also covered by ivy so as to entirely conceal them, giving them a very grave-like appearance. Hundreds of the graves as in the time of Gray, are mere hillocks of earth where "the rude forefathers of the hamlet sleep," as unpretentiously now as when the poet sung of them.

THE POET'S TOMB.

This, an unpretentious one, is near the front end of the church. The place was indicated as we approached by a group of visitors standing around it. The grass is kept trodden away near its sides by the multitudes of those who do homage to this shrine of the Muses. A tablet placed in the wall of the church near by, informs us that the body of the poet Gray, also that of his mother, lies in this vault. The quiet beauty of its surroundings is in keeping with the gentle, kindly nature of him whose body lies here.

Some three or four hundred yards from the church, in the edge of a wood where he loved to walk and commune with nature, is a handsome monument, erected by his admirers to his memory. The sides of the monument contain verses from his Elegy and other poems.

The granite, elaborate, costly and handsome tomb of Lord Beaconsfield is at the opposite end of the church, and although this contains the body of one of England's greatest writers, orators and prime ministers, it receives not half so much attention as the simple, unpretentious tomb of Gray.

The grounds, parks or lordly manor of Stoke Poges are exceedingly beautiful, with a palatial residence of its late owner, a most public-spirited and valuable citizen of great wealth and liberality, but who sadly, unfortunately, ruinously, fell into the habit, the bane of many an Englishman, of drinking and betting on horse-racing, and, like many of these before him, lost his entire fortune. His lordly estate with its stud of 200 horses, many of them the finest in the kingdom, flocks and herds of sheep and deer, all were sold at public auction under mortgage; a beggared family, wife and children, driven from their ancestral home, out upon a cold world, unprotected, perhaps unpittied. His misfortunes, as is not unfrequently the case, drove him to drinking deeper ever deeper and he died drunk in Paris a few months since, a drunkard and a pauper. The recital of his sad misfortune threw a sombre shadow over Stoke Poges, not relieved by the golden glories of a setting sun and which seemed to follow us along the trimmed hedges and shaded avenues along which we drove on our return home. The country over which we drove, from Windsor to Stoke Poges, is unsurpassed in quiet loveliness by any in the world. Much of the way was through shaded avenues or alongside of parks with large, old oaks that had battled with the storms of a thousand years. The entire country is fertile and the landscape the most English-like of all England. Leaving Stoke Poges, we drove to Slough, where we took cars for London.

LONDON BRIDGE.

The *Old London Bridge* was until the last 100 years the only bridge across the Thames, in or near London, and is yet the most important to the citizens of London, although now there are many bridges spanning the river within the precincts of the city. It is built upon the site of the old wooden bridge first built by the Romans. From the fact that all the early bridges were at this point, which separates the *Upper* from the *Lower* Thames, or constitutes the point where this distinction is made, we infer that there is a rock bed extending across the river at this point.

This bridge cost $10,000,000, and 15,000 vehicles and 100,000 foot passengers cross it daily, making it one of the most crowded thoroughfares in the world, and though fifty-four feet wide, so crowded was it that we found some difficulty in making our way across it. For many hundreds of years, at this point had been the only connection between the country lying on the opposite sides of the Thames, which for many miles above and below, quite to the sea, up to the eighteenth century remained impassable except by boats. Indeed it is yet the last or lowest bridge on the Thames. Below the bridge the river is as much crowded with steam, sail, and row vessels, barges, etc., as is the bridge with wagons, carriages, and foot passengers.

BANK OF LONDON.

The *bank* is a low, strong, stone wall of rooms running around and occupying with its rooms and inner court the entire block of ground, having on every side streets—crowded thoroughfares. There are no windows to be seen in the entire building, only blind walls, massive stone walls with no openings except an entrance or passway on two sides, and these are closed, at all other than business hours, by strong, double, iron doors, and guarded at all times by grim looking sentinels—soldiers in their red coats and muskets on their shoulders—standing as fixed and immobile as the iron posts or stone walls of the building. It is lighted from the inside court and by gas or electricity, and in its vaults is the wealth of a world. Its influence is not only felt to the ends of the earth, but constitutes the motive power by which runs the trade and commerce of the entire globe, and every money centre in the world, Paris, Berlin, Vienna and New York respond to the throbbings of this money heart of the globe, and the fortunes of millions rise and fall with the bullion in its vaults.

ST. PAUL'S CATHEDRAL.

The present cathedral which is the third largest in the world, only St. Peter's at Rome and the Cathedral at Milan being larger, was built in 1675–97 on the site of the old cathedral erected in the time of the Saxons and burned down in the great fire in 1666, and cost $3,750,000.

The cathedral is in the form of a Latin cross, with a nave 500 feet in length and 118 feet wide, with the cross bar or transept 250 feet long. The dome rises 363 feet above the pavement. This church though a grand old structure of the

Renaissance style, and really imposing, as the third largest cathedral in the world, owes its chief importance, to the tourist at least, to the fact that like Westminster Abbey it is a Temple of Fame, and fortunately much less marred by the presence of tombs and monuments of worthless or unimportant, unhistorical persons, as mere lords or rich men and their children, all of whom though very proper persons to bury, and even to have costly mausoleums built over them, if anyone wishes to build them, yet are out of place, and mar by their presence a Temple of Fame. In what possible manner does it concern the world to know that Lord Pomposity, Bart., or the millionare Thom. Jones, lived or died, how, where or when, if they did nothing more than merely to live while they could and die when they could not help doing so?

It is quite different with a king of England, as no matter how worthless he may have been, while and as king of England he represented the nation and at least some of the good or evil the nation did during his reign may well be attributed to his action or want of action.

Most of the names met with here on monuments are known to the world, among these we noticed that of Admiral Lord Nelson, at the mention of whose name the multitudinous ghosts of two mighty French fleets, in unshrouded terror fill the air and sea at Trafalgar and Abourkir, while shouts of victory by the English marines whose hearts are stronger than their all oak ships, startle old Neptune from his caverned depths with a fury that lashes oceans into maddened foam, that dashes the remnant of the French fleet to destruction, and denying sepulchre to her gallant dead casts their bodies upon the beach, and in the loudest requiem old ocean ever sung, the soul of the mighty Nelson leaves his flag-ship to bear aloft the battle-scared thrice-glorious flag of England's dear bought glory, and plant it upon the loftiest battlements of human fame from which the flag of victory ever floated. His splendid sarcophagus made of cannon, captured from England's foes is in the Cathedral Crypt. The pedestal of his enduring mausoleum is of grey granite brought from America, a worthy and time defying mausoleum this, that encloses this greatest of naval heroes, whose name and deeds shall live in song and story as long as ships shall dare the tempest and the flood. Next we meet the name and monument of *Marquis Cornwallis* (of Yorktown memory), *Sir Astley Cooper* (the great surgeon), *Gen. Sir John Moore* ("nor in sheet nor in shroud we bound him"), *Sir Ralph Abercrombie* (our Continental Wars), *Wellington*, whose splendid and costly sarcophagus is in the Crypt of the cathedral, resting on the durable iron car upon which it, containing the body of the Iron Duke, was drawn by twelve horses in mournful procession through the streets of London, followed by half a million of sorrow stricken people; it was then deposited here to bid defiance to the tooth of time. The whole structure which would weigh many tons is made of the metal of captured cannon. Next a monument to the heroes who fell at Inkerman, *Sir Joshua Reynolds* (England's greatest painter), *Lord Rodney*, *Napier* (History Peninsular War), *Gen. Sir Packenham.* This to the American is one of the most interesting monuments here. Gen. Packenham fell in the attack upon New Orleans, January 8th, 1815, after the Treaty of Peace between the two countries had been signed at Ghent.

In this memorable battle, Gen. Jackson, who had obtained some reputation in the Seminole war, and who, like Napoleon I., was by nature a military commander, first applied the principle of movable parapets, or breastworks, afterwards so successfully used by Gen. Price at the siege of Lexington, Mo., by seizing the cotton bales, many thousands of which had accumulated at New Orleans, placing them in line with his backwoodsmen armed with their deer and squirrel rifles, behind them. Gen. Packenham, after easily, with the powerful guns of the fleet, silencing the mud forts at the mouth of the Mississippi, landed 12,000 British regulars, and marched directly upon the American breastworks, not doubting of an easy victory. But he mistook the character of those behind the cotton bales, for though unused to warfare, they were deadly marksmen. They were ordered to reserve their fire until the enemy came fairly within range of their hunting-rifles. This they did, and not until the enemy were within a hundred yards, and had already thought themselves in possession of an easy victory, was the word given to fire. In an instant along the whole line of cotton bales ran a flash of light, and thousands of rifile bullets sped on their deadly mission, each ball hastening to its mark with unerring certitude. The whole front line of the brave British troops fell dead or mortally wounded. In vain those behind rushed over the dead bodies of their fallen comrades—these too were mowed down as fast as they came within the fatal line—a line 'twere suicide to cross. The metal of these hardy backwoodsmen was now fairly up, and these fearless pioneers, the sons of those who had driven the lurking savage from their wilderness homes, really enjoyed the deadly sport. Flash after flash lighted the line of breastworks, each flash of light hurrying thousands of bullets on their deadly mission. To meet or stand against this leaden hail were certain death, and the enemy, after a short, brave, but useless effort, fled from the field of death, leaving 3,000 dead and dying on the plain. Among the mortally wounded was their brave commander, Gen. Packenham, whose dead body was placed in a hogshead of rum and brought home for burial here.

Many other names known to fame are here. St. Paul, thus hallowed by the ashes of these noble dead, fittingly represents as a temple of fame, as well as by the noble architecture and grand proportion, the mightiest kingdom and people on earth.

LINCOLN'S INN AND TEMPLE BAR.

Sept. 27th.—Visited this immense law establishment, consisting of a great number of buildings covering a large area of ground, with a park and gardens extending quite down to the Thames. In approaching the halls we pass through a quaint old gateway, upon which, it is said, Ben Jonson worked as a bricklayer.

The building was not open at the time of our first arrival, but after walking around the building we fortunately met one of the members who kindly had the custodian show us through the halls and rooms. We first entered the library, with its 25,000 volumes of law books, in old oaken book-stalls. Next the great dining hall, built in the style of the Tudors. It contains many portraits of distinguished men. A fine fresco by Watts. Its most valuable painting is a Paul before Felix, by Hogarth. Fine portraits of Siddons, Goldsmith, Wm. Pitt, Lord Brougham. A part of this law establishment, the temple, was built in the twelfth century. For a great time it belonged to the Knight Templars, but has now long been a school of law. Oliver Goldsmith lived and died in one of its rooms, and the learned Blackstone occupied a room immediately under Goldsmith's, and it is related that the patience of Blackstone was often tried by the noise Goldsmith in his childish tricks kept up just above him. Dr. Johnson also occupied a room on Temple Lane, close by.

The historical building, Temple Church, formerly belonged to the Knight Templars, consists of two parts—a round Norman building some sixty feet in diameter, of the twelfth century, and a choir, in the early English style. In the round church are the bronze statues of eight knights, placed prostrate in full length on the floor, in full armor. Those who reached the Holy Land and did battle for the sepulchre, have their legs crossed, the others have theirs straight. The oaken stalls have rich carvings. We are brought face to face with the crusaders, as these knights are of those who accompanied Richard Cœur de Lion to Jerusalem. Numerous tombs in the yard around the church contain the bones of unknown crusaders. On the outside of the church in the graveyard, is the tomb, a simple unpretentious monument, of Oliver Goldsmith. We noticed beautiful wreaths of bright fresh flowers lying on either end of his tomb, immortelles, kept constantly here, placed by those who revere his muse. How fitting such emblems to his pure and gentle song. Sweet Auburn and the Vicar of Wakefield will be read and stir the heart as long as letters are cultivated.

THE CRYSTAL PALACE.

This is situated some twelve miles from Charring Cross, but so great is the city of London that most of the way is through it. We took the cars at Holborn viaduct, in the central part of the city, and yet the depot is so situated that it is not even seen from the street, and the railroad so placed as not to interfere in the least with the crowded thoroughfares in this vicinity. At first we are under ground, then coming out from under the covered way we find ourselves above the streets, crowded with the busy commerce and passengers of this part of London. We continued high above the streets, the cross streets running unimpeded under the road which crosses the Thames above the old London Bridge, and continues for many miles over the city, on a line with the tops of the houses, which stretch in compact masses as far away in every direction as the eye can reach. Multitudes of men, women and children fill the streets below us, and the houses to their garrets. In the streets these stolid masses are seen pressing, crowding or sauntering along, as they hurry or loiter in their ceaseless struggle for, or disregard of, life. Here beneath us in the midst of all this life and motion is a little church, with its small graveyard crowded with head and foot boards, recording the names of the long-since-forgotten thousands who sleep beneath its grass-grown surface. Yet these remain here, with their slumbers undisturbed by the carking wants of living men, with houses crowding upon their narrow cells, while the busy living masses are hurrying by thoughtless of its presence. Perhaps if any regard this presence of death in their midst, it is the few who, weary of life, wish that they too had finished their labors, while the great mass move thoughtlessly, heedlessly on, oblivious to the past, indifferent to the present, and thoughtless of the future, a moving mass of stolid humanity, a human sea, whose generations break and are lost upon the shores of time, as are those of ocean upon its strands, leaving scarce a trace in the sands of life. Alas,

> How many sighs, how many tears,
> How many hopes, how many fears,
> Are given to each passing wind,
> By these masses of humankind.
>
> How many thoughtless in the strife,
> Alike of death as well as life,
> Without a thought, without a care,
> Are drifting on, to God knows where.

After a run of half an hour over the city, through dense groves of trees, by flower gardens, clusters of houses, villages, towns, all alike, London and its immediate suburbs, we arrived at the Crystal Palace, standing on the margin of a beautiful, picturesque, undulating vale, like a stranded iceberg, a mountain of glory, alone unrivalled by any like structure in the world, a mountain of light, more like the work of fairy than of human hands—so fragile and airy that it looks as though intended as a gossamer palace for butterflies and humming-birds, and yet so strong that it trembles not at the weight of ten thousand men, and so spacious that its vast halls and recesses hold the restored palaces and works of art of a hundred cities, with goods of every description, and curiosities from every land, and in incredible quantities—lakes and fountains, with the fruits and vegetables of many gardens, together with whole forests of plants and flowers—and yet is not full.

This wonderful structure all of iron and glass, is 1,608 feet long, with two transepts, the one 370 long, with wings flanked by towers 250 feet high. It covers eight acres of ground and in some parts is three stories in height, giving twelve acres of flooring. Upon the great floor is a Pompeiian house restored, the court, the dining-room, reception room, kitchen and bed rooms, just as they existed in Pompeii, 2,000 years ago, with the mosaics on the floor and beautiful frescoes on the walls, just as we had seen them in Pompeii. A restored temple and palace from the long lost ruins of the city of Karnak, with halls, statues, frescoes and all much as they appeared in the time of the Pharaohs 5,000 years ago. The Moorish Palace, the Alhambra, all of great size, and yet occupying but a small part of this building.

The room of the Great Organ seats 4,000 persons; a large theater and concert hall, seat each 4,000 persons. A band of forty musicians were playing in the concert room, other halls contain ethnological groups, representing the persons and customs of all the peoples of the world least known to Europeans. Thousands of statues, casts and works of art constitute a wondrous museum of Greek, Roman, Norman and Renaissance art, forming for the connoisseur and student a connected school of these. Among these are fac simile casts of such works as of Laocoon, the destruction of the children of Niobe, Venus, of Milo, Michael Angelo's Moses and David, the gates of the Baptistry of Florence, the Parthenon and Colosseum of Rome, tombs from Italy and England, and an indescribable amount of other things in casts, almost as perfect and beautiful as were the originals we had seen in a hundred cities throughout Europe. Well may these have been collected for a world's exhibition, and well may they be retained here in this city that reflects in no mean microcosm the world and all it contains.

We spent the day wandering through these rooms and great halls containing much of the curiosities and art treasures (in casts) of the world, hurried from things of great interest to those of greater, missing many more of perhaps yet greater worth, until late in the evening, when tired in body, with brains overcrowded with sight-seeing, we returned home without being able to walk over and through the vast adjoining flower garden with its lakes, fountains, buildings, towers and works of art. The landscape view from the lofty galleries is among the most beautiful in the world. Through strong glasses this is seen as a long line of variagated smiling vale, enclosed with gently sloping hills, bespangled with hedges, fields, gardens, forests and palaces, like dissolving views or shifting panoramas, light as floating summer clouds and lovely as fields of Eden, and would well repay a visit to this place were there nothing else to be seen, and where we listened and scarce in vain to hear the song of birds of Paradise. It was doubtless here Milton wrote his Paradise Regained and where the Crystal Palace now is he placed his celestial city. What prophetic vision!

THE TOWER OF LONDON.

The oldest portion of this is the White Tower, built by William the Conqueror, in 1078, and is so named from being built of white stone, which, though yellowed by time, presents to the present day a conspicuous portion of the tower rising in a massive white square structure standing in the midst of the fortress.

This tower is said to be the glory and shame of England; its glory, however, is not so readily seen in its history, while the dark shadows of shame thrown across England's history by deeds done here, blur many a page for at least 500 years. Its rough, frowning walls fitly represent the dark and cruel character of England's tyrants, while its pavement and court are dyed, crimsoned with the blood of the noblest and fairest of the land, whom these tyrants seemed to think were born for no other purpose than to be butchered. The whole history of this tower cries in thunder-tones against the divine right of kings, warning the world against the danger, the fearful terror of placing absolute power in the hands of any individual whether he be called king or protector, of placing the purse and the sword in any power not directly amenable to the people. To learn that kings and priests are equally the enemies of freedom, has cost England, as it has other countries, rivers of its noblest blood and lighted the horrid fires of Smithfield. The block and axe being considered the best persuasive by kings, while flames and the stake were preferred for crushing out freedom of religious thought.

This place built as a palace, castle and strong fort, with twelve or fifteen strong, high towers and battlement walls while sometimes used as a palace, was more frequently a prison, with dark, gloomy and often subterranean passages and cells. Many of these cells were dimly lighted and some of them were only large enough for a person to stoop or sit in, without either light or ventilation. In these, unfortunate victims of tyranny were confined until relieved by death—either starvation or strangulation—or they went forth to meet a more merciful death on the block.

The first of a long line of prisoners beheaded within the tower, was the Earl of Huntington, who was beheaded in the reign of Henry IV. Previous to this it had been a prison, but not a slaughter-house as well. William Wallace and many of his brave nobles had been confined here and taken out to Smithfield and horribly beheaded during the reign of Edmund

I. During the reign of Edmund II., the king of France was long held a prisoner here, and during his entire reign the tower was filled with prisoners, many of whom only left it to be beheaded.

In entering the tower we passed over a wide moat, spanned by a stone bridge, and passed through the portcullis, the gate of which had been removed; but the grooves in which it fitted with the long iron spikes above are here yet. The entire fortress is surrounded by a deep, wide moat, which was formerly half filled with water. It is now dry, but can even now be flooded by hoisting the gates. In passing we stood at the Traitor's Gate, which has a flight of wide stone steps leading down to the river Thames. Formerly those accused of treason were brought by water and landed at this gate, from which they passed immediately into the prison, for the most part leaving hope behind.

It was at this gate Princess Elizabeth was landed on her arrest after the Wyatt rebellion, during the reign of Mary. Her fate, however, was less tragical than most of those who entered here. She owed her preservation perhaps less to the clemency of her sister Mary, who was at this time affianced to Philip II., of Spain, and much under the influence of the Spanish Catholic party, than to the fear justly entertained by these that if Elizabeth should be harshly dealt with, a far more formidable rising than that of Wyatt would hurl the Catholic party from place and power, would certainly prevent the hated and justly-feared Spanish Union, as Elizabeth was the hope of the Protestant cause, and therefore the idol of the English people. And then most likely deep schemes of those in power, and who were more anxious to serve themselves than the State, may have had much more influence in saving Elizabeth than can now be determined. And then we must do Mary the justice to suppose her influenced by natural ties and a sense of justice not unmixed with that delicate shrinking from acts of violence naturally associated with her sex. For while Mary was a bigot, believing her own salvation and all others' depended upon a strict adherence to the Roman Catholic Church, she was not the dark and bloody wretch history has painted her. Her faults as a woman, not directly attributable to her bigotry, were few—as a queen, scarcely more. Perhaps in both respects she was as admirable as "Good Queen Bess," whose virtues have been magnified in song and story from the day of her accession to the throne to the present times. At this, the Traitor's Gate, eighteen years before the Princess Elizabeth, another and more hapless prisoner was landed—the unfortunate Anne Boleyn, who fell a victim to the cruelty of one of the darkest and most bloody despots that ever disgraced a throne or human nature, Henry VIII. She was imprisoned, beheaded and buried here.

The White Tower, long a prison and slaughter-house, and whose every stone is big with human groans and incarnadined with human gore, is now a museum of ancient military weapons and armor. Full-suits, horse armor, as well as that for knights and common soldiers, are here in great quantity and completeness, both chain and plate, leaving nothing wanting to instruct us as to the ancient coat of mail, worn at tournament or on the battle-field. A complete study is also furnished of ancient, mediæval and modern weapons of warfare. And if we are astonished at the weight of some of these suits of steel armor, weighing ninety and one hundred pounds, we are not less so at the great weight and size of some of these battle-axes and spears and swords. Among the weapons that have played an important part in the English wars are long and crossbows, two of the former lately obtained from a sunken ship, where they had been for 300 years, are longbows made from the yew-tree, which from their great size and length must have required an arrow five or six feet long and a man of great strength to bend them. These longbows in the hands of the strong, well-skilled English yeomen were, as was proven on many a well-contested battle-field, a most formidable weapon against an enemy not clad in steel.

The study given here of firearms is most complete, interesting and instructive, from the old styles of match-lock and flint-lock, to the percussion-cap-lock and the present breech-loading rifle. Some of the old cannon are curious, being made of bars of iron placed in juxtaposition longitudinally and secured by iron bands wrapped around them and welded together as an external coat. Also are shown here instruments of torture used to wring from unfortunate victims secrets they often did not possess. Among these are thumb-screws, by which the fingers were mashed by means of a screw, the wheel and the rack upon which prisoners were broken, and then an instrument more kind than these, the block and axe, on, and with, which they were beheaded.

In front of the Traitor's Gate is the Bloody Tower, so named as being the place where the two children, Edward V., aged twelve, and his brother Richard, eight years old, were confined and murdered by their inhuman uncle, the Duke of Gloucester. They were buried here under the staircase, where their bones were found long afterwards. But these were not the only hapless victims of tyranny whose untimely taking-off this room has witnessed. Its blood-stained floor cries loud to heaven against England's kings and rulers.

From the Bloody Tower a stairway leads to St. John's Chapel, a beautiful Gothic room within the White Tower. It is interesting from its pure Norman architecture, the best now in England, with rows of heavy pillars, no two capitols alike, with square cornice and base. A wide triforium surrounds them. The historic importance of this chapel is great. The adjoining prison has upon its walls, as have most of the rooms, inscriptions and carved devices of their hapless inmates, who passed from here to execution. These sad mementoes, often all of those who wrote them that time has left us, speak in mournful accents from all these prison walls. In St. John's Chapel lie buried the headless bodies of the wives of Henry VIII., Catherine of Aragon, Anne Boleyn, and Catherine Hase. And here also is the grave of the lovely, innocent, pure and learned Lady Jane Grey, who fell a sacrifice to the ambition of the Duke of Northumberland, her father-in-law, and to that of her husband, Lord Dudley, both of whom were also beheaded and buried here; also the Lady Rockford, and the Countess of Saulisbury, the Duke of Suffolk, Duke of Norfolk, Earl of Arundel, Earl of Essex, and Sir Thomas Averly, all beheaded, and alike the victims of tyranny. But unfortunately this long list comprises not all, nor most. Some forty or fifty others, the noblest of the English nobility, lords and ladies, lie here, constituting this a frightful charnel-house, and also a slaughter-house, as they were beheaded here, murdered here. No other place on earth holds so many noble, wise and great victime of tyranny, so many murdered great men and women, making this tower the mausoleum of the murdered great. But those murdered and buried here and in the adjoining court, constitute but a small part of the victims this old tower has held, as most of them were led forth to public execution by the axe, or perished at the stake in Smithfield. For let it never be forgotten that while these bloody executions were going on Smithfield was lighted up by the sickly glare of fires that consumed those who died for opinion's sake—for their religion. While Henry VIII. was rioting in the blood of his wives and nobles who perished by the score on the block. Bishop Cranmer and Ridley urged the tyrant to strike and spare not those who deemed conscientous convictions dearer than life. And these two bishops stood by and mocked by exhortations, on patience and fortitude to their victims as they writhed or screamed amidst the flames, and as if in answer to the blood of these victims of Church, avenging heaven hoisted these two holy villians on their own petard, and gave them an opportunity of tasting the pleasures of the death they inflicted upon others, as the same bloody tyrant who burned their victims, in answer to their prayers, afterwards burned them also. Another instance of retributive justice this old prison witnessed, was the infamous Judge Jeffreys, who only escaped decapitation by dying in prison. It was almost a pity that this monster cheated the scaffold by dying in prison instead of on the block, where he had consigned so many others with a disregard of justice or mercy that disgrace alike the judge, the man and the nation.

Fortunately for our good opinion of human nature, and the hope that man is less cruel than ravenous wolves or hyenas, this dark and bloody spot, London Tower, has no parallel in the world's history. No other twelve acres has ever witnessed a like amount of cruelty and bloodshed of the fairest and noblest of the land by the unbridled, licentious, blood-thirsty, diabolism of rulers. And now that governors and the governed, tyrants and their victims, alike have long since passed away, have long since met in the grave, have moulded to common dust and been adjudged at a tribunal where no distinction is made between kings and their victims, may we not rejoice in the fact that, thanks to the age, the last sad dying groan has passed away, and the blood-stained walls and pavement have lost their crimson hue, the bloody axe and block are laid up as witnesses of the past, as mementoes of the strife through which man attained his freedom, while the fires of Smithfield have gone out, never again to be relighted by the bigotry of priests or tyranny of rulers, from both of whom the divine right of destroying their fellow-man, has passed forever away, fled before the new gospel that man alone is divine, and the prison converted to arts of peace.

KEW GARDENS.

Oct. 20th.—Visited this important Botanical Garden. Took the cars at Waterloo Station. Leaving this station we pass for many miles over, and by, crowded streets and houses—the city full and overflowing with people and all the hopes of busy life. We are hurried on, but still in the city, with its seemingly interminable crowded streets and houses. After a run of manp miles open spaces begin to appear—a garden, now a grove of trees, again clusters of houses, now open spaces, pastured lawns, meadows, fields. The Thames is crossed many times, when we reach Kew Bridge Station, and crossing over this on foot we enter Kew Garden, which with the pleasure grounds contain 300 acres.

The grounds are beautifully laid off in squares, circles, cubes and artistic flower-beds, and long pleasant shaded walks. There are some four large hothouses filled with ferns, orchids palms and cacti. The palm house, 362 feet long, 100 wide, and some 70 feet high, contains every known variety of palms, many of them of great size and beauty. Near by this is the tropical lily house, containing a great variety of lilies. The large central room is occupied by a tank fifty by thirty-five feet, 1,800 square feet, which contains the crowning glory of the lily world, the Victoria Regia, obtained from the river Amazon, South America. The main plant is in the center of the tank. From this long stems run off, reaching quite to the edges of the tank. These stems look like large ropes, and terminate each in a great leaf three to six feet in diameter. as much as eighteen feet in circumference, which rises to and floats upon the surface of the water as broad discs with turned-up edges like a plate or frying-pan. Some of the largest of these leaves would readily bear up a child. Other similar stems give origin at their extremity to the marvelously large and beautiful lily, which, like the leaves, floats upon the water surface. The season of flowering is in August, but though now October, fortunately one or two of these gorgeous lilies were in full bloom, and blushed in lovelier tints than Tyrean purple ever gave. Truly Solomon in all his glory was not arrayed like one of them.

There are also a number of botanical museums, One of these built by Miss North, has hanging upon its walls hundreds of drawings of plants made in all parts of the world by Miss North, placed in neat frames with written botanical descriptions, and arranged geopraphically—all done and presented to the botanical gardens, as well as the building, by this estimable, highly-gifted, cultivated and public-spirited lady. The vast amount of labor and time and expense necessary to accomplish this work is seen in the perfection, number, and wide geographical range of the collection.

At the far end of the grounds stands a beautiful pagoda ten stories high, from the summit of which a view of the grounds and adjoining country is given. We spent here the entire day—a beautiful October day, a day when every tree had put on its respective and variegated autumnal robe. The birch and ash trees blushed in purple and crimson, while maples and lindens shone in silver and gold, colors painted in hyaline tints caught not from earth, but heaven, the very bordering groves of Eden. And among flower-beds where roses and geraniums blushed as at the touch of the waning year they reluctantly left the parting stem to join their lovely companions that with fading blushes covered the ground and filled the air with sweetest perfume known to fields of Eden. We returned late in the afternoon quite tired but having had a most delightfully pleasant and instructive day.

ST. THOMAS HOSPITAL AND COLLEGE.

Oct. 11th.—Visited by invitation St. Thomas Hospital to witness an important operation by the surgeon in charge, Sir Wm. Makormac, well known to many of the physicians in St. Louis. The operation was beautifully and successfully performed.

St. Thomas is one of the oldest and most important of the many London hospitals. The new buildings are truly palatial in size and elegance, as also in the truly royal comfort of the apartments for patients. It is nearly a third of a mile in length, situated on the bank of the Thames opposite the House of Parliament, which it almost equals in elegance of construction. It consists of seven four-storied brick buildings connected by arcades. The buildings alone cost $2,500,000.

At 3 P. M. attended the hospital surgical amphitheatre to listen to the Inaugural Address of St. Thomas Hospital Medical College by one of the surgeons, Prof. McKeller. The address was truly English—able and practical.

St. Thomas Medical College is adjoining the hospital and well-furnished with valuable museums of anatomical and pathological specimens and preparations, and all other requisites for the successful teaching of medicine, while its connection with the wards of this immense hospital gives every facility for practical knowledge. With all these advantages, together with its present able, active, and zealous professors, we doubt not that the time is near at hand when a diploma from this institution will be a ready passport to the highest professional honors.

At 9 P. M. attended, by special invitation of Sir Wm. McKormac, and courtesy of the Faculty, the annual dinner of the older students, curators and professors of St. Thomas Hospital Medical College. It was a splendid affair, many distinguished physicians and surgeons belonging to, or older graduates of, the college ; among the number not a few Sirs or

Lords. Regular toasts were announced and many excellent speeches made. The dinner, speeches and all, were much such as in the United States. Perhaps the proceedings were a little more formal, dignified, than with us. The speeches, however, though clever, certainly were not any better than would have been with us in St. Louis, if as here the speakers had known in time what toast they were to reply to, while they lacked much of the ready wit that a like occasion would have called forth with us. There was, however, one distinction not observed with us on like occasions, all the guests were in full court dress. This gave it a rather formal court appearance— otherwise it was not at all so.

In attendance upon the clinics I noticed Sir Wm. McKormac speaking to the head nurses, or attendants, as Lady so and so. At the conclusion of the clinic I asked him if he here used the term *lady* in the American or English sense, when he assured me that he used it in the English sense, that these young women were of gentle birth and education, were the daughters of lords and ladies, and were here, some from in part necessity, but many for sweet charity; that every now and then a young physician married one of these, and indeed they were so gentle, refined and lovely that the term old maid was hallowed by association with some of these. And on my return to our hotel I got into trouble by telling my wife that I wished I was a young physician. Well, I told her that I did not mean it that way.

THE SCOTCH UNIVERSITY CLUB.

Nov. 11th, 1885.—Attended the annual dinner of the Edinburgh University Club, to which I had been invited by Prof. Wm. Playfair, physician to Her Majesty Queen Victoria, who introduced me to many of the most distinguished physicians and surgeons of London, among them Ericson, author of system of surgery—nearly all Scots and graduates of Edinburgh University. It was a really a grand feast of body and flow of soul, a most enjoyable occasion. Dr. Ericson who is a Scotchman, an Edinburgh graduate, is a candidate for Parliament, as is also Sir ———, the present Lord Advocate of Edinburgh, who was also present at the supper. These two distinguished Edinburgers are opposition candidates and were personally unacquainted with each other, having never before met. Both made most excellent speeches in which they alluded to their opponent in the most kindly and flattering terms, each complimenting the other, expressing delight in the fact that if defeated it would be by one so far superior to themselves. This of itself would have made the occasion a most enjoyable one, and received loud plaudits from their friends, most of whom at this supper being for Dr. Ericson.

Dr. Sierchenny, LL. D., was in the chair, and whose genuine Scottish wit and humor gave zest to the occasion, eliciting many brilliant scintillations from his fellows of the University Club. The short speeches given in reply to toasts were always classical and to the point, and often brilliant.

The banquet was given in the High Holborn Restaurant, said to be the finest dining hall in the world. It is lined with the most bnautiful and costly variegated marble, with numerous beautiful marble columns and brilliantly lighted with costly chandeliers. It is said that the marble alone cost more than half a million of dollars. The menu beginning with *Heutres* and ending with *Cafe Noir*, left nothing to be wished for. All kinds of costly wines and liquors were served at frequent intervals. The favorite drink, however, was a truly Scottish one, contained in the *Loving Cup*. The drink was something like hot champegne punch, and the Loving Cup a large silver pitcher with large handles on either side, and movable top. This is entirely Scottish, cup and contents, as well as the manner of using it. It is of great antiquity and redolent with deeds of daring and high carnival. Its very presence inspires a Scotchman with rememberance of bonny Scotland and University Club life. The Loving Cups filled with hot punch were passed up and down the long table at short intervals— each one of the guests doing it full justice, not only on account of its contents but also in remembrance of Auld Lang Syne. The manner of using the cup belongs to the Scotch clans, when Highland chieftains marshalled their kin and marched with Wallace or Bruce to death or victory. The cup is handed to the first man at the head of the table, who, turning around presents it to the next man, who removes the top, the first man holding the now open picture in both hands says *Alma Mater* and drinks. He then hands it to the next one, who goes through the same ceremony, repeating *Alma Mater* and drinking; and in this manner the pitcher passes around the table, and as it is a very agreeable as well as patriotic drink, it went around often.

We had fine music on the piano, accompanied with vocal music, the entire company joining in the more patriotic airs, the last of which was "Auld Lang Syne"; and as the Loving Cup had passed often this beautiful, touching, truly Scottish song was sung with much patriotic animation, all the company joining in the singing, and what may appear a little strange, all the company singing well, having greatly improved in this respect during the feast. The evening was a most delightful one, the company being of the highest literary culture and social position, including not a few of the Scotch nobility.

Nov. 12th.—Left London for Paris via Folkstone. Remained at Paris some three weeks, when we left Dec. 4th for Nice, where we remained until Spring.

NICE.

Nice is an old city, having been built by the Greeks in the fifth century, B. C. In B. C. 50 it fell, as did all other parts of

Greece, under the all conquering influence of Rome, a power that, in the providence of the world, was the hope of men— turning the darkness of savage forests into gardens. The Greeks have left little or no evidence of their existence here, but military Rome has left here, as in all parts of Europe, lasting traces of her occupancy and civilization, in walls of fortresses, amphitheatres, temples, roads and bridges, some of which, in a tolerable state of preservation exist here, and in almost every other part of the Rivera. After Rome had been sacked by the Goths and Huns and Vandals, who, in extinguishing the light of the world, were themselves illuminated by its dying embers. This part of the Rivera was overrun in the ninth century by the Saracens, and Nice became a Moslem city. These Mohamedans, like the Greeks have left little or no trace of their former occupancy. Rome, only Rome, asserts herself in her mighty ruins from the night of ages.

This city has about 80,000 inhabitants, is neatly built, and consists mostly of hotels and pensions, it having been for fifty years the favorite winter resort of the Rivera. The city is situated in the South of France, on the shores of the Mediterrenean, 670 miles from Paris, in a deep indentation of the shore line of mountains which surround the city in a semi-circle on the north, stretching from the southeast to the southwest, entirely protecting the city from the cold winds of the North, Northeast and Northwest. Its southern exposure is upon the Mediterranean, whose dark blue waters stretch southward, beyond the horizon. This beautiful sea, with its numerous white sails of pleasure boats or fishing smacks, with the occasional passing of a small coast steamer, gives an additional charm to Nice.

The city has no commercial or manufacturing importance, having only a small inland harbor, capable of admitting light crafts only. The old town was built to the east of the small river Paglione, a small mountain torrent, often dried up in summer. This stream has been walled in with high stone walls, and for a distance of half a mile has been arched over, and a beautiful garden planted with trees, shrubs and flowers, and a long, light, ornamental building erected, which is used as a museum and restaurant. To the north is the long, low line of mountains and foot hills, which immediately surround the city. Lying beyond is the loftier range of Maritime Alps, which present a long serrated line of snow, the higher peaks of which are seen from the city. The entire range, for many miles, is brought into view by ascending the high points of the hills that form the amphitheatre. The old part of the city, now occupied by the poorer class of natives, presents the high walls and narrow alley-like streets found in the mediæval cities of Europe. Many of the houses long antidate the discovery of America. The western part, or new city, has wide, neatly paved and planted streets, built by or for the English or other foreigners. This part of the city has every comfort and sanitary precaution, giving it a neat, pleasant and healthy appearance. Numerous orange and palm gardens are seen throughout the city. These orange trees, loaded with bright fruit, give, with the palm trees, quite a semi-tropical appearance. The entire coast, fronting the town, has been beautifully ornamented with a rude quay, well paved or graveled, and planted with palms and flowering shrubs. Much of this was laid out and planted by the English people, resident and visiting here, and is called the "*Promenade des Anglais.*" During fine weather, and the weather is nearly always fine here, multitudes of fashionable, gaily dressed people are seen on this promenade every afternoon. A beautiful, small, public garden, the "*Jardin Publique,*" near the fine stone bridge, the "*Ponte Napoleon,*" is on the "*Promenade des Anglais,*" and is quite a gem, embowered with palms, pepper and eucalyptus, globulus trees. In the middle of the garden is a music stand, at which a band plays every afternoon and evening. There are several public halls at which lectures are delivered by scientific and literary gentlemen every day, free. The English, also the Americans, have churches, there is a Protestant French church. There is also a fine Opera House, with an excellent company, the singing is very fine. Here is a theatre. These attractions with the villas, drives, walks, old Roman ruins, decayed castles and grottoes, render Nice, with its soft climate and beautiful shores, a favorite winter resort for the inhabitants of northern Europe. The orange and lemon trees are loaded with bright fruit all winter, while the open gardens are filled with bright roses, pinks, violets and other flowers, giving a summer-like appearance, not always in keeping with the weather, which is sometimes cold or disagreeably chilly. In the last of December we had a slight snow which remained on the ground several days with the ground slightly frozen, and yet, strange to say, the flowers and vegetables were not killed, and we have had green peas, fresh from the gardens, all winter. We have had fires all winter, while the natives, much less warmly clothed, almost never see a fire, we noticed this same thing last winter in Florence and Rome, where the natives seem hardly to know the use of fire for warming purposes.

Castle Hill to the west of the city rises 300 or 400 feet abruptly above the sea, and hangs directly over the little artificially prepared harbor. It affords a beautiful view of the city and coast range. Its summit is crowned with a ruined castle, with heavy old Roman ruined walls running around its crest, showing it to have been the site of a Roman Fort. A large stream of fresh water falls from its crest over the face of a ruined castle. in a beautiful cascade. Seen from the city it presents a most beautiful, sparkling silver appearance. The crest of this hill has been ornamented and planted in orange, lemon, palm and aloes. Numerous peafowls are kept here, whose bright plumage is only in keeping with their surroundings. To the north near the hills is the beautiful villa, Bermand, where died in 1865 Nicholas, heir apparent to the crown of Russia. Over the room in which he died has been erected a handsome memorial Greek chapel, containing some good Greek paintings and frescoes. The adjacent grounds are ornamented with orange, palm and eucalyptus trees and flower gardens.

A SILVER WEDDING.

Dec. 25th.—This being the twenty-fifth anniversary of Mr. and Mrs. Cupples' wedding day, who with their nieces were staying here, as were also Mr. Gregg and family, all of St. Louis, at the Hotel Grande, we were all invited to a sumptuous 6 o'clock dinner. The occasion was most enjoyable—the feast truly royal, with music, flowers, Yankee Doodle banners, etc. We remained feasting and talking over home and friends we had left behind us until a late hour, not forgetting to wish that our youthful friends might live to celebrate their golden wedding, and that we might be there to assist them. A few days after we with our niece, Miss Overall, were invited by Mr. Cupples to take the most delightful drive in the world, along the coast, over the high foot hills, with the bright blue Mediterranean spreading out in placid beauty a thousand feet below us. We were in two four-horse carriages, and these four horses were assisted by two others in steep places. The day was bright, clear, calm and warm. The road passes along the small river Paillon for some distance, when it ascends a lofty mountain ridge winding around the Observatory, which overlooks the city, and passes around the fort-crested summits that overhang the sea and where from an elevation of some 2,000 feet we have one of the most enchanting views in the world. On our right the sea, to our left and in front of us the long serrated snow-crested Alps. We passed numerous towns and villages. One considerable town, seen in the distance, near the head of a rocky ravine and surrounded by high, sterile, rocky hills, is deserted. Many houses, with their high rock walls and the roofs still upon them, have no inhabitants but the owl and bat. No children prattle in its streets, no maidens visit its wells—a city of the dead, standing as a shrouded spectre of the night—the voiceless ghost of mediæval times. How strange! Another, an old Roman village, Ezra, on a high rocky peak, with three of its sides, perpendicular rock walls of three or four hundred feet in height, and the fourth hillside so nearly perpendicular that it was easily made inaccessable to the assault of an enemy. Indeed, without the modern means of warfare, a few determined men could defend it against an army. During the times of the Saracens, and long after, even until the time of Louis XIV., it was a stronghold of pirates, who from this castle issued on their marauding expeditions, returning with their booty to this stronghold, where they could defy an army. It is now a peaceful village; the inhabitants subsisting on the olives and vines planted upon its terraced steep hillsides. A quaint old church with its curious old clock tower, that has battled with half a thousand years, attracts attention, because it looks like nothing of the present day. We arrived at Mentone at noon and partook of a sumptuous dinner at the fine " Hotel Anglais." Mentone is a beautiful little village nestled away in a niche in the mountains, with a southern sea exposure, well protected from the winds, and is even warmer than Nice. It is handsomely built and planted, and has numerous fine hotels and pensions with handsome walks, groves and gardens, which, together with the numerous splendid villas that surround, and the smiling irridescent sea in front of it, constitute it a very gem in the golden settings of this Arcadian Rivera.

Our return was along the sea-shore, whose babbling waters,

in very sport, often kissed the carriage wheels, through the far-famed gambling halls of Monte Carlo, whose gorgeous palace and tables of gold constitute a gilded stairway to a yawning hell where thousands fall. We reached home sometime after night—but the warm, bright evening, rendered softer yet by the laughing music of the waves, gave enchantment to night. As we were on a gala day excursion, with our four-horse carriages gaily decorated with numerous small star-spangled banners and Yankee Doodle streamers, we produced quite a sensation. Men quit work to stare at us, while all the women and children along the route ran out to see the sight, all wondering what could mean this new invasion of La Belle France.

The entire day, pleasant friends, gay surroundings; transportingly lovely scenery, strange manners and customs of the people we passed, with the jocund laugh of the young folks of our company, made this a most delightful excursion; an episode long to be remembered.

March 8th.—The Grand Carnival, which at Nice is the great occasion of the year, and since the Pope has been mad and refused to honor it with his presence, is much more pretentious here than at Rome. We had seen it at Rome along the Via Nazzionally on the Corso Roma, at Pisa, at Genoa and at Milan, where it is greater far than at Rome. We have in fact last winter, had carnival *ad nauseam*, for there never was anything more ridiculous, whimsical or worthless, leaving constantly the wonder that any but children could possibly be amused at it, much less to perform or pay for the farce. But notwithstanding these impressions, here at Nice the Carnival is really worth seeing and many things connected with it are really fine. We had secured seats at twenty francs each at the place du la Prefecture, where the night shows were to come off. It was necessary for the Carnival to have a king, and as the old king had been consumed in fire at the close of the last year's Carnival as is the custom, and his ashes containing his spirit placed in a sepulchre, it was necessary that he, phœnix-like, come forth from his ashes; consequently the first night the magicians had been assembled in this place and amidst bonfires, rockets, bombs, bengal lights and peals of artillery, King Carnival arose in great majesty and glory, and sat upon his throne to preside over the Carnival. All this was a very tame affair, much in keeping with what we had seen in Italy. Two days after this, the grand Battle of Flowers came off on the Promenade des Anglais. This was truly fine, beautiful. Thousands of splendid equipages, beautifully ornamented with flowers, fresh roses, pinks, violets and anemones, and bright ribbons passed along the quay that was lined with multitudes, perhaps 150,000, of people. The entire length of the Promenade, extending from the Paillon on the east, to the brook Magnon on the west, was occupied by a double row of carriages, all decorated and filled with flowers which the occupants of the carriages threw in great quantities of bright, beautiful bouquets among the crowd, while tens of thousands of bright, fresh flowers were thrown at the inmates of the carriages by their friends and others. This constituted a veritable " battle of flowers," which lasted for hours, in which millions of fresh flowers were thrown until the very air was filled with the odor of roses, pinks and violets, a very perfume garden. This occupied all the afternoon, and some two miles of the Promenade was pretty, fairy-like, beautiful. The beauty and loveliness of the flowers were surpassed only by the thousands of beautiful women, gaily dressed and radiant with smiles, brighter and lovelier far than the flowers. The Prince of Wales with the Princess, occupied one of the carriages, but thousands of gay equipages were so gorgeous, that the splendors of royalty could add nothing to them and were lost in the crowd. The day being bright and warm made the occasion the more enjoyable.

The next day was the throwing of confetta, or chalk. This is a chalk or white earth, so prepared as to resemble small peas of different colors, but when thrown, as it is, from small tin tubes with long elastic reed handles, a white powder. Every person passing on the streets on this day must have on a mask or domino or get his eyes filled and clothes whitened with this powder. Thousands of pounds are thrown. Every person provides him or herself with a wallet, tin cup and supply of confetta, and no age or respectability exempts one from this abominable nuisance. Indeed any appearance of respectability only invites an additional quantity. It is a childish, foolish, ridiculous custom, and one would suppose it could only exist among savages in some village in Zululand, but here in the center of European civilation it is not only tolerated but enjoyed. It is, however, but doing justice to this people to say that it is only the common that really enjoy it, the better classes only sympathizing with them in their childish sport. The last day of the Carnival, Wednesday, was a repetition of the Battle of the Flowers and the grand pageant at the Place de Prefecture. This latter was very pretty, and many of the designs and floats were really ingenious, grand, enjoyable. This was followed at night by the most splendid show of all, the burning of King Carnival, which took place at the grand stand amidst the finest exhibition of fireworks in the world. We had witnessed the great display of fireworks at Wiesbaden, Germany, last year, in which many things were done which we would have thought impossible, and were impressed with the idea that it could not be excelled, were in fact assured that this was the case. But this far surpassed everything at Wiesbaden. It was truly beautiful, grand, imposing, indescribable, and must have cost many tens of thousands of francs. Amidst the glare of red, blue and yellow rockets, Bengal lights, Roman candles, immense, variously-colored fire-boquets, volleys of artillery, and shouts of tens of thousands of people, in his burning palace, that far surpassed in seeming grandeur any other palace ever consumed by flames, King Carnival himself, with his sceptre, throne and all, was consumed by brilliant jets of flame that seemed to come from a spirit world. His ashes will be preserved for another carnival, when he will again arise from his ashes. Really this splendid exhibition of fireworks atoned for all the childish foolishness of the Carnival, and fully satisfied the wildest expectations, and, with the Battle of Flowers, it makes the Niciois carnival the principal one of Europe, a fact upon which the Niciois pride themselves very much and which brings here annually tens of thousands of people, not only from France and Italy but from moredistant countries.

On Februrary the 1st, with our niece, we took a long walk over the hills beyond Nice, where we gathered bouquets of bright flowers growing wild on the hillsides and saw peach trees and potato and pea vines in bloom; have endeavored elsewhere to account for this, and yet I cannot satisfy myself how it can be; I am quite sure nothing of the kind could be with us in St. Louis in the same temperature.

March 12th.—A SURPRISE.—This being the forty-first anniversary of our wedding-day, we were quite happy with the reflection that we had thus far climed life's hill together and that although far from home and friends, with only our niece, we were in the enjoyment of blessings greater than had fallen to many that we had known, not even thinking that we had other friends, when, about 7 o'clock in the evening, several ladies, seemingly by chance, dropped in, and to our great surprise we were invited into our dining-room to a beautiful but simple supper which these kind friends had prepared for us—tea, ices, cakes, wine, etc. We had a most delightful evening. These were ladies most of whom we had known only here, and yet, having learned that this was our wedding anniversary, they had taken all this trouble to render us happy. How lovely! None but women could or would have acted thus. Of a hundred male friends not one perhaps would have thus acted. I am young; if I were old, possibly I might not think thus. To me the one thing pure, holy and lovely is woman. Man in his viler states drags humanity down, ever down, until it lays hold on hell—is wont to consort with devils. Woman, in her purer moods, exalts human nature to the very gates of heaven; the angels, methinks, half fearing, half hoping, believe she may break through and take Paradise bodily. Tell me not of the gardens of the Hesperides, whose blossoms of silver and apples of gold are guarded by the ever-watchful dragon. Point me not to the roses of Sharon or the lilies that spring eternal in the vale of Shinar. The loveliest flower that ever blushed outside of Paradise is woman. In all the relations of life, as mother, wife, sister, friend, of priceless value, greater far than the Kooh-i-nor that glitters in the crown of England's queen, and her sweet, refining friendship more to be esteemed than gold, yea, than much fine gold. With her I had rather be stranded upon an iceberg drifting around the north pole than without her to be seated upon the banks of the river of life listening to the song of birds of Paradise.

MONACO.

Monaco is beautifully situated upon a high, rocky promontory, projecting into the sea, which surrounds it on three sides. It is the capital of the principality of Monaco, perhaps the smallest principality in the world— embracing, with Monte Carlo, some three or four miles square. It is a beautiful, well-built little city of some two or three thousand inhabitants; and the entire principality contains some 5,000 inhabitants.

With feelings inspired by the loveliness of the place, with our niece, Miss Overall, we strolled over this quaint city, along its neatly-paved, clean and almost deserted streets, in communion with, not the living, but the spirits of the dead; not the present, but the past; for Ichabod was written on tower and palace. We passed out on the parapets overlooking the blue sea, walked through the flower beds, along graveled walks bordered with flowering shrubs and palms, acacias and aloes, enchanted with the beauty, the stillness and loveliness of the scene. There are few places on earth more lovely than this. The gardens of the Hesperides were not, perhaps, half so beautiful; an earthly Eden that seemed an abode too fair for aught but disembodied spirits that fain might linger here, in no haste to leave it, even for a celestial paradise.

We returned to the palace—for the little town has a palace —and a most beautiful one, notwithstanding the meagre dimensions of the capital and principality, and its kings possess and exercise all the rights, privileges and prerogatives of sovereignty —are kings. We were shown through the palace, the court of which is entered through a strong iron gate, guarded by a sentinel who walks his beat with his musket just as though he were on guard at Windsor Castle, or the Palace of Kaiser William. The halls contain many portraits and paintings of the royal family, court beauties and others, some of them of historic interest. The furniture is exquisite—well becoming a palace. We were shown one bedroom of the time of the grand monarch, Louis XIV., with its quaint, rich furniture of that period.

There are none of the royal family here now. The present king, who is old and blind, is living with some friends or relations in the north of France; while his son, an only child, married the daughter of the Duke of Sutherland. His marriage was an unhappy one: his wife left him some time since and returned to England, taking with her their only child. The Prince, thus disappointed in life, with nothing to live for, left with a French expedition for the North Polar Sea, not wishing, perhaps, to return. Thus the palace, with its surroundings, has outlived its royal owners. A proud family—among the oldest of France—fallen to decay.

We descended the hill, along a highly ornamented and truly royal road, to the lower part of the town, near the sea, and known as Monte Carlo—famous as being now the only public gambling place in Europe. The gilded palace is more sumptuously furnished and its halls more gorgeously garnitured than those of kings. Its numerous tables, covered with gold and silver, occupy many rooms, and are surrounded by multitudes of men and women. Some of these were roulette tables; one seemed to be a faro bank. At these tables were many matronly, pious-looking, educated women, seated with the men, betting large sums of money. Indeed, gambling is followed here by men and women as a profession—a fine art—and entails no dishonor, especially if successful. Here, as in other places and in other callings, "nothing succeeds like success." It is, however, with all its gilded trappings, but a gilded hell, whose golden gates open wide and surely upon the road to death, while the feet of its votaries lay hold on hell. A gaping charnel house whose miry pits are filled with ghastly skeletons, and whose accursed altars have for incense crushed hopes, blighted lives, blood of suicides, tears of women, ruined families, anguish and remorse. These, like a shrouded pall of night, hang over its altars, and hide, with their spectre shrouds, its horrid images of death from its hapless votaries, some of whom daily add, by suicide, to its thousands of victims. I could but feel that there was a tangible spirit of evil in the very atmosphere of the place, caused by the ghosts of its murdered families, and was glad to regain the open air, where laughing nature, in sporting fountains and flowers, fanned by sea breezes, tokened nothing but kindness to man. The revenues of these gambling halls here support the palace on the hill. The licenses from these tables constitute the revenues of the principality of Monaco—support the palace and royal family. Possibly the religious, those who believe in a moral government of the world, and that the wages of sin is death, even in the present life, may find some connection with these facts, and the decay and desolation of the royal family of Monaco: even to the philosopher the relation might suggest that of cause and effect.

CANNES.

Canes is a city of about 20,000 inhabitants, and possesses in a rare degree many of the advantages and beauties of the towns in this part of the Rivera. Like Nice it is a winter resort for the inhabitants of the more inhospitable regions of Northern Europe, and even more than Nice, possesses the favor of the aristocracy. Like all the towns of this littoral, or shore line, it was long subject to the Romans, and after the fall of Rome shared its fate in being subjected to numerous destructive invasions by Goths, Vandals, Saracens and Franks, who in turn pillaged and destroyed the city. So great was this destruction that as late as 1831 it contained only a few mean houses and 3,000 souls, mostly sailors and fishermen. It owes its present prosperity to the lucky accident that in 1831 Lord Brougham, Prime Minister of England, on his return overland to England from Italy, where the cholera had broken out, was detained here on the frontier of France by the quarantine. At first he was greatly provoked by this detention, which with the then means of overland travel was a very great inconvenience, He was, however, soon so won by the soft climate and beauty and salubrity of the place that he determined to make it his winter residence, and built for himself and family a villa, and had many of his aristocratic English friends also build villas here, insomuch that Cannes became the favorite winter resort of the English aristocracy, which it continues to be to the present time with ever-increasing population and wealth. The Prince of Wales, among others, passed several weeks of the present winter here, and his youngest brother, Prince Leopold, died here at his villa, Villa de Nevada. English money and taste have done much for Canes. Many of its finest villas belong to English nobility or millionaires, while many of the finest hotels, such as the *Hotel de La Grande Britaine* and *Hotel Prince de Galls*, the latter the one at which the Prince of Wales stayed during his residence here, as well as many of the pensions and business houses have English names, or occupants. Nothing can well surpass the beauty and splendor of some of these villas and gardens that dot the hillsides in and around Cannes. We visited the lovely villa and gardens of the Duke de Vallambrosia, situated on an eminence overlooking the Gulf de Juan. It is indeed a very paradise, all that natural scenery, money, taste or skill in landscape gardening could do, has been done to render it enchantingly lovely. Fountains throw up crystal jets among roses, palms, mimosas and orange trees, with thousands of bright flowers arranged in artistic beds or clusters, or climbing up the graceful palms, flash as brilliant settings to this Arcadian scene. Cool grottoes, beautiful graded walks wind amidst this semi-trophical luxuriance of trees, vines, shrubs and flowers. I noticed date-palms loaded with clusters of ripe fruit, which, with lotus and other palms, reminded one of the banks of the Nile. The beautiful costly cottage villa is in keeping with the extravagance and beauty of the grounds. Altogether one feels here the reality of the wonders of Arabian tales. Surely if there be a Paradise on earth, where mortals, forgetting the cares and ills of life, might revel in Elyrian dreams, it is here.

Opposite the city, and some miles from the shore, rises the *Isles des Lerens*. On the largest of these, *Saint Margarite*, is the once strong Fort Monterey, famous in song and story as being long the residence of "the Man in the Iron Mask." This is one of the strangest and most inscrutable of the world's mysterious, cruel wrongs—a secret that remains and ever will remain a State secret. During the reign of Louis XIV., in 1686, a man was brought to this place with his face entirely concealed by an iron mask, which was never removed. He was never permitted to communicate with anyone but his keepers, who were State officers. He was of royal birth, as his demeanor and that of his attendants or keepers manifested. His plate was of solid silver and his furniture all such as betokened royalty. He remained here until his death, twelve years, in 1698, when his body was disposed of, as secretly as was kept the mystery of his life. No one knows who he was, from whence he came or where he was buried, or at least none but those who kept the secret. No public or private account of who or what he was, has ever been discovered, it was and is a State secret and doubtless one of great importance. The most reasonable conjecture of this strange occurrence, is that he was a twin brother of Louis XIV. and had been kept from infancy by the ministers in secret and finally thus disposed of to prevent rival claims to the throne. This fort is also famous in modern times as having been the prison of Marshal Bazaine, who, after the fall of Metz, was arrested for treason and imprisoned here from Dec. 1873, until the night of Aug. 9, 1874, when he made his escape, certainly through the connivance of his guards and the State authorities, as this was the best solution of the problem what to do with him. France overwhelmed by the disasters of their late war, felt the humiliation more keenly than any people ever had. All looked anxiously for some cause outside of themselves. Bazaine's misfortunes or faults pointed him as the scape-goat and the populace howled for his blood, while the government knew he could not be proven guilty of treason, yet were too weak to defend him, and not strong or wicked enough to murder him, hence his escape.

We were shown through the now unimportant and neglected, but once strong Fort of Monterey, saw the room in which the mysterious *Man in the Iron Mask* was confined 200 years ago. It is a strong prison with a strong iron door and a sufficiently large window opening out over the sea and guarded by double rows of iron bars. It was a prison that utterly forbid any hope of escape, otherwise not gloomy. We were conducted to the little fortress chapel where we were shown his chair and some other remains of the strange mystery. All these were royal in style.

It would be impossible to imagine anything more beautiful than this section of the sea coast, with its splendid and often palatial villas and gardens; called at the Villa Nevada, where died the Prince Leopold. It is a lovely spot, well becoming a prince. He was a most estimable young gentleman, the youngest son of Victoria and Prince Albert, was here on account of his bad health, died suddenly and while his young wife who was also in bad health, was absent from Cannes. His many excellent qualities as well as his high birth, had made him many friends, and much esteemed here.

After his escape from the Island of Elba, March 1, 1815, Napoleon I. landed near and encamped in Cannes. A column marks the spot where he landed and commenced his triumphant march to Paris. All France flocked to his standard, which inspired Frenchmen by the remembrance of former deeds of glory, forgetting that this glory had cost France hundreds of thousands of her bravest and best men, that the "old guard" slept with the grand army beneath the snows of Russia. After a struggle of 100 days against the Holy Alliance, the world, his standard was shrouded in endless night, and his star went down at Waterloo never to rise again.

FROM CANNES TO MARSEILLES.

March 23rd.—Left Cannes for Marseilles at 10 A. M., arrived at Marseilles at 5 P. M. Most of the way is along the enchantingly lovely shore of the Mediterranean with its deep curvatures and bright little bays, most of which are lined by small towns, with numerous villas, while the entire distance from Mentone to Antilis is lined with olive and orange trees, the hillsides are covered with dark forests of olives. At Antilis anciently Antipolis, a busy seaport of 6,000 inhabitants, we have an extended view of the coastline of the Rivera, as far as Nice and the Maritime Alps. Most of the Rivera, as far as Mentone, belonged to Italy until quite recently. In 1860 Napoleon III. with a well organized army marched into Italy to assist Victor Emanuel in driving out the Austrians. At this time the Austrians had possession of Northern Italy, including Milan, Verona and the world renowned gem of the Adriatic, the city of Venice. A great and decisive battle was fought between the French and Italians, on the one side, and the Austrians on the other. The Austrians were completely defeated and were compelled to sign a disastrous treaty by which they restored to Italy all their Italian possessions, including Venice, and in compensation for their services, without which it would have been impossible for the Italians to wrest from the Austrians much of the fairest portion of their country, they ceded to France all this lower part of the Rivera, as far as Mentone.

The Austrians attributed their defeat to the use of rifle cannon which the French here used for the first time. They accounted for their fearful defeat, a short time afterwards, by the Germans, by the use of needle guns, which the Germans first used in this battle. These two battles then introduced the formidable weapons of modern warfare—rifle-cannon and breech-loading rifles.

This entire coast from San Raphael is blighted by, cursed with, the great Mestral, a cold northwest wind, which blows with great violence and so continuously that the trees and shrubbery and grass are bent toward the southeast, and so chills this entire region as to produce a marked sterility, driving all foreigners from its inhospitable shores. Even the natives, who can, gladly flee to other sections, and those who remain have the forlorn appearance of a chronic chill. Ninety miles out from Cannes we reach Toulon, the war harbor of France, an important town of 80,000 inhabitants strongly fortified, every high hill or rocky eminence for miles around being crowned by strong forts. It was taken in 1793 by the English fleet under Admiral Hood, and was retaken a few months afterwards by the French under the artillery command of the then unknown young artillery officer, Napoleon Bonaparte. It is an unprepossessing place, cursed by the Mestral, and the brightest page in its history is that its possession by the English who defended it with their usual bravery, afforded an opportunity for the display of the then unknown abilities of Napoleon Bonaparte, at the time twenty-four years of age and artillery Lieutenant, and who instead of planting his artillery at the distance of a mile or more from the walls of the city, as was then the custom, ordered his siege guns up to within 200 yards of the wall, where he soon produced a breach, and leading the assault in person, he stormed and took the city, British valor being of no avail against this young lieutenant, who gave in the conduct of this siege and storming of Toulon, the sign and promise of the future emperor of the French, the modern Cambyses whose all-conquering car was to roll over Europe, crushing kings and emperors under its resistless, merciless wheels.

MARSEILLES.

Marseilles, 140 miles from Nice, is the third most populous

city, 319,000 inhabitants, and the second in commercial importance in France, and is to French commerce on and beyond the Mediterranean, what Havre is to the commerce of the Atlantic. We put up at the very excellent Hotel Louvre. The city is one of the oldest and most historical of all those of the Rivera, was founded by the Greeks from Phœnicia B. C. 600, or only 150 years after the founding of Rome. From Marseilles was founded numerous Greek cities along the Littoral as far as Nice, all these maintained the Greek language and culture down to the Christian era, when like all the other, with Greece itself, it fell under the power of Rome and became a part of the Roman Empire.

To the tourist Marseilles possesses but little interest. Most of the streets are narrow and the houses high and crowded together, much resembling Naples, which city it rivals in filthiness, and like Naples, pays for its utter disregard of all sanitary precautions by frequent irruptions of cholera. Last year and the year before, it, together with Toulon, was scourged with this plague, and as its filthy condition invites cholera, it is most likely it will be visited again the coming season.

We drove up the lofty hill to the foot of the long line of wide stone steps that ascend to *Notre Dame*, which stands upon a lofty, rocky eminence, overlooking the entire city and adjacent country. From here we had a fine view of the city and harbor almost immediately under us, also the adjoining rocky islands, upon all of which, as well as the adjacent hill are strong forts, bristling with cannon of immense calibre, including the Chateau, where Mirabeau was confined and which figures conspicuously in Dumas' *Counte of Monte Christo.*

This fine church, *Notre Dame*, (our lady) with its lofty tower crowned by a not very artistic colossal al bronze statue of the Virgin, holding the Infant in her arms, was built in 1860, and like the Temple of Diana Ephesus, it contains numerous votive offerings, the gifts of sea-faring men whom she saved from the dangers of the sea.

AVIGNON.

March 24th.—Left Marseilles at 2 P. M. for Avignon, where we arrived at 5 P. M. The route is uninviting, passing through a country more sterile than the desert plains of Colorado, we passed through several tunnels, one of which is three and a half miles long. The sterility of this country is quite remarkable, as the road passes over a level country, most of the way in the valley of the Rhone. Fifty-three miles out from Marseilles we pass through the once important commercial city of Arles, now a decayed, delapidated place of 25,000 inhabitants. Twenty-one miles farther on we arrived at the far famed historical town, the former residence of the French popes, Avignon.

Avignon was the residence of the Pope from 1309 to 1377. During this period of sixty-eight years Avignon had seven popes, the last of whom Gregory XI. transferred the See back to Rome. The city, however, continued under pontifical rule until 1791 when it was transferred to France. During this time the population had sunk from 80,000 to 17,000 inhabitants. The old city walls constructed in 1350 and which constituted an admirable defence during the reign of the popes, and through the middle ages, are in a good state of preservation, having been wisely preserved, reminding us much of the old German city of Nuremburg. The town is on the left bank of the Rhone, here a navigable but rapid river. It is connected with the opposite bank by a new and very fine suspension bridge. The old cathedral is adjoining the papal palace, which is an immense fortress structure erected in 1300, massive and constructed to withstand a seige. It is situated on a lofty summit with a perpendicular precipice on one side and the city wall next the river, of course it is not as large or fine as the Pope's Palace, the Vatican at Rome, and yet we may well suppose was adequate to acccommodate His Holiness and all his Cardinals and retainers: at present it is used for barracks, and so vast is it, that it contains sleeping, dining and hospital rooms, etc., etc., for 2,000 soldiers. We passed through its long corridors, great rooms and chapel. The rooms contain on their walls many frescoes of madonnas, apostles and saints, all of an early period, all faded, and present but little of interest. The whole building presents a gloomy fortress-like appearance. Behind the palace and still higher up the hill are beautiful gardens, from which we have an extensive view of the adjacent country—the Rhone and a long silver line the Durance, which enters the Rhone a short distance below the town. An old, so-called Roman bridge spans the Rhone from the city walls at the Papal Palace to within a short distance of the opposite bank, the last two spans being wanting. The portion standing is in a good state of preservation and the entire structure might be easily repaired, were it necessary. Local tradition and guide books inform us that this bridge was built by the Romans some 1800 or 2000 years ago, but on noting the arches, four or five of which are still standing, it readily appears that they are not the round Roman arch, but pointed Gothic arches, which dissipates this fable, and shows the bridge to have been built, at a period, most likely not earlier than the tenth or twelfth century. Indeed it is most likely this bridge was built by Clement VII. or his immediate successor in the fourteenth century. In front of the theatre are statues of Racine and Moliere. Medallions represent John XXII. and Petrarch. The great Italian poet, Petrarch, when quite a young man visited Avignon, where he saw and fell desperately, strangely, poetically and lastingly in love with a beautiful young French woman, with whom he never became acquainted nor revealed his consuming love. She married unfortunately, and many years after died, the mother of many children and bowed down with domestic affliction. Petrarch long reverenced her, but neither before her marriage nor after, ever received the slightest token of her attachment—indeed there is no evidence that she was even aware of it—and yet she was through his long life, even to old age, constantly present in his thoughts, in his affection; the constant image of his life-long worship, and the unconscious inspirer of many of his most beautiful songs and sonnets. This ideal love of the great poet for the idol of his affections; this beautiful, but stranger young woman is one of the most strange and touching of all love's strange romances. How different might have been the fortunes of this beautiful young woman—then only eighteen years of age as well as that of the poet, had he declared his passion. All the world has painfully regretted that a love so pure, so ardent, so lasting had not redeemed the sweet object of it from the cold hard fate of her life. This sweet, but sad remembrance of Petrarch constantly breathed forth in sweetest song, fills Avignon with sweetest recollections, and will live as long as may stand its massive Papal Palace. At Verona we visited, as have tens of thousands of tourists, the tomb of Juliet, made immortal by the genius of Shakespear in his Romeo and Juliet, a sweet recital of love that will outlive monuments of brass or marble, and yet all its incidents are less tender, less emotional than the strange, poetical love of Petrarch. We painfully regretted that the tomb of Petrarch's Laura had been destroyed. Her monument stands behind the museum buildings. We walked around one-third of the old city wall, beginning at the Old Roman Bridge, quite to the railroad depot. It is wonderful how well this wall has been preserved—indeed it looks as though it might have been built within the preseet century, and yet it is five or six hundred years old. It is fifteen or twenty feet high, flanked by lofty towers at every two or three hundred yards. The port-holes are for crossbow and arrows, these being, at the time this wall was built, the most effective defensive weapons, and with these walls were a strong defence.

PARIS.

March 28th.—Paris is, next to London, the largest city in the world, having a population of 2,500,000, and is altogether the most beautiful city in the world. All that art, that the most exquisite and cultivated taste, all that imperial pride could do to improve a situation naturally most beautiful, has been done, with the result of rendering this the fairest, the most enchantingly beautiful city on earth; forming, with its costly palaces, churches, public buildings, museums of art, its wide streets beautifully paved and artistically planted with trees, with its unequaled gardens, a habitation worthy of the gods, a very garden of Paradise, where wealth and culture have united in rendering its citizens, naturally polite, the most refined, polite and agreeable of all the inhabitants of earth. Indeed, society here, has doubtless in its culture and refinement, attained the *ultima thule* of human capability, and justly constitutes these people the arbitors of fashion for the world. A natural delicacy of taste, cultivated with ardor for centuries, has rendered these Parisian women the models of taste, as they are in personal beauty. The human form divine has here attained its highest perfection and loveliness, captivating us not more by their great beauty than by the softness of their manners and the faultless, unequaled taste in their attire. In a Parisian lady's dress there is no incongruous mixing of colors, no misfits, but each color, each bow and ribbon is so blended, so placed as to produce the finest effect, rendering the most beautiful forms and faces still more attractive, until each and every French woman walks, indeed a goddess, and looks the queen, a beauty and loveliness that scarce can fail to win our love and admiration.

The city covers an area of thirty square miles, divided into twenty wards. There are a number of large and beautifully ornamented parks within and immediately adjoining the city. The largest of these, the Bois de Bologne, 2,250 acres. In it are the race course and the Jardin d'Acclimation, which latter contains an almost infinite quantity and variety of animals, birds and plants, all of which are being taught, if not the French language, at least the climatic conditions of La Belle France. The Boulevard de Bologne, leading from the Arc de Triumphe to this park is 400 feet wide with quadruple rows of trees, a wide graveled way on either side for foot passengers. Within this and separated from it by rows of beautiful trees, is a wide Rotten Row for horses, with an open central space 200 feet wide for carriages. Of course this is the fashionable drive of the city, and on pleasant evenings tens of thousands of gay equipages crowd it through its entire length of two miles. So great is its width that it permits two rows of carriages, an outgoing and return row of eight carriages each, or sixteen carriages abreast, and yet so multitudinous are the vehicles found upon it that we were caught one evening in a carriage blockade sixteen carriages deep or wide, and extending from the entrance into the park to the Arc de Triumphe, so multitudinous are the pleasure vehicles of this gay city of two and a half millions of people, a number equal to the whole population of the State of Missouri. Besides these carriages filled with the elite of the city, the sidewalks of the boulevard were crowded with curious spectators.

In addition to its large parks there are forty open squares, beautifully ornamented with booths, trees and flowers. Many of the most popular boulevards within the most populous and finely built parts of the city are 200 feet wide, with double rows of trees. The most beautiful one of these, and indeed by far the most beautiful boulevard on earth, is the Avenue des Champs Elysees, which commences at the Arc de Triumphe and terminates at the Place de la Concorde, or at the Jardin de Tuilleries, near two miles in length. The lower half mile, or that next the Place de la Concorde, opens out into an extended, beautifully-planted forest and flower-garden, with wide graveled walks shaded by flowering trees, and bordered with flower-beds, with multitudes of gay booths, while numerous benches and chairs invite tired nature to linger yet another hour in this, the Jardin de Champs Elysees, the tessalated border of Elyseum, where in the very heart and centre of a great city, surrounded by the palaces of kings and emperors, and in the midst of a gay multitude, with splendidly ornamented fountains, throwing up their crystal streams, that flash as dazzling diamonds in the sunlight by day, and in the light of ten thousand gas jets by night, render this perhaps the most enchantingly lovely spot on earth—a very type of the ambrosial plains of Paradise. Beyond the Arc de Triumphe it is continued as the Avenue de Grande Armie, of equal width and of much the same beauty. At this point of divergence, on a commanding eminence, rises the Arc de Triumphe, surrounded by a circular vacant space some 300 yards in diameter. This space is named the Place de Etoile, or star, so called from the fact that from this point, surrounding the Arc de Triumphe, twelve wide avenues radiate like the spokes from the hub of a wheel or rays from a star.

The *Arc de Triumphe*, a triumphal arch, erected by Napoleon I., is the largest structure of the kind in the world. It consists of an immense arch sixty-seven feet high, with a transverse arch of the same height, the whole structure is 160 feet high, 146 feet in length and width; an immense structure, so large that it does not appear high, and so high that it scarcely appears large; so admirably is it proportioned, that forgetful of its immense size, we only think of the harmony of all its parts, blending in a beauty unsurpassed, unequaled by any like structure of modern times. From its lofty summit we have a commanding view of the City of Paris with its environs, even beyond the forts that cover the distant eminences around the city. It is ascended by a spiral staircase, within the structure, of 262 steps. All sides are beautifully ornamented with both *bas* and *alto* reliefs, of the battles of Napoleon I., while on the inner sides of the columns are engraved the names of 142 victories, constituting it a wonderful monument of French valor and glory.

The churches of Paris while of great size and beauty, fail to interest us as do the churches of Italy or even London. This is in part because most of the fine paintings, frescoes and statues, of which they were once possessed, have been destroyed by the vandalism of her mobs, communes, during the revolutions of 1792–3 and that of 1871, when most of the churches were despoiled of much or all that was most sacred or interesting, and converted into other and often unholy uses, and then there are but few of the churches now in Paris that are really old or hallowed by world memories. To this, however, *Notre Dame* offers a notable exception, both in its historical associations, which will live in the world's history as long as Paris itself shall stand, and in its venerable age which counts its centuries by more than half a thousand years.

This structure was first erected in the twelfth century, but has been subjected to so many repairs that but little of the old church remains as at first. It is situated in a low, flat district, on an island in the Seine, and fails to impress us as it would do were it more favorably situated. In 1793 its sculptures and paintings were destroyed and the church consecrated to the worship of heathen gods, or even less worthy objects. The image of the virgin was supplanted by the goddess of reason, and in the place of devout nuns, young women danseuses, demi-mondes, clothed in white garments and bearing torches, held orgies here, to the scandal of human reason, whose goddess they professed to worship, and of decency.

The façade dates back to the thirteenth century and is rather pretty. The church has a wide nave and two aisles divided by lofty columns supporting pointed or gothic arches. The nave is 417 feet long by 156 feet wide with a single transept near the High Altar, giving it the form of a Latin cross. In the Treasury we were shown some valuable relics that had survived the ravages of mobs and the tooth of time, among these were the relics of Napoleon I. and Charlemagne, also their crowns, together with some costly gifts of former kings, and the Virgin and Child in silver, given by Charles X., also the bloody robes in which the bishop of Paris was shot, murdered by the blood thirsty communes in 1871.

One of the wide avenues radiating from the Arc de Triumphe leads to the Palace du Trochadero, situated on an eminence near to and overlooking the Seine. The building consists of a circular central portion 189 feet in diameter and 180 feet high with semi-circular wings on either side 540 feet long. The towers are 300 feet high, beautiful gardens extend down to the river. The building is used as a museum and contains a great number of plaster casts and sculptures from the portals and foundations of churches and other buildings of the eleventh, twelfth and thirteenth centuries, together with many statues from France and Italy, all, however, of no great merit as works of art, but so arranged as to give a chronological history of the sculpture of the middle ages. It also contains an ethnological museum with many objects of interest from Oceanica. The great music hall has a fine organ and seats 6,000 persons. The view from the tower 500 feet above the river is the finest in Paris. Indeed from the top of this tower, which we reach by an elevator of singular construction, Paris is spread out as upon a map at our feet. During one of our visits to this palace, a Fair for charitable purposes was being held in booths on the covered piazzas of the wings of the building. All the booths were attended by beautiful young French women dressed in the peasant costume of the different provinces. The whole scene, booths, wares, and persons, was beautiful and very *Frenchy*.

April 16th.—Visited the Hotel and Musee de Cluney which occupies the site, and consists in part of the old Roman Fort constructed by Constantine in the third century, and where Julian the apostate was declared Emperor by his soldiers in 306. Much of it is still as Julian left it. It was long the residence of the early Frank kings. In the nineteenth century the Benedictine Monks built the present *Hotel de Cluny* on, and embracing the old Roman palace. Soon after its completion it was occupied by Mary, sister of Henry VIII. of England, and widow of Louis XII. of France. Her apartments are still shown and are called *La Chambre de la Riene Blanche*—The rooms of the *White Queen*. The museum contains a most valuable, interesting and instructive collection of objects of prehistoric and mediæval ages, in all 10,000 objects, weapons, tools, instruments, in flint and bone, found in caves and in lacustrine deposits. These last of course carry us back to prehistoric times when man had for cotemporaries in France the cave bear and reindeer, very possibly extending back into the dim, misty past, thousands or tens of thousands of years before the building of the pyramids of Cheops. Other rooms contain Flemish tapestries of the fourteenth and fifteenth centuries, remains of bishops' robes of the twelfth century, splendid, gaudily decorated carriages of the sixteenth century, handsome cabinets of kings and queens, potery and fayence wares of the the twelfth to the fifthteenth centuries, works in enamel and ivory, with shoes of different nations of the fourteenth to the sixteenth centuries, Limoges vases of the twelfth to the fourteenth centuries, small wooden images representing French kings from Clovis to Louis XIII., with many other things, giving other ages so perfect, that we seem to be living in their midst.

From the Cluney we visited the Pantheon, which is upon the highest point on this the left bank of the Seine, and occupies the spot where was formerly the tomb of St. Genevieve the patron saint of Paris. It was built as a church in 1770. In 1793 the Communes converted it into a Memorial Temple which they named Pantheon, and inscribed upon the façade in large stone letters, " *aux grande hommes la patrie reconnous*," which was removed, but again restored in 1830. The entire structure is well fitted for the purposes for which the Communes dedicated it, as it looks much more like a heathen temple than a Christian church.

The *Palace du Luxembourg* is an old structure of much beauty. It was erected by Maria de Medici in 1615, and was built upon the site of the old Hotel du Luxembourg. It is said to resemble the Pitti Palace at Florence, Italy, but we failed to see the resemblance, as this is a really handsome structure, while the palace Pitti is the least so of any building of like pretensions we have seen. During the revolution of 1791–'95 it was used as a prison in which were confined many of the most distinguished persons of France, among them Beauharnais and his wife Josephine, afterwards wife of Napoleon and empress of France, Danton and Robespierre. During Napoleon's time it was used by the Senate. It is now the Senate House. It contains many fine rooms in which are State paintings, frescoes, etc. To accommodate the large collection of statues and paintings by modern artists a large hall has been built, called the Musee. In this hall are placed all the works of living artists that have been adjudged by the Committee of the Palace l'Industrie as worthy of the prize and not sold by the artist or bought by the State. They remain here subjected to public opinion until 10 years after the death of the artist, when, if still approved as works of real artistic merit, they are removed to the Louvre, by which act the author is supposed to have received the highest honor in the gift of fame. The most beautiful of all these paintings, we thought, were two by Bougero, The Consolation of the Virgin and The Naissance of Venus.

Visited the *Palace du Champs Elysees*. 2,488 paintings by living artists are on exhibition in its halls, besides more than a thousand designs, cartoons, etc., and 1,200 sculptures, and nearly a thousand engravings, forming a collection of great works by living artists nowhere else to be met with. Here again, as at the Luxembourg, the best, we thought, were by Bougero. There is also some very excellent statuary by living artists.

Visited the *Jardin des Plantes*, to reach which from where we live, near the Arc de Triomphe, we take steamer at the Ponte l'Alma and run up the Seine four miles, passing, in this distance under fifteen splendid bridges which connect the different darts of the city situated on either side of the Seine.

Passed on our way the historic Isle de Citie, upon which are several costly and beautiful buildings, among them the Hospital Dieu and the Cathedral Notre Dame. The steamboat fare for this entire trip is only 10 centimes—two cents.

The Gardens, consisting of a museum, menagerie and botanical garden, contains 75 acres. The botanical garden is beautifully laid out in small beds artistically bordered. The medicinal quality of the plants are designated by labels or cards of different colors, which also contain the botanical name of the plant. Almost every known medicinal plant is found here. It would be impossible to find elsewhere so fine a field for the study of botany as we have here. The gardens are traversed by numerous wide gravel walks, shaded by beautifully trimmed trees. Besides the botanical gardens in the open air there are numerous hot-houses containing almost every known tropical plant and flower. The extensive menagerie contains a great variety of animals—elephants, rhinoceroses, lions, tigers, hyenas, bears, wolves, foxes, seals, sea-lions, deer, antelopes, Buffaloes, monkeys, swans, geese, cranes, eagles, vultures, pheasants, etc. At the far end of the grounds are extensive buildings containing the most extensive and complete natural history collection in the world, containing 200,000 specimens. The rooms containing the anthropoid and anthropological collections embrace lemurs, monkeys, ourang-outangs, gorillas, skeletons, male and female, of men, skeletons and crania, casts, portaits, paintings, photographs, busts, mummies and fossils of every nation, kindred, tongue and people on earth. Nothing can excel the perfection and beauty of this collection, containing, among others, the fine collection of skulls of the great phrenologist, Gall. We were much interested in the skeleton of the fanatical Solomon Hobbea, the assassin of the French general Blake in Egypt. We were quite certain that in the small, unsymmetrical head we could readily read the want of all moral instinct. Such a head, while it might make a fanatic, could never evolve the higher virtues.

THE LOUVRE.

The Palace of the Louvre, both on account of its great size and beauty and of the almost unrivaled treasures of art which it contains, will long remain the centre of attraction to persons visiting Paris. Commenced in 1541 by the splendor-loving Francis I., it has been extended and adorned by almost every subsequent ruler. It now constitutes, with the possible exception of the Popes' palace, the Vatican, in Rome, the largest and finest palace in the world. To form an estimate of its beauty it must be seen. Some idea of its vast proportion may be formed from the statement that the palace, with its enclosed court, covers 44 acres of ground, and to walk through its rooms without stopping to notice anything requires two hours —eight miles of rooms. The greater portion of this immense and splendid palace is now occupied by works of art, which in incredible quantities have been collected here by French monarchs since the time of Francis I. During the reign of Napoleon I., the spoils of Europe were collected here, constituting the Louvre galleries the most important in the world. Among these we may mention Potter's Bull; from the Hague, Raphael's Transfiguration, from the Vatican; and the Bronze Horses, from St. Mark's, Venice. We saw in the palace galleries of Italy many other great works that Napoleon had at one time carried off to the Louvre. All the most valuable of these works were returned after the downfall of Napoleon and yet the Louvre remains even now, in many respects, the most important art collection in Europe.

In its picture galleries all the schools are represented, and all the great masters have here, if not their greatest works, at least some works that are great. Raphael is represented here in five or six masterpieces, among them St. Michael, St. George and the Dragon, the great Holy Family and the La Belle Jardiniere, while most of the extant finished works of the most remarkable genius of his age and perhaps the greatest painter of any age, Leonardo da Vinci, are found in this gallery, chief among them his Madonna and Infant Christ with St. Anne, which if not *the* gem of the gallery is one of these. This immortal genius, Leonardo, who painted here during his last years, left but few finished works, because, while he readily satisfied all others, he could never please himself. His mighty conceptions of what a work ought to be were such as no human hand could accomplish.

The Spanish school is ably represented by its two greatest masters, Velasquez and Murillo. The Immaculate Conception, by the latter, is one of the master's greatest works. The Flemish and Dutch schools are fully represented in works by Rembrandt, Rubens, Dore, Van Dyck, Terberg and others. The French School is represented by numerous pieces by Vernet, Lesseur, Pyussin, Claude Lorrain, and many others. The English school by Constable, Lawrence, and others.

It would be idle to attempt an enumeration of even the best of the 2,000 paintings by the great masters, that adorn these galleries. Miles of wall are covered by them, and all placed at the disposal of students, who study and copy without let or hindrance. And all this vast art collection is open to the public, native or foreign, without money and without price. Every day in the week, Monday excepted, these galleries are open free from morning until night.

The Egyptian Museum is perhaps the most complete of any in Europe, but our remarks on this department in the British Museum, prevent the necessity of our more than referring to this. Let no visitor to the Louvre fail to visit it.

The rooms of ancient sculpture contain a most valuable collection of Greek and Roman statues, busts, friezes, etc. The gem of this collection, and, indeed, in the opinion of many, the glory of the Louvre, is the Venus de Milo, which is thought by many able judges to be the finest piece of ancient sculpture that has come down to us, and the most beautiful marble representation of the human form divine that is now in the world. Having seen and studied the Capitoline Venus at Rome and the Venus de Medici at Florence, I felt some anxiety to know what impressions this wonderful work, about which I had heard and read so much, would make upon me. It was, therefore, with feelings not unmixed with anxiety and doubt that I visited the room dedicated to this Aphrodite, whose only rival by common consent is the Venus Medici. On account of the loss of both arms, which are broken off near the shoulders, the statue is not at first sight, as imposingly, impressively beautiful as it otherwise would be, and I felt disappointed. Somehow the statue though surpassingly beautiful in many respects, failed to impress me as favorably as it had others. But after visiting it many times and studying it much and from different points in the room, I found its beauties growing upon me until I became as much captivated by its wondrous perfectron and beauty, as had been my niece and others.

I am now satisfied that the unfavorable impressions I had at first seeing it were the result of its mutilation in the broken arms and would advise others who may not be favorably impressed at first view, to visit it again and again, until the broken arms no longer appear as defects.

Like but one other work of the kind in the world, Raphael's Cistine Madonna at Dresden, we have here the most faultless, beautiful woman, in all the perfection and loveliness of woman, with the presence—the admixture of something more than the human, the divine. In both this statue and in Raphael's painting, the divine is as apparent as the human, both are unmistakably goddess as well as woman. Now what to me is the strangest part of all this, is that while we may know the most perfect type of female beauty, we positively know nothing of either the beauty or ugliness of a goddess, know the human, but are utterly ignorant of the divine, and yet we readily recognize in both of these great works that which we *cannot recognize*, the *divine* in the *human*.

This beautiful statue was found in the island of Milos—Milo. It is the work of Praxiteles or Scopos, of the school of Phidias, about the time of Alexander the Great. Among perhaps the best modern statues in the Louvre Museum, are a Cupid and Psyche by Canova.

VERSAILLES.

May 7th.—Visited this interesting place, with its costly palace, gardens and fountains so intimately associated with the *Grande Monarche*, Louis XIV., his son, Louis XV., and grandson, Louis XVI., and the beautiful, lovely, but unfortunate, queen, Marie Antoinette. It is situated ten miles from Paris and has 50,000 inhabitants. Louis XIV, who resided here, embellished it at a fabulous expense which severely taxed the resources of the nation. He is said to have expended the almost incredible sum of $250,000,000 in building the palace and ornamenting the grounds. The sumptuous palace, although among the finest in the world, lacks uniformity of plan, and is not as imposing as it should be, considering its great cost. The gardens were laid out by the world renowned landscape gardener, *Lenotre.* Its beautiful fountains, the water to supply which was brought from a great distance and at a fabulous cost, were long considered among the wonders of the world, while its extensive planted forests, long avenues, lakes, statues, etc., by absorbing their wealth and forcing the levying and collection of unjust and onerous taxes, impoverished the nation, led to that financial embarrassment and general distress which a few years later with more than cyclonic fury overthrew the French monarchy and deluged the land in blood.

The day of our visit was characteristic of the month of flowers, clothed in perfumed robes and fanned by the balmy breath of May. A cloudless sky and the air perfumed by forests of flowers enhanced the loveliness of the beautiful garden country over which we passed. On arriving at the Versailles depot we took carriage and drove to the palace, where we spent most of the day in threading its numerous rooms and great halls, walking five miles through rows of historical paintings, frescoes and sculptures. Many of the best of these paintings are by the greatest of French painters, Horace Vernet.

The enchantment produced in viewing these gorgeously decorated rooms. still retaining much of the antique and costly garniture of the times of the *Grande Monarche* and Louis XVI. and his queen Marie Antoinette, is greatly intensified by the speaking presence of their yet living history, stereotyped by the finger of time in ineffaceable characters upon their every wall and floor and ceiling.

We first enter the chapel, a large and costly ornamented room, richly adorned with sculptures and paintings, from this we pass into the galleries of historical paintings, containing 11,200 pieces, among them Charlemagne Submitting His Laws to the French, A. D. 779, by Delaroche; Charlemagne Crossing the Alps with His Army, A. D. 773, by Rouget. Saint Louis Mediating Between the English King and His Barons. But it would be idle to attempt either an enumeration or description of these thousands of fine historical paintings which form more than a mile of paintings lining these eleven rooms. Leaving these great rooms, we mounted a lofty flight of marble steps, some twenty feet wide, to the second floor, where after examining bust-portraits of most of France's great men, kings, generals, statesmen, poets, orators, writers and philosophers, we passed into the splendid room containing paintings of Louis XIV., XV. and XVI., together with nearly all the great battles of Napoleon, the Coronation of Josephine, with what to us was of yet more interest, a fine painting of the Taking of Yorktown, in America, containing fine portraits of well-known persons, Washington, LaFayette, etc. From here we passed into the bedrooms of Louis XIV.–XVI. and Marie Antoinette, in this we had pointed out the small, narrow stairway down which she, with her children, in terror fled, on that fearful night when the murderous mob, or patriots, broke into and sacked the palace, overthrew the monarchy, and shook the world by their mighty deeds. Adjoining this is the long, gorgeously-decorated ball-room in which was held a sumptuous georgeously-extravagant ball, at which were Louis XVI. and Marie Antoinette, with hundreds of gay cavaliers, lords and ladies and court beauties, representing the chivalry and beauty of France, only a few nights before the fatal irruption of the bloodthirsty mob, with the fearful cry of down with the monarchy, the aristocracy and priesthood. At this fatal ball, while dancing to the tune of soul-stirring music and intoxicated by the splendors of a court that had impoverished the people and oblivious to the distant howlings of the infuriated, starving masses, whose cry was " Bread or Blood," some one more thoughtful than his comrades paused to remark that they were " dancing over a volcano," but so blinded were the royal family by the false glory that surrounded them that they heeded not this fearful warning, but danced on. Alas! it was their last ball, the angry volcano, whose deep-toned bellowings might have been heard above the music of the ball, and whose vibrations were shaking France to its centre, burst only a few days after, with a cyclonic fury that not only destroyed the monarchy and deluged France in blood, but overthrew most of the thrones of Europe, broke up the foundations of the great deep and turned night and chaos loose to revel in hideous slaughter, until, glutted with the blood of its victims, it died of very repletion. Only a few days after this ball, Louis XVI. and Marie Antoinette were dragged from this splendid royal room, hurried by the mob to Paris, thrown into the Bastile, from the Bastile to the Guillotine, where their severed heads became the sport of a deeply-wronged people, who, in the blood of royalty blotted out the idea, at least in France, that there is a " divinity that doth hedge about a king," taught the world that not a king, but man alone, is divine.

A great many souvenirs of royalty are yet in these rooms. The death-bed-chamber, with its bed and furnishing of Louis

XIV., are much as he left them 300 years ago—numerous cabinets, marble tables, costly vases, mirrors, clocks, etc., of Marie Antoinette, Napolion, and other kings, queens and rulers of France. Leaving the palace we visited the gardens, the beauty of which in landscape gardening was never surpassed. Rows of beautifully trimmed box or cedar line the walks and squares with sculptures, lakes, fountains, flower-beds and avenues. We walked for an hour among these beautifully planned and planted palace gardens, when we took carriage and drove out a mile through a wondrously beautiful park through an avenue shaded by old lindens, to the grand Trianon, a handsome palatial villa of one story in height. We were shown through the rooms containing many souvenirs of former kings, queens and emperors, costly Sevres vases, Malachite vases and tables given to Napoleon by Alexander, Czar of Russia, the finely furnished room fitted up by Napoleon III. for Queen Victoria, on her visit to France. Victoria, however, for some cause, did not stay here. The finely furnished bed, as also much of the furniture remains much as it was prepared for her Majesty. It well represents the pomp and vanity of emperors in its costly fittings, which, of course, cost Napoleon nothing but the French people much. We were shown through the carriage house containing the most splendid carriages in the world, including the carriage of Napoleon I., that of the Prince Imperial, son of Napolean III. and Eugenie. Also the state carriage sent for Queen Victoria, together with many suits of splendid harness from the time of Louis XVI. to Napolean III., sleighs, Sedan chairs, etc. Went from here to the Petite Trianon, erected by Louis XVI., for one of his favorites, Madam Pompadour, and afterwards a favorite resort of the lovely, but unfortunate, queen of Louis XVI., which contains many costly baubles belonging to her and other queens.

These costly and splendid baubles, that have outlived the

the dynasty that impoverished the people, were first commenced by the splendor-loving, art-fostering Francis I. and were continued by the Grand Monarch, Louis XIV., who was not grand but, living in the halcyon days of the French monarchy, flattered himself and was flattered into the belief that he was really great, and by his son, Louis XV., by whom these gorgeous palaces were converted into dens over which reigned supreme his mistresses, Madames Pompadour and De Bray. This corruption of public morals by those who should have set the nation an example of virtue resulted in the downfall of the monarchy, the murder of Louis XVI. and his queen, the establishment of the Reign of Terror and the empire under Napoleon. Since the murder of Louis XVI. and Marie Antoinette, none of the French rulers have resided here. Ichabod is written on its palace gates and walls.

PARIS.
M. PASTEUR AND HIS TREATMENT FOR RABIES.

May 17th. 1886.—Had to-day the great good fortune to attend the clinic of M. Pasteur, at the Ecole Normale, being introduced by my friend Dr. Warren Bey, an eminent American physician now practicing here in Paris. Dr. Warren was knighted by the Sultan for his service in the Egyptian Army, and is also a fellow of many of the learned societies of Europe. He was not personallly acquainted with M. Pasteur, but in order to introduce me, as well as to see Pasteur and learn something of his discovery, he procured a letter of introduction from Professor Charcot, Physician in Charge at the Hospice de la Salpêtrière. This procured us ready admission to the clinic, where we saw one hundred patients treated for mad-dog bites, without being much the wiser for our experience.

The treatment consisted in putting into the cellular system,

on the anterior lateral portion of the abdomen, by means of
the ordinary hypodermic syringe, a slightly milky looking fluid
contained in wine glasses holding two or three ounces each,
carefully covered with thin pink-colored paper. The needle of
the syringe was passed through the paper, which was evidently
intended to prevent the free admission of air into the fluid.
The quantity used was half a drachm for adults, less for children
and ten to fifteen drops for infants. The operation was neatly
performed, not by M. Pasteur but by an assistant, M. Pasteur
standing near the door and calling out from a strip of paper
the names of the patients. After each injection the needle of
the syringe was very properly dipped in a hot solution of some
disinfectant, possibly a solution of salicylic acid, thus preventing the possibility of infecting other patients. The patients were a motely crowd of Greeks, Jews and Gentiles, from
Poland, Russia, Scandinavia, Italy, France, Germany, Austria,
and perhaps the remotest India—adults, children and infants,
mostly laboring peasant people, as these would naturally be
most likely to receive mad-dog and mad-wolf bites. But not
all were of this class, some of both the men and women were
of the better class of gentry. Well, of course, while all this
was interesting and easily seen, done and learned, it failed to
satisfy. What was the fluid that contained this antihydro-
phobic microbe, and how is it prepared? These to the physician were the all important points, and these I believe, M.
Pasteur has not revealed, *has kept a profound secret.* But,
really, while this at first thought, would condemn M. Pasteur
with the profession and, by a conduct so utterly at variance
with all medical ethics, would consign him to the list of quacks
and mountebanks, it may really result from the purest motives.
It may be that M. Pasteur is afraid that the unskilled or care-
less attempts to prepare the fluid might bring the treatment
into unmerited disrepute and that when he has perfected and

established it, under his immediate care, it will be time to publish his process. Well, is his process a cure or preventive for rabies? I fear not; certainly, it has not been proved; has not been sufficiently tested, and like Perkins' Metallic Tractors may fail to stand a rigid test.

He has now treated 1050 patients, bitten by mad, or supposed mad-dogs and wolves, and only a few of these thus for have died of rabies. Of the nineteen patients sent from Russia who had been bitten by a mad wolf, six or seven died here of hydrophobia and one or more since their return home. This frightful proportion, I learn, so frightened M. Pasteur that he insists that rabies in the wolf differs somewhat from the same disease in the dog. How does it differ?

Now, let us examine this wonderful discovery that has made M. Pasteur the most prominent professional man in the world, has, indeed, turned the eyes of all the world upon him, and by and through which he has received the highest honors, of stars and garters from the Czar of Russia and other kings and potentates, while the learned societies have been proud to do him honor. In the first place, perhaps not one dog in a dozen supposed to be mad, really has rabies. Dogs, like men, have fits, become insane, cranky. This condition in men may suggest pistols, daggers, etc., the so-called homicidal insanity; in a bull, it would manifest itself in a tendency to gore every person and animal that came in its way; in a ram, it would produce a butting furor; in the elephant, as is well known, it would result in the killing of its keeper; and, in the dog, as his habit in a sane condition is a biting one, would produce a morbid or exaggerated condition of this, his natural instinct, so that he would now be disposed to bite his friends as in a normal or healthy condition he would his foes. Then rabies is a disorder especially belonging to brutes, dogs, cats, wolves, etc., and is transmitted to man with not less difficulty than is cholera transmitted to dogs, horses, cattle, etc. So much is this the case that perhaps not more than one person in three or five, who are bitten by animals really rabid, go mad. And many of these really do so by the profound mental disturbance in the individual, the mortal-fright in having been bitten by a mad dog. Perhaps some of these last who go mad, and really die with many symptoms of hydrophobia have not rabies, nor had the dog that bit them, and here comes in perhaps much of the efficacy of M. Pasteur treatment, the patients are convinced that there is no possible danger, that they have been subjected to a treatment that knows no failure, that is specific, and if the same faith was given to Perkins' Metallic Tractors, perhaps the same result might be obtained. If rabies is not a neurosis, surely many of its symptoms are certainly so, and ally it in some of its phenomena to chorea. In both conditions the neurotic phenomena may kill; in both the causes producing the symptoms may do so. Now the power and influence of hope and fear, mental impressions, in causing or curing many of these diseases is well known. During the frightful epidemic of St. Vitus' dance that broke out in some of the monasteries and convents in Europe in the Middle Ages, many of the inmates of those institutions were seized immediately on seeing one effected with the disorder. Well, a wise doctor discovered that a *red hot iron* was a specific, not only in its application, but both preventing and curing the disease, by merely seeing it. He had the patients brought forward, placed a number of iron pokers in the fire, heated them to a red heat and ordered them applied to the first patient who had an attack. None were attacked. No one will infer by this that we do not believe that both rabies and chorea are real, any more than we would imply that cholera is not real when we say that during a cholera epidemic many persons die with *fright cholera* who would not have been sick but for their fright.

Again, many persons who are bitten by dogs really mad, and who otherwise might go mad are protected by their clothing wiping off the morbid material as the dog's teeth pass through it, previous to entering the flesh, just as persons are sometimes protected by their clothing having wiped off the venom of snake-bites, who would certainly have perished had they been bitten on a naked part.

While then, with all other men, we heartily wish that this claimed discovery of M. Pasteur's may be real and efficient, in the absence of all knowledge of how it is prepared, with its imperfect test, and with the known possibilities of error, we would prefer to wait further developments before giving our full assent, unmixed with fear or doubt, as to its efficacy.

M. Pasteur is about 65 years of age, some 5 ft. 10 in. in height, heavy set, with an iron constitution and extra inflexible will which images itself upon his visage, giving him almost a ferocious appearance, so that one could but feel when looking at him that he would have made a first class brigand, or an invincible commander of a privateer, where his victims would have been slaughtered without mercy ; But, as his life has been devoted to benefitting not injuring, to saving not destroying man, as we might well divine, he has been as successful in the latter as he might have been in the former direction, Independent of his present field, he has perhaps done more good than any other living man and is fully entitled to all the honors that have been heaped upon him. His exalted worth as a scientist, together with our undivided faith in the unlimited power of science to prevent or cure every disorder of a zymotic nature to which human flesh is heir, encourages the hope, despite the objections given, that he is now moving in the right direction, and that his labors may result in the prevention of this heretofore incurable and horrible malady, and that even now he may be in possession of the means to lessen the danger resulting from the bite of rabid animals.

It is indeed difficult to believe that of the nineteen patients sent him from Russia, who had been not merely bitten by a mad-wolf, but torn to pieces, fearfully mangled, by the enraged, monstrous, wild beast, only seven or eight should have died; Indeed, at first sight, it would seem scarcely possible, torn as they were, (one of the patients having the trachea torn open) with the immense absorbing surface exposed to the poison, that any of them should have escaped a horrible death; and yet it may be possible that as all these were bitten by the same animal in rapid succession, the first by wiping off with their clothes and flesh the saliva, may have protected those bitten later; just as we see if the most venomous snake is made to bite in rapid succession a number of rabbits or other small animals, only the first few die, the others being only slightly or not at all affected and then of these patient's who died of rabies after being subjected to Pasteur's treatment—may we not fear that some of them died of rabies *because* of the treatment—were unoculated with rabies? If, however, it is true he is really in possession of this miracle-working scientific discovery, it is impossible to overestimate its importance. Heretofore all hydrophobic patients have traveled the same road; from the dark, dismal labyrinths of rabies there have been no returning footsteps. Should then, this horrid disorder be exorcised by the almighty spell of science, the world's gratitude is due the wizard who evokes from science's alembic the wondrous spell.

LONDON.

LONDON—THE QUEEN'S BIRTHDAY.

May 29th, 1886.—This being the Queen's birthday, it is a half-holiday, with fetes and shows, military parade and illumination at night.

Attended in the morning a military parade of the Prince of Wales Regiment, at St. James Park. Officers and men were in their brightest uniforms, and a splendid looking body of men they were. The Prince of Wales, the Duke of Richmond, uncle to the Prince, General Wolseley and other distinguished officers and personages were present. The Prince, who is perfectly familiar with military tactics, reviewed the troops. The ceremony is called trooping the colors, and a very pretty ceremony it was. Nothing could excel the perfect evolution of the troops—horse and infantry. A military company of sixty musicians played "God Save the Queen" and other martial pieces. The Prince is a fine-looking, heavy-set, square-built English gentleman, forty-five years of age, a little bald, frank, open countenance, and will doubtless make a wise and good ruler as king. His general appearance is much like that of Henry VIII., with whose appearance we had been made quite familiar by Holbein's pictures of Henry, seen not only in the galleries here but also in Germany. I was forcibly struck with this resemblance, though I had never heard it mentioned, but when I mentioned this strong resemblance at table I was told that it was a general observation. The Prince is very amiable and is devoted to the Princess. I am really glad of this, as the Princess is a most lovely and quite handsome woman, the daughter of the king and queen of Denmark, to whom I, in common with other members, was introduced at their palace in Copenhagen, during the meeting of the International Medical Congress, in 1884, So gentle, easy and familiar were the entire royal family of Denmark, including King George, of Greece, and his wife, that all the American delegation fell quite in love with them and quaffed their health in a glass of wine and swore to protect them from Bismark and all the rest of mankind. As the wine was excellent aud the ladies quite handsome we took another drink in confirmation of this determination. As the baquet was truly royal and the kings more gracious and the queens and princesses more handsome than at first, to the toast " Long live the king and royal family of Denmark " we drank yet another glass. Now if Bismark or the Czar or any other power or potentate feels like interfering with the rights or privileges of these good people. I hope they will consult their own interests by first consulting the American delegates to that Congress. We are pledged.

In the afternoon there was a grand royal procession to Pultney to open a new bridge which is not as common a performance in England as with us, where we throw daily a dozen bridges across rivers, either of which would drown all England. With some English lady friends we took carriage to witness the royal cavalcade. First the royal body-guard came in a gallop, followed by the Prince, Princess and their two daughters in an open carriage drawn by four fine horses, in a sweeping trot, the Prince waving his hat and bowing to the loud enthusiastic and sincere salutes of the crowd that lined, in multitudinous masses, the roadsides for miles. If anyone supposes the English people tired of royalty, they would hardly have been strengthened in their belief by witnessing this hearty reception. We had a favorable position, within a few feet of the royal cortege, as they passed. The Princess was dressed in a grey suit. She and her daughters are rather handsome, resembling the royal family of Denmark, most of whom are handsome, as are indeed most of the ladies of Denmark, many of whom being the most handsome women in the world, and certainly have the finest complexions of all the *genus homo*. There is something in the high northern atmosphere or in the blood of these Scandinavians that gives to the women surpassingly-beautiful complexions, a blending of the lily and the rose nowhere else seen to a like perfection and loveliness.

After witnessing the royal cortege we drove back to Hyde Park to see the splendid equipages, and splendidly-dressed, beautiful women that throng that fashionable thoroughfare on such occasions. The aristocracy were out *en masse*. Thousands of splendid carriages, filled with the families of aristocrats and wealthy citizens, were drawn through the park along its extended wide, graveled avenues. Perhaps no place on earth could present an equal number of costly equipages, and beautiful, finely-dressed women and children. Now if anyone supposes that the English women are not handsome—and I have heard this stated—if they will drive out to this park on any fine evening, especially a fete day, during the fashionable season, and observe the women of the aristocracy and better classes, they will find themselves left on this opinion. Ours are the prettiest women in the world and we derive our national type of beauty from England.

After driving among and along with this splendid gathering for an hour or more, we drove to the Colonial Exhibition, South Kensington, where we remained until 11 o'clock P. M., when we returned home through the beautifully-illuminated crowded streets of London.

The Colonial Exhibition is just such a sight as only the British Empire could produce. From every part of her vast colonial possessions were multitudinous articles showing the natural resources and industrial products of the world. We remained in the great halls and large rooms entranced with sight-seeing until the illumination of the gardens. This was really a gorgeous sight, surpassing far the wildest dream of Arabian Nights. In an instant tens of thousands of small Edison electric lights flashed into view converting the gardens into those of the Hesperides literally, in which the trees at the same moment bore blossoms of silver and apples of gold and rubies. In every tree thousands of balls of glass of different colors, previously unseen, flashed into existence, loading the trees with blue, red, white and yellow flowers and fruits, while the beautiful fountains played now in jets of silver, now of gold lace, which breaking as cloud-dust fell in seas of sparkling diamonds, emeralds, pearls, fountains, fields of illuminated golden glory—such a scene as we might suppose the gods would prepare on festive occasions. The scene was surpassingly beautiful, gorgeous; just such a sea of irridescent glory as the wealth of the world could not have produced in any other age than this the marvelous nineteenth century.

www.ingramcontent.com/pod-product-compliance
Lightning Source LLC
Chambersburg PA
CBHW030601300426
44111CB00009B/1066